Managing Frontiers in Competitive Intelligence

Managing Frontiers in
COMPETITIVE
INTELLIGENCE

edited by
Craig S. Fleisher
David L. Blenkhorn

Q
QUORUM BOOKS
Westport, Connecticut • London

Library of Congress Cataloging-in-Publication Data

Managing frontiers in competitive intelligence / edited by Craig S. Fleisher and David L. Blenkhorn.

    p. cm.

    A collection of 24 papers by the editors and other researchers.

    Includes bibliographical references and index.

    ISBN 1-56720-384-1 (alk. paper)

    1. Business intelligence—Management. 2. Competition. I. Fleisher, Craig S. II. Blenkhorn, David L.

HD38.7 .M365 2001

658.4′7—dc21   00-037264

British Library Cataloguing in Publication Data is available.

Library of Congress Catalog Card Number: 00-037264
ISBN: 1-56720-384-1

First published in 2001

Quorum Books, 88 Post Road West, Westport, CT 06881
An imprint of Greenwood Publishing Group, Inc.
www.quorumbooks.com

Printed in the United States of America

The paper used in this book complies with the Permanent Paper Standard issued by the National Information Standards Organization (Z39.48-1984).

10 9 8 7 6 5 4 3 2 1

Contents

PART THREE
COMPETITIVE INTELLIGENCE AND ITS RELATIONSHIP WITH BUSINESS FUNCTIONS AND PROCESSES

PART FOUR
COMPETITIVE INTELLIGENCE AND ITS APPLICATION IN SPECIFIC CONTEXTS

PART FIVE
ORGANIZATIONAL ISSUES ASSOCIATED WITH
COMPETITIVE INTELLIGENCE

Preface

As we enter the new millennium, competitive intelligence (CI) has become an important management topic for senior decision-makers. This enhanced status is being fueled by increased global competitiveness characterized by heightened industry consolidation and fragmentation. Decision-makers entrusted with designing strategy for their enterprises in this environment must be more cognizant and vigilant than ever before in recognizing and understanding changing industry contexts, dynamics, and structures. Fortunately, advances in practice and technology have enabled data-gathering and -analysis for decision-making—the primary domain of those in the CI field—to be much easier and cost-effective.

As the discipline of CI grows, so does the research and published literature in the field, which to date is still very much in an emerging mode. Our contribution in this book is to assist in breaking new ground in CI—hence the title *Managing Frontiers in Competitive Intelligence*. The parts and chapters that follow cut across many dimensions of business practice with new ideas and techniques, opening up for managers new frontiers in competitive intelligence.

By almost any measure, the popularity of CI has continued to grow and interest in the area is high. This growth has been demonstrated in a number of ways. Among other things, there have been large increases in memberships in professional associations dedicated to the field, increased media visibility of the practice, expansion in the number of professional conferences and workshops offered around the globe, new degree and certificate programs being introduced at universities, and improved recognition of the value of CI by corporate senior-decision-makers.

Part One includes several chapters that address the frontiers being carved out by this growth. Managers are struggling with issues of making senior decision-makers aware of the potential value added by CI to the organization's competitiveness and bottom line despite the difficulty in providing definitive empirical indicators. Executives also struggle with the need for their organizations to be CI-sensitive—not only in doing its own CI tasks, but also in protecting itself from the CI efforts of competitors. Last but not least, the litmus test for many managers will be in demonstrating that the organization is actually performing CI well in the first place, or, in other words, that it is performing at best-practice levels.

Another frontier that has dramatically changed in recent years is the conduct of the actual CI process itself. Advances in awareness of CI, applications of new software and hardware, the Internet, and education in the field have led to exciting developments in collecting data, performing analysis, and in communicating CI findings. In Part Two, we show how managers face a number of prominent challenges in effectively performing the CI process. For example, managers must find the optimal balance between the human and technical elements of performing CI, the use of primary and secondary sources, the amount of time spent planning, collecting data and doing analysis, top-down (i.e., senior executive-directed) versus bottom-up (i.e., initiatives coming from the front line or CI personnel themselves) CI, and in focusing internally versus externally.

One frontier that may potentially offer great benefits to organizations is in establishing CI as a strategic process that cuts across all of an organization's traditional functional areas or processes. There are a number of critical challenges in achieving this potential. Competitive intelligence managers need to establish credibility with functional-area decision-makers. This is not always an easy task, because there is often interfunctional competition for access to a limited set of organizational resources. Another challenge is in finding a common language that demonstrates the benefits of CI coordinating its efforts with these functions, especially since CI must deal with both the "soft" (e.g., human-resources management, organizational development) and "hard" (e.g., finance, operations, production) skills specialties present in most organizations. Managers face difficulties in changing the culture of organizations that otherwise prefers to work in functional silos. Last but not least, how can managers create structures and processes that allow for CI to proactively engage the functions in both strategic and tactical decision-making? Assuming that these issues can be appropriately addressed, there are particularly strong opportunities for CI to work with the organization's management accountants, finance specialists, marketing area, and information-technology staff. These are the areas we focus on in Part Three.

Managers in a number of industries are questioning whether CI can be of benefit when applied to their particular competitive contexts. There is little doubt that CI has become prominent in the competitive arsenals of global leaders in industries such as aerospace, chemicals, communication and computing services, financial services, information services, and manufacturing. However, CI has not achieved the importance that some observers expect it can in several industries such as biotechnology, pharmaceuticals, and retailing. Also, CI is normally found in larger, private-sector, goods-producing firms, but has not become prominent in small-to-medium enterprises (SMEs) nor in the public and service sectors. In Part Four we demonstrate that the new frontiers in managing CI will likely occur in these underachieving industries, in SMEs, and in the service area.

The book's final part describes a number of critical and often thorny organizational issues associated with CI. At the frontiers, managers continue to face continuing challenges in addressing ethical issues that arise out of the uncertainty created in fast-moving global marketplaces. Issues of culture exist externally in dealing with global competitors, and also internally in helping employees understand the organizational need for effective CI. Another frontier that managers struggle with concerns the issue of change and how CI can continue to make contributions to organizations that, by competitive necessity, need to demonstrate continuous innovation in order to be successful. Finally, managers are always confronting the issue of what CI may add in the future. That may be the final frontier for CI managers.

We are genuinely interested in your comments and criticisms. We welcome contributions from you for future editions, including articles, examples, cases, or statistics. You can reach us by mail, telephone, fax, or e-mail, and are welcome to drop in on our classes for a face-to-face talk. Let us hear from you!

Craig Fleisher
Faculty of Business
University of New Brunswick Saint John
P.O. Box 5050
Saint John, New Brunswick E2L 4L5 Canada

telephone: (506) 648-5677
     fax: (506) 648-5574
  e-mail: fleisher@unbsj.ca

David Blenkhorn
School of Business and Economics
Wilfrid Laurier University
75 University Avenue West
Waterloo, Ontario N2L 3C5 Canada

telephone: (519) 884-1970
     fax: (519) 884-0201
  e-mail: dblenkho@wlu.ca

Acknowledgments

We are grateful to a number of individuals and organizations whose assistance was essential in completing this book. First, colleagues and students at Wilfrid Laurier University's (WLU) School of Business and Economics (SBE) helped us by assisting in the development of chapters and in allowing us opportunities to practice and/or test these ideas. Both of us have had the privilege of teaching Canada's only permanent MBA course in Managing Competitive Intelligence, and we have been extremely pleased with the results to date of our students and ourselves.

The WLU Research Office provided us with a book-preparation grant that was instrumental in our completing this effort. The School of Business and Economic's Elsie Grogan provided excellent word-processing outputs, while Margaret Dilworth helped us in the administrative-coordination tasks with our many contributors. Victor Knip greatly assisted in the preparation of the manuscript for publication. We also appreciate the support given to us from Eric Valentine and his capable team at Greenwood Publishing Group's Quorum Books.

We also gratefully acknowledge the authors who contributed chapters to this book. We have enjoyed working with our contributing colleagues and feel our dialogue with them has helped to add the needed breadth and depth to the final effort.

Finally, we owe a special debt of gratitude to our families and friends who had to put up with us while we completed this project. We appreciate their encouragement and support.

Part **1**

OVERVIEW OF
COMPETITIVE INTELLIGENCE
MANAGEMENT AND PRACTICES

1

An Introduction to the Management and Practice of Competitive Intelligence (CI)

Craig S. Fleisher

INTRODUCTION

This is a book about the management of competitive intelligence (CI). It includes two dozen chapters that should enhance any organization's ability to utilize CI, and more importantly to compete in an increasingly competitive global marketplace. However, the goal for managing CI more effectively shouldn't be to simply perform CI better, but to perform better in the product or service marketplace of today and tomorrow.

There are generally no happy surprises in today's marketplace. Management failures are frequently associated with the inability to: anticipate rapid changes in markets; respond to new and proliferating competition; or reorient technologies and the strategic direction of their business toward changing customer needs and new industry standards. A good analogy is to consider the *Titanic*'s senior decision-makers. Senior crewmembers could have benefited from early warnings about the location, shape, and size of the iceberg that claimed their ship and most of their lives. Surprisingly, many of today's supposedly well-educated business decision-makers choose to ignore competitor and market intelligence warnings. Perhaps this intelligence is flawed or their assessment of this intelligence is ineffective. These decision-makers are the *Titanic*'s business equivalents, and will take themselves and their passengers down with their ships!

Competitive intelligence has a long history, even though its use in the realms of commerce and business is more recent. Its origins most likely date back to

Confucius in China and to Moses in the West. For example, Moses is reported to have sent an expedition of Joshua, Caleb, and other men to scout out the promised land after the Jewish people had fled Egypt around 1500 B.C. A millennium later, the renowned Chinese military leader Sun-Tzu wrote a lengthy treatise on the value of military intelligence. Intelligence and competitiveness have a long association in warfare, and are gaining one in business. The following section will describe the application of intelligence to marketplace competition.

WHAT IS COMPETITIVE INTELLIGENCE?

The need for generating CI is not new. The benefits of successfully anticipating a competitor's future plans and strategies are generally self-evident. The consequences of making decisions based on information that is incomplete, inaccurate, or late are no less severe. In China 2,400 years ago, Sun-Tzu plainly stated the case for intelligence. He wrote: "Now the reason the enlightened prince and the wise general conquer the enemy whenever they move, and their achievements surpass those of ordinary men, is foreknowledge" (Sun-Tzu, 1988).

Competitive intelligence often rings up images of James Bond types using an array of sophisticated gadgets to eavesdrop on the business competition. In reality, CI can be equally exciting, but not because the CI practitioner gets an adrenaline rush from working in illegal skullduggery. Modern CI practitioners obtain excitement from using their unique set of skills, knowledge, and abilities to uncover relationships that may enable their organizations to compete more effectively in the product or service marketplace.

There are numerous definitions of CI in contemporary practice and scholarship. In general, CI is the process by which organizations gather actionable information about competitors and the competitive environment and, ideally, apply it to their decision-making and planning processes in order to improve their performance. Competitive intelligence links apparently unrelated signals, events, perceptions, and data into patterns and trends concerning the business environment. Competitive intelligence can be simple, such as scanning a company's annual report and other public documents, or elaborate, such as performing a fully digitized war-gaming exercise (Shaker & Gembicki, 1999) over continents and time.

Competitive intelligence uses public sources to find and develop information on competition, competitors, and the market environment (Vella & McGonagle, 1987). Competitive intelligence is *not* business espionage; it is ethical, legal, and legitimate, while business espionage is decidedly illegal, unnecessary, and not part of a CI professional's job description. Business espionage develops intelligence by illegal or cloak-and-dagger means such as black-bag operations (e.g., breaking and entering), bribery, coercion, deliberate deception (e.g., such as having one's employees claim they work for another entity or advertising "phantom" positions), electronic eavesdropping (e.g., bugging or tapping), network infiltration, or systems hacking. Competitive intelligence practitioners use public, but not necessarily published, information. In other words, the information the CI practitioner needs is readily available and identified through legal means of open sources such as public documents, interviews, published sources, and in-house expertise. Competitive intelligence becomes illegal espionage when it involves the theft of proprietary materials or trade secrets.

IN WHAT CONTEXTS IS CI APPLIED?

Most organizations in today's business environment perform CI at some basic level whether they acknowledge it as such or not. Competitive intelligence has existed commercially since the first salesperson got wind of a competitor's price reduction and decided to communicate this intelligence to his/her superior. In reality, most senior executives practice CI in their daily activities as they attempt to understand how to better position their organization's products or services in the marketplace. Few organizational founders can acquire the needed financial resources to launch their firms without having done at least some environmental scanning and identifying potential competitive threats. Even the search for patents, funding sources, initial customers, and employees will likely contain elements of more formal CI.

A reading of the burgeoning CI literature may suggest to the casual observer that CI is done only by large, public- or private-sector, well-heeled U.S. companies. This perception is misleading. In reality, many smaller private- and public-sector organizations both within and outside the United States perform CI whether they have substantial financial resources or not.

Much of the CI literature has focused on larger as opposed to smaller companies. For example, lists of the best CI performers frequently identify large multinationals such as AT&T, Coca-Cola, Eastman Kodak, Ford, General Electric, Hewlett-Packard, IBM, Intel, Kellogg's, 3M, Merck, Microsoft, Motorola, Procter and Gamble, Royal Dutch Shell, and Xerox as being among the best performers of CI (Harkleroad, 1998). Very rarely do these lists identify smaller firms as having superior processes, although the author can relate from his own experience and observations that many do it quite effectively. Large enterprises, with their cumbersome standard operating procedures and entrenched attitudes and functions, can have a harder time implementing CI processes than their smaller counterparts. Smaller companies are often more attuned to gathering and using CI effectively because they are leaner and "closer to the ground," often headed by a motivated entrepreneur accustomed to personally knowing as much as possible about competitors. Ironically, while these companies may lack the range of resources needed to launch and maintain sophisticated or automated CI networks, the fact that the chief executive officer and senior managers act personally and continuously on intelligence gives them a leg up in the competitive marketplace.

A casual observer of the CI literature may also get the impression that CI is only beneficial within certain industry contexts. For example, it is common to see case studies or articles written about CI efforts performed for organizations in high-stakes industries such as aerospace, biotechnology, chemicals, computer and information services, pharmaceuticals, and telecommunications. Although

CI can clearly be a substantial benefit to firms in these industries, it can be used with equivalent value in less "sexy" industries such as consumer products, electric or gas utilities, financial services, manufacturing, and basic resources. The literature does not necessarily reflect this reality; CI can potentially be of great value to organizations in any competitive industry.

Publicly owned, as opposed to privately owned, business enterprises have also received the lion's share of scholarly attention. This disproportionate academic focus should not suggest that private enterprises do not formally perform CI or cannot do it as effectively as their public counterparts. Again, the reality of global practice may suggest otherwise. Indeed, when it comes to countering competitors' CI efforts, private organizations have several advantages that make their public competitors' CI and strategy jobs more difficult.

Although the scholarship has primarily focused on private-sector organizations, the concepts and practices can also be effectively applied to public-sector organizations such as government agencies, universities, community and social organizations, and state/provincial or local decision-making bodies. Indeed, many of the earliest and still extant forms of formal intelligence processes were found in the military–industrial planning complexes of nation-states. Public-sector organizations require knowledge of competitive environments and interactions, since they must increasingly compete for scarce resources in the global marketplace. Nation-states or provinces compete to achieve higher standards of living for their citizens by using an array of competitive techniques, including tax or loan rates, grants or subsidies, well-educated human resources, and modern communication, information, and/or transportation infrastructures. One example of how governments have gotten into CI is Quebec's Ministry of Industry, Commerce, Science, and Technology, where twelve sector-based CI centers were set up in collaboration with private-sector companies, universities, trade associations, and research-and-development centers to provide value-added information on the sectors.

There is also a burgeoning market for CI consulting, software, and services solutions. There is no definitive market data available on the size of the CI market in these areas. Market sizing depends heavily on whether you use a restrictive (e.g., self-identified CI consulting services) or broadened definition of CI (including other related competitive information services). Narrow definitions suggest a growing global CI market of U.S.$100–200 million, while a broader definition places it over U.S.$1 billion. Add these amounts to the growing budgets devoted to corporate CI around the world and it becomes clear that the CI marketplace is a substantial one.

Why wouldn't an organization utilize CI? One research effort suggested that probably less than 10 percent of U.S. corporations know their way around the CI process and can effectively integrate the information into their strategic plans (Ettorre, 1995). Business professionals have been known to criticize managers harshly for ignoring CI. A case in point was Gary Costley, Kellogg's former North American division president, when he asserted that "managers who don't do competitive intelligence are incompetent" and that "it is irresponsible not to understand your competitors" (Ettorre, 1995). Costley is not the only one who casts this aspersion on some senior managers. Many of today's leading strategy scholars such as Michael Porter, Gary Hamel, and C. K. Prahalad repeatedly stress the importance of strategic positioning in this global age of brutal competition and declining profit margins. The failure to systematically pursue CI understandings is likely to put at a disadvantage those companies that must compete in the global marketplace. They will lose more than their share of marketplace battles to those that are doing CI.

MULTIPLE LENSES FOR RECOGNIZING CI

Competitive intelligence is frequently incorrectly associated with a number of other business disciplines. This error is often more than just a difficulty with business definitions or terminology. As someone who teaches master of business administration (MBA) courses in managing CI, I cannot tell you how many times my students come into the course with a variety of misconceptions about what CI is and is not. However, no single definition of CI is likely to be precise and universally accepted.

One way to understand CI is to view it as a progression from raw inputs to finished outputs. In this perspective, CI begins with scattered bits of raw, basic data. This raw material is then organized by CI practitioners and becomes information. Information becomes intelligence when it is placed into a format useful to a decision-maker's unique or critical intelligence needs (CINs); good CI is needs-driven. Intelligence is therefore information that is analyzed, interpreted, and infused with developed implications. Competitive intelligence is the refined intelligence product that meets a decision-maker's unique needs for understanding a competitive aspect of the internal and/or external environment. Competitive intelligence helps the decision-maker make a decision. Effective CI helps the decision-maker make a better decision!

Another way to understand CI is to view it as an organizational function. Effective CI activities range in scope between the broader area of business intelligence (BI) and the narrower competitor analysis (CA). They can provide the foundation on which market and nonmarket strategies and tactics are built, assessed, and modified. As a mostly staff-oriented function, CI will cut across and overlap other functions—in particular, those associated with marketing and planning.

Competitive intelligence activities are commonly organized programmatically within today's companies. Competitive intelligence programs (CIPs) can be defined as a continuously evolving integration of both formal and informal processes by which organizational members assess key trends, emerging discontinuities, the evolution of industry structure, and the capabilities and behaviors of current and potential competitors to assist in or develop a competitive advantage. Competitive intelligence programs support organizational decision-making and are focused on achieving competitive marketplace goals such as proactively detecting opportunities or threats, eliminating or reducing blindspots, risks and/ or surprises, and reducing reaction time to competitor and marketplace changes. Competitive intelligence programs attempt to ensure that decision-makers have accurate, current information about the organization's competitive environment, and a plan for using that information to the organization's marketplace advantage (McGonagle & Vella, 1990). In sum, CIPs can help business executives make better decisions than their competitors concerning:

- *Changing market structure*: entry into new businesses, new alliances, or partnerships
- *Competitive activities*: capacity expansion, mergers, and acquisitions
- *Competitive benchmarks*: both external and internal
- *Customer/supplier activities*: shifting needs and priorities
- *Emerging technology initiatives*: patent development, research-and-development planning
- *Global economic conditions*: major fiscal and monetary initiatives
- *Marketing planning*: new product developments or enhancements, entry into related product or service lines
- *Political and social climates*: shifting governments, public policies, and opinion
- *Regulatory and legal issues*: changing national and multinational administrative policies, alterations in laws or legal structures
- *Strategic planning.*

Prescott and Gibbons (1993) note that common to most CIPs is a focus on:

- Profiling industries and competitors for meeting a specific executive's decision-making needs: critical to this profiling are answering questions such as (Prescott, 1989):
    - —"who are my competitors both in the present and future?"
    - —"what are the critical characteristics of my industry and competitors?"
    - —"what are the current positions of my competitors?"
    - —"what moves are my competitors most likely to make?"
    - —"what moves can our organization make to achieve a competitive advantage?"
- Transforming gathered information into actionable intelligence
- Utilizing all members of the organization as intelligence "antennae"
- The evolution over time to address evolving critical issues and to facilitate organizational renewal
- Using ethical and legal means in the process of gathering, analyzing, and using publicly available data.

The domain of CI activity is both *external* and *internal* to the organization. In its external role, CI is focused on understanding:

- *Industry structure and evolution*: particular focus on the industry's attractiveness
- *The macro-economy*: otherwise viewed as the social, technological, economic, ecological, and political/legal (STEEP) sectors of the environment associated with one's business
- *Stakeholders*: those organizations that can impact or are impacted by the achievement of the organization's competitive objectives
- *Issues*: these are the gaps that exist between an organization's actions and the expectations of those (e.g., stakeholders) who can impact its competitive goals.

In its internal role, CI requires practitioners to have a detailed organizational understanding. Specifically, they will need to have a keen grasp of an organization's:

- *Strategy*: in particular, the organization's marketplace goals, posture, or competitive premise and scope of activity
- *Organization*: characteristics such as organizational culture, systems, structures, and staffing policies
- *Resources and capabilities*: financial, human, physical, reputational, structural, and temporal aspects
- *Values*: conception of decision-makers' desires that influences their selection from available competitive modes' means and ends of action.

Competitive intelligence practices are commonly structured in the following formats: 1) ad hoc; 2) continuous comprehensive; 3) continuous focused; and/or 4) project-based (Cartwright, Boughton, & Miller, 1995). *Ad hoc* CI is performed on an as-requested basis and produces outputs that are one-time in nature and focused on a particular competitor, event, or competitive product/service. *Continuous-comprehensive* CI is performed on an ongoing basis by a dedicated CI staff that assesses the broad competitive forces affecting the industry(-ies). *Continuous-focused* CI is also performed on an ongoing basis by dedicated staff, but is designed to investigate a selective set of specific issues as defined by key decision-makers. Finally, *project-based* CI is performed by a temporarily designated team that assesses how competitors and competitive conditions may affect the success of a particular project. Cartwright, Boughton, and Miller (1995) found that ad hoc was the most commonly used form of CI, although many firms simultaneously used multiple forms.

THE EVOLUTION OF CI PRACTICE

My MBA students often wonder why they had not heard of CI prior to taking my course in managing CI. Several have questioned whether the field can be that important, since CI courses are rarely offered in MBA programs. For example, my course in Managing CI at Wilfrid Laurier University's School of Business and Economics is the only CI course that is a permanent part of the graduate-business calendar in Canada. Even when CI courses are offered in MBA programs, they commonly focus on the data-gathering CI subprocess.

Competitive intelligence is not a recent phenomenon in either business practice or scholarship. The CI boom of the last decade was driven by the increasingly widespread recognition that good information has a direct impact on the bottom line. Competitive intelligence also evolved as part of the larger movement toward strategic management of organizations. Sammon, Kurland, and Spitalnic (1984) stated that ". . . by the 1980s, many business managers were wondering why it (strategy) worked so poorly. Part of the answer may be that strategy without intelligence had become a contradiction in terms."

Prescott (1995) identified three stages of CI development: *Stage one* occurred during the 1960s and 1970s and was mostly associated with data-gathering, informal and tactical. In this stage CI was poorly linked to decision-making and top management's concerns and involved little analysis. *Stage two* occurred mostly during the 1980s when competitor and industry analysis became popular. Competitive intelligence personnel switched from library functions to marketing or planning ones. Competitive intelligence activities remained tactically oriented during the second stage—the spy image of CI practitioners began to evolve, and there was still little quantitative data analysis. The *third stage* that began in the 1990s shows CI contributing to strategic decision-making that is built into dedicated formal units either on their own or within marketing or planning. Competitive intelligence activities are oriented to both tactical and strategic decision-making and include qualitative and quantitative analyses. Competitive intelligence receives moderate attention from top management and is often a valuable contributor to strategic decision-making.

Competitive intelligence has benefited greatly from influences generated within the marketing, policy, and strategy areas of business practice and scholarship. Competitive intelligence has profited from advances in the field of marketing, particularly in customer and market research and market planning. It has also gained a boost from the company-, environmental-, and industrial-analysis segments of the policy and strategy field. Competitive intelligence practice and scholarship have been augmented in recent years from advances in a variety of nonbusiness disciplines, including but not limited to anthropology, computing and informatics, engineering sciences, international relations, library and information sciences, psychology, sociology, and technology. Finally, CI is increasingly linked with intelligence of a strategic, competitor, market, or technical nature, as well as benchmarking, crisis management, and knowledge management among other things (McGonagle & Vella, 1999).

Competitive intelligence is commonly practiced in countries that have fought or have been fighting a war for their survival. France, Germany, Israel, Japan, Korea, and Sweden all have sophisticated intelligence networks, many of which have been transferred into the commercial and economic realm. Multinationals, especially those headquartered within Europe and Asia, are known to systematically leverage their employees as intelligence antennae (Hannon & Sano, 1995). Japanese semiconductor-industry competitors such as Mitsubishi, Mitsui, and Sumitomo have intelligence departments that purportedly rival the U.S. Central Intelligence Agency in ability and validity. Performing CI is seen as a natural extension of doing business and a part of their information- and intelligence-hungry cultures. That would not be the case in the United States or Canada. DeGenaro (1996) notes that the U.S. private sector stands in sharp contrast to other nations in that very few companies have "world-class" CI operations and that most are unaware that intelligence operations are being used against them. Kahaner (1996) further notes that many countries have been moving ahead with their CI activities, while North Americans have been slowed by ongoing ethical debates and sentiments.

My students' surprise about the international vitality of CI might have been unduly influenced by the relatively low profile of CI in North American companies. For example, many U.S. companies are oblivious to the fact that their current and future market opponents are using CI to systematically scrutinize them (McDermott, 1994). A 1995 study of American businesses by The Futures Group showed that 25 percent of their respondents were classified as "ostriches" because they did not think a competitor had ever used CI techniques against them (Harkleroad, 1996). That percentage fell to 5 percent in a similar study conducted almost three years later (Harkleroad, 1998), suggesting that American companies were quickly becoming cognizant of CI practices.

There is other evidence that CI has gained global prominence since the 1980s. Membership in the Society of Competitive Intelligence Professionals (SCIP) grew tenfold, from about 600 members in 1989 to over 6,500 by 1999. The number of conferences devoted to CI also grew about tenfold during that period, and not a week goes by without some organization hosting a meeting about CI or a related field. More articles and books were published about CI during the 1990s than the sum total of those previously published. Finally, globally in academe there have been an increasing number of courses and degree programs devoted to CI, including dedicated masters' degrees (e.g., the C.R.R.M at University Aix-Marseille in France) and doctorates (e.g., Lund University in Sweden). Finally, professional-development or executive-education seminars are also commonly offered by a variety of postsecondary institutions, conference organizers, and by CI-specialized private organizations.

WHICH INDIVIDUALS PRACTICE CI?

Competitive intelligence can conceivably be performed by any person or organizational department and not just by the marketing or strategy personnel who are most commonly associated with its practice (Ghoshal & Kim, 1986). The following lists a number of different practitioners who might commonly be associated with organizational CI:

- *Corporate, legal, and public librarians or library-information specialists*: they are frequently involved with the data-gathering process of CI

- *Decision-makers*: it is frequently their critical intelligence needs that CI is focused on meeting

- *Analysts*: the individuals who take the gathered information and make sense of it. These positions are frequently filled by newly minted MBAs who have up-to-date skills, knowledge, and abilities in this area

- *Consultants*: there is a large and growing CI consulting industry that includes many of the traditional strategy consultants (e.g., Booz Allen Hamilton, Boston Consulting Group, McKinsey, etc.), accounting consulting organizations (e.g., Ernst & Young, Price Waterhouse Coopers, etc.), management-information consulting organizations (e.g., EDS, IBM, SAP, etc.), and CI-specific consultants (e.g., Fuld and Company, Mindshifts Consulting Group, Washington Researchers, etc.)

- *Planners*: marketing and strategic planners in particular are frequently involved with CI

- *Researchers*: especially those associated on the market or marketing-research side

- *Development personnel*: those individuals looking for new business or corporate opportunities

- *Ex-military, intelligence community, or law-enforcement personnel*: frequently involved with CI from a security, counterintelligence or asset-protection basis.

A number of associations have also grown up around CI practice. Two associations focus on CI as their central interest: the Society of Competitive Intelligence Professionals (SCIP) in the United States and the European Union (EU)–based Association for Global Strategic Information (AGSI). Several other associations have related or overlapping interests in CI, such as the American Management Association (AMA), American Society for Information Science (ASIS), Association of Independent Information Professionals (AIIP), the Conference Board's Council on Competitive Analysis, Information Industry Association (IIA), the International Society for Strategic Marketing (ISSM), the Marketing Research Association (MRA), Special Libraries Association (SLA), and Strategic Leadership Forum (SLF).

TRAITS OF THE SUCCESSFUL CI PRACTITIONER

There is an ongoing question asked in the CI community as to whether effective CI practitioners are born or made. Although a number of observers would argue for the former, more would probably agree that they are made; nevertheless, the making of an effective CI practitioner can be a difficult task. Fuld (1995) suggests that experience and talent are more important than education. He notes how a business or engineering degree provides a general body of knowledge, but does not teach an individual how to pursue a line of questioning or to read the "rust on the rails." The traits associated with effective CI practice include:

- *Good listening and observation skills*: this is valuable when eliciting the information you want or need. Especially helpful in this global-business era is the ability to communicate in several languages
- *Creativity*: can identify the outlier information that others miss
- *Persistence*: not giving up even when the first ten contacts provide no leads
- *Strategy*: knowing how to plan in order to efficiently and effectively perform a designated CI task
- *Networking*: fat Rolodexes, knowing who to contact (note: these contacts are frequently within your own organization) for the insights sought
- *Information-related skills*: understanding databases, knowing the library, understanding relevant software programs such as spreadsheets or statistical analysis packages, writing and interviewing skills
- *Experience*: industry experience, knowing what questions to ask using the language understood by those with the answers you seek.

CORE TASKS OF THE CI PROCESS

- *Planning*: there are three critical aspects of planning for CI: gaining a clear understanding of the user's needs, including their resource constraints (e.g., budget, human, and time); a data-collection and -analysis plan; and an effort to keep the user informed
- *Data collection*: the gathering of data from and about sources or targets
- *Analysis*: allows the data collected to be reviewed, tested, and subject to challenge. The analysis process reduces the data into a usable form for decision-making
- *Implementation*: the actions taken to use the intelligence outputs to the company's advantage.

Since these four tasks form the critical core of the CI process, each is elaborated upon further in the following section.

Planning

The basic CI process should always begin with a decision-maker who has a specific intelligence need (i.e., critical intelligence need [or CIN]). It is important to determine what needs to be known, for whom, and how and when it will be used. Key internal clients for CI can include decision-makers with business development, financial planning, market planning or research, product planning, research and development, and strategic-planning responsibilities. By defining their information needs up front, the CI practitioner can generate a list of specific questions that helps focus the subsequent CI effort. Framed effectively, answering yes or no to these questions will lead to a decision.

Critical intelligence needs may be segmented into three objective types (Prescott, 1989): a) *offensive*—assignments conducted to evaluate the impact of a strategic or tactical move on the industry and competitors; b) *defensive*—understanding the potential moves that a competitor could make that would threaten the competitive position of the firm and developing responses to minimize or neutralize the threat; or c) *informational*—conducted primarily for the purpose of gaining a better understanding of an industry or competitor, although no apparent action is necessarily being taken. These three forms may be either operational or strategic: Operational decisions affect shorter-term goals and decisions made on a more-or-less daily basis, whereas strategic decisions influence the organization's longer-term mission and vision.

Another useful way to plan is to consider meeting the CI client's needs in terms of products. Dugal (1998) suggests that there are ten basic CI "products." They are: current intelligence, basic intelligence, technical intelligence, early warning intelligence, estimated intelligence, work-group intelligence, targeted intelligence, crisis intelligence, foreign intelligence, and counterintelligence. Each of these products are distinct from one another in terms of their "shelf life" (i.e., how long they remain useful), audience (i.e., to whom they are directed and most helpful), sources (i.e., from where the data underlying them is gathered), analytical tools (i.e., the means by which data is converted into outputs), modes of dissemination (i.e., modes and channels used for delivering the product), and relative cost. In sum, practitioners have different CI priorities depending on where their organizations want to go and who is expected to contribute future value; consequently, some companies focus on competitors, some on public-policy issues (Fleisher, 1999), some on technologies that impact their business (Ashton & Klavans, 1997), and others on new market development.

What does it take for a practitioner to successfully perform planning? There are a number of "competencies" that should be demonstrated, including (Society of Competitive Intelligence Professionals, 1999): understanding how to accurately identify and elicit the intelligence needs of decision-makers; developing effective communication, interviewing, and presentation skills; understanding basic psychology types so as to appreciate the different orientations of decision-makers; knowing the organizational structure, culture, and environment as well as the key informants; remaining objective; articulating intelligence needs into the intelligence cycle; knowing the internal and external capabilities; and conducting an information resource gap-analysis.

Data Collection

Most organizations are full of data, but starved for intelligence. The CI practitioner doing data collection asks: "Where can I access the information?," "Who produces the data I want?," "Who else collects the data I want?," "Who uses the data I want?," "How much will it cost?," and "How long will it take?" They have to manage the flood of information by storing, referencing, and manipulating it so that analysts can make sense of the often incomplete, fragmented data-mass. Managing the information is commonly done through e-mail, groupware, and/or document-management systems. As opposed to the problems of the preceding century, contemporary data collectors face challenges stemming from *too much* data, as opposed to dealing with data scarcity.

Sources for CI are numerous. Primary sources include speeches, financial reports, government documents, organizational homepages, product circulars, and other materials that come directly from an organization being studied. Key secondary sources include, among others, analysts' reports, magazine articles, books, edited TV or radio programs, and a variety of on-line sources. Among the highest-used sources are trade journals, on-line databases, external hardcopy documents, employees, industry experts, and trade associations/groups. Among the least-used sources are case studies, focus groups, mail surveys, or product purchases for reengineering (Society of Competitive Intelligence Professionals, 1997).

Data-gathering methods range from reactive, ad hoc methods where executives are irregularly sent pieces of information and analysis by employees, to automated and fully integrated digital-tracking systems. Most modern intelligence gathering is either electronic or human. Today's savvy data collectors are taking full advantage of the growing resources available on the Internet and World Wide Web (WWW). Despite the major impact of the Web, its efficacy as an investigative aid has yet and may never fully supplant good old-fashioned detective work of the human intelligence (HUM-INT) kind. The Web has leveled the playing field in terms of access to information and certainly makes information available quickly and often less expensively. Computers, software, the Internet, and databases cannot do it all. Human sources are commonly still the best sources from which to obtain the really critical intelligence fragments.

What does it take for a practitioner to successfully perform data collection? There are a number of "competencies" that should be demonstrated, including the ability to (Society of Competitive Intelligence Professionals, 1999): obtain knowledge of primary and secondary sources; know the various methods for accessing internal and external/primary and secondary sources; manage primary and secondary sources appropriately; know how to execute triangulated, multi-method, multisource approaches; ensure source reliability and validity; recognize anomalies in the information; know the difference between hypothesized and open assumptions; develop formal research skills; recognize corporate information-gathering patterns and collect accordingly; know the ethics associated with data gathering; and become keenly aware of security, legal, and counterintelligence issues as well as the effects of international and cultural issues.

Analysis

The items retrieved during data collection are not intelligence. They have to be processed into intelligence and then disseminated. The driving purpose of performing business and competitive analysis is to better understand one's industry and competitors in order to develop a strategy that provides a sustainable competitive advantage and achieves continuing performance results that are superior to one's competitors. The analysis outputs produced should be actionable (future-oriented), help decision-makers develop better competitive strategies, facilitate a better understanding than competitors of the competitive environment, and identify current and future competitors, their plans and strategies. The ultimate aim of analysis is to produce better business *results*, not achieve intermediate outcomes of better decisions or analyses. Good analysis provides an answer to the "so what?" test—in other words, the gathered information tells me something new or original that I need to know about the marketplace that can meet the decision-maker's CIN.

There are numerous formal tools and techniques available to help practitioners with the process of analyzing data (Fleisher & Bensoussan, forthcoming). These can take a wide variety of forms and require the analyst to be familiar with both qualitative and quantitative research methods. The business tools offered within a typical MBA program are only the analytical starting point and are generally insufficient in handling most CI-analysis tasks.

What does it take for an analyst to successfully perform analysis? There are a number of "competencies" that the analyst should demonstrate. One of the better summaries of these competencies comes from the Society of Competitive Intelligence Professionals (Society of Competitive Intelligence Professionals, 1999), which suggest that an effective CI practitioner needs to recognize the interaction between the collection and analysis stages, use creativity and alternative thinking, employ both deductive and inductive reasoning, understand the basic analytical models, introduce exciting and attractive models to elicit the discovery notion of analysis rather than the dry research approach, know when and why to use the various analysis tools, recognize the inevitable existence of gaps and blind spots, and know when to cease analyzing so as to avoid analysis paralysis.

Implementation

After the collected data has been analyzed it must be disseminated in an appropriate format to decision-makers. Competitive intelligence practitioners must format, deliver, store, and make available the intelligence for later access. Modes of dissemination, in order of perceived effectiveness, include: custom reports, personal communications, scheduled presentations, special memos, competitor files, computerized databases, newsletters, regular meetings, training seminars, bulletin boards, and special retreats (Society of Competitive Intelligence Professionals, 1997). The value of CI diminishes over time, making it important that the practitioner can flag the intelligence as critical and deliver it quickly to whoever requires it. Implementation usually also includes CI subprocesses such as assessment and reporting of the performance benefits and efficacy of the CI and decision-making process, feedback into future CI planning, and often a need to review or reassess the organization's strategy.

A good summary of dissemination competencies comes from the Society of Competitive Intelligence Professionals (Society of Competitive Intelligence Professionals, 1999) and suggests that an effective CI practitioner needs to use persuasive presentation skills, demonstrate empathy and use counseling skills when appropriate, organize findings and convey them with assertiveness and diplomacy, use the format or media appropriate for each end-user, recognize the effective volume and level of disseminating intelligence, and realize that listening can also be a form of presenting.

SUMMARY

It should go without saying that today's organizations compete in an increasingly dynamic global marketplace. Organizations frequently fail because they are unable to read the typically weak and ambiguous signals that are ubiquitous in their environments and markets (Gilad, 1996). A systematic, powerful CI and learning capability are competitive skills necessary for improving decision-making and market performance in this environment.

REFERENCES

Ashton, W.B., and R.A. Klavans. (1997). *Keeping Abreast of Science and Technology: Technical Intelligence for Business.* Columbus, OH: Batelle Press.

Cartwright, D.L., P.D. Boughton, and S.W. Miller. (1995). "Competitive Intelligence Systems: Relationships to Strategic Orientation and Perceived Usefulness," *Journal of Managerial Issues* 7(4): 420–34.

DeGenaro, B. (1996). "Counterintelligence," in *Advances in Applied Business Strategy,* supplement 2B, ed. B. Gilad and J. Herring. Greenwich, CT: JAI Press.

Dugal, M. (1998). "CI Product Line: A Tool for Enhancing User Acceptance of CI," *Competitive Intelligence Review* 9(2): 17–25.

Ettorre, Barbara. (1995). "Managing Competitive Intelligence," *Management Review* 84(10): 15–19.

Fleisher, C.S. (1999). "Public Policy Competitive Intelligence," *Competitive Intelligence Review* 10(2): 23–36.

Fleisher, C.S., and B. Bensoussan. (Forthcoming). *Business and Competitive Analysis for Strategic Management.* Upper Saddle River, NJ: Prentice-Hall.

Fuld, L.M. (1995). *The New Competitor Intelligence: The Complete Resource for Finding, Analyzing, and Using Information About Your Competitors.* New York: Wiley.

Ghoshal, S., and S. Kim. (1986). "Building Effective Intelligence Systems for Competitive Advantage," *Sloan Management Review* 28(1): 49–58.

Gilad, B. (1996). *Business Blindspots.* London: Infonortics.

Hannon, J.M., and Y. Sano. (1995). "Customer-Driven Human Resources Practices in Japan," *Human Resource Planning* 17(3): 37–53.

Harkleroad, D. (1996). "Too Many Ostriches, Not Enough Eagles," *Competitive Intelligence Review* 7(1): 23–27.

———. (1998). "Ostriches and Eagles II," *Competitive Intelligence Review* 9(1): 13–19.

Kahaner, L.K. (1996). *Competitive Intelligence: How to Gather, Analyze, and Use Information to Move Your Business to the Top.* New York: Simon & Schuster.

McDermott, M. (1994). "Is International Marketing a Game of Spy Versus Spy?" *Brandweek* (June 20): 31–32.

McGonagle, J.J., and C.M. Vella. (1990). *Outsmarting the Competition: Practical Ap-*

proaches to Finding and Using Competitive Information. Naperville, IL: Source-books.

———. (1999). *The Internet Age of Competitive Intelligence.* Westport, CT: Quorum Books.

Prescott, J.E. (1989). "Competitive Intelligence: Its Role and Function Within Organizations," in *Advances in Competitive Intelligence*, ed. J.E. Prescott. Vienna, VA: Society of Competitive Intelligence Professionals.

———. (1995). "The Evolution of Competitive Intelligence," *International Review of Strategic Management* 6(1): 71–90.

Prescott, J.E., and P.T. Gibbons. (1993). "Global Competitive Intelligence: An Overview," in *Global Perspectives on Competitive Intelligence*, ed. J.E. Prescott and P.T. Gibbons. Alexandria, VA: Society of Competitive Intelligence Professionals.

Sammon, W., M. Kurland, and R. Spitalnic. (1984). *Business Competitor Intelligence.* New York: Wiley.

Shaker, S., and M. Gembicki. (1999). *The War Room Guide to Competitive Intelligence.* New York: McGraw-Hill.

Society of Competitive Intelligence Professionals. (1997). *1997 Salary Survey* <http://www.scip.org>.

———. (1999). List of the CI cycle as published <http://www.scip.org>.

Sun-Tzu. (1988). *The Art of War.* Oxford: Oxford University Press.

Vella, C.M., and J.J. McGonagle. (1987). *Competitive Intelligence in the Computer Age.* Westport, CT: Quorum Books.

2

Competitive Intelligence and Strategic Decision-Making at the Chief Executive Officer (CEO) Level

Tabatha Martins

INTRODUCTION

The competitive intelligence (CI) function must be viewed as an efficient, effective, and relevant resource in the eyes of the chief executive officer (CEO). If this is not the case, and senior management confidence is not gained, then the CI effort is likely to fail. Chief executive officers want to know CI information; however, determining how much information is required and what depth of analysis is needed at each point can vary across time, budgets, companies, and industries. For this reason, the link between the CEO and the CI professional must be clear. For example, consider how CI can assist the CEO with the following types of decisions:

• Expanding into new foreign markets
• Acquiring or divesting a firm
• Engaging or terminating a strategic alliance
• Making trade offs in the adoption of technological advances.

This chapter will address how CI can be developed to directly assist the CEO with strategic decision-making. The objectives of this chapter are to review what is currently being done in various companies with respect to CI as a supportive corporate function, and how CEOs are utilizing this information. The case research method has been used to determine the CI processes of selected senior executives and their companies, as well as a literature review of published corporate CI practices. From this information a model has been developed for CI professionals and CEOs to use as a starting point for the development of their relationship, the purpose of which is to make informed decisions. Although this chapter will refer to the decision-making of the CEO, other senior managers will also benefit from utilizing these findings in their corporate roles and responsibilities.

CI AND STRATEGIC DECISION-MAKING AT THE CEO LEVEL

Current Practices

There have been many debates on how to use CI to make informed decisions. Articles and studies have reviewed which format and process best utilize CI information (Berger, 1997; McGonagle, 1992). Many studies have gone further to recommend the practical aspects of physically accomplishing this task; however, it would seem that a review of what actually happens at the CEO level, and how CI information is managed at this level, would lend itself to deny or confirm the actual practice of these theories (Costley, 1996; Eger, 1996).

Many corporations promote the need for cross-functional, integrated, ongoing, CI gathering of information; however, the findings have shown that CEOs are often actively involved in doing their own CI activities and that this information is not always filtered throughout the organization. There are, of course, always exceptions. The following case reviews describe the CI function from a variety of sources, including literature reviews of published practices as well as through primary sources using formal and informal interviews.

This chapter addresses the case studies that have been done with respect to the practices of CI within corporations and, where information is available, how these processes are filtered back to the CEO. In addition, the research will show what is actually done at the CEO level by the CEO, and what is not filtered back throughout the rest of the organization. Each case will be presented on its own merit in a framework that follows the information-gathering stage, the management of the CI results, and the impact of the process on the strategic decisions of the CEOs.

This chapter includes CI practice information from CEOs of eight small and large corporations that have made public their processes, and in some cases the expected result of this practice. In order to generate useful information and gain the trust of this study's participants, every effort has been made to protect the identity of the participants.

The objective of this chapter is to understand whether CI practices are being used by companies as a direct input into CEO decision-making, and whether or not the processed and analyzed results are being used by the CEO for the purpose of strategic development. This chapter would not be complete without a review of the type of information that is being collected in order for a CEO to consider the information actionable.

Gathering Information

The one source of information that all involved parties used was the Internet. Everyone in the study appeared to use it slightly differently. Varied use of the Internet for CI did not appear to be an industry effect, but to a larger extent it was a personal priority decision. For example, one individual used the Internet to download a variety of demos or videos of a particular product or service. Most individuals used the Internet to obtain press releases, speeches, upcoming events, and general company overviews. Some companies used the Internet to check staff changes; however, some companies used corporate telephone directories as well to identify any differences. Many individuals were interested in personnel profiles. Few companies found website traffic to be a source of significant information with respect to the potential customers that were interested in the company and the specific competitors that were reviewing information.

A major source of information that many of the CEOs relied on was analysts' reports. Their confidence was in the "expert" level of information. Although many used the published analysts' reports, some went further to interview experts in the field, join networking groups to develop contacts in their respective areas, and others contracted marketing-research companies or consulting agencies to customize their CI project to their needs.

Competitive intelligence information needs were also met through trade shows, suppliers, and distribution channels. All of these sources were used to a lesser extent than the Internet or analysts' reports because the CEO was not directly involved in this data-gathering. There was a general consensus that these sources were excellent for determining sales-related information; however, the senior executives interviewed relied on reports from middle management to summarize and provide insights into the information found, as opposed to their own form of analysis. Generally, CEOs felt that any strategic information of significance from these events would be brought to their attention by their middle managers.

Although there has been a significant amount of literature that suggests that internal employees are the largest source of CI information, only half of the interviewed CEOs formally or purposefully used such sources. Of the CEOs who did use their employees for CI information, most contacted their sales staff and limited themselves to that group.

Other less-commonly used sources of CI information consisted of customer interviews—depending on the type of product or service—competitor seminars, and surveys. Generally this information was gathered from the company's marketing department and was filtered to the CEO through the vice president of marketing. This information was not strategic in nature, and although most CEOs wanted to be informed of the results, most indicated that this source was generally used for tactical adjustments, as opposed to strategic direction.

One source of CI information that CEOs used personally and on a regular basis was magazine and newspaper reviews. CEOs were also involved in panel discussions, CEO conferences, industry forums, and personal contacts. There was also some indication that contacts were made through strategic alliances. Many of the CI sources for CEOs were very qualitative, and confirming the accuracy of a piece of information was generally done through a more formal CI group within the firm, or through the marketing department.

To a much lesser extent, some forms of intelligence came from buying the product or service. Some parties were interested in what functions the product provided; however, some were interested in what it felt like to be the customer. As a customer, intelligence was gathered about service guarantees, customer-service levels, price negotiations, and after-sale follow-up. In addition, some companies used focus groups to ask questions about competitors. Chief executive officers found this information useful because the participants were generally being given firsthand information.

In addition to the above methods of intelligence gathering, a few individuals used physical monitoring as a source of information. Depending on the product or service, a sales location was identified as a valuable source of information for statistics on traffic patterns, consumer-buying patterns, supplier deliveries that would occur, and the demeanor of staff arriving and leaving work. Surprisingly, none of the participants in this study mentioned contacting past employees as a CI source.

Managing CI Information

Developing an understanding of how CI information is managed has proven to be a very fragmented process. Although all individuals who participated in this study understood the necessity of having a system in place to manage the information, only a few of the CEOs interviewed indicated that they had such a formal or semi-formal system established within their company. The reason for this lack of institutionalized CI did not appear to revolve around the challenges of changing organizational culture into one in which competitive information was shared; nor did there seem to be any issues surrounding obtaining the information. The most common concern indicated a need for systematic understanding of the compiled material. Many of the CEOs interviewed did not have a frame of reference for setting this up. This type of integration problem is also reflected by executives in the Society of Competitive Intelligence Professionals (SCIP) Symposium (Society of Competitive Intelligence Professionals/Rutgers CEO Roundtable, 1996): They had no previous formal CI training and didn't understand how best to utilize the information other than to make it available internally in some central location.

Given the above situation, the CEOs were asked how they managed the CI information that was gathered. Most of the responses indicated that an intranet was used to post information as it was gathered. In this system, the individuals within the organization were responsible for reviewing the material and understanding its implications for their functional areas. There were a couple of indications that this information was made public to the press with prior corporate authorization.

Most companies were using filing cabinets, bookshelves, and corporate libraries to store the information. Many of the functional areas kept their own segment of information in their own areas, although there was some indication that the information was still open and shared among staff. In most of these cases there was one central person responsible for managing the information. There was no particular employee whose title or role included this task as part of their job description; however, the majority of the CEOs indicated that this responsibility was held by someone they worked closely with and trusted.

Some of the larger published companies indicated that a Lotus Notes database was their choice for information management. The majority of the respondents in this study also indicated a preference for this database software; however, the structure of the database varied by the individual needs of the corporation (Society of Competitive Intelligence Professionals/Rutgers CEO Roundtable, 1996).

Strategic Decision-Making

Decision-making is becoming more complex as industries move toward faster product lifecycles and globalization, where strategic decision-making is made more complex with the incorporation of new regulatory frameworks, cultures, and methods of conducting business. In this respect, decision-making can vary according to the needs of the corporation and the industry in which it operates; however, strategic decision-making responsibility is still primarily held at an upper management level. For this reason this chapter will focus on the types of final decisions and trade offs that are made by the CEO.

With this changing economy in mind, the findings given below should be considered with two things in mind: First, the CEO who is making the strategic decision must consider CI from a multifaceted viewpoint to adequately cover the different effects of the decision on the entire gamut of competitors worldwide. Secondly, these decisions must be made faster than ever. The CEOs almost universally believed that the best form of CI is the one that is vague enough to cover these many areas, yet still functional to the point of being useful. To further complicate the above situation, the decisions that are often made involve tactical, strategic, and operational issues. For the purpose of this chapter the decisions that the CEO makes or influences will be reviewed, and to a larger extent the level of impact that CI information has on those decisions.

Chief executive officers were asked to describe how the CI function related to their decision-making. Many of the participants viewed CI as a general method of collecting information about their competitors. In this respect, the results showed that CI is used periodically on an as-needed basis. The CEOs also viewed CI as a method for tactical refinement. The CEOs generally agreed that CI gathering kept their company in touch with the softer aspects of what was going on in their respective industries. Armed with this type of information about industry trends, they were better able to respond to competitive actions in a manner that had been tried by others or would be considered acceptable. At the strategic level, CI was described as a basis for the development of tacit knowledge.

Chief executive officers typically felt that their strategies did not change due to CI information because the path that they described for shareholders was always the same. The CEO's primary goal is to maximize shareholder value, and as such the path that is often chosen is based on where the industry is going. Competitive intelligence comes into play to determine where the industry is going by following the "big players." For many, the events after this goal is established are often thought of as tactical.

How Do CEOs Use CI Information?

The literature shows that many corporations use CI data for benchmarking larger companies; however, little work has been done on the extent of influence this process has on the leaders of the organization and their decisions. The participants in this study primarily used CI information at times of structured change. For example, business planning generally happened annually, and it was at this time that CEOs wanted to know what the competitors were doing. This apparent lack of congruence suggests that CI resources are being underutilized, because the goal of the CI professional would be to anticipate what the competitor is going to do. Furthermore, the limitation of this path occurs at the point when the company becomes a leader in the industry; there are few competitors to strive to "beat." The literature points to some companies that have risen above this problem. For example, Xerox has a strong CI function where competitors from different industries are benchmarked globally, nationally, and locally (Vezmar, 1996).

For planned business cycles, CI is critical for the development of the corporate business plan. Competitive intelligence is not a function that can easily be done periodically. Competitive intelligence is best used when information and trends have been analyzed over time for the purpose of anticipating future competitive moves. The participants in this study generally did not engage in systematic renewal of CI information. The CI information that was sometimes reviewed systematically focused on sales, prices, promotions, and marketing efforts.

THE CEO-CI MODEL

The CEO-CI model begins with a review of the significant research areas that a CEO could find useful in future decision-making. Determining what specific type of information can be acquired in each of those areas is important and has been previously reviewed by many CI professionals (Flynn, 1994; Galvin, 1997). The central goal of that research should remain the focus of the efforts (table 2.1). Being overwhelmed with details makes it difficult for the CEO to understand the valuable items that have been found and how to analyze the information in a relevant and actionable way. The services of a trained CI professional would be extremely valuable in this circumstance.

Competitive intelligence professionals are poorly utilized if all they are paid to do is to gather information from the Internet. They are better utilized when they are able to organize and analyze the information offered to them and make recommendations regarding the future of the industry via competitive or environmental changes or with respect to the anticipated moves the competition is expected to make. For this reason, the value of the CI professional for the CEO's purposes is to communicate the information that has been gathered in a useful, accurate, and strategic fashion that is actionable.

Under these guidelines, table 2.1 broadly outlines the minimum areas of research a CI professional would need to understand to offer a CEO reasonable predictions on competitive actions. In this respect, a CEO should be able to rea-

Table 2.1
THE CEO-CI MODEL

Area of Research	Goal
Management Profiles and Motivations	The goal in finding information in this segment of research is to determine how your competitor thinks. Ideally, if you know what motivates your competitor, the culture of the organization and the CEO, who the primary influencers are, their tolerance for risk, who is on the board of directors, shareholders, stakeholders, and the history of the key persons, then you could offer fairly accurate ideas about what types of decisions a company will make.
Organizational Framework and Reporting Structures	The goal in researching this area is to determine how quickly a competitor can respond to changes in strategy and key tactics. Knowing the organizational structure of the company and the level of interaction among key functions in the corporate environment allows the CEO to determine what the lead and turnaround times are for a competitive change from the time the decision is made to the time it is implemented.
Resources: Human, Financial, and Organizational Capabilities	The reason for finding out about a company's resources is to determine the company's abilities and capabilities. Knowing whether a corporation is potentially able to take on substantial debt, or if it is in the midst of changing their management structure, or investing in new areas for training tells the CEO how well the competitor is positioned for the future as well as specific areas for which it is preparing.
Environment and Industry Issues	The goal here is to find information with respect to the flexibility offered within an industry and the necessary areas to be mastered to influence any trends. Ideally a CEO would want to understand the networking abilities of their competitors, and the amount of flexibility available if key contacts are exploited. In addition, industry regulatory environments must be monitored to ensure that CEOs are aware of any upcoming legislative changes that may affect the future direction of the corporation.
Strategic Direction and Synthesis	Strategic direction is determined by synthesizing all of the above information. Armed with the profiles of the executive management and how decisions are made, supplemented with their level of bureaucracy, available resources, and the ability to coordinate and implement plans in specified regulatory environments, a CEO will be able to understand what the environment is that they are dealing with and the probable direction in which it is headed.

sonably expect that their CI professional be well versed in their industry and the players who influence it, as well as the expected outcomes of changes in their environment. The CEO-CI model outlined in the table does not specifically outline what methods are needed to answer those questions but rather what the information should be describing.

APPLICATION OF THE CEO-CI MODEL

The CEO-CI model has been developed to demonstrate how CI fits in with the general framework of doing business analysis. In choosing someone to perform these tasks, there has been some research done that discusses what traits best suit this role; however, the CI professional must primarily be a macrothinker. In addition, the CI professional should understand the vision of the CEO and what information would be beneficial to assist him or her in arriving at that goal. In a situation where there is a group working on the CI function, it is best to have a point of convergence for the CEO (Eger, 1996; Galvin, 1997).

At this point, the reporting structure needs to be implemented. For a single individual performing the task of answering the questions in the model, the process is clear. The individual begins gathering information according to the different areas in the model, and synthesizes the material to arrive at some potential recommendations regarding how competitors will behave in the future. For larger groups, the structure can be more difficult.

Larger groups have the opportunity to be divided according to the specialist areas of the model. For example, one individual, or a cross-functional team of individuals, will investigate the management profiles, while another will evaluate the capabilities of the firm. The convergence point described above that is required to maintain the relationship with the CEO must still be established. For this reason there should be a group leader providing the liaison between the CEO and the CI group.

BARRIERS AND OBSTACLES

The implementation of this CEO-CI model follows the fundamental rules of CI according to Fuld (1991) and Eger (1996): The CI role should not have allegiance to one functional area; and the success of a corporate CI operation depends on the ability of the CEO to remove it from the existing departmental areas and allow independent operation. The resulting independence is necessary because the CI function cannot have any vested interest in performing according to any particular departmental needs.

Senior management must be in full support of the CI function. Eger (1996) provides a checklist for the successful implementation of a CI operation that explains a number of the pitfalls of developing this type of function, and how to avoid these issues:

• Lack of senior management support

• Lack of modern technology

• Lack of a formal independent budget

• Lack of one convergence point.

In addition to the consideration of the above items when implementing the

CEO-CI model, there are some limitations to consider. The CEO-CI model is based on an ongoing relationship of trust that is expected to develop over time between the CEO and the CI professional. Many CEOs move from company to company, and a reasonable level of trust is difficult to develop under those conditions. Perhaps during the evolution of the CI profession the function will gain credibility as a necessary part of doing business rather than a "spy game," and as such, the CI professional will not need to continuously defend their position.

In addition to the above limitation, the model is still untested. It is the author's hope that this model can be tested with existing groups of CI professionals who may provide feedback on the feasibility of implementing such a system. For the purpose of building confidence in the model, CI professionals must be comfortable using it and CEOs must understand what will be changing in terms of information flow.

Conclusions: A Valuable Model for CEOs to Best Utilize CI

The main purpose of this chapter was to give CI practitioners and corporate leaders a means of building a framework that satisfies the needs of the CEO and best utilizes the skills of the CI professional. A secondary purpose was to identify the information gaps between CI professionals, who are providing exceptional work in their respective fields, and the ultimate decision-makers who act on that information. In this regard, the model outlined here provides the basis for a practical application of CI practice—perhaps not in terms of a specific "how-to" process, but to a larger extent in outlining the goals of the CEO. It is the author's view, based on her review of the literature, experience, and research described in this chapter, that the CI profession is undergoing a shift toward a more practical application of CI analysis, and as such can help companies and their leaders achieve new marketplace advantages.

APPENDIX: SOURCES OF CI WITHIN THE CEO MODEL FRAMEWORK

Specific methods of gathering information have been reviewed in the current-practices segment of this chapter; however, some additional practices that have been cited in relevant periodicals include those listed below.

For Management Profiles and Motivations, consider the following sources:

Analyst Reports	Personal Memberships with Networking Groups
Speeches, Interviews	Accomplishments
Magazine Articles	Biographies
Press Releases, Resumes	

For Organizational Framework and Reporting Structures consider the following sources:

Annual Reports	Investment Reports
Websites	Published Articles
Brochures	Recruiters
Value Line	Human Resources Departments

For Resources: Human, Financial, and Organizational Capabilities consider the following sources:

Financial Statements	Regulatory Filings
Management Profiles and Career Paths	Investment Reports
Alliance Announcements/Partnerships	Value Line
OEM Relationships	

For Environment and Industry Issues consider the following sources:

Sales Representatives	Census Bureau
Customers	Political Reviews
Analysts' Reports	Trend Reports
Strategis Canada	Industry Handbooks

For Strategic Direction and Synthesis consider the following sources:

Patent filings	Speeches
Panel Discussion Groups	Press releases
Annual Reports	Trade Shows

REFERENCES

Berger, A. (1997). "Small but Powerful: Six Steps for Conducting Competitive Intelligence Successfully at a Medium-Sized Firm," *Competitive Intelligence Review* 8(4): 75–77.

Costley, G.E. (1996). "An Executive Perspective of Competitive Analysis," in *Advances in Applied Business Strategy*, supplement 2A, 87–92. Greenwich, CT: JAI Press.

Eger, M.C. (1996). "The CEO and the CI Professional: Big Impact Partners," in *Advances in Applied Business Strategy*, supplement 2A, ed. B. Gilad and J.P. Herring. Greenwich, CT: JAI Press.

Flynn, R. (1994). "Nutrasweet Faces Competition: The Critical Role of Competitive Intelligence," *Competitive Intelligence Review* 5(4): 4–7.

Fuld, L.M. (1991). "Total Quality Through Intelligence Programs," *Competitive Intelligence Review* 2(1): 8–11.

Galvin, R.W. (1997). "Competitive Intelligence at Motorola," *Competitive Intelligence Review* 8(1): 3–6.

McGonagle, J.J., Jr. (1992). "Patterns of Development in CI Units," *Competitive Intelligence Review* 8(1): 11–12.

Society of Competitive Intelligence Professionals/Rutgers CEO Roundtable. (1996). "Symposium: Understanding the Competition: The CEO's Perspective," *Competitive Intelligence Review* 7(3): 4–14.

Vezmar, J.M. (1996). "Competitive Intelligence at Xerox," *Competitive Intelligence Review* 7(3): 15–18.

3

Reducing Vulnerability Through Counterintelligence

Peter Barrett

INTRODUCTION

Counterintelligence is the process of countering, or preventing, the intelligence-gathering effort of other parties—often, but not necessarily, your competitors. Understanding counterintelligence requirements means understanding the competitive intelligence (CI) process itself to reveal how others might collect information about your firm. By definition, the CI process is legal and ethical (Nolan, 1997), but not everyone involved is ethical and legal. Therefore one must also have an understanding of the aims and methods of industrial espionage.

Counterintelligence requires differentiating between information management and security. It requires understanding what is valuable, which parties pose a threat, how you are vulnerable, and what counterintelligence means to the company. And, most importantly, counterintelligence means understanding what you should do about it.

This chapter will aid managers who are concerned about information security within their organizations in understanding the ways in which they are vulnerable to counterintelligence, and how they should deal with it to minimize risk. This chapter will lay out a simple counterintelligence program that will show the kinds of information that might be sought by competitors, the manner in which they might seek it, and the methods to make those efforts less effective. It will also heighten awareness of the different ways our mundane daily activities can communicate our broader intentions to those who may be listening.

THE COMPETITIVE INTELLIGENCE PROCESS

Understanding the CI process and how it is used to gather data is key to understanding how to manage information within the company. Companies leave a paper trail of their day-to-day activities that is usually easy to follow. Most of the information your competitors want is available from publicly available channels. In fact, some estimates say 80 to 90 percent of the required information can be collected from public sources, and, when analyzed carefully, makes the remaining percentage insignificant (Richard Combs Associates, 1998). It has to be recognized that your competitors can collect information about you in the same way that you collect information about them.

To get a better sense of the type of information that you are making available, it is useful to look at the CI process itself. If you understand where someone looks for information and what they do with it, you can better manage *what* information you put *where* and the conclusions you draw from it.

THE COUNTERINTELLIGENCE PROCESS

Your competitors, both old and new, always have their eyes trained on you and your operation. Countermeasures must be thought of as part of an ongoing process, and, beyond the initial setup, not as a one-time project.

Before undertaking a countermeasures program, it is essential that there be top-management buy-in. They will allocate resources and provide the line authority that will support the policies that arise. The difficulty will be in measuring the contribution that countermeasures will make to the bottom line. If the process is effective, losses to competitors due to their intelligence efforts will be minimized, and the countermeasures will look like a cost on an income statement. It is difficult to measure the value of a competitive edge lost or not lost or, perhaps, unknowingly lost. However, through examining the counterintelligence process and seeing the costs associated with not having an effective program, the value should become clear.

Tasking

Many corporations rely on security to protect their assets, assuming that if the physical assets are protected, then the valuable assets are protected. This emphasis on security has been referred to as the "gates, guards, guns, and dogs" approach and isn't surprising when you consider that over 50 percent of today's security managers have a background in law enforcement (Nolan, 1996d). Although physical-assets protection is necessary, this type of security cannot protect the company's intellectual capital except through the reactive apprehension and capture of criminal perpetrators (if they can be found at all), usually long after the damage has been done.

Security should be viewed as a proactive and integral part of the overall counterintelligence program. But because of the very close tie between the CI process and the counterintelligence process, the primary responsibility should be with the CI team. As discussed earlier, their in-depth knowledge of CI gives them a key understanding of how outside interested parties might interpret the company's activities.

Define Requirements

Defining requirements means understanding *what* really needs to be protected. The degree of protection will vary greatly from company to company, as will the types of information requiring protection. This stage of the process requires some corporate self-assessment. A good starting point is to define what you consider your company's "crown jewels"—those few key components or capabilities that give you the competitive edge and would cost you dearly were they available to everyone (Nolan, 1997). These core competencies could encompass proprietary product technology, manufacturing processes, training techniques, or internal operational systems. It could also include new product launches, mergers and acquisitions, research and development, financial details, or strategic plans. In other words, anything that might allow someone to out-maneuver your business.

It is important to note that the size of the firm is not related to the need for protecting sensitive information. Many companies mistakenly believe that they are too small to be thought of as having valuable information. A good example of how that assumption can lead to disaster is the story of a small, 20-person software engineering firm in Palo Alto, California, that was infiltrated by an agent of the French government (Nolan, 1996b). Although the perpetrator was caught and charged, the firm had no idea that they might be a target of intelligence gathering until their proprietary information was "out there."

Assess Competition

In this stage, you need to grasp who poses a threat to your organization. Who would want to know more about you and want information you have? In many cases they are competitors in your business, or want to be. Assessing this threat is a classic CI function, and you may already have most of the information you need from your regular CI processes. The analytical requirements here, though, are a bit more particular.

Primarily, you want to understand your competition's (or potential competition's) intelligence-collection capability and its underlying, governing philosophy (Nolan, 1997). In the long run, you cannot assume your competition is any less vigilantly investigating you than you are investigating them. First, things change—they could get better. Second, what if, with whatever degree of enthusiasm your competitors perform their CI, they stumble across that one piece of information you would not like them to have? Third, and worst of all, they could actually be much better at CI than you are. Therefore a thorough understanding of their CI capability can let you know exactly what you are up against, and perhaps provide the opportunity for you to control the information they get. Understanding their underlying philosophy can give some insight into how they might react to information they obtain. You also will want to be able to estimate how much they already know about you.

Competitive intelligence professionals are thorough and tough. Assume that if information regarding your company is out there, they will find it. Most wise companies know this and act accordingly. A good example of this understanding is demonstrated by a situation recently faced by Gay Lea Foods Co-operative Ltd. More than a year ago, Gay Lea applied to the Ontario Ministry of the Environment for approval to build a new emission stack at their Teeswater, Ontario, plant that would help improve the plant's efficiency. Ontario's Information and Privacy Commission ruled that the detailed technical information submitted in support of the application for provincial approval of the upgrade be publicly released. However, company president Charles MacDaid said that "[t]here is some information in that document we didn't want our competitors to have. They could infer certain things about our operations" (*Daily Commercial News and Construction Record*, 1999). MacDaid now must decide whether or not to seek a judicial review of the decision. Perhaps those applications might have been submitted in a less-detailed fashion—perhaps not, but MacDaid knows if the detailed plans are made public, his competitors will examine them closely and any competitive edge he had hoped to gain will be lost.

It must be remembered that not everyone interested in what your organization does is ethical. The possibility that illegalities might be undertaken to harm your company must be seriously considered. Espionage is "an act or activity directed towards the acquisition of sensitive or proprietary information by the use of clandestine collection methods" (Tracey, 1998). These threats can come from a wide variety of organizations with a surprising variety of reasons for wanting to damage your business. They can take an assortment of forms, from simple break-and-enter to the more sophisticated hacking into computer systems or electronic eavesdropping.

The Federal Bureau of Investigation estimates that in the last six years 1,100 known cases of corporate espionage have resulted in losses of over U.S.$300 billion (Tracey, 1998). In one form or another the principal reasons for this sort of activity are money and power, whether to gain technology to advance revenue or to support political ideology.

Whatever the reasons, there is a long list of entities that could pose a threat to your organization. This list could include foreign-government intelligence services (both hostile and friendly nations), foreign or domestic corporations, criminals (organized or otherwise), terrorists, and activists. One common methodology is to introduce people (known as moles or agents) into the company. Another common methodology is to exploit people already within the company. Candidates for this method could include such insiders as on-site nonemployee workers (contract personnel), regular employees who may be in need of money or are just plain greedy, regular employees who have something to hide (blackmail), disgruntled employees, thrill seekers, activists, ideologues, departing employees, or former employees (Winkler, 1997). In short, anyone against whom some leverage could be used.

These people need not necessarily be exploited by an outside agency. Personal motivations could lead them, of their own volition, to commit the thefts and then look for buyers. Most commonly, insiders will remove, copy, photograph, download, or otherwise steal sensitive information from your organization. They might also simply overhear, electronically bug, or eavesdrop conversations (Tracey, 1998).

Recent events that are interesting examples of threats coming from noncompetitive sources are groups that have been dubbed "hacktivists." These groups launch software attacks on companies involved in activities to which they are politically opposed, such as nuclear proliferation or pollution, and perform acts of sabotage as a form of protest. An electronics company manufacturing electrical components used in a nuclear power plant could suddenly find itself under attack and its business stability threatened by an enemy it didn't even know it had.

Estimate Vulnerabilities

Vulnerabilities refer to any weaknesses within your organization that will provide an opportunity for a threat of exploitation. They fall into four broad categories: operations, physical, personnel, and technical (Winkler, 1997). Estimating vulnerabilities thoroughly requires a considerable amount of corporate self-examination and honest soul-searching. You need to find as many of your weaknesses as you can, because if you know about them, you can deal with them. When assessing vulnerabilities, remember without fail that *information is information*—the source is irrelevant (Richard Combs Associates, 1998).

Operations vulnerabilities refer to weaknesses in the way your firm does business on a day-to-day basis. They refer to the way the actions of the company reveal its future plans, and how the company goes about giving out information. The Gay Lea incident is a good example of an operational vulnerability. In the normal course of doing business, Gay Lea risked making proprietary processes public. A similar example is the chief executive officer who was trying to show the Environmental Protection Agency that his company could not afford the large fine that it was being assessed. In attempting to do so, he brought his financial spreadsheets to the hearing. As part of the minutes from the hearing, they became part of the public record (Richard Combs Associates, 1998).

Many operational activities can telegraph your secrets. Companies generate large volumes of formal documents, both public and in-house, from the aforementioned government-regulatory applications to securities exchange (SEC) filings, strategic plans, manufacturing and product specifications, and financial reports. These documents often include drafts with associated working papers, often regarded as trash once the final document has been generated. There are many other documents that can also give clues to your firm's activities. Travel records could indicate the occurrence of meetings you might not want everyone to know about. Bills of lading, often not regarded as very sensitive, could reveal who is buying what from whom, which could be significant in the context of other information (Winkler, 1997). The same daily activities that are carried out for business purposes can indicate what those purposes are.

The most significant operational vulnerability is the lack of awareness among employees of what exactly constitutes sensitive information. All people have what can be termed "exploitable motivations," which, using legal methods, can cause them to reveal information they shouldn't be revealing (Green, 1999). Many things can be learned simply because somebody phoned and asked for the information. Most of these informational calls go unreported to those for whom the pattern of inquiry may make up a picture. People also take work with them to do in public places, such as the commuter train, where interested parties could simply read over their shoulder. Casual conversations in public places can be very revealing as well.

Physical vulnerabilities can be another significant area that can easily be exploited. Many companies fail to have suitable access control, and if they have some security guards, they are not properly trained in what to look for. The biggest vulnerabilities on the physical side come from not using readily available security measures such as locks on drawers or doors to rooms that contain sensitive materials. Computers may be left on or contain no password protection so that anyone gaining physical access could make use of the system. A similar vulnerability is the messy desk where papers that should be stored away are left sitting in the open or lying in an inbox for any passerby to read. Such vulnerability can be compounded by poor disposal procedures. "Garbage surfing" or "dumpster diving" is a common method of locating information (Winkler, 1997).

Personnel vulnerabilities differ slightly from operational vulnerabilities. Rather than focusing on the way people work and function within the organization, personnel vulnerabilities focus on the way in which companies hire and manage their employees. Once hired, people have, or can, obtain relatively free access to most areas of the company. Failing to check claims about background on resumes can result in the hiring of unsuitable people. These could be people with criminal intent at the time of hiring or people who could be exploited later in their tenure at the company. In addition, if it is not well known that a person's employment has been terminated, this person could continue to gain access to the company and inflict vast damage (Winkler, 1997).

Technical vulnerabilities can be likened to physical vulnerabilities that exist in cyberspace. They are essentially vulnerabilities that can allow the organization to be compromised through the computer system. Dr. Loki Jorgenson, Research Manager for the Center for Experimental and Constructive Mathematics at Simon Fraser University (SFU) and former systems administrator for both SFU and McGill University, says that the average system is secure "in the same way that the average house is secure—in other words, not very, aside from being locked [most of the time]" (Jorgenson, 1999). Each computer system on the market has known vulnerabilities that hackers try to exploit. Failure to secure known weaknesses in the systems with readily available patches is a very significant problem in many organizations. For example, most UNIX-based systems that have not been deliberately secured against attack are vulnerable (Jorgenson, 1999). The risk associated with insecure computer systems is why—when advertising to hire technical people—it is a bad idea to list the systems on which you would like them to have had experience; it essentially tells people, in print, what they need to know to hack your systems.

Dr. Jorgenson tells an anecdote that illustrates the basic vulnerability of a system (in this case the system at SFU, which hosts the North Atlantic Treaty Organization [NATO] information site) to which access can be obtained by way of the Internet:

> The one serious hacker that came in would never have been caught (he sniffed the password) and would have done a lot of serious damage (capturing passwords in other systems) if I hadn't fluked onto his plant. He came in, planted a backdoor very fast, and got out—the plant worked in such a way that, even if found, he would never be caught on the system (it shipped the captured information out of the site on request). Because it was sniffing FTP accesses and we run a very busy FTP site, his plant process showed up on the process logs as taking a lot of central processing unit (CPU) time. And I didn't recognize the name of the program . . . so I tracked it down. (Jorgenson, 1999)

Poor password protocols, not closing unused accounts, uncontrolled modem accesses, and poor systems-administrator (or other personnel) training are other factors that create technical vulnerabilities (Winkler, 1997). Internal personnel can exploit these without using the Internet by having access to your local area network (LAN). Someone could copy poorly protected information or alternatively create the holes for it to be removed externally, either alone or with co-conspirators.

Develop/Employ Countermeasures

The development and employment of countermeasures is the process of addressing your vulnerabilities to protect your company's assets in a manner consistent with its value. Reliance on law-enforcement agencies is a reactive strategy; they can't do anything until after an illegal act has occurred. And if the act isn't illegal, as properly conducted CI isn't, then law enforcement is powerless. Countermeasures need not be expensive but they must be appropriate, and they are your responsibility.

The most important operational countermeasure is an awareness program. All personnel need to realize that they have a direct relationship to, and investment in, the company's well-being. This direct employee impact means their understanding the relationship of what they do, not only to specific projects or assignments, but also to the on-going operations of the company relative to its competitors.

The focus of an awareness program should be to educate, not threaten, employees. Threats will only result in poor morale and create more vulnerabilities. The key facts to communicate are the value of information (both to the company and to the competitor), how competitors collect it, how competitors assess it, and the employees' role in the countermeasures to prevent it (Winkler, 1997). If they understand the relationship between the value of the information and corporate performance, self-interest should lead to heightened awareness.

To support the higher levels of awareness, communication channels must be established, such as an incident-reporting protocol. Requests for information should be dealt with on a callback basis. The name, telephone number, and company of all such callers should be obtained along with the specific information being requested and the timeline for the needed response. Each of these incidents should be reported to a CI gatekeeper. The gatekeeper can collate and assess the information for any patterns and properly coordinate the response. Requests for information could indicate not only who is looking, but also what specific information they are looking for. An incident-reporting protocol will have the additional advantage of actively engaging employees in countermeasures by giving them a real part to play in foiling the competitors' CI processes (Nolan, 1996c).

A good training program will address many operational vulnerabilities. Employees will begin to treat information differently. Management must also treat information differently. Not all information has the same value, so not all information warrants the same degree of protection. By categorizing information by level of sensitivity and value, others will know how to treat it differently. Place more-sensitive information in more-controlled environments, and encourage reporting of unauthorized access (or attempted unauthorized access). Any document containing an employee name should be considered "company confidential." Information relating to specific projects or that is considered proprietary should be restricted to those who need to know it. Sensitive financial information should be restricted to senior executives. The need for information with respect to both internal and external requests should always be verified (Winkler, 1997).

Managers should ensure that basic security activities occur to address physical vulnerabilities. Security guards should be properly trained, and copier use should be restricted. Computers should be shut off, doors and drawers should be locked, desks and in-boxes cleared, papers suitably shredded prior to disposal, and unusual activity questioned. In addition, business conducted away from the office, where unknown ears and eyes could intercept it, should be conducted in a more discrete manner (Winkler, 1997). These countermeasures are also effective measures that can make an unfriendly interested party's job more difficult.

Other simple measures can restrict private information from becoming public. Papers to be published or speeches to be made should be reviewed for unsuitable content. Establish nondisclosure agreements with suppliers so that they do not reveal crucial component or usage information. Do not post every detail possible onto your website, where the whole world can read them. In regulatory documents and filings, report only the minimum necessary to comply (Winkler, 1997). This step alone might have saved Gay Lea a big headache, potentially lost profits, and substantial legal bills. Simply put: Think about what you say in public before you say it.

The human-resources function (HR) can be a big asset when addressing personnel vulnerabilities. Proper background checks on applicants can quickly reveal suspicious or false claims, and prevent infiltration by an unfriendly mole or agent. Coordination with security and the information-systems function on terminations should be used to prevent hazards such as continued postemployment access or a remote or local area network (LAN) computer account remaining open past termination date. The placing of employment advertisements, and the kinds of information those ads contain, must also be restricted to prevent revealing too much. Vague ads may lead to reviewing more unsuitable resumes, but, given the alternative, it may be time well spent. Categorizing employees (such as temporary and contract) and imposing appropriate restrictions on what they have access to will help prevent those with less interest in the company's future from taking advantage of such intelligence-gathering opportunities (Winkler, 1997).

The single biggest failure in addressing technical vulnerabilities is not closing known holes in your system. The well-known weaknesses of systems are the first target of any technical penetration and constitute about 95 percent of the problems (Jorgenson, 1999). Lack of awareness on the part of systems administrators is probably most at fault. There are more systems needing good administrators than there are good administrators, and most are very overworked anyway (Jorgenson, 1999). The primary source to learn of known system vulnerabilities is the Computer Emergency Research Team (CERT), which publicizes recently discovered vulnerabilities and archives older, known ones for almost any system at its website (<http://www.cert.org>). This resource should be consulted regularly and its recommendations for system repair followed. This countermeasure by itself will prevent most of the uncreative intruders.

Education is a key factor in preventing technical intrusions. Employees need to be taught not only that passwords must not to be given out, but also that they should not use ones that can be easily guessed. Protocols of giving out access passwords only in person, strong password-change mechanisms, and regularly expiring passwords will demonstrate the importance of security issues (Jorgenson, 1999). In addition, you should have in place policies related to where and how proprietary information is stored within the system, as well as access controls. A well-trained systems administrator will be invaluable for this.

Other basic countermeasures to protect technical intrusion will depend on budget and system complexities. These can include antivirus software, intrusion-alert software, and mirrored logs. Some can be expensive to install and monitor, so again, they should be considered in light of the value of information requiring protection. However, as Dr. Jorgenson's anecdote suggests, a systems administrator with a good sense of what is right and wrong within the system will be a very effective countermeasure.

However, the question arises: If we know how they get the information and from where they get it, then can we influence the picture they see? That is, could we, or should we, deliberately deceive the competition?

The goal of such a strategy is to "confuse your rival's CI organization—the eyes and ears of his strategists—so that the decision-maker makes the wrong decisions about what they should do in response to the incoming information" (Nolan, 1996a). This deliberate action can be thought of as *perception management*. Done well, your competitors will begin to distrust their CI department and its recommendations.

Deception, though, is very labor-intensive and requires a great deal of attention to detail. In order not to give the game away, nearly all potential sources of CI must be managed to convey the desired impression. The risk is that your competitor may simply replace one collection method with another. Diversionary tactics are usually employed on a project-specific rather than an on-going basis, such as misleading a competitor on a coming product launch with respect to timing, pricing, or the technology involved.

Great care must be taken—especially in a publicly traded company—when creating false impressions. For example, a recent case of faked website postings by a company's employee implying a coming merger caused the stock to skyrocket and led to a charge of securities fraud (Wyatt, 1999). That being said, misinformation that isn't illegal is not necessarily immoral. After all, you don't owe someone the information just because they asked for it.

Analysis

A regular and rigorous review of your success in prevention, and your competitors' successes in obtaining information, is essential to prevent new sources from springing up. You can be sure that if a competitor doesn't get information from one source, it will try another. The collection of information should be difficult enough that the true CI professional will not be able to form a full or clear picture of your intentions in a timely manner. The collection of information by those using less ethical means should be difficult enough that they will go elsewhere to seek easier prey. The self-analysis process must be continuous. Each activity must be thought of in terms of what it might tell someone else, and then, conversely, how it might be done so as not to be too revealing.

CONCLUSION

Companies no longer operate with assets that are purely physical in nature. The new measurement of corporate value is intellectual capital. It is knowledge that creates revenue and profits. Understanding your competitors and their competitive edges can go a long way to helping you make better decisions about how to compete with them. However, not remembering that the same information about you and your operations is of equal or greater interest to them can be fatal.

REFERENCES

Daily Commercial News and Construction Record. (1999). "Firm Wants to Keep Details of Stack Secret," *Daily Commercial News and Construction Record* 72(123): A5.

Green, W. (1999). "I Spy," *Forbes* 164(1) <http://www.forbes.com/forbes/98/0420/6108090a.html>.

Jorgenson, L. (1999). Research Manager, Center for Experimental and Constructive Mathematics, Simon Fraser University, personal communication, June 24, 1999.

Nolan, J.A. (1996a). *Is It Better to Give than to Deceive?* <http://www.intellpros.com/lib/deceive.html>.

———. (1996b). *You Don't Have to Be General Motors to Be a Target.* <http://www. intellpros.com/lib/gm.html>.

———. (1996c). *Now That You Know How They're Getting It, What Do You Do Next?* <http://www.intellpros.com/lib/next.html>.

———. (1996d). *What Does Our Competition Know About Us and How Did They Get It?* <http://www.intellpros.com/lib/know.html>.

———. (1997). *Is Somebody Dulling Your Competitive Edge?* <http://www.strategis. ic.gc.ca/SSG/mi03945e.html>.

Richard Combs Associates. (1998). *The Axioms of Competitive Intelligence.* <http://www. strategis.ic.gc.ca/SSG/mi03988e.html>.

Tracey, M. (1998). *The Threats of Corporate and Economic Espionage and How the Threat Can Be Countered by the Effective Use of Intelligence.* <http://www.strategis. ic.gc.ca/SSG/mi06117e.html>.

Winkler, I. (1997). *Corporate Espionage: What It Is, Why It Is Happening in Your Company, What You Must Do About It.* Roseville, CA: Prima Publishing.

Wyatt, E. (1999). "Fake Web Posting Leads to Fraud Charge," *New York Times* (May 16, 1999) <http://www.scip.org/news/newsbriefs_artic...ORD=924562111&XP_FOR-MAT=newbriefs_article>.

4

The Use of Counterintelligence, Security, and Countermeasures

Alain Francq

INTRODUCTION

John Nolan, a leading authority on the subject, defines counterintelligence as "[a]ctive measures, undertaken by a commercial firm—sometimes in cooperation with Federal counterintelligence services—to protect its operations by anticipating and neutralizing the intelligence operations of a competitor" (Nolan, 1997).

"Active measures" means not lying back and waiting for something to happen, and then trying to find the culprit who has injured the firm. It means that counterintelligence is *anticipatory* and *business-oriented*. We want to determine and understand everything about the competitor who is going to try to penetrate a company and gather its secrets. This level of counterintelligence is several orders of skill beyond the typical "gates, guards, guns, and dogs" approach that characterizes most company security programs in which the orientation is defensive and involves law enforcement and protection from criminal types of attack.

No discussion of counterintelligence is complete without addressing the pros and cons of the U.S. Economic Espionage and Protection of Proprietary Information Act passed in 1996. The Act was intended to finally federalize the many different trade-secrets misappropriation laws that existed at the state level. It was intended to criminalize espionage and therefore make the penalties much more severe. The legislative intent of the Act was to allow companies that were being attacked by illicit means to call upon the Federal Bureau of Investigation (FBI) to investigate and the Department of Justice to prosecute the perpetrators of such crimes, whether they be domestic industrial espionage types or the economic espionage practitioners from abroad (U.S. Congress, 1996).

U.S. NATIONAL SECURITY

The American FBI's counterintelligence mission is set out in a strategy known as the National Security Threat List (NSTL). The FBI identified eight categories of foreign intelligence activity that were deemed to be significant threats (U.S. Federal Bureau of Investigation, 1998):

- Terrorism
- Espionage
- Proliferation
- Economic Espionage
- Targeting the National Information Infrastructure
- Targeting the U.S. Government
- Perception Management
- Foreign Intelligence Activities.

However, there are several problems with enlisting Federal counterintelligence support:

- It takes time to investigate and prosecute one of these kinds of crimes. Federal agencies thrive on budgets that are supported by statistics. Statistics are comprised of arrests, and more arrests equals more funding. You can catch a lot more bank robbers in a shorter period of time than you can industrial spies. A higher priority assigned by federal agencies to conventional crime limits the amount of resources available to help commercial counterintelligence practitioners.

- There has not been a significant increase in the number of agents trained to do counterintelligence. The counterintelligence squads at most FBI offices are small when compared to those of bank robbery, terrorism, or kidnapping.

- Very often the FBI only comes in to participate in the final apprehension of the criminal party (parties) and appears at the press conference to share the spotlight. This limited participation points out not only the inability of government to be the answer to everything, but also that it comes down to the company's leadership to protect its assets in the first place.

- Furthermore, if a company hasn't paid the appropriate amount of attention to protecting itself in ways that are consistent with the threat and environment, then no court in the world is going to provide relief. That's like the judge asking someone, "Why should I give greater value to your company's private information than you did?"

- The issue of the courts is also problematic because companies are sometimes forced to reveal more than what they lost in the first place in the discovery process. If a company is charging another party in a theft case, the defendant has the right to ask for all information about the way the plaintiff was doing business. In many cases, the plaintiff has to reveal so much about itself and its operations that it was better off doing something else.

- Last is the matter of why companies might not want to reveal in the public domain that they failed to take the steps necessary to protect themselves from information loss. The results of this action could be diminished shareholder value, diminished shareholder confidence, loss of public face, and a whole host of other considerations.

CANADIAN ECONOMIC SECURITY

The cost of economic-espionage activities to individual firms and the Canadian economy runs into billions of dollars annually. Canada, as one of the world's most open and trade-dependent countries, is one of the most vulnerable to penetration by economic spies from the intelligence services of both friends and enemies. If the growing damage to Canada resulting from the theft of Canadian technology is to be reversed, a number of changes will have to take place, including the following (Canadian Security Intelligence Service, 1998):

- The domestic legal framework covering economic espionage will have to be modified and strengthened
- Intelligence services will have to focus more on monitoring the corrupt business practices of other nations and their firms
- Intelligence services will have to take a more aggressive approach to countering economic espionage.

According to the Canadian Security Intelligence Service (CSIS), the SVR, which replaced the Soviet KGB in 1991, sends highly trained "illegal" intelligence officers to Canada who take up residence and spend years collecting political, economic, technological, and military information (Canadian Security Intelligence Service, 1998).

To summarize this discussion: A company must manage their own counterintelligence system.

GETTING OFFENSIVE: THE USE OF DECEPTION

Perhaps the most proactive, aggressive, and effective countermeasure is deception. Deception is often called "perception management" in counterintelligence. The end result of this process is to confuse your rival's competitive intelligence (CI) organization (the eyes and ears of their strategists) so that the decision-makers make the wrong decision about what they should do in response to the incoming information (Nolan, 1997): "When enemy agents come to spy on you, fool them into passing on false information. The enemy will make preparation according to this information" (Sun-Tzu, 1988).

During the Desert Storm campaign, General Norman Schwarzkopf depended heavily on intelligence about the Iraqi military forces—the number and capabilities of their weapons and their deployment—to formulate his strategy and battle plan. He then purposely created a different perception about his battle plan in the minds of the Iraqi military leaders by revealing to them and their intelligence units what he wanted them to know (Herring, 1992).

When the Iraqi counterintelligence unit discovered that U.S. intelligence-gathering efforts included satellite photography, the Iraqi military strategists recommended placing balloons shaped like tanks in the desert to feed misinformation into the U.S. intelligence effort. In both cases, competitive intelligence and counterintelligence played a very important role in formulating, protecting, and executing strategy.

A very important aspect of counterintelligence is that if you become aware that you are a target of CI gathering or espionage, special steps must be taken to avoid alerting your surveillant to the fact that you know they are watching.

PERCEPTION-MANAGEMENT EXAMPLES

Creating False Impressions

A competitor was able to anticipate one company's production changes by simply having someone sit in a car some distance from the gate of the factory and record the traffic flow. An increase in cars, and thus number of people, indicated an increase in production (Nolan, 1997).

What should the company do? Call the police? No, don't let them know you know. You do not want to have the competitor replace one collection methodology with another one that would take longer to detect and neutralize.

Instead, the company provided incentives for employees to car pool just as the company was increasing the number of people hired for increased production. The distance was such that the surveillant could not detect the number of people in the cars, and the number of cars remained relatively constant. The company was able to realize a significant increase in market share during that particular cycle, and the increase in earnings more than offset the costs of the perception program (Nolan, 1997).

Creating Confusion

Another effective deception countermeasure is to influence the target's behavior. One company set up an in-house security-awareness and -training program. Through real-world examples, employees became quite familiar with the kinds of questions and interests that CI practitioners had about their company's operations. Within a few weeks, numerous employees had reported suspicious calls. By the time the next series of inquires came in, the company's leadership set up a plan to confuse the rival's management. Instead of just creating a false impression to mislead the rival firm, which is the typical approach of perception management, it wanted to sow uncertainty and disequilibrium. Therefore, when the rival firm's intelligence collectors called they obtained a tremendous amount of information, much of it contradictory, which led to general confusion in deciding what the information meant (Nolan, 1997).

This confusion did several things: First, it reduced the confidence of the rival firm's leadership that it was getting quality information from its intelligence unit on a timely basis; second, it caused the intelligence collectors to be unsettled and uncomfortable with information that it obtained from reliable sources; and third, it caused the rival's collectors to develop other sources in the target company, some of which were "dangled" in front of them, so that the target company could control the information the competitor was receiving (Nolan, 1997).

It is important to note that use of deception must be done with great caution. For example, companies can assume competitors are closely scanning websites for indications of strategic direction or changes. It is tempting to use your corporate website as a method of conveying false information. However, not only are your competitors looking at the site, but so are your customers and industry analysts—to name a few.

COUNTERINTELLIGENCE MIND-SET

It is very important to establish a corporate counterintelligence mind-set. This is not to instill paranoia, but rather to get people to think proactively by asking questions such as: What are competitors looking for? How are they trying to get it? What can we do to reduce their chances of getting it?

To gain insight into these questions, the following six ways of how "open" sources could be exploited exist (Nolan, 1996):

• Deduce the probable production dates for a new product from a review of newspaper classified advertising for new employees

• Gain an understanding of the technique that would be used in the production from a review of the same advertising

• Gain an appreciation of the strategic role that a new product would play in the direction of the company and how it could relate with other product lines, derived from a review of remarks that senior executives make to the local chamber of commerce

• Obtain the layout of the manufacturing line for the new product from documents filed with the local emergency-management office

• Gain an understanding of some advanced manufacturing techniques to be employed in making the new product, derived from an article in a technical journal written by a member of the engineering staff

• Gain a clear picture of the penetration strategy to be employed by a company, complete with how the pricing and distribution decisions were made, derived from an article in a professional journal written by a member of the market-research staff.

Five ways of how "human" sources could be exploited are (Nolan, 1996):

- Identify the subassemblies associated with the new product by talking to the subcontractors who made them and discussing delivery schedules, quality, reliability, pricing, volume issues, and weak points in the relationship
- Estimate annual production rates based on data obtained from the company that would be producing the packaging materials for the new product
- Confirm the production rates, launch dates, and customers based on conversations with the transportation company
- Identify various patterns concerning market testing based on follow-up conversations with participants in those test-marketing activities
- Reveal that others had interviewed the test-market participant to collect the same kind of data.

There is no such thing as coincidence. Whether you use link analysis or pattern analysis to determine the extent and nature of the threat to your business, you will observe too many coincidences to dismiss the connections out-of-hand (Nolan, 1996). Assess the threat by looking for motive, opportunity, and method. Counterintelligence involves monitoring and identifying CI modus operandi. The modus operandi (National Counterintelligence Center, 1995; 1996; 1997; 1998; 1999):

- *Elicitation*: a ploy whereby seemingly normal conversation is contrived to extract information about individuals, their work, and their colleagues. It is difficult to recognize, and is easily deniable
- *Eavesdropping*: listening to other people's conversations to gather information. It can occur within a radius of ten feet and often does in restaurants, bars, and public transportation
- *Technical eavesdropping*: use of audio and visual devices. Relatively cost efficient, low risk, and easy to conceal
- *Electronic interception*: conducted against modern telecommunications systems. Telephones, fax machines, and computers can be easily monitored
- *Unsolicited requests for information*: the most frequently used modus operandi for collection because it is simple, low cost, nonthreatening to the recipient, and low risk to the collector. Can be as simple as a telephone call, fax, e-mail, or letter
- *Inappropriate conduct during visits*: this is the next most-frequently reported modus operandi. Once in the facility, collectors may attempt to manipulate the visit to satisfy their collection requirements. Beware of hidden agendas, unannounced persons, "wandering" visitors who become offended when confronted and conversation with escorts beyond the approved scope of the visit
- *Solicitation and marketing services*: there is an increasing trend involving "headhunters" who solicit information from targeted employees for information-gathering purposes

• *Exploitation of joint ventures*: often members of a joint venture are competitors or may become competitors. Joint efforts place competitors in close proximity and afford potential access to information

• *Acquisitions of companies and technology*: the acquisition of key competitive partners such as suppliers provides access to competitors' operational information

• *Using the Internet to identify and target information for collection*: the Internet is the fastest-growing modus operandi. It opens many avenues of access to a company's employees and corporate information and intentions

• *Targeting at trade shows, exhibits, seminars, and conventions*: these functions directly link programs and technologies with knowledgeable personnel

• *Marketing survey ploys*: competitors may send out a "fake" survey that solicits information concerning corporate affiliations, market projections, pricing policies, names, or purchasing practices

• *Co-opting of former employees*: former employees who had access to sensitive proprietary information remain a potential counterintelligence threat. Nike and Reebok, the athletic-apparel companies, have complex nondisclosure and anticompetition agreements that prohibit employees from disclosing any corporate information or working for the competition for one year after leaving.

Table 4.1 summarizes these modus operandi and lists the measures for countering them.

SECURITY

By analyzing your daily security procedures, whether personal or company-wide, a detailed overview of strengths and vulnerabilities related to operational threats can be developed. Focused analysis of access controls, security-team procedures, data and communications, emergency response, employee relations, facility integrity, and other vital areas of daily operation need to be monitored by executives so as to achieve effective tactical security management. The following is a list of counterintelligence security essentials (Bernhardt, 1993) that should be secured:

• access control
• conversation
• communications
• document handling and destruction
• computers
• filing systems
• corporate employees.

Table 4.1
CI MODUS OPERANDI AND COUNTERMEASURES

Modus Operandi	Security and Countermeasures
Elicitation	Training in what is appropriate in conversation, and techniques to deflect questions
Eavesdropping	Assume conversations are never entirely secure and speak accordingly
Technical eavesdropping	Assume conversations are never entirely secure and speak accordingly. Try not to place materials or conduct activities in areas where they can be photographed. If you are aware of the surveillance, you may use perception management techniques to sow misinformation
Electronic interception	Assume that all telephone, faxes, and e-mails are intercepted
Unsolicited requests for information	Implement an information-protection program (IPP) that trains employees to recognize and report suspicious requests. Company leadership or a counterintelligence unit may set up a perception-management or -confusion program to sow misinformation or disequilibrium. Be careful!
Inappropriate conduct during visits	Beware of hidden agendas, unannounced persons, "wandering" visitors who become offended when confronted, and conversations with escorts beyond the approved scope of the visit
Solicitation and marketing services	Limit access to sensitive information and provide incentives to employees to report a valid solicitation attempt
Exploitation of joint ventures	Tightly monitor shared information and attempt to deduce what the partner is doing with the information (e.g., using it to develop their own product)
Acquisitions of companies and technology	Monitor agency filings and mergers and acquisitions. Analyze whether the acquiring firm could become a competitor, especially if the company acquired is a proprietary supplier
Using the Internet to identify and target information for collection	Recommend not using corporate websites to convey strategic or sensitive material. Do not use as a channel to sow misinformation
Targeting at trade shows, exhibits, seminars and conventions	Very rich source of intelligence. Competitors will be collecting information! Do not show or discuss products yet to be released. Try to discuss benefits and not the details behind the service or product
Marketing survey ploys	Ensure that surveys and participation in research are carefully screened before proceeding. If you are aware the survey is of a CI nature, you may use perception management to sow misinformation
Co-opting of former employees	Implement nondisclosure and noncompete clauses in employee contracts. If you are aware of former employees talking to, or working for, competitive firms, ensure that everyone knows not to discuss corporate issues with them. Furthermore, deception techniques can be employed

INFORMATION-PROTECTION PROGRAM

An information-protection program (IPP) will educate key employees on what needs to be protected and what their responsibilities are to prevent the loss of classified intellectual property or proprietary information. It will also help educate all employees on counterintelligence-awareness issues. Good risk-management practices will ensure the proper training of employees and empower them to recognize and report suspicious activity.

Continuous intelligence monitoring should be conducted by employees utilizing such activities as: contacts with field reps, communication with suppliers and customers, discussions with joint-venture partners, former employees, competitors' disenchanted employees, and scrutinizing of relevant analysts' reports and regulatory filings, among others.

COUNTERINTELLIGENCE APPROACH

Counterintelligence is sometimes confused with security, and therefore often countermeasures are entrusted to security personnel, if they are thought about at all. But as previously defined, security seeks to protect a firm's assets by a combination of policies, procedures, and practices. Counterintelligence aims to engage and neutralize a competitor's collection efforts through a variety of imaginative and active measures. An organized counterintelligence approach can help ensure CI integration.

The military's five-step operational security (OPSEC) approach for assessing risk and establishing countermeasures has been adapted for CI. However, corporate efforts to protect proprietary information that follow the classified-protection models developed to thwart clandestine or illegal intelligence operations leave firms unprepared to defend themselves against an organized collection effort that analyzes information routinely gathered in the course of business (Mark, 1997).

A better counterintelligence approach is to review what you consider worth protecting about your business and the environment within which you operate. Identify and assess your vulnerabilities by performing a strength, weakness, and vulnerabilities analysis of your company. Survey information-handling systems and procedures and test your defenses by running an intelligence operation against yourself. Aggressive countermeasures can then be developed and implemented.

Counterintelligence should move away from the government clandestine model to an approach based on learning (during routine CI activities) about the intelligence activities competitors are directing at your company, and to analyze any potential damage. The process described above becomes on-going and integrated into the CI effort. An information-protection program can be developed and communicated throughout the corporation (Pattakos, 1997). The critical steps in counterintelligence are:

- identify critical information
- analyze threats
- analyze vulnerabilities
- assess risks
- apply appropriate countermeasures.

CONCLUSION

Counterintelligence is anticipatory and business-oriented. It aims to engage and neutralize a competitor's collection efforts through a variety of imaginative and active measures. Security, on the other hand, seeks to protect a firm's assets by a combination of policies, procedures, and practices. In summary, security is aimed at *reducing corporate vulnerability*, while counterintelligence and countermeasures are aimed at *reducing a competitive threat*.

While the threat of illegal espionage has increased, so too has the new threat of legal or systematic CI. Companies must be aware that both legal and illegal intelligence techniques may be used upon them. When it comes to enlisting government help in issues of espionage, companies should rely on and manage their own counterintelligence efforts.

Perhaps the most proactive, aggressive, and effective countermeasure is *deception*. The end result of "perception management" is to confuse your rival's CI organization so that the decision-makers there make the wrong decision about what they should do in response to the incoming information (Bernhardt, 1993).

It is very important to establish a corporate counterintelligence mind-set to get people to think proactively about how to identify, and consequently thwart, CI-gathering operations.

Intelligence-gathering threats should be assessed by looking for motive, opportunity, and method. Counterintelligence involves monitoring and identifying CI modus operandi for intelligence-activity indicators. If an intelligence-gathering effort is discovered, countermeasures and security can be developed and implemented.

The five steps of counterintelligence can provide a framework for a company to develop its counterintelligence system, which can be integrated into an existing competitive-intelligence and security system.

Competitive intelligence can provide a competitive advantage; however, to enhance and sustain that competitive advantage, a company must incorporate the defensive and offensive elements of security and counterintelligence.

REFERENCES

Bernhardt, D. (1993). "Counterintelligence: Defending Your Company's Secrets," in *Perfectly Legal Competitor Intelligence: How to Get It, Use It and Profit from It*, ed. D. Bernhardt. London: FT Pitman Publishing.

Canadian Security Intelligence Service. (1998). *Canadian Security Intelligence Service's 1998 Public Report.* Ottawa, ON: Canadian Security Intelligence Service.

Herring, J. (1992). "The Role of Intelligence in Formulating Strategy," *Journal of Business Strategy* 13(5): 54–60.

Mark, D. (1997). "Competitive Intelligence and the Corporate Jewels," *Competitive Intelligence Review* 8(3): 62–70.

National Counterintelligence Center. (1995). *Annual Report to Congress on Foreign Economic Collection and Industrial Espionage* <http://www.nacic.gov/fy95.htm>.

———. (1996). *Annual Report to Congress on Foreign Economic Collection and Industrial Espionage* <http://www.nacic.gov/fy96.htm>.

———. (1997). *Annual Report to Congress on Foreign Economic Collection and Industrial Espionage* <http://www.nacic.gov/fy97.htm>.

———. (1998). *Annual Report to Congress on Foreign Economic Collection and Industrial Espionage* <http://www.nacic.gov/fy98.htm>.

———. (1999). *Annual Report to Congress on Foreign Economic Collection and Industrial Espionage* <http://www.nacic.gov/fy99.htm>.

Nolan, J.A., III (1996). "What Does Our Competition Know About Us?" *Security, Technology and Design* 6(2): 69–71.

———. (1997). "Confusing Counterintelligence with Security Can Wreck Your Afternoon," *Competitive Intelligence Review* 8(3): 53–61.

Pattakos, A.N. (1997). "Keeping Company Secrets Secret," *Competitive Intelligence Review* 8(3): 71–78.

Sun-Tzu. (1988). *The Art of War.* Oxford: Oxford University Press.

U.S. Congress, 104th. (1996). "United States Economic Espionage Act of 1996," *Competitive Intelligence Review* 8(3): 4–6.

U.S. Federal Bureau of Investigation. (1998). "Welcome to ANSIR on the Internet: National Security Threat List," *Federal Bureau of Investigation Awareness of National Security Issues and Response (ANSIR) Program*, April 6 <http://www.fbi.gov/programs/ansir/ansir.htm>.

5

Overview of Best Practices in Competitive Intelligence

Julia Madden

INTRODUCTION

Many companies realize, or are beginning to realize, the potential and benefits of competitive intelligence (CI). The Society of Competitive Intelligence Professionals (SCIP) defines CI as "the process of monitoring the competitive environment" that "enables senior managers in companies of all sizes to make informed decisions" (Society of Competitive Intelligence Professionals, 2000). Like any other process or function, CI has methods and techniques for improving its effectiveness; like any other function, it also has best practices. Although measuring the effectiveness of CI is difficult, best practices in CI have been identified in companies that are perceived by expert observers to be performing CI better than anyone else.

What is a *best practice*? The American Product and Quality Center (2000), a resource for process and performance improvement for organizations, defines a best practice as "a practice that has been shown to produce superior results, selected by a systematic process and judged as exemplary, good or successfully demonstrated" (American Product and Quality Center, 1998). Best practices are not the "best" because they are for everyone. They must be adapted to fit each specific organization. Several studies, models, and speculative theories have evolved around best practices in CI, but a greater understanding of CI is still needed.

By looking at several different studies, models, and current best practices, several common or similar factors should appear to be crucial to effective CI regardless of the organization, size of organization, or industry. Each organization should look at these similarities as the foundation on which to base its efforts in adapting CI practices.

CURRENT BEST PRACTICES

American Product and Quality Center (APQC) Consortium Study

In 1996, International Benchmarking Clearinghouse (IBC), a service of APQC, performed a "best practices" business and competitive intelligence study across several industries (O'Dell & Grayson, 1996). Twenty-two companies participated in the study, of which seven were selected as best-practice companies. The seven companies were used as benchmarks with which the other companies could compare themselves. From this study, seven findings were identified as components to best practices in competitive intelligence. The companies considered having best practices in CI included Bell Atlantic, Eastman Kodak, Fidelity Investments, Ford Motor Company, Merck & Company, Pacific Enterprises, and Xerox Corporation. The seven key findings from the study of these best-practice companies are:

- *Evolving, stable CI infrastructures*: Best-practice companies have CI mechanisms and structures in place that have evolved over time. The stability of these structures is usually held together by key people who have experience in their respective industries and the development of networks. Key people or champions ensure that there is continuity and that the CI function is maintained. For example, in the APQC study, the Merck and Fidelity corporations were revealed to have personnel with long term experience and certain personality traits. Where champions are not available to drive CI, best-practice organizations have developed policies, mission statements, or other means of substituting these individuals and integrating CI into the organization. Best-practice organizations also plan for the evolution of their CI to continually adjust to new trends and industry changes.

- *Decentralized, coordinated networks*: The study determined that decentralized networks have to develop for several reasons: they better address the company's diverse intelligence needs; they capture the realization that all employees are not knowledgeable about every area of the business; and they allow for use of resources and personnel that exist throughout the company. Various methods are used for forming networks; some develop from grass roots while others are more formal. Kodak, for example, has a matrix of different groups performing CI in different areas such as manufacturing, competitors, and technology. When information is needed it can be drawn from any of these sources by either individuals or groups. Best-practice companies developed their networks slowly. Because of the length of time required for effective CI functional development, companies starting CI and adapting best practices should focus on areas where there are the greatest competitive threats and build from there.

- *Responsive information-technology systems*: For best-practice companies, information technology (IT) usually makes the transfer and sharing of information more effective and efficient. The platforms used in best practice companies provide databases that catalog studies and other information already owned by the company, while easy-to-use discussion forums allow the organization to get rid of unwanted data and coordinate diverse information systems. Topics are added and taken out as necessary, which allows individuals to share their knowledge with others in the organization. Information technology helps organizations deal with information in a timely manner and keep up with the changing competitive environment. It may be wise for companies to develop the CI program with existing IT first, and then determine what is needed to make the system better and more flexible to accommodate CI and information sharing across the company.

- *Linkage between strategic and tactical intelligence*: Tactical intelligence comes from the day-to-day operation of an organization. Operational-level employees see trends, new technology, and have personal contact with suppliers and customers. Information gathered at this level of the operation must flow upward to be incorporated into the strategic level of the organization, and be examined for future strategic decisions. Strategic decisions must flow downward and have support at the tactical level. The two types of intelligence rely on each other and must be linked. Strategic intelligence looks at how the organization can change and respond to changes in the industry and environment. There should be a link between these two types of intelligence, because they feed into and augment each other. Best-practice companies realize the trade off between the two types of intelligence and work to keep them in balance. Often, strategic intelligence is overemphasized, to the detriment of tactical intelligence or vice versa. Companies need to keep up with current strategy but allow for new information to affect future strategic direction.

- *Customer feedback and implementation link*: Best-practice CI programs ensure that there is feedback and dialogue with the customer. The customer refers to the requester of information within the organization. Competitive intelligence requests must be well defined and *re*defined until the request is actionable. For CI to be of value to the customer it must be in a form that can be used and ideally is measurable. For example, at Bell Atlantic the CI project is only considered complete when management uses the information. Feedback from the customer also allows CI to develop better services and products that are useful to the decision-maker. Measurement of CI is still very difficult; however, with clearer defined deliverables, CI projects may be measured more effectively. Customer/CI feedback is two-way and hopefully nearly symmetric in volume. The customer should be able to determine what specifically they require of CI, and CI must be able to determine what it can provide in return.

- *Hypothesis-driven recommendations*: Competitive intelligence programs (CIP) should add value to the company. They should generate a positive return on the resources invested in developing it. The information should be infused with some analytical insight or strategic direction to assist managers in making decisions. Analytical thinking is critical for best-practice companies. The APQC study indicated that very few of the studied companies could explain how they perform analytical thinking, but stated that it was important. In other words, analysis has the classic elements of "tacit knowledge." Competitive intelligence products and services in an organization should answer questions or provide information to an executive, which helps him or her make better decisions. Many best-practice companies analyze their CI findings relevant to their current strategic position to determine if change is needed.

• *Institutionalizing intelligence cultures*: Best-practice companies develop ways to make CI a part of everyone's job. The top managers need to be involved and drive the organization's culture to institutionalize CI into the company's culture. This process takes time and commitment on the part of senior managers, but is necessary for the continuous implementation of CI. This area is where the most resistance and difficulty in instituting CI is found.

THE NEXT PHASE OF BEST-PRACTICES UNDERSTANDING

During 1997–1998 a follow-up study, *Managing Competitive Intelligence Knowledge in a Global Economy* (APQC, 1998), was conducted. Again, the study used 22 companies, with seven chosen as best-practice-partner companies with which to benchmark. From this second APQC study an enhanced model was developed to demonstrate the best-practice CI process.

Five Steps of the FIICH Model

• *Focus*: Develop a clear set of goals and objectives for CI-knowledge activities

• *Implement*: Create an organizational culture conducive to implementing actionable CI knowledge

• *Institutionalize*: Incorporate CI knowledge-management practices into the daily activities of managers

• *Change*: Modify thought processes, behaviors, and performance in ways that help achieve organizational goals and objectives

• *Hone*: Make the CI knowledge-management process a dynamic, evolving activity with a bias toward continuous improvement.

In this study, researchers were interested in what "attributes of CI were most valued by managers" (APQC, 1998). Different findings were determined for best-practice companies under each step of the FIICH model's framework:

• *Focus of CI Efforts*. Best-practice CI organizations:
   —focus their CI efforts on decision-making areas that are critical to their business
   —have actively involved senior management in CI, rather than having it just ask for moral support of CI
   —allow the critical intelligence needs (CIN) focus to drive the output of CI products and services

- *Implementation of CI*. Best-practice CI organizations:
  —establish a systematic, documented process that clearly defines roles and responsibilities for those involved with CI
  —follow practices that include a sensible approach, built-in redundancies, future orientation, global perspective, integration of informal and formal networks, and a concern for ethics

- *Institutionalize CI Knowledge*. Best-practice CI organizations:
  —spread CI by providing a variety of products, services, and practices throughout the organization

- *Change*. Best-practice CI organizations:
  —provide training in information technology (IT) and human networks
  —encourage managers to make more decisions using CI knowledge and embed CI processes in the organization culture

- *Hone*. Best-practice CI organizations:
  —coordinate and strive for continuous improvement across diverse business units
  —measure, or attempt to measure, the economic impact of CI.

In a recent study in the United Kingdom, researchers found from their survey of firms and competitive intelligence professionals that there is a "scarcity of models of CI in action" and that "there is a problem of knowing what was needed for the CI unit" (Wright, Callow, & Pickton, 1999). The FIICH model simplifies the approach to CI; however, it does not express how to apply this knowledge to actual decisions. This model has been added as an item to the seven key findings of the 1996 APQC study (Wyckoff, 1999). However, tacking the model onto this list does little to provide a clearer understanding of best practices in CI, and the adaptation of these best practices in organizations. The first study explains seven significant components to CI in best-practice companies. In combining the seven components into the FIICH five-step model, a more detailed process identifies how each component fits into the process. The detailed combination may help organizations better determine how they can incorporate a best practice into their business (figure 5.1).

DIFFICULTIES IN IMPLEMENTING BEST PRACTICES FOR CI

One difficulty with transferring best practices in CI is that the best practice for one company may not become a best practice for another (if any of the seven elements described above are missing). There are several problems and difficulties in establishing and adapting best practices in CI to businesses.

Companies must recognize their limitations and be prepared for the length of time it takes to develop the necessary components for a successful CI program. Time is required for CI to become institutionalized and integrated into a company's culture to allow the processes and practices to be adopted and incorporated. For companies just getting into CI, this time element may be discouraging and detrimental to the development of a CI program. If results from CI are not

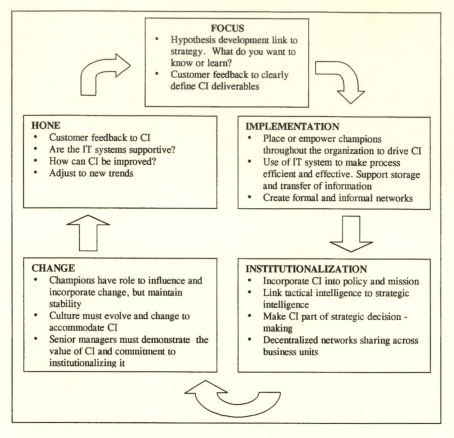

FIGURE 5.1 Combining the 1996 APQC study with the FIICH model.

visible, a CI program may lose its credibility before it has a chance to become established in a company.

The lack of key people or champions to carry the momentum for a CI program may also be a difficulty. Best-practice companies have large, established networks with experienced CI champions. Companies new to CI may not have people with the necessary qualities to execute an effective CI program or carry forth the momentum.

The difficulty of measuring the economic benefits of CI is another problem of transferring best practices in CI. How should a company determine which best practice will suit them if measurement of CI is elusive? To get CI started there must be some tangible results and definite benefits derived from the intelligence collected or the CI program will lose credibility and acceptance in an organization. Well-defined CI needs, deliverables, and goals will help determine whether the CI product/service provided was actionable and/or useful in making a decision.

Organizational structure and culture need to be arranged so that communication occurs across business units. If an organization is not already communicating cross-functionally, it will be more difficult to implement an effective CI program.

It is much more difficult to identify and transfer *tacit knowledge* rather than *explicit knowledge*. Tacit knowledge, as defined here, tends to be the intuition and experience combination that leads to useful CI analysis. In best-practice companies this tacit knowledge is there, but how it is passed on and used is not clear (Prescott, Herring, & Panfely, 1998). This element of a best practice is difficult to adapt and must be discovered by each company individually.

In the studies conducted it was evident that active involvement by senior management is a strong key to the success of a good CI program. Senior management must commit to, see the value of, and integrate CI into the company's decision-making process.

OPPORTUNITIES AND BENEFITS

Companies can learn a great deal from other companies with well-developed and -defined CI programs. Organizations must remember that no individual best practice is suitable for all and that it needs to be evaluated within the firm planning to implement it. From the APQC Best-Practices White Paper Report (O'Dell & Grayson, 1996) on identifying and transferring internal best practices, four expectations of networks should be addressed. These expectations can be applied to the transfer and adaptation of best CI practices:

- The really important and useful tacit information is passed on through human contact and face-to-face information sharing. Information-technology systems can be used to assist in this information exchange. For example, the AMP Inc. database system identifies the source of information, name and brief description of the information entered, when it was entered, who entered it, and a person to contact for more information. This type of system points people in the right direction to obtain needed information. The IT in this case supports the various people talking to one another.

- A framework for classifying information should be established. A framework helps with the process of collecting, sharing, and adapting CI best practices. Each company may have its own classification system that feeds into its specific structure or industry.

- Entering information into the system must be part of everyone's job—whether they work in CI or not—if CI is to be institutionalized throughout the organization. Anyone who enters information should be responsible for ensuring that the information is accurate and credible. Unchecked information can potentially lead to poor decision-making.

- Culture and behaviors can be difficult inhibitors or drivers of information sharing in a company. For example, at Chevron, teams were formed to work on adopting best practices and benchmarking. The teams had a difficult time explaining to co-workers the time they were spending on these projects. Management had to communicate the investment of time that these teams were spending on information-sharing processes. Involvement of senior management and commitment assists with a company's overall adoption of CI and the sharing of information.

SUMMARY

Like any other functional adaptation of best practices, the adoption of CI best practices is tricky. No one best practice is suitable for every organization. Each practice must be modified and changed to suit an organization's industry, culture, and level of diversity. Several studies and models have been developed to determine some of the best practices in CI. These studies indicate that developing and institutionalizing good CI programs takes time and commitment to build into the organization. This time commitment, combined with weak measurement of the economic benefits of CI, makes it difficult to justify resource allocation to CI. However, best-practice companies have demonstrated that CI programs produce actionable intelligence that leads to competitive advantage. Companies embarking on CI programs should realize that the long-term benefits of a good CI program can keep the company in tune with the competitive environment and changes that may affect business strategy.

REFERENCES

American Product and Quality Center (APQC), Consortium Report. (1998). *Managing Competitive Intelligence Knowledge in a Global Economy* <http://www.apcq.org>.
American Product and Quality Center (APQC). (2000). *APQC Benchmarking Terms* <http://www.apcq.org/free/terms>.
O'Dell, C., and C.J. Grayson, Jr. (1996). *Identifying and Transferring Internal Best Practices.* American Product and Quality Center (APQC) Best Practices White Paper Report <http://www.store.apqc.org/cgi-bin/vsc.exe/Jacket/cmifwp.htm?E+Book Store>.
Prescott, J., J. Herring, and P. Panfely. (1998). "Leveraging Information for Action: A Look into the Competitive and Business Intelligence Consortium Benchmarking Study," *Competitive Intelligence Review* 9(1): 4–12.
Society of Competitive Intelligence Professionals (SCIP). (2000). *What is CI?* <http://www.scip.org/ci>.
Wright, S., J. Callow, and D. Pickton. (1999). *Competitive Intelligence in Action.* Leicester, UK: DeMontforte University, Competitive Marketing Practice Research Group.
Wyckoff, T. (1999). *Benchmarking Competitive Intelligence.* Washington, DC: Special Libraries Association.

IMPROVING THE
COMPETITIVE INTELLIGENCE
PROCESS

6

Using the Internet for Gathering Competitive Intelligence

Richard McClurg

INTRODUCTION

This chapter explores how *push* and *pull* methods on the Internet—more specifically, the World Wide Web (WWW)[1]—can be used for gathering information as part of the competitive intelligence (CI) process. By using these methods, the CI professional can save valuable search time, which can then be directed towards the more critical analysis stage of the CI process.

The discussion will first focus on the role that the Internet plays in CI. Particular attention will be given to the types of generic CI products with which the Internet can assist, and the importance of assessing the value of information. The inherent advantages and disadvantages of the Internet will also be outlined.

Push and *pull* methods will then be explained, followed by general tips that will assist the CI practitioner in focusing their search and locating relevant information. Next, specific *push* and *pull* methods and resources will be identified for gathering information on targeted competitors. Finally, some of the newest resources will be highlighted, as well as a discussion on the future direction of Internet tools for conducting CI.

Although the Internet can also be used for disseminating information to decision-makers and clients, this chapter will focus specifically on the data-gathering capability of the Internet.

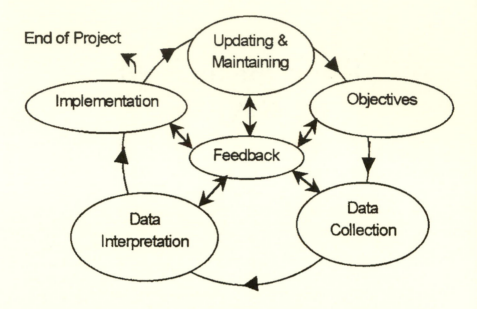

FIGURE 6.1 The competitive intelligence process (from Prescott [1989], reprinted with permission of the Society of Competitive Intelligence Professionals).

THE ROLE OF THE INTERNET
FOR COMPETITIVE INTELLIGENCE

A competitive intelligence program is a "formalized yet continuously evolving process by which the management team assesses the evolution of its industry and the capabilities and behavior of its current and potential competitors to assist in maintaining or developing a competitive advantage" (Prescott & Gibbons, 1993). From figure 6.1, the steps involved include setting objectives, collecting data, interpreting the data, implementing, and possibly updating and maintaining the system.

Using the VRIO model for analyzing resources, Cory (1996) argues that the data-collection phase in the CI process has a low probability of resulting in a sustainable competitive advantage. Data-gathering activities are generic in nature and can easily be imitated by competitors. Only if competitors are not performing CI can data collection provide a competitive advantage. The highest probability for developing a sustainable competitive advantage, however, is derived from superior analysis.

A substantial amount of the entire CI effort is spent in the data-gathering stage at the expense of the other tasks. That being the case, data-gathering tools that save the CI professional time will be beneficial. The time saved can be redirected to critical tasks such as analysis and gaining insight.

The Internet is one such tool that can reduce the amount of time spent gathering information. Used wisely, the Internet will allow the CI professional to spend more time on the analysis stage of an intelligence product, which Cory (1996) argues can lead to a sustainable competitive advantage. Examples of intelligence products are identified below.

To summarize, the Internet offers a CI professional many advantages in gathering information, but its disadvantages should not be ignored. The trick to effectively and efficiently use the Internet for CI may be in the utilization of *push* or *pull* methods discussed in the next section.

PUSH VERSUS *PULL* METHODS OF UTILIZING THE INTERNET FOR CI

The Internet offers a multitude of tools that can help the CI professional gather information either through *push* or *pull* methods as summarized in table 6.1. Just like they sound, *pull* methods are used to bring the information to a user, while *push* methods automatically send or notify a user of newly available information.

Most information is *pulled* from the Internet. Information is pulled whenever a user utilizes a browser such as Netscape Navigator or Microsoft Internet Explorer to download and display a page of information on the user's desktop (Leonard, 1997). In the case of the *push* method, an application will automatically search for user-defined information. A Web server will then automatically

Table 6.1
SUMMARY OF *PUSH* AND *PULL* METHODS

Method	Category	Types
pull	search engines and directories	meta-searchers major search engines webliographies specialized engines
	specific search resources	background information financial information news coverage other resources
push	specific push resources	browser-based services client-based services push e-mail e-mail alerts personalized Web pages

send (or *push*) the information when and where the user directs (Gustitus, 1998). This *push* can be in the form of a specific Web page, file, e-mail, or even information sent to a pager or cell phone.

The advent of *push* technology can therefore save the CI professional time. Instead of actively having to search through vast amounts of information, the information is automatically delivered. This information delivery is especially useful for monitoring the activity of a competitor or industry. It is, however, less useful for gathering information to answer a specific intelligence request.

The CI professional should follow specific search strategies and become adept at utilizing the various search engines, CI resources, and *push* techniques to maximize the efficiency and effectiveness of environmental scanning and targeted intelligence-gathering. Examples of *push* and *pull* methods for gathering CI are discussed in the following sections.

PULL: USING SEARCH ENGINES AND DIRECTORIES

A number of CI authors have offered advice on how to conduct effective Internet research. These tips will help the CI practitioner find the information with the greatest benefit while minimizing search time.

- *Articulate the question or requirement* (Shaker & Gembicki, 1999): It is imperative to exactly define what information is being sought. Although the Internet offers the benefit of hypertext links for easy navigation, these links can easily lead to dead ends that take the CI practitioner off topic. While information may be stumbled upon that proves very useful, more often vital research time is wasted. Therefore it is wise to periodically ask: "Is this really the information that is needed?"

- *Think about who may be able to answer the question* (Fuld, 1995): Although a CI practitioner's initial reaction will probably be to start from scratch, there are likely others who have already gathered the required information. These may include industry associations, local media, government agencies, financial analysts, special-interest groups, labor unions, and academic institutions. The CI practitioner should search these websites before reinventing the wheel.

- *Identify search terms that state the question or could lead to the answers* (Shaker & Gembicki, 1999): A simple example is if a new competitor has been discovered in a particular market, and the CI practitioner wants to know their technological capabilities. A common start would be to search the Internet for the "competitor's name" and "research and development." It is advisable to phrase the question and key words in several different ways, because the search results may differ dramatically.

- *Be inventive—deviate from the expected* (Shaker & Gembicki, 1999): Sometimes after conducting an exhaustive search, the CI practitioner will still come up empty-handed. It may be time to try something different that contradicts the first point of focusing the search. However, if all other avenues have been exhausted, trying searches with dramatically different search terms and following obscure links can sometimes lead to the desired information. This method of searching should be done only as a last resort.

- *Utilize advanced searching techniques* (Shaker & Gembicki, 1999): It is important to become familiar with, and fully utilize, the advanced searching techniques available on major search engines. Since every search engine is unique—requiring different symbols and operators to fine-tune the search, it is advisable to invest some time in learning the intricacies of the advanced searching techniques. Review the search engine "help" section for this information.

- *Mark the trail* (Calishain & Nystron, 1998): It is easy to develop the habit of bookmarking every website that is uncovered. By following this strategy, however, a bookmark file will quickly "evolve into a huge unusable mess." The CI practitioner should consider creating folders for each specific research project. Alternatively, Website addresses could be cut and pasted into a separate project file with a brief description of the type of information contained in the site for future reference. This information should be backed up on a regular basis to avoid losing the data.

Overall, when pulling information from the Internet, Shaker and Gembicki (1999) recommend starting by taking a broad or "macro" approach, and then refining the search to the "micro" level. This broad approach involves starting with meta-search engines, moving to major search engines, using sites with webliographies (or list of links), and finally using specialized search engines (Shaker & Gembicki, 1999). This macro-to-micro approach is more fully described below.

Meta-Search Engines

According to a February 1999 study by Lawrence and Giles, the publicly indexed World Wide Web contains over 800 million pages with 6 trillion bytes of information. That is a significant increase from the 320 million pages that they reported in their December 1997 study. However, the top eleven search engines were found capable of locating just 42 percent of all sites, with no one search engine covering more than 16 percent of the Web. In addition, their study showed that on average it takes more than six months for a new Web page to be added to a search engine's listings.

Meta-search engines search through multiple engines at once. For example, a meta-search engine will use ten other search engines to search on the keywords that have been entered. The researcher will be presented with a consolidated list of the best results from each engine.

Meta-searches appear to be an essential tool for locating information on the Web, since no single search engine indexes the Web completely. Some of the better known meta-search engines include:

- *Metacrawler* (http://www.go2net.com/search.html): combines searches from ten other search engines

- *Dogpile* (http://www.dogpile.com): compiles results from eleven search engines

- *Profusion* (http://www.profusion.com): combines searches from nine other search engines

- *Ask Jeeves* (http://www.askjeeves.com): an easy-to-use natural language meta-searcher that prompts the user to enter a search query in the form of a question.

Using meta-searches to search multiple engines simultaneously saves the CI practitioner time. However, they don't always support the advanced search options offered by individual search engines that can really help fine-tune a search and yield more relevant results. Consequently, search engines will be discussed next.

Major Search Engines

Currently, there are over 300 search engines available on the Internet. Each one has a unique way of searching the Internet and can yield different results. Some cover more of the Web and add new documents to their database faster than others.

According to the Lawrence and Giles (1999) study, the following search engines index more of the WWW than others:

- *Northern Light* (http://www.northernlight.com)

- *Snap!* (http://home.snap.com)

- *Altavista* (http://www.altavista.com)

- *Hotbot* (http://www.hotbot.com).

From time to time the CI Internet researcher should review sites such as Search Engine Watch (http://www.searchenginewatch.com) to assess which search engines may yield optimal results. When selecting a search engine, Shaker and Gembicki (1999) recommend keeping in mind that:

- Each engine has limitations to what is searched. Some only search the document title, Web address text, or image description tags

- There are peak usage times for search engines. Noon to 3:00 P.M. (EST) is usually the slowest time for conducting searches

- The order of words placed in the search phrase greatly affects search results.

Webliographies

A "webliography" is a site that contains many links to other sites. Most university libraries now provide webliographies that are useful to students in the disciplines encompassed by the institution. These sites can be particularly useful in becoming familiar with the tools and resources available on the WWW. Webliographies of particular interest to CI professionals include:

* *Fuld & Company* (http://wwwfuld.com/i3/index.html): provides links to over 600 CI-related websites. The links are divided into three broad categories: general-business Internet resources (includes links to macroeconomic data, patents, and financials), industry-specific resources, and international resources.
* *AWARE* (http://dspace.dial.pipex.com/aware/competitiveintelligence.shtml): provides an extensive and current list of sites for finding competitive intelligence. As is pointed out on the website, however, the links are "biased towards UK/English-language resources."
* *Michigan State University Center for International Business Education and Research* (http://ciber.bus.msu.edu/busres.htm): provides a comprehensive collection of resources for finding global business information.

Specialized Search Engines

Some search engines focus specifically on business information, which enables the researcher to search specific industries. Examples of these include:

* *Livelink Pinstripe* (http://pinstripe.opentext.com): utilizes "slicing" technology that allows the researcher to go directly to the business topic of interest.
* *Northern Light's Industry Search* (http://www.northernlight.com/industry.html): enables the researcher to fine-tune the search by selecting specific industries, time frames, and information types such as press releases and job listings.

Going from the macro to the micro is an effective way of finding information on the Internet. However, using specific search resources may yield even better results. Specific search resources of particular interest to the CI practitioner are discussed next.

PULL: USING SPECIFIC SEARCH RESOURCES

There are numerous *pull* methods for both environmental scanning and for gathering information on specific targets or stakeholders within the task environment. Given the vast number of resources and wide variety of needs for macroeconomic scanning, it is helpful to use the webliographies listed above for finding the information that is required. The following are specific search resources that can be used by CI professionals to gather information on the task environment and, specifically, on targeted competitors.

Background Information

There are many ways to find information on competitors. The best place to start is to go directly to the company's website, if one exists.

COMPANY WEBSITE. There are two primary ways for finding the Internet address (or Uniform Resource Locator [URL]) of a company's homepage—guessing or performing a Web address search.

Guessing the website may be the fastest method. Most company website addresses are formed as www.*companyname*.com. Therefore, simply substituting the target company's name in the *companyname* part of the address should yield up its homepage. For Canadian companies, try substituting a ".ca" extension instead of ".com"[.] It is also important to keep in mind when searching for international companies that their addresses may end with a country-code domain such as ".se" for Sweden or ".de" for Germany. International companies may also have an extension such as ".co.uk" for a company from the United Kingdom or ".co.jp" for a Japanese-based company. Therefore some experimentation may be required.[2]

The Amnesi search engine (http://www.amnesi.com) is a particularly useful tool for finding a Web address. This specialized engine helps the researcher locate a complete address if only a portion of the address is known. A "best guess" is entered and the engine provides a list of Web addresses that most closely match the search parameters. Alternatively, URLs associated with a particular company name are listed by Whois (http://www.networksolutions.com/cgi-bin/whois/whois).

COMPANY PROFILES. On-line company directories can be used to identify competitors and provide the CI practitioner with a profile of a targeted company. Each directory has different search features and ways of organizing the data into categories such as by industry, name, location, size, North American Industrial Classification System (NAICS, formerly SIC) codes, and products.

Companies Online (http://www.companiesonline.com) is an especially good resource that allows a researcher to search for information on over 100,000 public and private companies. A convenient feature of this site is a link to Dun & Bradstreet, where one can order a company background report for a minimal fee. When searching for U.S. companies, Hoover's Online (http://www.hooversonline.com) may be the best place to start. This searchable database contains over 12,600 public and private companies, including financials, key competitors, and other general information.

For a more international focus, try Kompass (http://www.kompass.com). This highly flexible database contains product and company profiles on more than 1.5 million companies from around the world. Corporate Information (http://www.corporateinformation.com) is also a specialty website that contains many links to public and private companies from around the world. It includes a search engine that accesses a database of over 300,000 companies. Search results indicate a source of information and provide links. If, however, the CI practitioner is looking specifically for information on high-tech companies, then Corp Tech (http://www.corptech.com) may yield up the best results.

FINANCIAL INFORMATION. Much information about a competitor can be gleaned from the annual reports and financial information that public companies must file. Sources for these include:

EDGAR, the Electronic Data Gathering, Analysis, and Retrieval System (http://www.sec.gov/edgarhp.htm). This database contains filings such as 10Ks that are required by the U.S. Securities and Exchange Commission (SEC). In addition to financial information, these filings also contain valuable information on products, markets, and operations.

The Public Register's Annual Reports Service has links to more than 2,100 annual reports that are either available on-line or can be downloaded in Adobe PDF format (http://www.annualreportservice.com). A search can be performed by company name or industry.

If looking for financial information on Canadian companies, try searching SEDAR (http://www.sedar.com/search/search.htm), the System for Electronic Document Analysis and Retrieval that is similar to EDGAR.

Analysts who closely monitor public companies are an excellent source of information as well. They periodically provide analysts' reports on-line. However, most of these are fee-based. Normally, these services can be subscribed to without fee for a limited period of time to assess their value. Analysts' reports are available from sites such as First Call (http://www.firstcall.com) and Zacks Investment Research (http://www.zacks.com).

News Coverage

As part of an on-going program of monitoring the task environment, a CI professional should also monitor press releases, company news, and newspapers and magazines.

PRESS RELEASES. If available, start by searching through the "press release" section on the target company's website. Most company websites offer this information. Companies also issue press releases to news services. These are often picked up by Internet news services such as Business Wire (http://www.businesswire.com) and Reuter's business briefing (http://www.bizinfo.reuters.com). PR Newswire (http://wwwprnewswire.com) also offers a searchable database containing stories that have appeared on the Internet over the past three years.

COMPANY NEWS. Transium Corporation's Business Intelligence website (http://www.transium.com) is an excellent source for news abstracts. More than 1,000 business and trade journals are regularly scanned, and Transium claims to have information on over 300,000 private and public companies from around the globe. When a keyword search is conducted, a collection of abstracts is presented. Full text documents can be purchased, but typically there is enough information contained within the abstract. Search results can be grouped by categories such as job functions, industries, and products.

Two other good sources for company news include Infoseek's News Center (http://www.infoseek.com/news) and IndustryWatch (http://www.industrywatch.com). Infoseek provides industry-related daily news drawn from over a hundred news sources. The best feature about this site is that it provides executive summaries about the featured companies.

NEWSPAPERS AND MAGAZINES. Major newspapers and magazines often contain searchable archives of articles written about companies. Try searching the archives of magazines such as *Business Week* (http://wwwbusinessweek. com), *Fortune* (http://www.fortune.com), and Wall Street Research Net (http:// www.wsrn.com).

A source that is often overlooked, but can contain the most valuable information about a competitor, is local newspapers. AJR Newslink (http://ajr.news link.org) provides links to over 9,000 local newspapers and magazines from around the world and is searchable by country, state/province, and city. Drill down to the home city of the targeted company and link to the local newspaper. Most newspaper websites will offer a keyword search utility that can be used for finding information on the target company.

Also consider publications that are specifically industry-targeted. For example, the publication *Television Broadcast* has a website (http://www.tvbroadcast. com) that contains a search tool that can be used to find information about a competitor that supplies equipment to broadcasters. Most industries have similar specialized publications.

OTHER INTERNET CI SOURCES

News Groups

Most information on a competitor's products or services can be gathered from a news or discussion group. However, carefully consider the credibility of this source, because many rumors originate here. Sometimes, though, these rumors can provide valuable insights for the CI practitioner.

One of the best ways to search through newsgroups is to use Deja.com, formerly known as Deja News (http://www.deja.com), which covers 45,000 discussion forums and Usenet groups. Reference.Com (http://www.reference.com) is also an excellent source for finding discussion groups, mailing lists, and Web forums pertinent to the company that has been targeted.

Intellectual Property: Trademarks and Patents

If the CI practitioner is gathering technical intelligence and wants to monitor patents issued by competitors, the following free resources should be considered: U.S. patent search (http://patents.uspto.gov/access/search-adv.html); IBM patent server (http://www.patents.ibm.com/ibm/html); and the Strategis Industry Canada, Canadian patent-search database (http://patents1.ic.gc.ca/intro-e.html).

Help-Wanted Ads and Resumes

By searching on-line competitor job advertisements and employee resumes, a CI professional can discover the kinds of technology competencies that a company has or is lacking. In addition, one can ascertain in which markets the targeted company is growing, or seeks to expand. Furthermore, on-line resources can be used for locating primary sources of information, such as former employees who may provide insightful information (Kassler, 1997). Some of the largest resume and job-posting databases that can be used for searching this type of information include: Monster Board (http://www.monsterboard.com); Career Path (http://www.careerpath.com); and Career Mosaic (http://www.careermosaic.com). Alternatively, Job Search Engine (http://job-search-engine.com) can be used to meta-search up to ten U.S. and Canadian job boards simultaneously.

Having highlighted the major *pull* methods for gathering CI, the next section will discuss *push* methods.

PUSH METHODS

There are several variations of *push* methods that prepare and/or send information automatically to the CI professional. Some of these methods can also be thought of as *automatic pull*, depending on whether the type of information is preselected by the recipient or whether the information provider selects which content to send. *Push* methods therefore range from *pure-push*, such as client- and browser-based services, to alerting services and websites that generate personalized content:

- *Browser-based services* (Calishain & Nystron, 1998): Preselected content is sent directly to the browser. Netscape's Netcaster is a popular example of this type of service. The user simply selects the desired "channel" of information; the service will then broadcast the information to the user's Web browser. For example, if the CNN Financial Network channel is selected, breaking financial stories and market information will be sent directly to the browser, which can then be viewed, even if the user is off-line.

- *Client-based services* (Calishain & Nystron, 1998): Preselected content or "channels" of information from the Internet are sent to special software on the user's computer. The software must be downloaded and installed before receiving the *push* content. Pointcast (http://www.pointcast.com) is a well-known client-based *push* service.

- *Push e-mail*: Information that has been subscribed to is sent to an e-mail account. For example, a competitor's website may allow a user to join a mailing list for new product announcements, or a trade magazine may issue periodic e-mail newsletters. CI practitioners should fully explore the potential of their e-mail software. Programs such as Microsoft Outlook include an "inbox assistant" that will sort and filter incoming messages into folders to make the information more manageable.

- *E-mail alerts*: An e-mail message is sent "alerting" the recipient to new content. Typically, hypertext-enabled e-mail includes the links to the website that contains the information that is sought.

- *Personalized Web pages*: Examples include Yahoo (http://www.yahoo.com) and Excite (http://www.excite.com). Selected information is presented in a personalized Web page. A CI practitioner may choose to have financial information on a targeted company displayed on a customized Web page in addition to business and industry news.

Before having information *pushed*, traditional *pull* techniques will generally have to be employed to first find, and then determine the good information sources. Automated tools of particular interest to CI professionals are provided below as a starting point. These tools allow for efficient monitoring of competitor websites, financial updates, breaking news, new published material, and job announcements:

- *NetMind* (http://www.netmind.com): automatically informs a subscriber by e-mail, pager, cell phone, or personal digital assistant (PDA) when a competitor's website is updated.
- *Watchlist/Edgar Online* (http://www.edgar-online.com): alerts a subscriber with an HTML-enabled e-mail message when a target company files with the SEC. This is a fee-based service.
- *InQuisit* (http://www.inquisit.com): sends an alert by e-mail when target-company news or industry-related news is released on the major newswires or by international and national newspapers. This service is also fee-based.
- *Excite's NewsTracker Clipping Service* (http://nt.excite.com): continuously hunts through over 300 international on-line newspapers and magazines. Users can create up to 20 customized topics such as an industry or target company.
- *Company Sleuth* (http://www.companysleuth.com): combs through several of the previous day's trademark, patent, domain name, SEC filings, company news, and Usenet postings for targeted public companies. An e-mail report is sent daily alerting subscribers to changes. Following the links in the e-mail takes the user to a customized Web page that provides the details.
- *BusinessVue* (http://www.businessvue.com): delivers CI directly to a user's desktop, including profiles, news, SEC filings, forum postings, and website changes on public and private companies. The software required to retrieve the information can be downloaded free from the website.
- *Big Board* (http://www.bigboard.com): provides a service that automatically informs a subscriber when a competitor posts a job.

It is recommended that if a CI practitioner has information *pushed* or subscribes to various automated services, the registration information is tracked in a centralized file. Buchwitz (1997) recommends recording the name of the website or source of information, the Web address, frequency of information delivery, cost, user identification, and passwords. In addition, it is important to record, for future reference, how to subscribe and unsubscribe to each particular service.

Using *push* methods for gathering CI has its advantages. Information is sent in a timely manner, the type of information can often be customized, and the information can be received in a variety of formats. Most of all, *push* methods can improve a CI professional's productivity by automating some of the search. However, there are some negative aspects of *push* technology that need to be carefully considered (Gustitus, 1998). First of all, the CI professional could quite easily become inundated with information that cannot be reasonably evaluated. Second, having vast amounts of data coming across an organization's computer network may clog the system, depending on the available bandwidth.

FUTURE DIRECTION

There are many evolving technologies and new tools and services that will greatly assist the CI practitioner in gathering relevant and timely information. The following are some of these new developments.

Bots

Robot technology will greatly assist CI professionals in fully mining competitive information on the Internet. Robots are "programs that travel across the Web's hypertext structure and search and retrieve documents" (Shaker & Gembicki, 1999). Other names for robots include *spiders, intelligent agents, web wanderers, web crawlers*, or just *bots*.

Customized *bots*[3] can be created to retrieve specific information of interest to CI professionals. *Intelligent agents* are a type of *bot* that travels among sites and uses past experience to guide decisions. The opportunities for *bots* are immense; however, their use and potential misuse raise legal and ethical questions. Search-engine developers that use *bots* for indexing websites have formed standards for their use. Competitive intelligence professionals should also adhere to ethical guidelines when using bot technology.

Companies such as Intelligent Automation Inc. are developing a suite of tools, including *bots*, that can be customized to the CI professional's needs. These tools will automatically gather information on competitors and report back the relevant data on a continuous basis (Shaker & Gembicki, 1999).

Given the extremely high potential of this technology, it is imperative that a CI professional keep abreast of any new developments.

XML

A new development that is taking hold now is the use of extensible mark-up language (XML). An alternative to the existing hypertext mark-up language (HTML) that simply formats Web pages, XML describes the content of Web pages. Microsoft Office 2000 software supports XML, and Sun has modified Java to be compatible. The broad adoption of this language will make it easier and faster for search engines and bots to locate information. XML will help correct the lack of a comprehensive indexing system, which makes it difficult for CI professionals and all users of the Internet to locate the most current and relevant information.

Other Tools and Services

There are a growing number of tools available to CI professionals for monitoring competitor and macroenvironment activity on the Internet. Some of the new, intriguing tools and services include:

- *Current Analysis* (http://www.currentanalysis.com): a highly value-added service that delivers relevant news, rates its importance and impact on the industry, and provides analysis by industry experts that allows the CI practitioner to make decisions. This service is currently only available for key segments in the information-technology and telecommunications industries.

- *NewsMaps* (http://www.newsmaps.com): this site displays a topographical overview of keyword density on the Internet. This intriguing tool provides a CI professional with a graphic display that illustrates hot topics during the past week, month, or year. For example, if there has been a lot of news on *wireless networks*, those keywords will be displayed as a mountain. A user can then drill down to specific information on that particular news topic.

- *Intelliseek's BullsEye* (http://www.intelliseek.com/prod/bullseye.htm): this is a desktop application that allows users to efficiently find, analyze, filter, report, track, and manage information. BullsEye utilizes a collection of custom intelligent agents to search both the visible and invisible Web.

There are also fee-based services that will do all the Internet monitoring, compile the information, and prepare daily reports for the CI practitioner. Examples include *Ewatch* (http://www.ewatch.com) and *Cyber Alert* (http://www.cyberalert.com). These types of services may be suitable for organizations that lack adequate staffing to produce the required CI.

What Lies Ahead?

The number of Internet-related tools and services available to CI professionals for gathering and analyzing data is dramatically growing. It is expected that over the next three years, new software such as intelligent agents will come to be used more frequently than they currently are (Fuld, 1998).

In addition, more websites are expected to offer alerting services that inform users when content is changed or added. These alerts are a mixed blessing for the CI professional. Although it saves search time, the amount of time spent wading through new information could grow exponentially. In fact, "there is already evidence that analysts can easily spend 80 percent of their time just fiddling around with monitoring or performing activities such as gathering and sorting data that don't involve interpretation and analysis" (Finegan, 1998). Therefore new relevancy tools will be needed to help the CI professional determine the most valuable information for specific CI needs.

With respect to monitoring activities, there is huge potential for the new data-visualization technologies such as NewsMaps. Competitive intelligence professionals can quickly gain insight and "see" relationships among data when it is presented as a "picture." With the rapid globalization of business from freer trade, relaxed capital-flow restrictions, and advances in communications technology, it is becoming increasingly challenging and imperative for the CI professional to track changes in the competitive landscape. Data-visualization technology can facilitate this task.

Finally, it is clear that the opportunities for *push* technology will continue to be explored. *Push* will be used not just for gathering information, but also for disseminating information to those who "need to know" within the organization (Finegan, 1998).

CONCLUSIONS

There are many valuable resources available on the Internet that help a CI professional monitor the business environment and gather data on specific targets. Some of these tools are easier and faster to use than others and provide more valuable information. It is therefore recommended that the CI practitioner experiment with the different services and resources to determine which ones best suit his or her needs. Most fee-based services provide a free trial period for evaluation purposes. However, registering with them all at once is unwise, as the researcher will be inundated with information that cannot be evaluated effectively.

The CI professional must perform due diligence when evaluating sources of information derived from the Internet. Like any source of information, the credibility, bias, and timelines of the information must be evaluated.

Finally, the CI professional should not forget about the other sources of information for competitive intelligence. The Internet can be effectively used for initial research and monitoring, but contacting primary sources such as industry experts, customers, executives, and colleagues should remain a key data-gathering method.

NOTES

1. The terms "Internet" and "World Wide Web" are generally used synonymously. The World Wide Web (WWW), or simply "Web," is a system that uses hypertext links and graphical links for navigating among different information sources. The Internet on the other hand includes a full range of utilities including e-mail, Gopher, WWW, Telnet, and file-transfer protocol (FTP) that encompasses browsing, searching, retrieval, and communication across computer networks. The use of the term Internet in this chapter refers to just the Web and E-mail functions.

2. Visit the Internet Assigned Numbers Authority at <http://www.iana.org/cctld.html> for a listing of country name domains.

3. For additional information on *bots*, visit <http://bots.internet.com>.

REFERENCES

Buchwitz, L. (1997). *Monitoring Competitive Intelligence Using Internet Push Technology* <http://tor-pw1.netcom.ca/~lillyb/CI_paper.html>.

Calishain, T., and J. Nystron. (1998). *Official Netscape Guide to Internet Research*, 2d ed. Toronto: Coriolis Group.

Cory, K. (1996). "Can Competitive Intelligence Lead to a Sustainable Competitive Advantage?" *Competitive Intelligence Review* 7(3): 45–55.

Finegan, J. (1998). "License to Know," *CIO Magazine* (March 15) <http://www.cio.com/archive/031598_cia_content.html>.

Fuld, L.M. (1995). "Getting Started: The Basic Approaches and Techniques," in *The New Competitor Intelligence: The Complete Resource for Finding, Analyzing, and Using Information about Your Competitors*. New York: Wiley.

———. (1998). "1998 Customer Satisfaction Report and Survey," *Competitive Intelligence Magazine* 1(3): 18–33.

Gustitus, C. (1998). "The Push is On: What Push Technology Means to the Special Librarian," *Information Outlook* (January) <http://www.sla.org/pubs/serial/io/1998/jan98/push.html>.

Kassler, H. (1997). "Mining the Internet for Competitive Intelligence," *Online* 21(5): 34–45.

Lawrence, S., and C. Giles. (1999). "Accessibility of Information on the Web," *Nature* 400(6740): 107–9.

Leonard, D. (1997). "Channel Turf: Push Content Stakes out Your Screen," *CNet* (February) <http://www.cnet.com/Content/Reviews/Compare/Push/index.html>.

Prescott, J.E. (1989). "Competitive Intelligence: Its Role and Functions Within Organizations," in *Advances in Competitive Intelligence*, ed. J.E. Prescott. Alexandria, VA: Society of Competitive Intelligence Professionals.

Prescott, J.E., and P.T. Gibbons. (1993). "Global Competitive Intelligence: An Overview," in *Global Perspectives on Competitive Intelligence*, ed. J.E. Prescott and P.T. Gibbons. Alexandria, VA: Society of Competitive Intelligence Professionals.

Shaker, S., and M. Gembicki. (1999). *The War Room Guide to Competitive Intelligence*. New York: McGraw-Hill.

7

Analysis in Competitive Intelligence: Process, Progress, and Pitfalls

Craig S. Fleisher

INTRODUCTION

In light of the tremendous growth and inexpensive availability of data or "raw competitive intelligence material," analysis and communication of intelligence as opposed to data gathering will increasingly differentiate organizations' competitive intelligence (CI) capabilities in the future. Called by one expert (Herring, 1998) the "brain" of a modern CI system, analysis is one of the more difficult roles a CI specialist is called upon to perform and a manager is called upon to oversee. Although great strides have been made in recent years in terms of planning CI projects and collecting data, the same cannot be said for analysis.

In its undigested state, copious amounts of competitor data and competitive environmental information can be a potentially dangerous resource. Vast amounts of such information can be one of the most damaging resource wasters (e.g., in terms of money, opportunities, people, and time) present in an organization. Intelligence is the analytical process that transforms this undigested information into accurate, relevant, and usable knowledge about competitive conditions and competitors' capabilities, intentions, performance, and position. In other words, the real value of intelligence is essentially the analytical interpretation of sufficient, accurate, and timely data rooted in the knowledge of the future plans and intentions of competitors. This analysis is what is useful for organizational policy-makers.

The analysis of CI consists of processing the data into intelligence by evaluating and interpreting it. Processing the data requires the analyst to perform the time-consuming task of cataloging, filing, "recording," or otherwise document-ing the raw data. The analyst must also understand the merits of the cataloged material. The analyst interprets the cataloged data by sifting and sorting through the collected items in order to understand what is happening in the competitive environment and to competitors.

DEFINING ANALYSIS FOR COMPETITIVE ANALYSIS

Herring (1998) states that "today when I ask a new group of CI practitioners for their definition of intelligence analysis, I am usually given a rambling list of quantitative business-school techniques or some fuzzy definition akin to com-petitor profiling . . . in fact, I find most definitions not only wanting but rather misleading." Definitions of analysis can resemble former U.S. Supreme Court Justice Potter Stewart's response about pornography, who, when asked to define the term, stated that *he may not be able to define it, but he knew it when he saw it*. What then is analysis?

It would be unwise to get the definition of intelligence analysis from the dic-tionary, since dictionary and intelligence community definitions have a funda-mental distinction. An official U.S. government definition says that "intelligence analysis is a process in the production of the intelligence cycle in which intelli-gence information is subjected to systematic examination in order to identify sig-nificant facts and derive conclusion therefrom." Dictionary definitions of analy-sis suggest the analysis process begins with the "whole," and seeks to separate it into its component parts. Intelligence analysis begins with the parts and seeks to fashion the "whole" of the situation.

I define analysis as "the multifaceted combination of processes by which col-lected data are systematically interpreted to produce insightful intelligence find-ings and recommendations for actions." Analysis answers that critical "so what?" question about the data gathered, and brings insight to bear directly on the deci-sion-maker's needs. It is both a process and a product.

As a process, analysis consists of the sequence and totality of steps that the analyst goes through in taking collected data and turning it into analytical out-puts. Langley (1995) notes that the analysis process serves intermediate decision-making purposes such as reducing the number of input variables, providing more time for decision-making as opposed to facts absorption, providing connections among seemingly unrelated data and information, providing a context by relat-ing information to organizational mission, objectives, and strategy, and creating a "working hypothesis" by making a story out of disparate business-environment information.

As a product, analysis usually takes on one of a number of common formats: current intelligence, basic intelligence, technical intelligence, early-warning intelligence, estimated intelligence, work group intelligence, targeted intelli-gence, crisis intelligence, foreign intelligence, and counterintelligence (Dugal, 1998). Godson (1987) states that analytic outputs serve four organizational purposes: they predict future developments and explain the implications to decision-makers; they make data more meaningful and provide guidance to decision-makers considering goals and the alternative means of achieving them; they provide warnings of major developments, events, trends, and assessments based on empirical evidence, thereby helping policy-makers avoid unpleasant surprises; and they provide pieces of current information on specialized topics of concern to decision-makers.

The increased use of computers and availability of on-line data have given organizations the ability to access and manipulate data in volumes and at speeds that were not even dreamed of a couple of decades ago. Because of advanced modeling, computational, display, and interaction tools we have seen in recent years, a vast increase in the speed, capacity, and comprehensiveness of intelligence analysis has taken place. With these increases come corresponding opportunities for innovation, entrepreneurship, and profit-making.

THE PURPOSE AND PRACTICE OF COMPETITIVE ANALYSIS

The purpose of competitive analysis is to better understand one's industry and competitors in order to develop a strategy that will provide a sustainable competitive advantage and achieve continuing performance results that are superior to one's competitors. Analysis done properly can also have a number of intermediate outcomes that can help the analyst and his or her organization. Despite the obvious importance of these outcomes, the ultimate aim of analysis is to produce better business results, not just better decisions.

Successful intelligence analysis requires the practitioner to effectively perform a balancing act among a number of different continua. For example, the practitioner has to simultaneously balance between:

- *Creative and scientific.* The analyst must understand how and when to use his or her judgment in combination with proven (scientific) techniques to arrive at the best conclusion. Much of the "scientific" aspect of analysis can be taught by exposing the practitioner to the tools and methods for conducting analysis, but the creative aspect may be more *trait* than *trainable*. Werther (1998) observes this balance when he notes that part of successful analysis is the "art of knowing what to look for, selecting wisely, understanding the degree of rigor that the particular material will support, and then drawing from this delimited understanding the best 'qualified' conclusions that one can."

- *Deduction and induction.* Over time, the effective CI analyst will have to utilize both deductive and inductive reasoning in his or her approach to the analytical task. Deduction requires the practitioner to make inferences from a general rule or theory to specific instances or examples. Induction is the process of making inferences from some specific observations to a more general rule that is commonly used in constructing theories.

- *Precision and perspective.* Does it really matter whether the competitor has 23.465 percent of the market, or about a quarter of the market and is growing its share at a 2 percent per year clip? The successful analyst almost always seeks both precision and accuracy in generating analytical outputs; however, they cannot sacrifice the usefulness of the outputs by making the outputs accurate at great expense of resources, timeliness, or general understanding.

• *Qualitative and quantitative.* Recent years have seen the analytical task become far more quantitative in character due to the explosive growth of numerical data available on the Internet and in on-line databases. However, numbers cannot and do not necessarily tell the entire story. In fact, any accountant or economist will tell you how numbers can distort or hide the true competitive picture. It is also problematic when analysts try to package imprecise raw data in a way that is made to look precise, and then perform rigorous-looking analytical "magic" on the resulting mass (Werther, 1998). It is critical, therefore, for the CI practitioner to also utilize an array of qualitative methods in performing analysis as a way of developing a richer picture of the situation.

Many competitive analysts unsuccessfully perform the required balancing act, and their failure frequently shows up in poor public results. Werther (1998) notes a number of recent spectacular intelligence-analysis failures—such as the steep Asian decline from what had only recently been viewed as a "miracle"— that have prompted considerable criticism of analysts in public agencies. He suggests that private-sector analysts may want to avoid a similar fate. Why then has analysis received a bad rap?

DIFFICULTIES IN GENERATING SUCCESSFUL ANALYSIS

Besides the previously established fact that few people can adequately define it, there are a number of other reasons that potentially explain why analysis is not the most popular process for CI practitioners to perform:

• *Analysis is hard to do for most people.* In today's turbo-charged digital world it is far easier to collect a lot of data than it is to figure out what to do with it. Analysis can also be very time-consuming, is seen by some to be a "dry" or unexciting activity, and the feedback from analysis efforts may not show up for an extended time. As in nature, people tend to prefer taking the path of least resistance when it comes to putting forth effort or expending energy on tasks that may not be easily recognized or quickly rewarded.

• *Few people have publicly recognized or established analysis expertise.* Even those who do may not necessarily be able to "teach" or disseminate how to do it. Analysis skills can be developed over time as one grows in experience and knowledge, but some analysis expertise will require a degree of tacit skill or inherent creativity that is "born and not made."

• *There are few frameworks for understanding how the analysis component can be managed as part of the larger CI process.* Analysis cannot be performed successfully when distinct from CI planning and data collection. Successful

CI managers recognize this interaction between the collection and analysis stages. Finally, few individuals can thoughtfully explain how analysis can be successfully managed according to the three "Es": efficiency, effectiveness, and efficacy. For example, some organizations spend, and frequently waste, untold amounts of financial resources to perform analysis at high levels of precision, compared to what could have been saved resource-wise in overall systems terms with a slightly less precise and more smartly managed analytical processes.

In my experience, there are a number of prevalent empirical symptoms that suggest why analysis is not performed successfully. Several of the most common ones include:

- *Tool rut.* Like the man who has a hammer and begins to think everything he sees looks like a nail, people keep using the same tools over and over again. We describe this tendency to overuse the same tools as being in the "tool rut." This overuse is counter to the principle that, in addressing the complexity of this ever-changing world, the CI analyst needs to consider numerous diverse models to provide value. Successful analysts understand the basic analytical models and know when and why to use the various analysis tools (Society of Competitive Intelligence Professionals, 1997).

- *Blind spots.* Zahra and Chaples (1993) note that many analyses are flawed due to an organization's mistaken or incomplete view of its industry or competition, the poor design of the analysis system, or inaccurate managerial perceptions. Their research suggests that these six blind spots are most common:
    —misjudging industry boundaries
    —poor identification of the competition
    —overemphasis on competitors' visible competencies
    —overemphasis on where, not how, rivals compete
    —faulty assumptions about the competition
    —paralysis by analysis
  Successful analysts recognize the inevitable existence of gaps and blind spots, and actively address the issues associated with their existence.

- *Business-school recipe.* Many individuals charged with doing analysis come out of master of business administration (MBA) programs where they have been taught tried-and-true recipes from instructors with financial- and management-accounting backgrounds. Business and competitive analysis are as far different from accounting analysis as strategy is from accounting, and not the least of which because one looks from the present backwards (e.g., accounting), while the other looks from the present forwards (e.g., CI). This backward-looking analytical orientation may help explain why few accountants lead CI or strategy functions and vice versa.

- *Ratio blinders.* Most businesspeople do analysis based on historical data and financial ratios. Historical analysis of the financials can at best only provide comparison and tell the analyst the size of the gap (the "what") between two organizations on a particular data point or data set. It does not help the analyst explain the reasons why the gap exists, or how to close it.

- *Convenience shopping.* Individuals frequently do analysis on the basis of the data they happen to have easily on hand, as opposed to the data they should have. Because the analyst has certain data at his or her disposal, he or she uses the analytical technique that suits the data rather than focusing the analysis on the client's question and/or the intelligence actually required. This bias towards analytical convenience is especially true when accountants are asked to do analysis, and they provide outputs that only reflect financial manipulations.

- *Microwaved preparation.* The perceived and real pressures driving many organizational decisions today mean that analysis is undercooked and not ready to eat when it needs to be served to decision-makers. Successful analysis commonly requires thoughtful and substantial consideration. Decision-makers who ask for and expect analytical outputs from their CI practitioners "yesterday" are cooking a surefire recipe for decision-making deficiencies.

- *Organizational spin cities.* CI outputs are commonly used today as a means for exercising influence or power over others rather than for finding new insights. Several academic studies (Langley, 1995; Mintzberg, 1989) have noted the politicization of formal analysis whereby managers tread the fine line between ill-conceived, arbitrary decisions ("extinction by instinct") and an unhealthy obsession with numbers and reports (i.e., "paralysis by analysis"). Successful analysts have the judgment to know when to cease analyzing and when not to "shoot from the hip."

Not every CI practitioner can become a successful CI analyst. This is because successful analysts are a product of both nature and nurture. Sawka (1999) notes that the wiring of the practitioner's brain is more important than his degree or prior work experience. Herring (1998) notes that three critical elements have been identified as characterizing the best government intelligence analysts: knowledge about the subject being analyzed, clarity of thought in describing how the analysis was conducted, and judgment or the ability to arrive at the correct conclusion.

Government studies of successful analysts suggest that they are frequently characterized as "NTs" (i.e., intuitive thinkers) using the Myers-Briggs Personality Type Indicator. NTs are individuals who demonstrate strong intuitive-thinking abilities. NTs have strengths in organizing data and facts in ways that allow them to spot discontinuities and link related observations, and can use their ability to "see the big picture." Other observers have noted how successful analysts also demonstrate the qualities of forward-looking mindsets, logic, perseverance, comfort with ambiguity, insight, and big-picture-pattern thinking (Sawka, 1999).

CATEGORIES OF COMPETITIVE ANALYSIS TECHNIQUES

Just what is the CI practitioner likely to be analyzing in the first place? A great deal must be learned about an organization and its environment so that strategies may be effectively formulated. Although the broader strategy-formulation process would include both external (e.g., environment, industry, competitors, etc.) and internal (e.g., resources, values, organization, etc.) analysis, most analysis within CI is focused outwardly on competitors and elements that affect or can potentially affect the competitive situation. This chapter will not specifically cover traditional strategy formulation done at the corporate, business, or functional levels, because they are more than adequately covered in a variety of good textbooks (see, for example, Grant, 1998; Hax & Majluf, 1996; Thompson & Strickland, 1999).

Nearly every CI analysis technique requires the practitioner to accurately define its competitors and industry. These definitions are much more difficult to distinguish in reality than most people believe. Part of the problem stems from the fact that the definitions of competitors and industry overlap one another. I'll briefly touch upon them below, even though these issues are too large to adequately address in this chapter.

In general, an industry is nothing more than a cluster of economic units that are grouped together for analytical or cooperative (e.g., trade associations) purposes. One of the more commonly used taxonomy schemes is the North American Industrial Classification System (NAICS) (formerly SIC) that clusters and codes establishments together on the basis of the primary activity in which they are engaged (e.g., normally a product or service category). Another common way to identify an industry is to determine close product or service substitutes that exhibit high cross-elasticities of demand. However, as a practical matter, geographic boundaries, customer types, needs satisfied, suppliers, technologies, or other peculiar dimensions of a business may better serve the purpose of clustering organizations for analysis.

Identifying competitors is critical because if you know who they are, you may be able to predict their behavior; however, competitor identification is difficult, in that there are numerous extant taxonomies of competitors. Common taxonomies include current versus potential competitors, direct and indirect, single and multipoint (e.g., the rival competes against the organization in several product/service lines), or national and multinational. Although Fahey (1999) suggests that competitors may be identified by the locales of rivalry such as factor arenas (supplies, components, labor, etc.), customer arenas, geography, channel arenas (e.g., wholesalers, distributors, retailers, etc.), or institutional arenas (e.g., governmental agencies, social groups, community groups, etc.), there are essentially two broad approaches for identifying competitors (Aaker, 1998): The first approach organizes competitors according to the degree with which they compete for a buyer's choice (e.g., product-use associations), while the strategic-group approach organizes on the basis of their strategies (e.g., along the lines of posture, characteristics, assets, competencies).

For example, one method of competitor identification depends on the nature of the competitive interaction an organization has with a rival (Clark, 1998). There are three types of interactions possible between two organizations: an explicit interaction (each firm is aware of the other and attempts to manage that relationship to its advantage); an implicit interaction (customer response to the two organizations' actions creates certain outcomes for both organizations, but each organization is ignorant of the other's effect on its business); and an asymmetric interaction (an *aware* organization has the opportunity to exercise stealth, taking actions that the *ignorant* competitor will not perceive).

An organization and its managers can use a wide variety of techniques to combine, process, and sort collected data in order to produce relevant and timely information for impacting strategy. Recent years have seen an evolution of thought, practice, and analysis tools. There are several hundred analytical tools that have been classified as being useful in CI applications, and that number is probably conservative in light of the many tools that have been custom-designed to serve some organizations' proprietary CI purposes.

An easy way to classify CI analysis techniques would be to use my working list as follows:

- *Strategic.* Companies usually earn superior returns by either entering profitable industries or by establishing competitive advantages over their rivals. How these are achieved is usually done in the domain of corporate ("which business should we be in?") or business ("how should we compete within a specific market or industry?") strategy. Therefore major tools of analysis will include such items as industry-classification analysis (e.g., five forces analysis), driving forces or industry-maturity analysis using S-curves depicting lifecycles, core competencies and capabilities, resource analysis (tangible and intangibles), future analysis, key success factors, strategic-group analysis, or competitor-gap analyses.

- *Product-oriented.* In light of the ability of competitors to quickly imitate innovations, and the decreasing time that companies are able to maintain competitive advantages, it is important for the analyst to understand competitors' products or services. This insight is gleaned through the analyst's application of such tools as reverse engineering, tear-down analysis, blind testing, and mystery shopping.

- *Environment-oriented.* Today's competitive global marketplace requires the analyst to understand how the broader impacts of an industry's environment can impact an organization's competitiveness. This understanding is gained through the analyst's application of tools such as country risk, issue mapping, policy analysis, STEEP analysis, political and social risk, and media-content assessment.

- *Customer-oriented.* Organizations are frequently able to develop competitive advantage by constantly delivering better customer value than their competitors. Organizations use several tools to help them determine how they are delivering customer value relative to their competitors. The primary tools used for this task include customer-value analysis, preferences benchmarking, customer-value mapping, price-performance mapping, and customer-value management.

- *Financial-oriented.* Financial strength can often be a key factor underlying the competitiveness of a marketplace player. It is almost impossible to do an effective competitor analysis without assessing its financial condition in depth. Several financial-analysis techniques can be successfully used within CI. Although these, like all other techniques, have limitations, thoughtful analysis can help the analyst to understand a competitor's economic and financial character, capabilities, and its potential direction. Some of the more effective financial-oriented tools are ratio analysis, sustainable growth-rate analysis, disaggregated financial-ratio assessment to understand the economic characteristics of a corporate competitor's business units or product lines, competitive-cost analysis to understand how firms are establishing low-cost positions, and value-chain analysis.

- *Technological-oriented.* Firms are increasingly achieving competitive advantages through their ability to out-innovate their competitors in the marketplace along both process and product/service lines. These dual advances mean that the analyst must regularly assess the technology and technological environment for organizations of all types. Some of the tools commonly used for this task would include patent analysis, application of the scientific method, and discovery curves.

- *Behavioral.* Qualitative data about a company's culture and management can often provide the keys to the story about a competitor's success. The more the analyst knows and understands about a competitor's management and its key employees, the more he or she will also likely know about the firm and its possible marketplace actions. Some of the key tools the analyst uses in understanding management style, culture, and values are shadowing, leadership profiling, and values analysis.

The use of tools from each of the seven categories is important so that organizations do not become over-reliant on a competitor, customer, environment, or product focus, and instead retain a healthy market orientation (Kotler & Turner, 1998).

THE ANALYSIS PROCESS WITHIN THE LARGER CI CYCLE

How is the process of analysis conducted within the larger CI cycle? *What* practitioners analyze and *why* matters as much as how the collected data is processed. The formula for placing CI analysis into context is: *Understand Business Situation and Client's Needs*—determines → *Type of Analysis*—determines → *Type of Data Needed*—determines → *Type of Data Collection.*

The depth and complexity of analysis are dependent upon the business situation and client's needs. It is the CI analyst's up-front responsibility to determine the situation and critical intelligence needs (CINs). This determination may be harder to do than say, as it is not uncommon for the client not to know his or her own needs. Analysis must be user-driven, and users want intelligence that offers insight and a guide to action that helps them gain competitive advantage.

Data should be evaluated after it is collected, filtered, and entered into the organization's CI system. Unfortunately, this formal evaluation of data that is commonly done by military and public intelligence agencies is rarely done by business. Evaluation includes the determination of the *relevance, reliability*, and *validity* of the collected data. *Relevance* suggests that the analyst must assess how well (in terms of what, when, and why) the raw data addresses the CI clients' CINs and the organization's mission, objectives, and strategy. *Reliability* is an evaluation of the data source and whether it has a good track record for providing useful information. In particular, the analyst tries to determine whether biases are present that might affect the quality of the data. *Validity* requires the analyst to assess the "truthfulness" or accuracy of the data itself. Validity can be assessed in terms of face validity, triangulation whereby the collected data are compared to data available from alternative sources, and searching for surrogate indicators.

The evaluated data are then transformed into intelligence. Transformation occurs through a variety of approaches, including transmission, accumulation, aggregation, relational checking, and pattern recognition.

Transmission

Transmission is the movement of data from one source to another. It is important to the analyst because communication channels frequently introduce "noise," and thereby distort the data. The resulting distortion can be especially critical when data is transmitted among analysts, data collectors and analysts, and the analyst and the client.

Accumulation

Accumulation refers to how data is stored and retrieved. Organizations trying to analyze competitors or the competitive environment with incomplete and inefficient storage-and-retrieval systems create difficulties for the analyst. Many individuals are reluctant to enter what they perceive to be personal or "soft" information into the CI system; others find the systems too difficult to bother with. Individuals may want to maintain the data for their own selfish purposes. The implications for the design of a CI system and for the efficiency and effectiveness of analysis are large.

Aggregation

Aggregation is the function in which larger data points are reduced to smaller, more pertinent sets. This is the first function in which analysts actually act on the data. Most organizations do this by putting the filtered information within a variety of permanent categories on the organization-wide CI system. For example, many aggregate data by competitor, issue type, product/services, industry, or the broader environmental (e.g., STEEP) sectors.

Relational Checking and Pattern Recognition

Relational checking and pattern recognition happen when the analyst perceives and determines patterns among the disparate collected data. Relational checking is the more formal and logical process by which the analyst seeks to find and measure the relationships among collected data. The level of pattern checking and relational checking varies among companies and industries: Some companies generate competitive balance sheets for benchmarking their organization against its competitors, while others use it to identify opportunities or anticipate potential threats. Relationships commonly tracked and analyzed include those between advertising or promotional activity and sales, research-and-development expenditures and new-product development, industry capacity and sales volumes, or market share and profitability, etc.

ASSESSING THE ANALYSIS PROCESS AND ANALYTICAL OUTPUTS

How would a decision-maker know whether the analyst has done these processes effectively? A successful analysis will demonstrate the following five characteristics:

- *Comprehensive.* The analyst will not have selectively chosen facts to support a preordained conclusion, but will have considered *all* available data.

- *Credible.* The analysis is internally consistent and will not contain contradictions in either content or logic.

- *Clear.* The decision-maker can understand the rationale for and process of analysis employed. In other words, the language of the analysis can be easily explained to the nonanalyst.

- *Garbage In, Garbage Out (GIGO).* The analyst can demonstrate the use of reliable and trustworthy inputs, and can vouch for the quality of the data-evaluation process employed.

- *Actionable.* The resultant analytical outputs inform the decision-maker's business judgment without being a substitute for it. The analysis must pass the decision-making client's face validity or "common-sense" test.

In addition, the analytical outputs themselves can be subjected to tests of quality. Fleisher and Bensoussan (2000) describe their FAROUT system for assessing whether analytical outputs demonstrated insightful trade offs among the following qualities:

- *Foresight.* The best analytical outputs will be forward-looking and future-oriented, helping the decision-maker to understand how competitive matters will be transformed from the present onward.

- *Accurate.* This is an important determination of how well the outputs are likely to explain subsequent events. It also suggests that alternative findings and views have been elucidated, and that the conclusions have been challenged, compared, and tested.

- *Resource efficient.* This is a measure of analytical productivity that requires the analyst to demonstrate that they were able to generate the analytical outputs in the fastest time possible using the minimum amount of resource inputs.

- *Objective.* This assesses how well the outputs dealt with perceived or actual biases that were likely to be present either in the raw collected data or the analytical process itself. Objectivity demands that underlying assumptions and uncertainties have been identified and addressed. This quality is crucial so that the analyst can maintain his or her credibility with decision-makers, who will rely on his or her analytical outputs in decision-making.

- *Useful.* This is the decision-maker's assessment of how well the analytical outputs met their CINs. Satisfying CINs also requires implications to have been developed for the client, and were presented in an effective format for planning. Successful analyses are always useful in the decision-maker's development of tactics and strategies.

- *Timely.* Timely analyses mean that management can act on the outputs with enough time to make a competitive difference. Analytical output that arrives to the decision-makers after it has gone stale is not intelligence at all, but merely information and a waste of resources.

SUMMARY

During the last few years we have witnessed a vast increase in the speed, capacity, and comprehensiveness of intelligence analysis because of advanced modeling, computational, display, and interaction tools. Speed has increased the administrative gains such as wider acceptance of CI in companies and better training of analysts, as has new computer-based analytical tools, databases, and communication methods. Capacity has improved because more participants from diverse locations can be involved in CI; consequently, the number of analysts, tools, or data sources that can be linked is increased. Comprehensiveness has improved because we are better able to integrate a broader range of perspectives or viewpoints on the input data.

Despite these advances, CI-practitioners' exploitation of analytical processes and techniques looks very much like the *iceberg principle*: We use the bulk of processes and techniques that exist above the water, but the ones underwater are what we should be most concerned about. Even though the field has made substantial strides over the last two decades, there remains substantial room for improvement in CI-practitioners' performance of intelligence analysis.

Last but not least, I should conclude by noting that useful analysis exists only when combined with responsible decision-making. Decision-makers who are unwilling to put their trust and faith in responsible CI analysis must be willing to live with the consequences of ineffective decision-making, unsuccessful tactics and strategies, and poorer marketplace performance.

REFERENCES

Aaker, D. (1998). *Developing Business Strategies.* New York: Wiley.

Clark, B. (1998). "Managing Competitive Interactions," *Marketing Management* 7(4): 9–20.

Dugal, M. (1998). "CI Product Line: A Tool for Enhancing User Acceptance of CI," *Competitive Intelligence Review* 9(2): 17–25.

Fahey, L. (1999). *Competitors: Outwitting, Outmaneuvering, and Outperforming.* New York: Wiley.

Fleisher, C.S., and B. Bensoussan. (2000). "A FAROUT Way to Manage CI Analysis," *Competitive Intelligence Magazine* 3(2): 37–40.

Godson, R. (1987). "Intelligence: An American View," in *British and American Approaches to Intelligence*, ed. K. Robertson. London: Macmillan Press for Royal United Services Institute.

Grant, R.M. (1998). *Contemporary Strategy Analysis*, 3d ed. Malden, MA: Blackwell.

Hax, A., and N. Majluf. (1996). *The Strategy Concept and Process: A Pragmatic Approach*, 2d ed. Upper Saddle River, NJ: Prentice-Hall.

Herring, J.P. (1998). "What Is Intelligence Analysis?" *Competitive Intelligence Magazine* 1(2): 13–16.

Kotler, P., and R. Turner. (1998). *Marketing Management*, 9th Canadian ed. Upper Saddle River, NJ: Prentice-Hall.

Langley, A. (1995). "Between Paralysis by Analysis and Extinction by Instinct," *Sloan Management Review* 36(3): 63–76.

Mintzberg, H. (1989). *Mintzberg on Management.* New York: Free Press.

Sawka, K. (1999). "Finding Intelligence Analysts," *Competitive Intelligence Magazine* 2(1): 41–42.

Society of Competitive Intelligence Professionals. (1997). "Competencies for Intelligence Professionals," from the education-modules section of the Society of Competitive Intelligence Professionals (SCIP) website at <www.scip.org>.

Thompson, A., and A. Strickland. (1999). *Strategic Management: Concepts and Cases*, 11th ed. New York: Irwin/McGraw-Hill.

Werther, G. (1998). "Doing Business in the New World Disorder: The Problem with Precision," *Competitive Intelligence Magazine* 1(2): 24–26.

Zahra, S., and S. Chaples. (1993). "Blind Spots in Competitive Analysis," *Academy of Management Executive* 7(2): 7–28.

8

A Toolbox for Communicating Competitive Intelligence via the Internet

Robert Cunningham

INTRODUCTION

Competitive intelligence (CI) has become a necessity in the world of business. Competitive intelligence increases the probability that a company will maintain or enhance its competitive advantages. Competitive intelligence relies heavily on an effective structure and system that assimilates and disseminates accurate and timely information. Communication is the backbone of this structure.

Various strategic alliances have been suggested as necessary business relationships in this accelerating frontier: consortia that set standards for industries, joint ventures on various areas of research, technology, and market efficiencies, along with mergers and acquisitions resulting from such alliances. There is an obvious trend in today's global environment of corporations needing to connect with other corporations that can enhance their strategic objectives on a global platform. Simply put, today's competitor may be tomorrow's ally, and if you are not ready to communicate with it, another competitor will.

Corporations are becoming aware of what communication means to their CI department. Competitive intelligence professionals need to make informed decisions about what is going on in the world, the environment, and how this relates to their company's strategic planning and strategic thinking, along with the adaptation of a sustainable corporate milieu.

The Internet is truly the only frontier that is global. No country has been able to, nor will be able to, say that they own or dominate this frontier. The standards, rules, and laws that are familiar to a CI manager do not necessarily apply to the Internet.

Many articles and books have been published on how to manage the flow of communications internally using the Internet as a vehicle. This chapter will examine the external environment—how a company can better position itself in communicating in this global environment.

The focus of this chapter will be on the Internet as a public domain. Consideration will be given to the practicalities of positioning information on the Internet and communicating information to various competitors/allies and potential allies. Several issues will also be discussed that are important to CI managers, including how to validate information, trademark and intellectual-property issues, and an evaluation of various interactive or otherwise useful websites and newsgroups. The purpose of discussing these domains on the Internet is to illustrate the use of the Internet as a vehicle in communicating with the outside world, and to show the value of communicating on the Internet to the CI executive in disseminating and gathering CI data.

The Internet can be used as a tool to communicate with other corporations in many different ways to enhance global partnerships. Initially there may not be the level of trust that would allow these meetings or negotiations to happen via Intranet communications, nor the need. One function of the CI department should be locating suitable companies that may match the requirements of any possible alliances. These companies may not be multinational corporations (MNCs); they may be regional or national companies, and as such not easily locatable. The advantage of communicating on the Internet is the ability to extend the reach of communications. There are several ways to start the process, and there are several things that a corporation and a CI executive in particular need to be aware of when they start these communications over the Internet.

The Internet can be used as a tool to scan the environment, but there is a blurring between what is external and what is internal. Certainly companies use the Internet as a (CI) tool for scanning the competitive environment. This usage makes sense considering the comparative low-cost advantage of compiling information (Graef, 1996). In addition, the Internet can be used as a pull mechanism, capturing information on regulations, financial markets, and competitor behavior and signals. Technology trends and patent updating is also possible using Web databases that help in assimilating information (Malhotra, 1997). This information assists in supplementing strategic planning in regard to joint ventures, mergers and acquisitions, and various business function activities.[1] Defensive CI actions are also very important, and caution should be used when disseminating bits and pieces of information about your company across the Web. A shrewd assimilator can quickly observe patterns from this information (Harkleroad, 1994).

However, once done, how does a CI executive venture outward on the Internet to meet professional colleagues? In addition, what should be known about the Internet's particular idiosyncrasies before the company makes an informed decision? Given the vast number of sites, links, search engines, etc., this search for an informed decision can become an onerous task. Further complicating the situation is the complexity of considering any alliance or consortium. As this relationship evolves, as does the use of the Internet, these competitors, now allies, may have a need to know how you have positioned yourself on the Internet and what networks or links you may be involved with. The evolution of alliances needs to evolve at the same pace as the ability to respond using the Internet as a function of doing business; communicating with other businesses will become an integral part of this function.

The purpose of this chapter is to advance additional information on what is needed in any CI toolbox, and to further elucidate on the need to become interactive on the Internet—becoming comfortable in knowing how to communicate, where one can communicate, and being secure in what is being communicated.

COMMUNICATING INFORMATION ON THE INTERNET

The Internet places few restrictions on what kinds of information are contained in the millions of pages and websites that can be accessed by anyone with a personal computer (PC), browser, modem, and an Internet service provider (ISP). This editorial freedom means that CI executives need to realize the importance of communicating accurate information on the Internet, and in recognizing what is reliable information. Various authorities have established criteria in the field of library science that will increase the integrity and the timeliness of such information.

Given the likelihood for the need to interact with those who could become allies or partners, CI executives need to make sure that the information they are communicating is positioned properly and in a way that is considered credible. Furthermore, any information that is used in additional communication needs to be relied on for its content and documentation. There are several questions that should be asked (Smith, 1997):

- What is the scope of the resource: its breadth, depth, timeliness, format restrictions?

- Is the information content indeed fact? Is this original information, or is it useful for its links? How have you expressed your intent and is it clear to the reader?

- If the value of your page is the links, are the links updated? Have all links that are in frames been secured so that there are no copyright issues?

- Is the information presented accurately, and can it be checked against other resources that the viewer may have?

- On what authority are you speaking, and what standing do you have in the field? Do you have an e-mail address that you can be reached at on the page that is active?

- Does the information need to be updated, or is it static? If it needs updating, is the last update visibly posted?

- What advantage is there in reading the information you have posted? Can this information be derived in some other format that complements it?

- Have you written well what you are saying? Has it effectively managed the transition into HTML in appearance and positioning on the page?
- Is the page interesting to look at? Are the graphic or multimedia effects distracting, or do they enhance the content?
- What is the purpose of the page or site? Is it clearly stated? Do you fulfill this purpose?
- What reviewing services have made comments on your information? Are they linked to your URL?
- Where have you positioned this information? Is it part of your company website or have you created an ancillary site for the alliance and the general public?
- Is your site convenient to use? Does it take too long to load? Can the viewer get what it needs quickly and efficiently and exit feeling that it was worth the time?
- Is your information easy to read, and if you offer additional resources, are they easy to use?
- Do you need to attach special requirements for accessing the information (e.g., passwords, software)?
- Have you linked your information to the various search engines, and, in certain instances, do you want to do this?
- Can the site be accessed on a regular basis, or is it often overloaded or off-line? Have you mirrored the site to reduce time and bandwidth delays and restrictions?
- Are there any costs associated with connecting to the site or associated with acquiring the intellectual property that you are presenting?

Information communicated on the Internet is far more complex than a simple e-mail. Just as with any article that is written, one must consider the style necessary to communicate what is being said. The effective documentation and usefulness of data on the Internet is continually being updated. It is suggested that the World Wide Web (WWW) Virtual Library is a good place to start to get more information. In addition, it may be useful to become involved in future discussions on standards associated with communicating information over the Internet. Several sources of information on what is considered credible documentation can be found in the WWW Virtual Library located at <http://www.vuw.ac.nz/~agsmith/evaln/evaln.htm>.

USENET

One of the better definitions of Usenet is the following:

> Usenet is a world-wide distributed discussion system. It consists of a set of "newsgroups" with names that are classified hierarchically by subject. "Articles" or "mes-

sages" are "posted" to these newsgroups by people on computers with the appropriate software—these articles are then broadcast to other interconnected computer systems via a wide variety of networks. Some newsgroups are "moderated"; in these newsgroups, the articles are first sent to a moderator for approval before appearing in the newsgroup. Usenet is available on a wide variety of computer systems and networks, but the bulk of modern Usenet traffic is transported over either the Internet or Unix to Unix Copy Program (UUCP). Usenet is the set of people who exchange articles tagged with one or more universally recognized labels, called "newsgroups" (or "groups" for short). There is often confusion about the precise set of newsgroups that constitutes Usenet; one commonly accepted definition is that it consists of newsgroups listed in the periodic "List of Active Newsgroups" postings which appear regularly in news lists and other newsgroups. (Note that the correct term is "newsgroups"; they are not called areas, bases, boards, bulletin boards, conferences, round tables, Special Interest Groups (SIGs), echoes, rooms or use-groups! Nor, as noted above, are they part of the Internet, though they may reach your site over it. Furthermore, the people who run the news systems are called news administrators, not sysops. If you want to be understood, be accurate.)[2]

Usenet can be a valuable ally to a CI manager. By using software programs such as Outlook Express by Microsoft one has access to an e-mail program and a newsreader. On a recent compilation of the newsgroups available, Outlook Express recognized over 31,000 newsgroups.[3] One advantage of using Outlook Express is the built-in search mechanism. This simply means you have only to type in a word—e.g., "research"—and all group names with this name in it will appear in alphabetical order. Suddenly you have access to various topics that may be of interest to you. These newsgroups are then instantly accessible by either clicking on them or clicking on the "go to" command. But beware—the contents of some of the posted information is questionable, and as such needs to be further documented. The plus side to using this resource may be the contacts you will make that may not be available otherwise. In addition, you can use this environment to create newsgroups on subjects of interest to you and your company. It is advisable to post in your introductory article some disclaimers acknowledging your intent and whatever your professional code of ethics requires you to state.

Informal contacts established in this form of communication are, and can be, used to develop ongoing business relationships or networks that may help in bridging alliances in the future.

INTERACTIVE WEBSITES, AND WHAT THEY MEAN TO A CI MANAGER

Several websites are available to the CI executive in which to share information and monitor what other CI professionals are saying. One can expect these sites to evolve into partner-forming relationships that can be taken further than the sharing of information. If the objective is just to share information, they can still be used to create consortia on various issues such as standards or larger global concerns that will affect your company. The following are examples of such websites:

- *The Top Management Corporate Development Center*
<http://www.mcb.co.uk/topman/gateway.htm>

This site provides an interactive participatory way to share in the current and future issues of management with other professionals. One area of interest to CI is the discussion on continuous improvements. There is an excellent probability of sharing and acquiring a variety of solutions to current issues, accessing articles, and learning about activities that will enhance the CI department's information and communication reach.[4]

- *Emerging Markets Companion* <http://www.emgmkts.com/>

Given the ongoing change in the global environment, this website offers information pertaining to emerging markets. It is updated daily and offers financial news and investment information from Asia, Latin America, Africa, and Eastern Europe. This site links its information to well-respected news and investment organizations such as Reuters, Bloomberg, Stone and McCarthy, Credit Lyonnais, and NatWest Markets. Conferences and events in these spheres are also offered, along with background data on emerging markets. There is a search facility that allows for an easier search of the content of the website. By using this website, international CI professionals will have access to information in a more concise manner than they would otherwise. Although currently not interactive, the value of the information available makes it worth mentioning.[5]

- *Management-Research*
<http://www.mailbase.ac.uk/lists-k-o/management-research/>

Management-research methodology is the basis for the discussion forum provided by this site, along with the networking capabilities and the dissemination of research findings. Full instructions are given on how to join this website's listserver. Management-research's archives are completely searchable, which enables new users to catch up on debates prior to joining. The added incentive is in knowing who is saying what about the topics in which you are interested. Others who have used the site have said that they are impressed by the quick response to the topics of discussion.[6]

- *@BRINT.COM* <http://www.brint.com/>

Brint or Business Researcher's Interests is a very valuable site for any CI professional. Besides the ease of searching for relevant materials on the hottest topics in business, Brint offers a comprehensive database on several aspects of the Internet and related issues. Brint also offers a comprehensive array of information on CI that will prove invaluable to any CI executive. Brint also provides an online searchable discussion forum where existing discussion forums can be accessed, or new forums can be created. Examples of ongoing discussion forums include:

—technology, competitive intelligence, and conversations
—impact of waste of knowledge
—project-knowledge management and boundary objects

—on knowledge and patterns
—knowledge in documents: social and technological issues
—databases and knowledge management
—outsourcing and helpdesk management
—intangible assets and intellectual capital
—knowledge-management architecture and unified theory
—meaningful role of (CKO) and knowledge managers
—enterprise architecture of knowledge
—translation, meaning, and trust
—virtual teams and knowledge sharing
—retaining knowledge of contract workers
—mapping of organizational knowledge
—knowledge economy: diverse perspectives
—knowledge-management software capabilities[7]

- *Booz, Allen & Hamilton, Inc.* <http://www.strategy-business.com/index.html>

  Billed as "the gathering place for today's and tomorrow's business leaders," this site is an extension of *Strategy and Business* (*S&B*) magazine and forms part of the wider website of Booz, Allen & Hamilton; by its own reckoning, one of the world's largest management- and technology-consulting firms. The site is split into articles, quotes, book reviews, upcoming issues, and "beyond *S&B*." The "articles" section enables you to access and search past issues of the journal, while the "beyond *S&B*" patch provides "hot links" to a large number of other top sites. Here you will find the Fortune 500 companies ranked and dissected, two sites chosen for their strategy and management expertise, top sites for various industries, the top ten business schools, and top search tools. Numerous links are included to sites such as the *Economist* magazine, Harvard Business School, and the Yahoo homepage. This website is graphically pleasing, well-organized, and appears to be updated regularly.[8] In addition, the ideas-exchange page offers a forum that allows you to challenge the authors of several articles, pose questions, or ask them advice.

- *The Center For Intelligent Information Retrieval (CIIR)* <http://ciir.cs.umass.edu/>

  The University of Massachusetts at Amherst CIIR carries out basic research and technology transfer in the areas of text-based information systems. It was created to address the problem of effective use to the growing quantities of electronic information throughout our society in business, health care, international trade, government, and other areas.[9]

- *TechnoGate* <http://www.technogate.com/>

  TechnoGate is an internet-based business-growth tool developed by the global advanced-technology industry for technology companies focused on accelerated growth and global expansion. In the fast-paced world of global competition and technology convergence, no organization can "go-it-alone." Success on the world stage demands world-class products and services, financing, staffing, preparation, and execution.[10] TechnoGate is an industry-led business network that connects technology enterprises to strategic partners, and expert suppliers to the technology industry. This site also provides high-value information critical to business growth. TechnoGate is now used to access contacts, source and post opportunities, advertise and source companies' capabilities, and for numerous deal-making resources (e.g., on-line discussion, brokerage, compensation benchmarks, surveys, electronic payment, news clips).[11] TechnoGate also gives you access to various databases that will be useful to any international ventures. Any company that is considering allying itself in the areas of research and development (R&D) and technological advances should give this network serious consideration.

• *CEO Express* <http://ceoexpress.com/>

CEO Express is not an interactive site, but it is one of the most comprehensive websites made up entirely of links to other very useful websites. Any CI professional will need to be able to gather reliable information on the Internet, and CEO Express offers this on one site, listing hundreds of different links to very reliable organizations whose offerings are on a multitude of topics and areas in business.

Intellectual Property and Trademarks

The Internet is ripe for disputes over intellectual property and trademarks. Good defensive posturing is needed, and this is a function of the CI department. In this context, CI is responsible for minimizing a company's risk of entering into litigation over name disputes and information ownership on the Internet. All companies on the Internet should take judicious care in ensuring that they are protected from such problems. Protection is not as easy as one would think.

Domains are Uniform Resource Locators (URLs), where the letters after the final period indicate the domain; for example, ".com"; ".net"; and ".org"[.] For many years people have owned these names, and now they are ripe for litigation. For example, on January 14, 1997, Wired News announced that Harrods of Great Britain had won a lawsuit concerning its name "Harrods" by another company as a domain name.[12]

This legal success has led the way to further international litigation. Who will win and lose is still open for discussion. Given the premise that companies need to position themselves on a global platform, it is important for the CI function to make sure that its company is ready to accept and move on any strategies necessary to adapt to the WWW. The burgeoning growth of e-commerce implies the need to be aware of any constraints that may be involved in using a domain name.

This ruling also implies that if you use your initials or name for a domain name that you may have had since the Net was flat, and a company comes along claiming rights to that name, you might be faced with a very expensive lawsuit and a claim of trademark infringement.[13]

Several options are available for solving any name disputes. Competitive intelligence managers should consider the problems associated with Internet property rights, since they will likely escalate over the course of the next few years. This issue becomes even more complex once you consider that domain disputes are still being negotiated on a country-by-country level.

The InterNIC (http://rs.internic.net/) secures domain names and registers them, focusing on the domain ending with ".com"[.] In the United States and to a large extent globally, it has become the premiere domain-issuing agency.[14] The InterNIC recognizes the registrants of any domain as being the businesses that are listed in section three of its template. Most companies on the Internet have registered with the InterNIC. However, the roles and responsibilities of the administrative contact, technical contact, and billing contact have been given specific responsibilities. Over the course of the next few years these roles will have much more significance to any company that owns a domain, and the CI department should monitor the evolution of these requirements. The correct registrant information or organization should be listed in section three of the domain template during the initial registration; if there are any discrepancies, they should be remedied. There is always the possibility of entering into an unpleasant domain dispute; the objective is to minimize the risks and the consequences.[15]

As mentioned, domain disputes are exacerbated once a company enters into operation in foreign markets. It is suggested that any company that wishes to fully use the Internet should consider any domain issues that may be confronted when using the Internet on a global level, and especially if they are creating a joint website—domain names should be secured on a country-by-country basis.

There are several websites that can offer assistance in this area:

- *Internet Gold-Rush* <http://www.igoldrush.com/>: offers considerable information on domain disputes and continually updates its articles on any information dealing with government, agency, and judicial actions.

- *Network Services* <http://rs.internic.net/help/domain/tools.html>: offers a site for extracting information on any questionable sites.

- *EFF* <http://www.eff.org/pub/Intellectual_property/Internet_address_disputes/index.html>: a valuable website offering an archive on how to manage Internet disputes.

CONCLUSION

The world of business is changing. Global pressures have recently made odd bedfellows of competing companies. Restrictions on resource allocations or requisite knowledge have increased the need for allying corporations in different functions and geographic regions. Those who were once competitors are now becoming allies. The risks associated in not communicating with potential allies have also increased. The Internet continues to become a necessary factor in communication. The CI executive needs to know the idiosyncrasies of communicating on the Internet. By enhancing one's toolbox with the ability to communicate more efficiently, and understanding the standards and security issues that go along with evolving the communication base over the Internet, the CI department can better position itself for these possibilities and offer key insights into the consequences of such alliances. The tools are only a start, but they at least give some direction on where to go in the future. After all, understanding what the future will unfold is the competitive premise of any CI department.

NOTES

1. Malhotra, Y. (1993). *Competitive Intelligence Programs: An Overview* <http://www.brint.com/papers/ciover.htm>.

2. Moraes, M. *What Is (Is Not) Usenet?* <http://www.comm.arizona.edu/Groups/whatsnot.html>.

3. Research carried out on July 11, 1998.

4. ANBAR Electronic Intelligence <http://www.anbar.co.uk/>.

5. Ibid.

6. Ibid.

7. @BRINT, Knowledge Management Think Tank: Archive <http://www.brint.com/wwwboard/wwwindex.htm>; <http://www.brint.com/wwwboard/wwwboard.html#post>.

8. ANBAR Electronic Intelligence <http://www.anbar.co.uk/>.

9. Ibid.

10. TechnoGate Homepage <http://www.technogate.com/>.

11. *TechnoGate Content Providers* <http://www.technogate.com/proposals.htm>.

12. Vesely, R. (1997). *Harrods Wins Domain Name Ownership Suit,* Wired Digital Inc. (January 14, 1997) <http://www.wired.com/news/news/politics/story/1460.html>.

13. Ibid.

14. *EFF, Internet Address & Domain Name Disputes Archive* <http://www.eff.org/pub/Intellectual_property/Internet_address_disputes/index.html>.

15. *Domain Dealers* <http://www.reignyourdomain.org/tips.html#dealers>.

REFERENCES

Graef, J. (1996). "Sharing Business Intelligence on the World Wide Web," *Competitive Intelligence Review* 7(1): 52–61.

Harkleroad, D. (1994). "Making Intelligence Analysis Actionable," *Competitive Intelligence Review* 5(2): 13–17.

Malhotra, Y. (1997). "Internet Enterprise Strategy and Design: A Real-World Introduction to Electronic Commerce, an Online Guide for Net Entrepreneurs and Managerial End Users," Katz School of Business, University of Pittsburgh <http://www.brint.com/enterprise.htm>.

Smith, A.G. (1997). "Testing the Surf: Criteria for Evaluating Internet Information Resources," *Public-Access Computer Systems Review* 8(3) <http://info.lib.uh.edu/pr/v8/n3/smit8n3.html>.

9

Using a Marketing Framework to Communicate Competitive Intelligence Results

Victoria Turner Shoemaker

INTRODUCTION

Businesses today have to be increasingly aware of what their competition is doing. The stories of business failures in newspapers, business journals, and stock markets constantly illustrate the importance of keeping abreast of industry trends and the early identification of potential opportunities and threats. Given the ever-increasing growth in globalization, telecommunication, and technology, the ability to react quickly and effectively is vital for a company's survival (Hitt, Keats, & DeMarie, 1998; Youngblood, 1998). All factors that can improve a company's strengths in this area are eagerly sought. As a result, competitive intelligence (CI) has been gaining more attention and credibility in the business world.

The development of corporate CI capabilities is gaining increased attention in business journals and seminars. However, while a great deal of attention has been devoted to the collection and analysis of competitive information, little focus has been given to the communication of the results. Additionally, most investigation into this area deals either with the technical elements of dissemination, or simply stresses the importance of clearly communicating the results. Very little attention has been given to "how to" communicate the results of CI to its recipients in such a way as to garner their attention, support, and action.

The communication stage is crucial in the CI process. Even the most vital information that is analyzed expertly and made openly available to the appropriate people, will have little effect unless the recipients will actually read and give attention to the report. And even then they still must be made aware of the benefits they will receive from acting upon the information. Unfortunately, many CI practitioners feel that most of the information they present to the company is ignored or dismissed, since other employees feel that they don't have the time or resources to follow up on the reports. This chapter will offer a framework for CI practitioners to use to effectively communicate their findings. It is intended primarily for start-up CI departments or CI departments that are having difficulties gaining credibility and recognition.

ANALOGY TO MARKETING

Marketing professionals face problems similar to those of CI professionals: Unless a customer can see the tangible results of a purchase, structured in such a way that he or she can clearly perceive the resulting benefits, the sale will be lost. Through market segmentation (tailoring the messages about the features and benefits of their product to the needs, wants, values, and perceptions of their target market), marketers lead their audience to value the product.

The primary challenge that faces CI departments and practitioners is the uphill battle for the consideration and resources of the rest of the organization. Using a marketing perspective to communicate the CI findings and recommendations will result in more attention and credibility being gained. Of the "4Ps" of marketing (see below), the element of *promotion* is the one that is often neglected. Little effort is given to showing the customer why the CI *product* is worth the *price*, which is time. After researching to understand who the aggregate CI "customer" is, a series of market segmentations can be used to identify the best target audience. Through a cover letter, executive summary, e-mail, or other method, the report can be customized to demonstrate to the customer why it is worth its *price*.

APPLYING THE MARKETING FRAMEWORK

The fundamental principles of marketing are commonly known as the "4Ps." The discipline can be broken down into these four areas: *product*, *place* (distribution), *price*, and *promotion*. These four areas, as applied to CI, are examined below.

Product

The CI products are the reports and information that are generated through CI activities. The process of gathering and analyzing the data has been studied from multiple perspectives (Barndt, 1994; Dugal, 1998; Youngblood, 1998), and a marketing perspective toward the product is being developed.

Dugal (1998) classified all outputs of CI as one of ten products:

- current intelligence
- basic intelligence
- technical intelligence
- early warning intelligence
- estimated intelligence
- work group intelligence
- targeted intelligence
- crisis intelligence
- foreign intelligence
- counterintelligence.

Each "product" is defined by description, shelf life, and primary audience.

By treating CI results as a "product line," the potential customers can develop a better understanding of the types of CI that they need and want. By using terminology all business managers are familiar with, many of the confusions and misunderstandings about CI are resolved. However, as in all marketing situations, while an appropriate product is required, if the other elements of the marketing mix are not present the product will not likely be a success.

Place (Distribution)

The dissemination of CI results to the appropriate target has been studied through an examination of distribution channels. Different methods for distributing the results of CI have been studied, including intranets (Laalo, 1998), bulletin boards, presentations (Baumard, 1994), and "fast channels" (Fuld, 1994).

While each method has its strengths and weaknesses, all stress the importance of the audience being able to access the information. Unless your audience understands the importance of the CI results and how the reports will influence them, they will pay it little or no attention. This chapter will offer a solution to that problem.

Price

When looking at CI from a marketing perspective, the *price* paid by the customer is *time*. Managers have increasing demands upon their resources, of which time is the most constrained. Unless your potential customer (the recipient) understands the product and the benefits to be received, he or she will not pay the required price—time to read the report and act upon it if necessary.

The CI practitioner must ensure that the price is reasonable for the product: First by having a good product and not wasting the time of recipients with information they cannot use, or that is inaccurate. Just as importantly, the CI practitioner must make the recipients aware of the features and benefits they will receive from the product. Competitive intelligence, however, frequently fails to effectively market its "product line."

Promotion

The *promotion* of CI results, which involves making your audience aware of why the product will benefit it, has been neglected in the industry literature. Although many articles discuss the importance of effectively communicating the results to the intended audience (Herring, 1999; Laalo, 1998; Linville, 1996), very few offer advice on how to do so.

Promotion is what attracts the attention of "seekers" and stimulates interest in "nonseekers," both of whom are potential customers. Competitive intelligence reports compete with other reports, meetings, duties, and projects for customers' time. Unless CI is promoted as offering direct, tangible benefits, it will be passed over in favor of "products" that are more clearly recognized as having value. CI practitioners must learn how to promote their product so that it is recognized as good value for the price. The deficiencies within the 4Ps when applied to CI can best be remedied with the utilization of marketing research, which is addressed next.

MARKETING RESEARCH

One of the first stages of marketing is *marketing research*, in which you attempt to determine: Who is your audience? What are their wants and needs? Why do they need your product? How can they use it? What benefits will they gain from using it?

Substantial research has been done to guide the CI professional in assessing the needs of its audience (Herring, 1999). Once the type of CI product has been defined, the gathering and analysis completed, and method of dissemination decided, gaining your audience's attention is the next step. Determining the most effective way of conveying the important benefits of the report[1] to potential customers is necessary. The following models and processes will help CI professionals in this task.

THE PROCESS OF MARKET SEGMENTATION

The smaller and more specific the audience, the more relevant the competitive intelligence benefits can be. A sequential process of market segmentation[2] can be developed to target specific departments, project groups, and individuals. As a general guideline: The more targeted you become, the more effective your message. As a warning, however: If the target market has been incorrectly identified, then the effectiveness of the message will be lost. The depth of segmentation will vary according to the type of information, the type of organization, and the confidence the CI practitioner has in his or her targeting process.

Learning about the market segments (who and where to target) can be very complex. It takes time and patience to learn the most effective methods with which to target. A database will help to coordinate the research results. Information management is key for all elements of CI, including "customer marketing-research" results.

The use of market-segmenting techniques may appear to be overwhelming; however, it is not necessary to format the entire report for each recipient. A cover letter, executive summary, e-mail, or short meeting can be tailored for each targeted customer, demonstrating the specific benefits and points of interest in the report. These briefs will give the recipient the incentive to read the report and a framework of reference to use in comprehension. These concise preambles to any CI communication should also ensure that, although each recipient receives the tailored product, the overall content is consistent.[3]

Stage One: Defining Your Organization

Before market segmentation can be started, the organization's aggregate style must be defined. An organization's personality can be conservative or daring, formal or casual, centralized or decentralized, integrated or modular, geocentric or ethnocentric, or any combination of these and other descriptions. The first step is to make sure you are fitting the norms of your organization.

ORGANIZATIONAL FOCUS. Once the tone is set, you must define the focus of your organization. As shown in figure 9.1, organizations can be internally or externally focused. The challenge is to ensure that the CI information meets the needs of the organization. This is not to say that internally focused companies do not need or want marketing intelligence, but that they prefer a concentration in their area and will inherently value more readily this type of information.

Determining where the information is needed most is also necessary. Are most of the decisions made at the upper levels of management, or does middle management play a vital role in the direction of the company? Understanding where the bulk of decisions are made further specifies the tone of the report. Information should be generally classified as *strategic* or *tactical* in nature, and directed to the level of management best able to respond to it. Although the CI results may be widely disseminated, ensuring that the key individuals and departments understand its impact and application is vital.

Internal focus. An internally focused company generally concentrates on processes such as research and development, engineering, and manufacturing. Its premise is that if you produce a good product, people will buy it. A product *push* strategy is frequently used. These types of organizations will concentrate CI resources on the processes of other organizations. Most information will be judged by how much it helps the company to improve in these areas.

	Internal Focus	External Focus
Top-Level Management	Strategic-Process– Oriented	Strategic-Product– Oriented
Middle- or Lower-Level Management	Tactical-Process– Oriented	Tactical-Product– Oriented

Internal Focus   **External Focus**

FIGURE **9.1** Organizational focus.

External focus. Externally focused companies concentrate on areas such as sales and marketing. Market share is their primary concern and they usually follow a *pull* marketing strategy. These organizations devote most of their CI resources to understanding how other companies are positioning themselves and their products. The introduction of new products, promotional strategies, and new market entrants are favorite areas of investigation. Competitive intelligence will be evaluated according to how well it allows the company to react to or preempt competitor actions in the market.

DECISION-MAKER LOCATION. The position of the recipient in the organizational structure also affects how the report is promoted. Using Dugal's (1998) model as a guideline, determine the location of the target audience—the decision-makers and influencers. Is this information that the top-level managers need to make decisions, or would middle managers find it more useful?

Top-level managers. Top-level managers need information that is strategic in nature. They need to see the "big picture" and know the information that will affect the company in the long term. Generally top-level managers also need to know information that will have a dramatic effect on the company, and need to understand how to maximize opportunities and minimize potential threats.

Middle- and lower-level mangers. Middle-level management deals with the organization's tactical issues. They need competitive information that will affect departmental and functional operations. The decisions made at this level affect the company's short- and medium-term performance and usually do not dramatically change the company.

Challenges. Initially it can be difficult to determine the level of management to which to direct the report. It helps to have an advocate in the upper levels who can assist with this stage until the process becomes more familiar.

Stage Two: Functional Perspective

All business professionals have a frame of reference by which they judge the usefulness of information. A functional or departmental perspective is the most common. The CI practitioner can quickly attract the attention of a manager if the report is presented in such a way as to address his or her concerns. Using functional/departmental terminology and references will generate immediate issue-comprehension. Moreover, different departments place different relative values and importance on different issues.

For example, the sales department may be very concerned over the new promotional campaign offered by the market leader, while the engineering department is far more interested in its next generation of product and not as interested in the current market situation.

Research into the department will also reveal issues and concerns, both immediate and long term. If the results of the report can be shown to help resolve some of these issues, its value will be perceived immediately. Understanding the functional perspective is vital to communicate this value.

A cross-functional CI team will have the ability to understand the departmental perspective and have members who are familiar with the terminology and frameworks used. Moreover, they will have an insight into the areas of concern for the department.

CHALLENGES. Be sure the reports do not contradict one another across the functional boundaries. Although each report may have different implications for each area, ensure that if different functions see other reports, it will not create confusion or undermine the credibility of the report.

Stage Three: Decision-Makers/Influencers

Identification of the decision-makers regarding a project or proposal is usually not too difficult.[4] However, they are not the only individuals you should target. Influencers can have a strong effect upon decision-makers, but influencers are sometimes far more difficult to identify.

Hanson and Krackhardt (1993) suggest developing an influence or trust map to identify individuals who may have an effect on the manager you are targeting. Informal paths of influence are typically as strong as, if not stronger than, the formal paths and must be understood in order to be properly navigated. Understanding "why" the influencer has power is also critical—don't target an influencer who would not have credibility or consistent values in the area addressed in the decision-maker's report. To effectively target a decision-maker, the appropriate formal and informal influencers must be targeted.

To target an individual, an understanding of that individual's wants, needs, and values must be understood. The basics of this information can be gathered from memos, reports, pet projects, meetings, general observations, etc. This information should be collected in a database that will help highlight the issues and concerns to emphasize in the report.

CHALLENGES. Once again, the primary challenge is consistency. The balance between customizing the report and delivering noncontradictory information is delicate and must be managed carefully. When in doubt, lean toward keeping the tone and emphasis of the influencers' report similar to the decision-maker's one.

Stage Four: Early Innovators

An alternative or supplement target to decision-makers and influencers is early innovators. These are the individuals who are willing to try new ideas and take greater risks than the average manager. This market segment can be difficult to define and tricky to manage, but the results can be substantial. The same processes of information-gathering can be used for early innovators as for decision-makers.

CHALLENGES. Understanding the motivations of early innovators can be difficult. Do they enjoy trying new ideas, but easily get bored and move on to another idea immediately? Ensure that the early innovators targeted have credibility with others in the organization, particularly concerning the topic addressed.

IMPLEMENTATION

The use of cross-functional CI teams is vital when applying these market-segmentation methods. Not only does the "inside" person know the terminology and general concerns, but identifying the key individuals and their personal preferences also becomes easier. Moreover, the credibility of the CI information is higher as it is perceived to have been analyzed from the perspective of someone who "understands" the issues.

RESULTS

These marketing models, used effectively, will aid CI professionals in communicating the results of investigation and analysis. As CI becomes more accepted and recognized in organizations, the need for such in-depth market research and segmentation diminishes. The monitoring of key values, concerns, and importance indicators needs to continue, but the need for detailed targeting becomes less necessary as credibility becomes established. The process of organizational acceptance takes a substantial amount of time, but the wait is worthwhile because accurate reports will produce positive, measurable results for many companies.

Eventually, as awareness of the benefits of CI become known throughout the organization, a reverse flow of information will result. Departments and individuals, seeing the concrete benefits of CI, will be more likely to supply unprompted

the CI practitioners with information. Since it is commonly believed that approximately 80–90 percent of the information needed for CI is contained within the
firm, leveraging the existing in-house intelligence will dramatically improve the
firm's CI capabilities and effectiveness.

SUMMARY

By tailoring the introduction to the report such that the benefits to the recipient are clear, better understanding and comprehension of CI will result. The
implementation of necessary actions will become more effective and common,
developing an organization that is more proactive in its response to competitive opportunities and threats. Additionally, the CI department will be better
able to serve the needs of the organization as the projects become more specific.

NOTES

1. The CI reports referred to in this chapter are typically unsolicited reports, or reports
meant for general dissemination. It is only through showing the specific benefits of these
reports to departments and individuals that they become valued.

2. These stages involve a substantial amount of research on the firm. The process will
be very similar to performing CI internally.

3. Warning: Do not attempt to target a group or individual who would not gain a true
benefit from the report. Doing so would only discredit the CI process, and would undermine future attempts to target them.

4. The following stages deal with individuals. This degree of market segmentation
should be used sequentially after functional segmentation. The exception is when dealing
with top management—it needs the overall perspective. However, understanding the
functional background from which it emerged may accelerate the next stages.

REFERENCES

Barndt, W.D., Jr. (1994). *User-Directed Competitive Intelligence: Closing the Gap
Between Supply and Demand.* Westport, CT: Quorum Books.

Baumard, P. (1994). "The Intelligence Dead End: How You Present It!" *Competitive
Intelligence Review* 5(2): 53–55.

Dugal, M. (1998). "CI Product Line: A Tool for Enhancing User Acceptance of CI,"
Competitive Intelligence Review 9(2): 17–25.

Fuld, L.M. (1994). "Talk It, Show It, Write It," *Competitive Intelligence Review* 5(2): 56–
57.

Hanson, J.R., and D. Krackhardt. (1993). "Informal Networks: The Company Behind the
Chart," *Harvard Business Review* 71(4): 104–11.

Herring, J.P. (1999). "Key Intelligence Topics: A Process to Identify and Define Intelligence Needs," *Competitive Intelligence Review* 10(2): 4–14.

Hitt, M.A., B.W. Keats, and S.M. DeMarie. (1998). "Navigating in the New Competitive

Landscape: Building Strategic Flexibility and Competitive Advantage in the 21st Century," *Academy of Management Executive* 12(4): 22–42.

Laalo, A. (1998). "Intranets and Competitive Intelligence: Creating Access to Knowledge," *Competitive Intelligence Review* 9(4): 63–72.

Linville, R.L. (1996). *CI Boot Camp.* Johnson City, NY: Competitive Horizons.

Youngblood, A.H. (1998). "CI: Focusing Management on What Matters," *Competitive Intelligence Review* 9(2): 1–2.

10

Effective Approaches to Assessing Competitive Intelligence Performance

Craig S. Fleisher and David L. Blenkhorn

> *If I could only improve something just by measuring it, I'd start losing weight every time I hopped on the scale.*
>
> —Unknown Author

Imagine being the skipper of a large and luxurious passenger liner, and seeing only one or two gauges and instruments in the bridge of the ship you were assigned to captain from England to New York on its maiden voyage. How would you make it there safely, even assuming the weather was clear, tides right, and visibility high? Does this sound like *Titanic* revisited? You'd probably either have to be very lucky or pray quite hard! Needless to say, the absence of instrumentation and gauges would put the skipper at a distinct disadvantage in terms of planning the trip and getting the ship to its destination in the most efficient and effective manner.

Many competitive intelligence (CI) programs operate like this two-gauged passenger liner, with their managers playing the role of the unfortunate skipper. Successfully planning and managing CI programs and activities without the proper measurement and evaluation tools are akin to piloting a complex liner without gauges. Of course, you may argue that most CI managers at least conduct some modicum of evaluation research to limit the amount of "steering blind" they perform; however, even in this case, the evaluation-research component of most CI programs is frequently poorly, inappropriately underutilized—or simply unused.

Assessing performance is doubtlessly among the most difficult tasks CI managers have to tackle in the course of doing their jobs (Herring, 1996). The simple fact that people are asking for performance assessment, whether it is the managers doing the job or those ultimately authorizing its existence, is a marked advancement in the practice. When most people thought of CI as only getting reports or briefs done as part of the strategic-planning process, there was little question about how to assess it. Essentially, you looked at the plans that were produced, assessed which parts used and did not use the information from CI briefs, and gauged the proportion of the plan impacted by CI inputs. Now that CI has become integral to a more comprehensive and integrated approach to influencing the competitive environment, it is much more difficult to evaluate what achievements have been made.

Managers need to know what they are managing or measuring in order to manage or measure it. A lot of the debate around assessing CI performance reveals confusion about what CI is and why it is practiced. Competitive intelligence has come to mean different things to different people and organizations. For example, many organizations utilize an executive approach to CI whereby it is predominantly conducted by the senior executive, while some use faux-CI approaches (e.g., marketing employees flooding executives with compendia of articles about competitors found on the Internet). Others prefer selective competitive education of their employees: some use formalized, computer-driven approaches, while others use informal 3 × 5 card-based ones.

Regardless of what you choose to do in terms of pursuing a particular definition of CI for your organization, you still may or may not choose to evaluate it. You likely don't need to devote valuable resources to performance assessment if your CI program regularly improves itself, is self-sustaining, never has a breakdown or letdown, works consistently, helps every time, and everyone that matters knows that the program was directly responsible for positive decision-making outcomes. Unfortunately, few individuals have ever experienced such a program, and we've seen some pretty good ones in action in nearly two decades of studying CI efforts around the globe. So why would we need to be concerned about CI performance assessment in the first place? Simply because we feel a need or want to improve our CI management. If there is no room for, or need of improvement, then there is likely no need to be concerned about its assessment. Also, following the continuous-improvement philosophy means that processes and practices are continually monitored and updated where appropriate.

RELATING ASSESSMENT TO SUCCESS

Understanding the vagaries of CI strategy and tactics is not something for the faint of heart. What does it take to be successful at CI? Answering the vital question—*"what are the critical factors for successful CI performance?"*—is never a simple one. At a minimum, the critical factors for success at CI:

- Are difficult to identify and capture accurately in the first place
- Depend on the definition, goals, scope, and competitive premise of CI in use
- Change as the organization's competitive objectives and strategies evolve
- Shift as the nature and processes associated with influencing stakeholders in the competitive environment change
- May be dependent on many variables, some of which are not easily counted, measured, or quantified.

Numerous studies of CI practitioners and their units within organizations have shown a moderate degree of dissatisfaction with the evaluation or measurement aspects of the CI task (Prescott & Fleisher, 1991; Prescott & Bhardwaj, 1995; Simon & Blixt, 1995). There are several reasons specific to CI that may help explain the lack of, or dissatisfaction, with CI performance assessment, including (Fleisher, 1991):

- The relative newness of the function to many organizations
- Lack of time to do performance assessment due to the pressing demands and importance of conducting day-to-day CI activities
- Failure to design appropriate CI performance-assessment systems
- Inability to conduct CI performance assessment
- The level of resources required to conduct an appropriate or valid assessment
- No demands for accountability from senior management
- Lack of data available to perform the assessment
- Absence of defined performance-assessment goals.

Regardless of these variables, a useful assessment of CI performance must minimally include an evaluation of relative performance compared to that of competitors, and must also demonstrate the linkage between performance measures and critical-success factors.

So what is the secret to measuring CI performance? Ultimately, it is to assess, evaluate, measure, and manage CI in the same ways we would other successful programs. In most cases, this means we should utilize a number of different approaches, as opposed to a "single" or "all-or-nothing" approach. The next section will outline a variety of CI performance-assessment approaches that have been or may be used.

PERFORMANCE MEASURES AND OBJECTIVES

Four aspects of performance factors can be managed and controlled: *quantity*, *quality*, *cost*, and *time*. Much of this information can be readily collected, especially if it is built into the design of the program in the first place. Other data will emerge through the utilization of digital tracking through software programs, surveys, benchmarking exercises, and interorganizational comparisons. These categories are all important in and of themselves, but become even more vital to providing necessary management information when they are used in wise combination.

- *Quantity:* This can be measured by any ratio created combining quantities of output/inputs (e.g., 12 competitors actively monitored/19 competitors in the industry). It is also known as the "measurement of productivity." The CI manager should be looking here to raise the output/input ratio. For example, an annual objective may be to raise from 80 to 95 percent the number of CI network participants that have added to a competitor database within the last month. Still, quantity or productivity alone cannot tell the whole story of performance. It must be balanced by the other measure categories, because nothing is more wasteful than doing with great efficiency that which is totally unnecessary.

- *Quality:* This requires the CI manager to assess the satisfaction of customers (e.g., decision-makers), CI practitioners, key external contacts, department heads, and other executives who both use and could potentially use CI outputs, etc. Ultimately, the manager needs to increase levels of quality achieved by the CI program if it is to maintain its success over time. One caution is that many satisfied CI members may still be ineffective in achieving the program's goals, because they either lack the capability—the understanding of how to make CI contributions—are socially inept, or poor communicators. One of the authors of this chapter recalls an insurance-company CI executive relating that she had a group of satisfied CI-network participants, but never seemed to influence her company's decision-making. Her comment about the relationship between satisfaction and performance was telling. She noted "no matter how hard you rub, you can't polish horse manure" and proceeded to seriously address the human-resource elements that were keeping her CI program from succeeding.

- *Cost:* This factor may be calculated in terms of person hours, materials, opportunity, etc. The CI manager should be looking for every way to reduce the cost of achieving CI program objectives. He or she should be gathering comparisons of the financial cost of employing different techniques for assessing cost/benefit decision trade-offs (e.g., making calls to contacts at other companies to get data, compared to getting similar information from the World Wide Web).

- *Time:* This may include calculations of time such as: amount of lead time we have with respect to the decision being considered, amount of time needed to activate the CI network, amount of time required to receive feedback from network participants, etc. Ultimately, the CI manager should be looking to *reduce total cycle time* across the range of variables in which speed of response is critical in achieving CI success. Still, CI managers need to avoid the trap of getting out more products in less time, and failing to recognize that being busy is not the same as being productive. Some of the too-quick-to-market products may fail, caused in part by the haste.

METHODS FOR ASSESSING CI PERFORMANCE

Because most performance-measurement experts agree that multiple methods of assessment are far superior to single methods, we will attempt in this chapter to provide you with a range of tools you can use to assess CI performance. We recognize that some of these may fit your situation, and some will not; however, any of the methods or tools described here can be successfully used in assessing CI performance. Below are listed ten of the more popular assessment approaches.

A good starting point in the quest to assess the performance of the CI function is to address the effectiveness issue: Is CI doing the right job?

Measuring the Effectiveness of the CI Function

There seems to be broad agreement that part of what constitutes *effectiveness* is "achievement of goals." Effectiveness can be defined as the extent to which an organization is responsive to constituent preference for performance and is doing the right job. Effectiveness includes the human impact of the system on its individual members. An effective organization is one that can build consensus between policy-makers and implementers so as to create joint commitment to the goals of the organization. The CI function provides intelligence to the policy-makers that often includes recommendations for implementation. So how do we know that the CI function is doing the right job? How can we measure the effectiveness of the CI function?

An input to effectiveness evaluation is *accountability*, a management term that is gaining increasing importance in meaning. Implicit in being accountable is to have relevant, realistic, preset goals, the achievement of which are readily measurable. The CI function can make a more significant contribution when its value added to the whole organization can be quantified. In today's competitive, global business environment, no organization can afford second-rate CI performance. The continuing support the CI function needs to perform exceptionally well hinges on evidence of current performance—being effective in all that it does. Traditional formal reporting systems often do not effectively communicate CI's accomplishments, nor are the numbers produced by such systems effective in elevating the views non-CI managers have of this key function.

The question of how to measure and evaluate CI effectiveness is not easily answered. A major problem is that to date, a practical approach that produces consistent results in different types of organizations has not been developed. One tested methodology (Blenkhorn & Gaber, 1995) to measure organizational effectiveness—and we suggest it is applicable to the CI function—obtains a rating on 11 attributes:

- management direction
- relevance
- appropriateness

- achievement of intended results
- acceptance
- secondary impacts
- productivity
- responsiveness
- working environment
- protection of assets
- monitoring and reporting.

Obtaining meaningful quantifiable measurement of the above attributes should give an evaluation of the CI function's effectiveness within the organization. We will now provide thumbnail sketches of methods that we or others have successfully used in assessing CI performance.[1]

AUDITS. Audits are methodical investigations of the organization that produce factual data for decision-making, with an eye on making recommendations to improve CI management performance. The objective of the audit is to evaluate the organization's total CI effort in achieving its competitive-strategy objectives. One form of an audit that could be performed on a CI program is *communications*. For example, communication elements that are commonly audited within a CI context would be:

- *Types of messages circulated* (both between CI managers, employee network and competitive-environment stakeholders); content of messages (e.g., actionable, decision-oriented, etc.)

- *Forms of messages* (e.g., informational, defensive, offensive, strategic, tactical, etc.)

- *Frequency* (e.g., just-in-time, hourly, daily, weekly, bi-weekly, monthly, irregularly, etc.)

- *Media/channels used* (e.g., bulletin boards, face-to-face, letters, faxes, e-mails, reports, etc.)

- *Relationships among individuals both inside and outside the organization, and networks.*

Most audits utilize a four-step process involving audit design, data collection, analysis/interpretation, and interventions/recommendations.

BALANCED SCORECARD APPROACH. The balanced scorecard promotes the establishment of tangible objectives and measures that relate to an organization's mission, vision, and strategy. The balanced scorecard emphasizes strategic process over routine processes. Priorities are set within the major categories, first at the corporate level and then at division, department, team, and even individual levels. It typically requires the analyst to establish and track performance across four or five specific areas. The four critical success indicators most commonly utilized are:

- *Competitive intelligence network members* (i.e., those individuals formally or informally involved in the organization's CI data-gathering efforts): In this category we would ask questions such as: Do we understand members' needs/ motivations? Are members satisfied with our program? Are we making it easy for them to work with the formal CI team?

- *Financial accountability:* Are we getting the best possible return on the CI investment? How do we look to our CI budget allocators?

- *Internal work efficiencies:* Are we getting the job done as efficiently and pro-ductively as possible? Have we improved our capacity to deal with increased volumes of information? Are our CI systems utilized by a high percentage of employees?

- *Learning and growth:* Are we getting better over time and improving our capability to deliver desired results? Are we employing the best learning available about CI management practices?

BALDRIGE-MAPPING. This technique requires you to assess the program rel-ative to the seven Malcolm Baldrige National Quality Award (MBNQA) criteria of world-class organizations, adapted to the level of the CI organization. As in the genuine Baldrige process, the assessor(s) would be looking for data covering three factors in each answer:

- actual results
- implementation
- deployment.

Categories assessed using a Baldrige-type application may include the fol-lowing:

- *Competitive intelligence leadership:* This section would examine the extent to which the chief executive officer and other senior executives of the com-pany become involved in creating a focus on competitors and the competitive environment, and in establishing and disseminating CI values. The section would also attempt to determine how CI values are integrated into the com-pany's everyday management activities.

- *Competitive intelligence information and analysis:* This would require an examination of the scope, management, and use of data and information to drive CI excellence and improve CI performance. Also examined would be the adequacy of the organization and the CI unit's data, information, and analysis system to support improvement of the company's competitive focus, products, services, and internal operations.

- *Strategic CI planning:* The purpose of this section is to list and briefly discuss the planning process for CI, and the ways in which performance targets and continuous-improvement measures are initially built into plans and updated.

- *Competitive intelligence human-resources development and management:* This section examines how the CI unit encourages its members to achieve their potential while pursuing departmental and corporate goals of high performance and continuous improvement. The section also examines what the organization is doing to develop employee potential and promote superior execution and continuous improvement.

• *Management of CI process:* This section examines the processes used by the CI unit to ensure quality products and services and continuous improvement of product quality and service levels.

• *Operational and organizational results:* This section looks at the quality and achievement levels of the CI unit and its external contractors and whether they are improving. Also examined is how the unit is doing vis-à-vis the CI areas of other companies.

• *Competitive intelligence network member/target focus and satisfaction:* This section examines the unit's relationships with its clients, how determinations are made of what clients want, and whether the unit's members know what quality criteria are important in satisfying them.

BENCHMARKING. This method requires the systematic comparison of CI practices between two or more organizations. Successful CI benchmarking (note that this is benchmarking *of* the CI unit, not benchmarking performed *by* the CI unit) is achievable in two steps:

• understanding the definition of benchmarking
• thoroughly completing the benchmarking equation.

We define CI benchmarking as an ongoing systematic approach by which a CI program is measured and compared with higher performing and world-class programs in order to generate knowledge and action about CI roles, processes, practices, products/services, or strategic issues that will lead to performance improvement. This definition is one that establishes several requirements and criteria for successful benchmarking that are beyond the scope of this chapter.

The benchmarking equation is:

$$\text{Demographics} \times \text{How it works} \times \text{Why it works} = \text{Benchmarking results}$$

Demographics represent the basic unit/organizational and industry information, budget, staff sizes and reporting relationships, organizational positioning as per organizational charts, communication content/frequency and channels, network nature and size, number and type of CI products, etc. *Demographics*, combined with *how* a CI unit accomplished its tasks and goals, provide a glimpse of new opportunities and potential areas for improvement. Multiplying *why* certain practices, roles, processes, etc., are acted upon provides an even clearer picture. The product of these three items is the *benchmarking result*. Most benchmarking efforts of CI units that we have experienced have focused on the *demographics* and *how* parts of the equation, without much regard being given for the *why* part of it.

It is optimal to determine best or proven CI practices, adapt them to your own organization, and perform the practices at levels surpassing those that were emulated. A key to making benchmarking helpful is to look outside your own organization and industry.

COMMUNICATIONS APPROACH. In this approach the assessor seeks to evaluate the quality of communications between CI program managers and CI network participants. Hence, assessment would focus on three critical communication elements of the sender, medium, and receiver. Using this approach, the CI manager or an outside party would look at assessing such things as: Was the audience carefully targeted for inclusion in our effort? Have our messages been appropriate for our audiences? Have we carefully selected those individuals we want to receive our messages? Have we sent our messages in the proper (most efficient and effective) form/medium? How effective are our newsletters, faxes, snail or electronic mailing? A key to using this method is to do pre- and posttesting and to encourage the generation of as much feedback as possible.

A variant of this approach is to assess the levels of performance the organization achieves among its CI network members and/or their intended communication targets both within the CI area and in the senior decision-making team. A key to using this approach is to identify your members, their needs, and to continuously assess and close gaps between needs and satisfaction. One form of member response worth considering is notes from decision-makers on the positions they are taking, and acknowledging these letter writers. One way to measure the satisfaction achieved in your CI communications is to utilize a CI adaptation of the "pyramid of quality" that was developed in the communications area at FedEx (Robertson, 1991).

HUMAN-RESOURCES-BASED METHODS. This approach requires the manager to assess the performance of a CI program in terms of attracting, recruiting, motivating, and training/developing CI employees or network participants. This assessment requires the collection of data (and a resultant flexible database) over time for comparison purposes. It also requires the manager to understand, typically through research, the objectives that individuals have for participating in CI programs and how the programs themselves may be aligned with the achievement of an individual's career and/or personal objectives.

MANAGEMENT BY OBJECTIVES (MBO). This approach assesses the alignment and congruence of CI with broader organizational/competitive strategy goals. The ultimate CI program objective is to influence the decision-making process. Intermediate objectives should assess how each CI alert, communication, presentation, and activity can potentially impact the way a decision-maker reacts on competitive issues that affect your organization.

There are six criteria for setting "good" objectives:

- *Specificity:* they are easily understood by all CI participants
- *Flexibility:* they should allow modifications to accommodate unanticipated opportunities or threats
- *Measurability:* the objectives must be stated in terms that can be evaluated or quantified

- *Attainability:* they should simultaneously motivate and challenge, but should also be realistic and attainable
- *Congruency:* they should be congruent with one another; that is, obtaining one objective should not preclude obtaining another
- *Acceptability:* they should be acceptable to those achieving them and to the firm's other key stakeholders.

QUALITY-RELATED METHODS. These methods refer to the application of quality-management principles to CI performance assessment. As such, they generally focus upon the four common elements of customer satisfaction: *measurement, processes, continuous improvement,* and *empowerment.* Achieving the quality maxim of "doing the right thing right the first time every time" should provide dollar benefits in the form of cost savings, productivity improvements (more proactive decisions and enhanced CI environment), elimination of waste (duplication, redundancy), and reduction in future uncertainty.

One variant of the quality-related methods is the hierarchical CI quality assessment, which requires the manager and/or independent verifiers to assess:

- Did we get there *on time*?
- Did we get to the *right people* on time?
- Did we get to the right people with the *right intelligence* on time?
- Did we get to the right people with the right messages on time *and in the manner (e.g., e-mail, phone, fax, letter, face to face) they preferred to be reached*?

STRATEGIC-MANAGEMENT METHOD. This refers to the family of processes that lead to adjustments in the CI mission, goals, strategies, or implementation plans when necessary. It requires the assessor to evaluate aspects such as congruency between the CI goals and other organizational (strategy) activities, alignment of CI plans with CI implementation, synergy between CI and other decision-making-influencing activities, and the accuracy of the environmental analysis (e.g., did we use the CI initiative for the right issues, at the right times, etc.?).

SYSTEMS METHOD. This approach requires the manager to track CI program-activity inputs, processes, outputs, and impacts over time and/or against other CI organizations (including internal units or departments). It can be done in both absolute and relative terms. Here again, the idea is to develop trends in these elements over time that you can use to perform comparisons and set challenge targets.

SOME GUIDELINES FOR BUILDING IN ASSESSMENT TO CI PROGRAM MANAGEMENT

All the methods in the world will not lead to effective performance if they are not guided by a systematic plan and overall strategy. The following are some of the key characteristics of effective measurement systems[2]:

- *Fewer in number:* the best measurement systems do not generate excessive data on a daily basis, but rather generate data across a few key areas using a few key measures

- *Linked to critical success factors:* measures used should allow for those very few vital changes in tactics or strategy that can "make a difference" in whether the CI program performs successfully or not

- *Chronologically balanced:* measures should look at the evolution of the program (i.e., what was done in the past), what is being done in the present, and what may be done in the future (i.e., closing the gap between your program and the best-practice programs)

- *Based around the needs of all stakeholders:* assessment should provide information to support all CI program stakeholders, including those persons authorizing the program, those persons managing it, those persons participating in it, and those persons who receive the program's outputs (e.g., decision-makers)

- *Goals based on research:* any effective measurement system values facts and data above speculation, opinion or hearsay; therefore some degree of research will always need to be conducted, along with the measurement and evaluation of the program that is conducted, to ensure that findings are valid and reliable

- *Change with adjustments to environment and strategy:* measurement and benchmarking systems will change along with the strategy and environment. Measurement systems that are incapable of change or inflexible are costly and inefficient and only serve to reduce the possibility of generating valuable management-improvement insights.

The following are some helpful managerial guidelines for performing successful CI measurement:

- *Handle-as-a-change strategy:* measurement is typically something that has to be "bolted on" to most programs, as opposed to having been built in. As such, it generally is associated with a change in the common modus operandi of most programs and hence should be treated similarly to other organizational interventions in terms of how it is planned and implemented

- *Create a vision for performance improvement through measurement and benchmarking:* stakeholders will need to understand how measurement and benchmarking will be used to improve the management of the program, and not to become another burdensome aspect of participating in it or another means for pre-justifying an increased budget allocation (see next bullet point)

- *Get senior-management buy-in:* when senior managers value the benefits that can come out of CI measurement and benchmarking efforts, others in the organization will also value it and facilitate its completion

- *Aim initial efforts at high success-probability areas:* don't try and measure the immeasurable, make radical changes through measurement, or try to identify the "magical silver bullet" with your earliest efforts. You will only frustrate subsequent efforts and become discouraged. Instead, identify some measurement or benchmarking aspects that are likely to be easier to do and provide incremental improvements first

- *Strategically manage the measurement and benchmarking process:* measurement and benchmarking are processes. Like all processes, they need to be systematically managed and integrated with other ongoing processes so as to maximize their potential effectiveness

- *Be alert to political ramifications:* measurement is done to improve management. Improving management generally means changing something that is currently being done. Many people become fearful or anxious about measurement, because they assume it will mean changes to them that they may not understand or support (see next bullet point)

- *Build in ongoing communications:* one way to reduce the anxiety described in the previous point is to regularly communicate with your stakeholders what you are measuring and why you are doing it. Findings should be shared with them and explanations given as to how the measurement and benchmarking will lead to improved outcomes. Be sure also to communicate with others how your measurement led your program to take actions that were associated with CI successes

- *Assess your measurement and benchmarking system:* measures, like plans, need to be evergreen and change every now and then to reflect fundamental changes in a program's underlying strategy or environment

- *Accept delayed gratification:* the results achieved by effective measurement or benchmarking are not always immediately obvious, especially when they are applied to improving programs like CI that are devoted to influencing the dynamic competitive marketplace. You have to plant before you can harvest, and that's particularly true when it comes to things like measuring or assessing CI programs!

NOTES

1. We have provided thumbnail sketches of the principal methods that can be utilized to assess CI performance. The authors of this chapter can be contacted for more in-depth explanations and examples of their successful implementation.

2. Additional guidelines for integrating measurement into an overall organizational system may be found in W. Christopher and C. Thor, eds., *Handbook for Productivity Measurement and Improvement* (Portland, OR: Productivity Press, 1993).

REFERENCES

Blenkhorn, D., and B. Gaber. (1995). "The Use of 'Warm Fuzzies' to Assess Organizational Effectiveness," *Journal of General Management* 21(2): 40–51.

Fleisher, C.S. (1991). "Applying Quality Process Evaluation to the CI Function," *Competitive Intelligence Review* 2(1): 5–8.

Herring, J.P. (1996). *Measuring the Effectiveness of Competitive Intelligence: Assessing and Communicating CI's Value to Your Organization.* Alexandria, VA: Society of Competitive Intelligence Professionals.

Prescott, J.E., and C.S. Fleisher. (1991). "SCIP: Who We Are, What We Do," *Competitive Intelligence Review* 2(1): 22–27.

Prescott, J.E., and G. Bhardwaj. (1995). "Competitive Intelligence Practices: A Survey," *Competitive Intelligence Review* 6(2): 4–14.

Robertson, E. (1991). "Doing Right Things Right," *IABC Communication World* 8(9): 32–35.

Simon, N.J., and A.B. Blixt. (1995). "Emerging Issues in Competitive Intelligence, 1994," *Competitive Intelligence Review* 6(2): 42–56.

COMPETITIVE INTELLIGENCE
AND ITS RELATIONSHIP WITH
BUSINESS FUNCTIONS AND PROCESSES

11

Competitive Intelligence and the Management Accountant

Victor Knip

INTRODUCTION

This chapter will address the important strategic links between competitive intelligence (CI) and management accounting. Contemporary strategy theory will be analyzed to support actionable recommendations for synergistic collaboration between these two disciplines.

COMMON GOALS

The first and most obvious link between CI and management accounting is that the two professions share very similar goals. Both professions function to accumulate and analyze a variety of information in the interest of providing strategic executive recommendations. This similarity suggests significant opportunity for functional integration and cooperation. Moreover, within the context of contemporary strategy theory the process of sharing this information and analysis is of immense strategic value to the firm.

IMPLICATIONS OF CONTEMPORARY STRATEGY THEORY

Achieving a sustainable competitive advantage is generally regarded as the defining mark of successful strategy. Contemporary strategy theory offers the resource-based view (RBV) of the firm as the premiere analytical model to deliver strategic success. This conceptual framework holds potential for both the

CI professional and the management accountant in their cooperative support of corporate strategy, because it is rooted in economic theory.

The RBV model theorizes that successful corporate strategy depends on the ownership or control of valuable competitive resources. These resources may be tangible, intangible, or they may be the organizational processes of the firm. For these competitive resources to be valuable they must lie at the intersection of three market-determined forces: demand, scarcity, and inimitability (Collis & Montgomery, 1995). It has been noted that tangible assets rarely meet this definition of value, simply because they can usually be acquired through purchase or benchmarking, thus stripping the asset of its inimitability (Cory, 1996). Hence, competitively valuable resources are usually composed of intangible assets and unique activity sets. Proponents of the RBV model assert that it is the ownership of such valuable resources that, when deployed in a well-executed strategy, "enable the company to perform activities better or more cheaply than competitors" (Collis & Montgomery, 1995).

In his article "What is Strategy?" in the *Harvard Business Review*, Michael E. Porter (1996) further explores just what is required to perform activities better than competitors. He argues that the essence of strategy hinges around a company's ability and deliberate decision to perform interlocked systems of activities that deliver a superior value proposition to the chosen customer. In Porter's parlance, this means "choosing to perform activities differently or to perform different activities than rivals." He goes on to defend his assertion with this elegant reasoning: "The probability that competitors can match any activity is often less than one. The probabilities then quickly compound to make matching the entire system highly unlikely ($.9 \times .9 = .81$, $.9 \times .9 \times .9 \times .9 = .66$, and so on)." Using Porter's logic, one can quickly see why a complex activity-based positioning strategy rooted in RBV theory is so important to securing competitive advantage.

The RBV model provides robust theoretical support for the proposed collaboration between the CI professional and the management accountant. The conceptual rigor of the RBV theory stems from its combination of internal corporate analysis with external analysis of the competitive environment (Collis & Montgomery, 1995). Central to the internal analysis in the RBV model are the firm's interdependent activity systems. The management accountant is well placed in the firm to offer expert internal analysis. Equally important in the RBV model is the external analysis of the market forces that validate the firm's chosen activity-based positioning strategy. The CI professional is well placed in the firm to offer expert external-market analysis. More importantly, the collaboration and overlap of these two disciplines at the external/internal interface of the firm's RBV strategy are essential for corporate success. What is needed, however, is an implementation framework to make this collaboration actionable. Enter the *balanced scorecard*.

THE BALANCED-SCORECARD APPROACH

The *balanced scorecard* is a performance-measurement system that combines traditional financial metrics with three additional types of operational measures that drive future financial performance (e.g., "How do our stakeholders view our financial performance?"): *customer satisfaction* (e.g., "How do our customers perceive us?"), *internal processes* (e.g., "Are our processes both efficient and effective?"), and *innovation and learning activities* (e.g., "Are we able to leverage our knowledge?") (Kaplan & Norton, 1992). For each of the four perspectives tracked within this scorecard approach, the user develops a set of goals and the associated measures needed to assess goal achievement.

The central methodology in this model is to first determine and explicitly map out the activity systems that drive the firm's competitive strategy. The outcome measures and performance drivers in the four perspectives should incorporate only these activities (Kaplan & Norton, 1996). This selectivity allows for the explicit recognition, measurement, and management of the interrelated activities that support the firm's competitive advantage. In this way, the balanced scorecard allows for the testing of *if–then* statements that clarify the underlying cause-and-effect structure of strategy, because "ultimately, causal paths from all the measures on a scorecard should be linked to financial objectives" (Kaplan & Norton, 1996).

In this respect, the balanced scorecard has a strong alignment with the concept of strategic trade-offs that Porter argues is the essence of strategy. He stresses that trade-offs force management to choose a set of unique activities that is the root of the competitive strategy (Porter, 1996). These trade-offs boil down to the fact that the firm cannot excel at everything: it must decide to concentrate on its core competence. The cause and effects embedded in the four perspectives of the balanced scorecard are, in effect, these same strategic trade-offs. The balance scorecard encourages management to explicitly recognize and manage these trade-offs during strategy formulation. Market validation of the correct choice of trade-offs will be revealed through the causal links to the financial metrics in the balanced scorecard. This motivates management to craft strategy responsive to the market forces that determine whether the firm's competitive resources are truly valuable, and thus capable of securing a sustainable competitive advantage.

The balanced scorecard's inherent recognition of these market forces integrates it with contemporary RBV-strategy theory. In fact, the design of the balanced scorecard transcends the realm of measurement systems by also becoming an intrinsic part of the strategy it was designed to measure as well as encouraging competitive breakthroughs (Kaplan & Norton, 1996). The balanced scorecard, then, promises to be an effective tool to help the CI professional and the management accountant cooperatively develop, implement, and monitor corporate strategy that is consistent with RBV theory.

STRATEGIC BENEFITS OF COLLABORATION

The external focus of the balanced-scorecard approach creates demand from the management accountant for continuous competitive intelligence of the firm's external environment. Implementing this model requires much information, analysis, and strategic collaboration between the functional boundaries of the firm. Within the context of the balanced-scorecard approach, one of the most important collaborations is between the CI professional and the management accountant. The CI professional is well versed in such techniques as industry-structure analysis, environmental scanning, issues management, competitive analysis, scenario analysis, and technology forecasting (Sullivan, 1997). These skills aptly provide the external analysis needed to compliment the internal analytical requirements of the balanced scorecard. In this way, the CI professional is indispensable in providing the external analysis of the market forces needed to determine if the firm's interdependent activity systems are indeed a competitively valuable resource.

The internal focus of the balanced-scorecard approach creates demand by the CI professional for a point of reference needed to frame his or her CI activities. By working closely with the management accountant in developing and monitoring the balanced scorecard, the CI professional will be able to acquire an intimate knowledge of the firm's activity-based positioning strategy. The balanced-scorecard approach offers this perspective to the CI professional, because it borrows heavily from one of the most powerful analytical techniques developed by the management-accounting profession—activity-based management (ABM). This is not surprising, given that one of the originators of the balanced scorecard, Robert S. Kaplan, is also considered to be the grandfather of ABM. Collaborating with the management accountant through ABM, then, gives the CI professional a valuable opportunity to witness firsthand the strategy of the firm reduced to its lowest common denominator of competitive premise—the activity systems that drive the competitive advantage. As a result, the CI professional is provided with a strategic context for his or her CI-gathering activities and analysis. Acquiring such an intimate knowledge of the firm's activity-based positioning strategy from the vantage of an eye-level resource-based view of the firm will foster more effective and efficient CI efforts.

This proposed interdisciplinary collaboration will leverage the expertise of both professions in their support of the firm's strategy. Moreover, the ensuing synergy through analytical dialogue at the external–internal boundary of the firm is necessary to meet the challenge of addressing each perspective of the balanced scorecard.

Customer Perspective

The *customer perspective* of the balanced scorecard asks the question: "How do our customers perceive us?" The CI professional can be very helpful here in at least two ways: The CI professional is well placed to determine exactly what the firm's chosen customers value. The management accountant can then use the techniques of ABM to translate this information into determining the correlating set of activities that will profitably produce this value. Together, the CI professional and the management accountant, along with the firm's marketing professionals, can then determine if the total value of ownership of the firm's products and services is consistent with the goal of customer delight.

This component of the balanced-scorecard approach also asks a relative question. Customer perceptions of a company's products and/or services will almost always be impacted by a relative comparison to competitive offerings. More value from the CI professional could be delivered here to determine the strategically consistent performance measures that incorporate external competitive considerations. This analysis will help to devise either a successful low-cost or differentiated activity-based positioning strategy that exceeds the relative expectations of the firm's chosen customer segment.

Internal Business Perspective

The *internal business perspective* poses the relevant question "are our processes both efficient and effective?" to guide the selection of performance drivers and outcome measures. This is also a consideration that begs the question: "Compared to what or whom?" The CI professional is again well placed to provide the external informational and analytical input to answer this question. Periodic benchmarking and continuous monitoring of the operational excellence of "best-in-class" firms are the types of value-added input that the CI professional could provide. Then the management accountant, the CI professional, and the firm's operations function could work together to ensure that the firm's business-systems focus is supporting a superior value proposition.

Innovation and Learning Perspective

The *innovation and learning perspective* of the balanced scorecard asks: "Are we able to leverage our knowledge?" The environmental scanning of the CI professional is indispensable in fostering the conditions necessary to build a learning organization. The early identification of threats and opportunities could then provide the lead-time necessary for the CI professional, the management accountant, and the firm's human-resources function to collectively formulate a strategic response. Armed with this analysis, they could proactively train personnel, provide the appropriate motivational incentives, and develop the management controls needed to acquire the organizational capabilities in order to evolve with the rapidly changing business environment.

Financial Perspective

The *financial perspective* poses the question: "How do our shareholders view our financial performance?" This component of the balanced-scorecard approach will validate the success of the three operational components of the model in creating shareholder wealth. In order to attract capital, the firm must decide upon an optimal combination of risk and profitability. This is a relative proposition that the CI professional can place in context to competing firms in the capital markets. Value could be added by the CI professional by continuously monitoring the financial statements and analyst reports of firms that are drawing from the capital pool. The CI professional can then use this analysis to estimate the causal links between the operational and financial metrics of competing firms. Then, the management accountant and the CI professional can work together with the finance department to approximate a balanced scorecard for competing firms. This could be used to determine the relative attractiveness of the firm's equity in the capital markets, as well as offer an excellent insight into the strategy of rival firms. In effect, this analysis would be akin to benchmarking against an estimated balanced scorecard of competitors in order to test the strength of the firm's unique activity-based positioning strategy.

Contemporary RBV-strategy theory as implemented through the balanced-scorecard approach validates the proposed collaboration between the CI professional and the management accountant. As summarized in table 11.1, the opportunities for sharing information and analysis are ample, varied, and of strategic significance.

PROFESSIONAL BENEFITS OF COLLABORATION

On a more personal level, CI professionals currently seeking corporate employment would be well served to seek out a company that has a balanced scorecard already installed. It has been observed that a TQM environment or one that uses a process-driven organizational philosophy would be much more receptive to the value of competitive intelligence (Sullivan, 1997). In some organizations the strategic value of CI as a distinct functional area has been questioned due to a perceived lack of internal demand. To a diminishing and misinformed minority, it is still seen as nothing more than a sexy new label for the marketing-research function. The strategic benefit of collaboration between the CI professional and the management accountant that is the central argument of this chapter could be used to further validate the strategic role of the CI professional. The internal demand for CI could help the CI professional establish him- or herself as an equal member of the firm's strategic team. Chances are that the management accountant at an organization with an established balanced-scorecard approach would be the first to lobby the hiring committee on behalf of the CI professional.

Similarly, career-seeking management accountants would do well to seek out firms with established CI capabilities. For many years now the management-accounting profession has made a conscious effort to move away from its increasingly irrelevant backward-looking control focus, towards a more forward-looking strategic role through ABM. A recent article in *CMA Magazine* reflects this trend: "[ABM] is the device that will secure management accountants, correctly, in the role of organization performance-knowledge integrator" (Sharman, 1996). Similarly, witness the title of an article in *Management Accounting* that

Table 11.1

OPPORTUNITIES FOR STRATEGIC COLLABORATION

Balanced-Scorecard Category	Strategic Intent	How the Management-Accountant Assists	What the Management-Accountant Needs	How the CI Professional Can Assist	What the CI Professional Needs
Financial Perspective	—Shareholder-wealth maximization by ensuring that total investment returns more than invested capital —Value-based management —Ratio analysis	—Analysis of linkages between financial and operational metrics of the firm —Approximation of the balanced scorecard of rival firms to estimate the linkages between their financial and operational metrics	—Analysis of linkages between financial and operational metrics of rival firms	—Analysis of financial statements, quarterly reports, market intelligence, and analyst reports of rival firms —Approximation of the balanced scorecard of rival firms to estimate linkages between their financial and operational metrics	—Analysis of linkages between financial and operational metrics of the firm
Customer Perspective	—Ensuring value proposition is consistent with the goal of customer delight —Actionable measures of the total value of ownership of the firm's customer offering	—Analysis of the value of activity systems that the firm owns, controls, or must acquire to ensure customer delight	—Relative comparisons of competing value propositions	—Analysis of competitive customer offerings —Determining exact definition of customer value	—Analysis of the firm's existing source of competitive advantage that sustains customer delight —Point of reference for customer and market research
Internal Perspective	—Measures of core competencies needed to support the business systems focus that drives the proprietary value proposition	—ABM analysis to provide optimal activity-based positioning strategy	—Continuous benchmarking of operational excellence of best-in-class firms	—Determining if the business systems' focus of firm is superior to rivals' through competitive benchmarking	—Witness the competitive strategy of firm reduced to the lowest common denominator of competitive premise
Innovation and Learning Perspective	—Measures needed to transform firm into a learning organization	—Proactive development of motivational incentives, management controls, and organizational processes needed to compete in changing value chains	—Analysis of economy-wide value chains and technology impacts on current ABM analysis	—Expertise in economy-wide value-chain analysis combined with technology forecasting	—Analysis of firm's existing capabilities and resources —Feasibility of preparing for competition in changing value chains

refers to management accountants as "strategic resource managers" (Birkett, 1995). Collaboration with the CI professional within the balanced-scorecard approach will do much to support these professional aspirations. The mutual professional benefits are yet another reflection of the rich synergy that exists between these two disciplines.

FUTURE IMPLICATIONS

Information technology is creating a fundamental change in traditional economic theory underlying many business models. In a 1997 article in the *Harvard Business Review* entitled "Strategy and the New Economics of Information," Evans and Wurster (1997) convincingly argue that information technology is revolutionary because it allows information to become unbundled from its physical carrier. As such, the authors assert that the traditional trade-off between the richness and reach of information will be obliterated. They predict that many value chains will be destroyed as a direct consequence. Despite these challenges, this harbinger only serves to reinforce the legitimate strategic alignment between the CI and management-accounting functions.

As traditional sources of competitive advantage become threatened, overtaken by nimble technology-enabled competitors, or simply disappear, the strategic collaboration between the CI professional and the management accountant will become even more central to strategy. These two functional disciplines must be prepared to collectively reevaluate entire value chains. In the words of noted strategy guru Peter F. Drucker (1995), "[a] company has to know the costs of its entire economic chain and has to work with other members of the chain to manage costs and maximize yield. Companies are beginning to shift from costing only what goes on inside their own organizations to costing the entire economic process, in which even the biggest company is just one link." In the new economics of information, the next competitor with a totally novel activity-based strategy could appear tomorrow without warning from virtually any industry or market.

In this fundamentally altered competitive landscape, the CI professional must now search for threats and opportunities from any and all economic sectors. Similarly, the management accountant must remain alert to the very real possibility of developing an activity-based positioning strategy to compete in radically different value chains. Together, the CI professional and the management accountant must think outside of the proverbial box by challenging the competitive assumptions inherent in the firm's current strategy (figure 11.1).

It is helpful here to borrow and expand on an idea developed by Kenneth Cory (Cory, 1996) that applies RBV theory to determine if CI analysis can be considered a valuable resource. The collaborative activities in response to the new economics of information presented in figure 11.1 will themselves become one of the valuable resources that helps to form part of the unique activity-based strategy of successful firms. The analytical dialogue between the CI professional and the management accountant at the internal/external interface of the firm

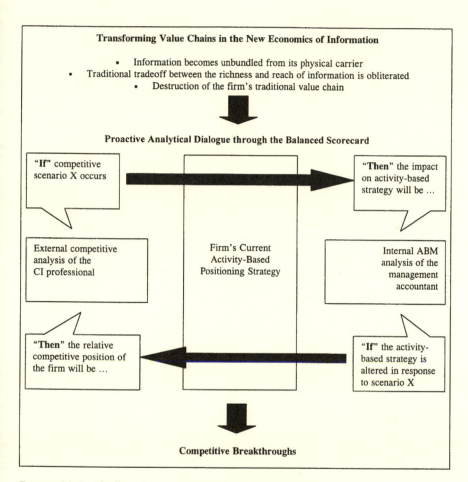

FIGURE 11.1 Challenging strategy through collaboration.

passes the valuable resource tests of scarcity, inimitability, and demand. These cooperative efforts can then be viewed as yet another way in which the CI professional and the management accountant contribute to the firm's competitive advantage.

This potential economic reordering associated with the new economics of information should not be viewed as a negative impetus for exclusively defensive strategy. Rather, these developments should be optimistically embraced with aggressive strategies designed to take advantage of the tremendous opportunities for competitive breakthroughs that information technology affords. Through collaboration within the balanced scorecard, the CI professional and the management accountant are fully capable of rising to this challenge.

SUMMARY

Contemporary strategy theory strongly endorses increased collaboration between the CI professional and the management accountant. This chapter offers both professions an actionable model to craft business success by working together through the purest distillation of corporate strategy—the firm's interdependent activity systems. Collaborative activity between the CI professional and the management accountant is a promising way to grow the intellectual capital necessary for success in the exciting knowledge economy that will define the new millennium.

REFERENCES

Bernhardt, D.C. (1996). "Competitive Intelligence: Lifeblood of Competitive Strategy," *Competitive Intelligence Review* 7(1): 38–44.

Birkett, W.P. (1995). "Management Accounting and Knowledge Management: Management Accountants Are Becoming Strategic Resource Managers," *Management Accounting* 77(5): 44–48.

Collis, D.J., and C.A. Montgomery. (1995). "Competing on Resources," *Harvard Business Review* 73(4): 118–28.

Cory, K.D. (1996). "Can Competitive Intelligence Lead to a Sustainable Competitive Advantage?" *Competitive Intelligence Review* 7(3): 45–55.

Drucker, P.F. (1995). "The Information that Executives Truly Need," *Harvard Business Review* 73(1): 54–62.

Evans, P.B., and T.S. Wurster. (1997). "Strategy and the New Economics of Information," *Harvard Business Review* 75(5): 71–82.

Horngren, C.T., G.L. Sundem, W.O. Stratton, and H.D. Teall. (1996). *Management Accounting.* Upper Saddle River, NJ: Prentice-Hall.

Kaplan, R.S., and D.P. Norton. (1992). "The Balanced Scorecard—Measures that Drive Performance," *Harvard Business Review* 70(1): 71–79.

———. (1996). "Linking the Balanced Scorecard to Strategy," *California Management Review* 39(1): 53–79.

Porter, M.E. (1996). "What is Strategy?" *Harvard Business Review* 74(6): 61–78.

Sharman, P. (1996). "Activity/Process Budgets: A Tool for Change Management," *CMA Magazine* 70(2): 21–24.

Sullivan, M. (1997). "Using Competitive Intelligence to Develop a Strategic Management Action-Oriented Measurement System," *Competitive Intelligence Review* 8(2): 34–43.

12

Using Competitive Technical Intelligence Techniques to Complement Research-and-Development Processes

Jeffrey Murphy

INTRODUCTION

Ownership and effective exploitation of leading-edge technologies are widely recognized as a critical foundation of global competitive advantage. Success is frequently the product of an efficient and well-funded research and development (R&D) program.

To effectively use R&D resources, organizations are turning to programs that incorporate more focused elements of competitive technical intelligence (CTI) into their corporate strategy. Strategic decision-making is typically centered on issues of future customer needs, company resources, and competitor activity. These programs require support by analytical techniques that can minimize management uncertainties.

This chapter explores CTI within organizations and its role in supporting R&D processes. Executives and competitive intelligence (CI) professionals alike are provided with a brief overview of how CTI is evolving with the technology-maturation process. In particular, the field of *technology scouting* and the practice of *technical literature analysis* are reviewed with respect to their complementary role in a firm's R&D efforts.[1] As a final note, the role of CTI in organizations and its future in R&D decision-making are discussed in a global context.

THE ROLE OF COMPETITIVE TECHNICAL INTELLIGENCE IN RESEARCH AND DEVELOPMENT

Superior technology is a source of considerable competitive advantage, making competitive intelligence for R&D essential. Technology intelligence reaches beyond topics directly related to competitors to include early identification and understanding of breakthroughs in science, technology trends, and changes in the technology bases of suppliers and customers (Brenner, 1996).

New technology may take years to develop; therefore effective technology intelligence frequently focuses on early indicators of change to optimize response options. Early signals often emerge in scientific and technical discussions, in "gray literature," or in corporate releases stating that resources are being directed in certain areas. Later signals are evident in scientific publications and journals, which might occur a few years after the research has been completed. This delay is continually abbreviated with improvements in technology (Brenner, 1996).

Scientific reports often follow rumors of R&D alliances, joint ventures, or partnerships. Later patents are issued representing work that was performed years earlier—clearly not timely indicators for identifying and addressing technology changes. Process-and-development efforts on the new technology might be rumored next. The strongest signals occur near the end of the development cycle, and may involve a product announcement, competitive product sales, and a loss of business (Brenner, 1996).

Leading-edge technologies give important competitive advantages. An early mover into a market with a new product or service can establish a commanding lead and can be very difficult for competitors to dislodge. But there are also disadvantages associated with being a technological leader: The costs of implementing and debugging new and unproven technologies are high, because later competitors may gain from your experience at no cost and with little risk (Industry Canada, 1999).

The strength and timing of technology signals correlate with the well-established "S-curve" path of product development, serving as a useful tool in technology prospecting (see figure 12.1). Small-business innovators look for the inflection before the curve turns upward, because it is an excellent time to acquire a technology or partner with the inventor to bring a technology into the mainstream. First-mover advantages at this point can yield superior price-and-performance characteristics in the eyes of consumers (Industry Canada, 1999).

In the early stages of R&D there is a lot of investment in a technology. This is the no-growth stage represented by the initial flat part of the S-curve. The technology is next embodied in some early marketable products, processes, or services. Early models tend to be expensive, with small market penetration and low returns. As the S-curve turns upward, the new technology begins to have an impact on the marketplace. Growth eventually slows as wide market penetration is achieved. The curve levels off again once market saturation has been reached (Industry Canada, 1999).

Significant progress occurs as resources are applied to technological devel-

Signal Intensity

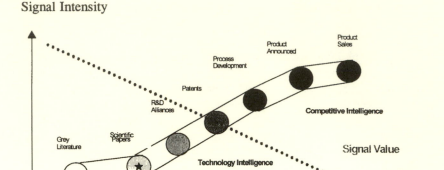

FIGURE 12.1 Competitive technical intelligence in the product lifecycle. (*Source:* Adapted from Brenner [1996].)

opment. The main focus of technology intelligence concentrates in this stage.[2] Competitive advantages are realized by innovation in marketing, after-sales service, or training rather than in the technology itself. Later stages of product development are within the realm of competitive intelligence. The technology has been commercialized and it has become a strong competitor in the marketplace (Industry Canada, 1999).

Technology prospecting refers to monitoring new technological developments. Holding off from investing in new technology until it is ready for full-scale commercial application yields the most success. At that point, the innovator must be agile and leap past competitors who have spent resources developing the technology through its early stages. This strategy carries smaller risks, requires lower investment, and demands shorter lead times. Financial returns are large and relatively certain because the new technology has demonstrated its potential. Entrepreneurs employing this strategy are usually able to beat competitors with successful new or improved product/service offerings (Industry Canada, 1999).

With the increasing number of international technological powerhouses, it is impossible to follow all the key players and their developments. Learning about technological development at your own pace will not bring much success either. Companies may miss the opportunities to exploit advances in technology, or perhaps they may even invest in the wrong technology (Paap, 1994). Fortunately, there has been increased focus on formal techniques to gather and assess technological progress. The field of *technology scouting* and the practices of *technology forecasting* and *technical literature analysis* are becoming more important in supporting R&D efforts.

Technology Scouting

Technology scouting is geared toward identifying trends and opportunity generation rather than problem-solving (Brenner, 1996). With the current pace of technological change, scouting is evolving from tracking market opportunities to compiling information on how to manage the technologies located in the search (Tibbets, 1997). Examples of organizations using technology scouting are Air Products and Chemicals, Inc. (APTECH) and the BOC Group (Ashton, 1997).

Successful technology scouting can provide new paths to achieve the same objectives already being pursued in an organization. Focused technology-intelligence efforts can help companies avoid the potential surprise of a competitive product launch, and can reduce uncertainties during the expensive development period. False leads can be avoided by uncovering failed attempts while accessing inventions that can save much time and effort (Brenner, 1996). Scouting is particularly important when a company does have technical expertise or when the technology is perceived to be "cutting edge."

Trend tracking involves environmental scanning of the business world and focuses on providing awareness of happenings outside a certain niche or field (e.g., federal regulations, consumer trends, and economic/political environments). Because trends usually develop as a result of larger-scale movements, trend analysis should include contextual data to support interpretation. Experienced technology scouts are aware of emerging trends and are prepared to generate reports within a short timeframe (Tibbets, 1997).

Research techniques used by technology scouts need to support more adaptive strategic decision-making. Techniques must help manage uncertainty about the range of technological choices. The most useful analytical tools are those that are part of an integrated strategic-planning process that helps management make well-informed technology decisions with respect to the future business environment, customer intelligence, competitor intelligence, organizational goals and resources, and the technology alternatives that currently exist (Thomas, 1994).

INTEGRATED COMPETITIVE TECHNOLOGY ASSESSMENT

The CTI Process

Monitoring efforts must be organized and conducted in ways that define specific objectives, resources, and projects. These analytical criteria are fundamental to the CTI process. Successful technology-scouting programs will influence the highest levels within the organization. Thus intelligence services should focus on findings or ideas that affect key decisions.

A common shortcoming of many monitoring programs is the low priority assigned to it by management or insufficient allocation of resources. To avoid early pitfalls, create a multidisciplinary team around a project that will demonstrate value (Society of Competitive Intelligence Professionals [SCIP], 1999).

Assigning gatekeepers and/or champions to the process is the best way to ensure that monitoring works.

Sources of information typically come in the form of reports, briefings, or e-mail, but these are usually not sufficient to ensure impacts on decisions by themselves. Enormous volumes of CTI data can create information that can be analyzed to develop strategic insights. However, ineffective data-analysis of organizations is identified as the most significant cause of intelligence failures (Brenner, 1996).

Various levels of integrated analysis are commonly cited in the CI literature. Several terms are often cross-referenced and appear to be used interchangeably among practitioners of innovation forecasting. Common terms used to describe integrated analysis of CTI include: *technology forecasting*, *scenario analysis*, and *technical literature analysis*. An overview of the various terms and levels of analysis is presented in figure 12.2.

Technology Forecasting

Technology forecasting needs the context of strategic goals and consumer needs, plus the focus of specific future products/services. The technique must be easily integrated into a process that can be adjusted as required. Numerous market-research techniques are based on extrapolative analyses of current trends. Most techniques can support decisions about future products and their component technologies, but are less effective when nonestablished products are being modified, the forecast horizon is distant, and the competitive landscape is unknown (Thomas, 1994).

Focused competitive technology *forecasting* is most useful when the forecast horizon is distant or hazy (e.g., multiple product lifecycles of 5 to 15 years), and when customer requirements are less certain. The assessment should begin with the "pull" of the future customer to address questions related to relevant technologies and competitor positioning. Scenario-based analysis is used to provide planners with goals that are viable over a wide range of futures and plausible business environments (Thomas, 1994).

After forecasting, the second task is to find the enabling technologies that are required to develop the future products. Competitive technical intelligence practitioners need to identify and focus on the few technologies that are critical to sustaining a competitive advantage (Thomas, 1994). The third phase of the assessment involves technology *backcasting*. The goal here is to identify all of the alternative technology-development paths that may lead to the future product. Bibliometrics and patent analysis are two common techniques used by technology scouts to identify historical trends, and can be incorporated into the forecasting/backcasting analysis. These techniques fall into the realm of *technical-literature analysis*.

Technical-Literature Analysis

BIBLIOMETRICS. Bibliometrics is an approach to innovation forecasting that involves the counting of publications, patents, or citation activity. Researchers

Specialty	Strategic Purpose	Implementation Process	Resources

Scouting	*Targeted* (short-term)
	
	Reconnaissance (long-term)
		• Online database search
		• Literature review
		• Expert interviews
		• Patent Search
		• Networking with selected contacts
		
		• Same as above.
		• Emphasis on maintaining, expanding and refining existing leads.
		• "Trend tracking"
			• Electronic databases
			• The Internet
			   www.townhall.org
			   www.riceinfo.rice.edu/
			   www.loc.gov
			   www.nsf.gov
			   www.carl.org
			   www.corptech
			
			• Bulletin Boards
			• Literature Reviews
			• Trade Shows
			• Bibliometrics/Patents
			• Company Directories
			• Manufacturers' Directories
			• Universities

Forecasting	*Scenario Planning Analysis (Future)* Segmentation Analysis – purchasing behavior of future target segments is explored one scenario at a time.		Modeling Software • Technology Sequence Analysis (TSA*)
Backcasting	Identify alternative technology development paths that may lead to future products.		* This is a management tool – does not provide a definitive prediction of what "will be".

Technical Literature Analysis	
Bibliometrics	Databases: • LEXPAT (legal searches) ◄ • ESPACE • CA SEARCH (abstracts) • U.S. Patents (US) • U.S. PATENT SEARCH (US) • CLAIMS (US) • FPAT (France) • JAPIO (Japan) • INPADOC (International) • PCI (International) Online • Knight-Ridder Information Inc. • Questel-Orbit • Mead Data Central • STN International Technical Library • CISTI (Canada)

FIGURE 12.2 Overview of integrated competitive technical assessment.

have studied innovation success from the perspective of technology transfer, diffusion, and substitution to understand significant factors that promote technological success.

Watts et al. (1998) published a case study synthesizing various innovation concepts. A useful model was derived to explore aspects of technological change in ceramic engines. Technology *lifecycle* indicators examined the development path of the technology, the growth rate, and the status of the technologies on which it depends. Innovation *context* factors considered socioeconomic influences on business and the target technology. Product *value-chain* issues focused on the potential returns and the enabling requirements.

Innovation indicators consider the specific content of applications rather than using a general counting procedure. The Watts et al. (1998) study looked at the evolution of keywords for maturing technologies poised for commercialization. Technological activities were examined by generating lists of keywords over a specified time period. Common keywords were eliminated across periods to examine the evolution of changing keywords as indicators of technological maturation.

Analysis of technology maturity versus keyword diffusion suggests that innovation sequences often start with a lot of hype, followed by disillusionment and then a period of reduced interest—signaled by a reduced number of publications related to the associated technology. Over time, there is a gradual increase in the number of publications, and the richness of the information improves as indicated by a greater number of associated keywords. Terms eventually evolve toward the analytical sciences (e.g., computer-modeling applications) along with materials and processes applications (Mogee, 1997).[3]

In short, bibliometrics represents a cost-effective means to critically track innovation progress, and can provide a solid basis to gauge a technology when the information is combined with expert opinion. By combining bibliometrics with other intelligence information, CI practitioners can spot competitive threats, uncover relationships between technologies and key players, and identify emerging trends.

PATENT ANALYSIS. Patent intelligence is a unique public source of information used to study technological change. Companies often use patent information either as a current awareness tool or as more quantitative pattern analysis used in conjunction with other technology-intelligence methods. It is the process of examining large numbers of patents, quantifying key aspects, and identifying patterns and trends in the data.

A parent company sacrifices the secrecy of the invention by publishing complete technical documentation of its features in exchange for legal protection (i.e., a patent) from potential copiers. Worldwide patents do not exist, so it is necessary to obtain protection in each country that a company plans to make, use, or sell an invention. Under international law, inventors must file all foreign applications within one year in order to preserve the "priority date" of original filing (Mogee, 1997).[4]

Patents are distinguished from other scientific publications in that they signify perceived economic potential. Careful study of patent information is advantageous, because the information generally appears before a new product is introduced, making it possible to track and provide an early warning of a competitor's R&D plans. With the exception of personal information sources, patents are the most current innovation intelligence available on new technologies. Patent analysis should be considered a critical component of a company's CI program if the core competency of the firm is an innovative R&D program (Mogee, 1997).

By studying patents, managers can gain a measure of foresight as to where

R&D time should be focused and directed. Usually, the first step in patent analysis involves analyzing current research positioning relative to the competition. This analysis involves benchmarking one company's patenting activity against another. But one of the most common errors made at this stage is to simply count the number of new publications by companies, and then to use that number as an indicator of R&D productivity. Not all inventions are patented or patentable, and the propensity to patent inventions varies according to a host of factors (e.g., time, country, industry, and company). Comparisons across technologies should be strictly avoided (Mogee, 1997).

Interpreting the results correctly requires a thorough understanding of the types of databases available in order to determine the best one for the purpose and avoid making misleading interpretations. Many patent databases exist, mostly covering the patents issued by a single country. Because worldwide searches are usually impractical, searches of the U.S. Patent Office are typically conducted first, because of its large volume of well-classified "prior art" patents. Examples of the largest and most commonly used databases are listed in figure 12.2.

The average *patent family size* for a company is an important indicator of the extent to which the company intends to exploit its inventions internationally. This size also points to the commercial value of the work that a company is conducting. The family size tends to be larger for companies that are based in countries with small domestic markets (e.g., Canada), but with strong trade ties with other industrialized countries. Because patenting is expensive, companies with deeper pockets are more likely to have more patents.

Patenting activities are also different in companies from different countries. A good way to compare international companies is to measure the number of patent applications outside the home authority. Regardless of the strategy, the most commercially viable patents receive the added protection of application in other countries (Mogee, 1997).

A *patent-citation analysis* is one of the best ways to establish a base of "prior art" patents for a new line of research, and is a good initial step in obtaining a feel for the important patents in an industry. Citations can highlight seminal technologies in an industry, because patent examiners are likely to cite and be familiar with them repeatedly. A patent is more likely to be commercially relevant if it is frequently cited in the industry literature.[5]

Analysis can often involve comparing the *patent-to-product ratio* relative to competitors. A lower ratio suggests an efficiency problem is occurring within R&D. If competitive patents are consistently blocking progress, it's probably not coincidental. Large patent blocks might show strategic-level technical trends, signaling that a competitor is preparing for commercialization of a new product. For example, in a cross-licensing scenario, Japanese companies frequently create larger patent clusters to surround domestic or competitive patents. These clusters create a "minefield" that blocks competitors or boxes them in depending upon how they are positioned (Cantrell, 1996).

Some companies patent in wide clusters while others are more secretive, and some do not patent at all. The existence of patent clusters by a single company and connected by a large number of intercitations reflect an attempt to develop and protect a niche. If a company cites its own patents, it is adding to its own work and has successfully protected its technology from being used by others. Patents that are heavily cited in other related patents indicate that the technology is teaching others (Mogee, 1997).

Changes in a firm's patenting levels are important. Comparing patent classifications in a particular industry is used as an indicator of core technical competence. For example, if automobile companies are being compared, the analyst might consider each company's technological profile in terms of the proportion of patents in engines. An increase or change in research staff could indicate a major innovative effort. Yearly variations in patent data make it difficult to use this type of trend analysis to gauge short-term trends (Mogee, 1997).

STRENGTHS AND WEAKNESSES OF TECHNICAL-LITERATURE ANALYSIS. Given that various models and methods are used in business literature to explore alternatives, it is useful at this stage to highlight the key strengths and weaknesses of technical-literature analysis using the popular FAROUT evaluation criteria (Fleisher & Bensoussan, 2000):

- *Future oriented:* Technical-literature analysis inherently looks at historical documentation. However, the technical intelligence can be incorporated into the "backcasting function" of scenario analysis so that emerging opportunities and future customer needs are identified.

- *Accuracy:* Bibliometric studies (i.e., keyword diffusion) indicate that published information is rather subjective. Innovation sequences evolve from periods of hype to reduced interest. Key terms eventually move toward the analytical sciences along with materials and processes applications. Information that is perceived to have high economic potential becomes harder to obtain.

  Patents yield the most accurate and detailed information. A major short-coming of patent data is that not all inventions are patentable. Companies usually consider the cost–benefit of filing a patent and defending it versus losing control of the technology in the absence of legal protection. To account for the significance of the patent, it is necessary to distinguish between basic and improvement patents and their clusters by considering renewal rates, looking at subsequent patents, and identifying members of the international patent family.

- *Resource efficient:* Technical-literature analysis consumes time and resources. But the efficiency of the process is enhanced when management needs are clear and an organized process is in place. Small multidisciplinary "knowledge teams" headed by a process manager are common. Building larger resources such as internal "war rooms" is costly, but may be worth the effort for larger organizations.

- *Objectivity:* Technical-literature analysis is pseudoscientific in nature. Content obtained from journal articles, magazines, and newspapers is subjective, but an element of objectivity is gained if systematic processes of data collection and analyses are applied in the research. Observations and trends can be quantified and subsequently used to support long-term strategic decision-making.

- *Usefulness:* Technological competition is increasing, and effective exploitation of leading-edge global technologies is a critical foundation for competitive advantage. Research-and-development programs require focused efforts to survive and grow in the future. Analytical tools are needed to manage these uncertainties and avoid misdirected investments.

- *Timely:* The CI function must be held accountable for its performance so as to be taken seriously in an organization. Intelligence of strategic significance has to be available when needed. Technical-literature analysis is often criticized as not being timely enough for CI purposes; using international databases that cover patent applications can reduce response times.

THE FUTURE OF COMPETITIVE TECHNICAL INTELLIGENCE

Competitive technical intelligence is emerging as a separate discipline that is poised for rapid growth. Improvements in computer and communications technology will significantly affect the way competitive intelligence is produced and managed. Organizations will naturally mature and adapt to the new demand for these services as CTI becomes more widespread.

Integration of CTI in Organizations

Organized processes can contribute significantly to the CTI function. Flexible teams led by an intelligence-process person often produce the best intelligence. The process manager is someone who can link management's intelligence needs back into the organization as effectively as possible. Several organizational structures have evolved, but no single model is always effective (Society of Competitive Intelligence Professionals [SCIP], 1999). Common structures include central units, decentralized groups, combined operations, and diffused groups (Ashton, 1997).

The CTI unit is dependent on library resources and systems. Some larger organizations, including the U.S. Department of Defense, have developed multidimensional technical "war rooms" that provide a wide array of information resources, analytical tools, and staff capabilities. These information-analysis centers (IACs) are current with pertinent information and thus provide senior technical staff, lab managers, and executives more confidence in their R&D decision-making abilities (Ashton, 1997).

An emerging informal concept with potential for CTI applications is the "knowledge cell," which is a topic-specialized group dispersed throughout an organization. Groups are designated to research a business-intelligence topic in order to arrive at a common understanding, identify actionable items, and prioritize needs. This system has been successful in generating multiple points of view about a topic, and to develop and execute marketing strategies for emerging technologies (Ashton, 1997).

Future Trends

Companies operating in technologically dynamic industries have a stronger need for formalized CTI programs. Competitive technical intelligence industry trends are directly tied to the future direction of public and private R&D. Technical intelligence is particularly important when changes are imminent, rapid, and driven by advances by companies outside the incumbent firm's main technical field. Many companies scout technology activities to track R&D advances and to develop profiles of competitor strengths and weaknesses as part of the overall business-intelligence function. The evolution of the CTI field as a specialization depends on a continuing demand for services and the investment in research and resources that is needed to deliver useful technical-intelligence products (Ashton, 1997).

The future looks promising, with organizations seeking methods to improve the flow of scientific and technical information to help R&D decision-makers prioritize their needs.[6] There are few educational or training opportunities for CTI in business or engineering schools, and advanced training for practitioners is virtually nonexistent. As the requirement for CTI grows, the availability of professional education and training courses must increase to meet the demand for technological intelligence (Ashton, 1997).

An integrated approach to analysis permits several types of input data to be synthesized for simultaneous evaluation. Future integrated techniques are likely to provide new ways of collecting and analyzing intelligence data. Advanced modeling, computational displays, and interactive tools will increase the speed, capacity and overall comprehensiveness of the analysis process. Competitive technical intelligence practitioners will likely benefit from increased computer-technology advancement and the convergence of the "content-centric" information-technology industry. Gains will also be realized with a wider acceptance of CTI in organizations, better training of analysts, and new tools. Nevertheless, hardware and software for these emerging applications can only be enabling components, and not ends in themselves (Moschella, 1997). The intelligence function is not a turnkey operation—in some cases it may take 10 to 15 years to fully integrate CI into the firm. By most expert accounts the benefits are definitely worth the effort (Miller, 1999).

SUMMARY

Tracking technological developments in other firms and industries is an important subset of CI activities. Competitive technical intelligence is undertaken to monitor and interpret key events and to provide a continuous awareness of science and technology trends. Technology intelligence can help companies detect potential threats to the firm's success, or can lead to the development of new processes, products, or alliances. An effective program can help a firm avoid redundant research efforts, respond to competitor actions, take advantage of technological breakthroughs, and enhance the overall competitiveness of an organization.

NOTES

1. For a more comprehensive review of CTI trends and practices, the reader is referred to W. B. Ashton (1997) (see reference list).

2. An alternative strategy is to be a technological follower—waiting until other companies have developed and commercialized leading-edge technologies before you adopt them.

3. It is interesting to note that there is frequently a reduction of publicly available data, implying that firms are holding onto competitive information that is perceived to have high economic potential.

4. A patent generally has a lifetime of 20 years, dating from the patent-application filing date. In the United States and Canada only issued patents are published, and the application remains proprietary if the patent is not granted. In many European and Asian countries, patent applications are automatically published after 18 months.

5. Examiner citation is fundamentally different than the references in the literature articles by authors. Examiners are using citations to make the case for or against relevant claims. They are usually younger and less experienced than the scientists and lawyers who are applying for the patents. Company researchers can provide better insight upon reviewing the full patent.

6. Most notably SCIP (Society of Competitive Intelligence Professionals) and the CENDI (Commerce, Energy, NASA, NLM, Defense, and Information Group).

REFERENCES

Ashton, W.B. (1997). "Future Directions in Competitive Technical Intelligence," in *Keeping Abreast of Science and Technology—Technical Intelligence for Business*, ed. W.B. Ashton and R.A. Klavans. Columbus, OH: Battelle Press.

Brenner, M.S. (1996). "Technology Intelligence and Scouting," *Competitive Intelligence Review* 7(3): 20–27.

Cantrell, R. (1996). "Patent Intelligence—Information to Compete Before Products Are Launched," *Competitive Intelligence Review* 7(1): 65–69.

Fleisher, C.S., and B. Bensoussan. (2000). "A FAROUT Way to Manage CI Analysis," *Competitive Intelligence Magazine* 3(2): 37–40.

Industry Canada. (1999). "Innovating For Success—Part 4, The Second D: Design," *Canadian Management Network* <http://strategis.ic.gc.ca/cgi-bin/basic>.

Miller, J.P. (1999). "Some Competitive Intelligence Advice," *Information Today* 16(7): 56.

Mogee, M.E. (1997). "Patents and Technology Intelligence," in *Keeping Abreast of Science and Technology: Technical Intelligence for Business*, ed. W.B. Ashton and R.A. Klavans. Columbus, OH: Battelle Press.

Moschella, D.C. (1997). *Waves of Power: The Dynamics of Global Technology Leadership, 1964–2010.* New York: Amacom-American Management Association.

Paap, J.E. (1994). "Technology Management and Competitive Intelligence: New Techniques for a Changing World," *Competitive Intelligence Review* 5(1): 2–4.

Society of Competitive Intelligence Professional's 2nd Annual Competitive Technical Intelligence Symposium. (1999). "Developing Processes and Infrastructure to Meet Upper Management's CTI Needs: A Roundtable Discussion," *Competitive Intelligence Review* 10(3): 4–18.

Thomas, C.W. (1994). "Foresight in Strategic Technology Competition," *Competitive Intelligence Review* 5(1): 17–26.

Tibbets, J. (1997). "Technology Scouting," in *Keeping Abreast of Science and Technology —Technical Intelligence for Business*, ed. W.B. Ashton and R.A. Klavans. Columbus, OH: Battelle Press.

Watts, R.J., A.L. Porter, and N.C. Newman. (1998). "Innovation Forecasting Using Bibliometrics," *Competitive Intelligence Review* 9(4): 11–19.

13

Applying Competitive Intelligence to Mergers and Acquisitions

Angus Stewart

INTRODUCTION

Mergers and acquisitions (M&As) continue to be a popular solution to a variety of problems faced by businesses coping with global competition and other changes in their competitive environments. As an indication of the magnitude of this activity, U.S. mergers set a record in 1998, hitting $1.61 trillion—a 78 percent increase from 1997 (*Business Wire*, 1999). However, it has been well documented that as a business alternative, M&As have not been very successful. One report states that "barely half (54%) of large-scale mergers resulted in a combined entity that outperformed industry averages for shareholder return. Fewer than 25% could be counted as a success from a shareholder perspective" (Keenan & White, 1982).

The shareholders of acquiring companies have virtually no legal recourse in the event of a failed merger or acquisition if due diligence has been satisfactorily performed. However, the shareholders of the target firm who are on the receiving end of the transfer of wealth can hold the officers and directors of their firm liable for not making an informed decision about the appropriate selling price of the company. This is as a result of the landmark 1985 U.S. case, *Smith v. Van Gorkem*.

The purpose of this chapter is to examine how competitive intelligence (CI) could be used in the pre-acquisition or pre-merger planning stage in order to determine and/or improve the chances of success that, for our purposes, will be defined as either maintaining or increasing shareholder value.

COMPETITIVE INTELLIGENCE IN THE INITIAL STEPS OF THE M&A PROCESS

M&As as a Strategic Alternative

When M&As are a strategic alternative to developing competencies, markets, or products from scratch, management should consider other alternatives that could help the organization reach its desired goal(s). Competitive intelligence can play a crucial role here by providing information on those alternatives. This might prevent executives from automatically assuming that M&As are the only solution worth considering.

Is This the Right Target and/or the Right Market?

Competitive intelligence can be used to explore the nature of both the business and the market that the acquirer is looking to enter. Lisle and Bartlam (1999) contend that there are subjective intangibles that are often hidden during due diligence that often become huge obstacles during the integration phase. These are:

- Market growth of the target is lower than expected
- Industry margins are less than expected
- Market position of the target is weaker than expected
- Competition is tougher than expected
- Pre-acquisition research is inadequate and inaccurate
- Management at the target is weak
- Profit margins of the target are narrower than expected
- The systems of the acquired company are not as developed as expected
- Post-acquisition capital requirements are larger than expected
- Strategic planning is lacking.

Information that deals with the above points might lead the firm to conclude that there are many reasons to avoid either the target firm or the market under consideration.

Using CI to Locate Suitable Targets—"Search and Screen"

Competitive intelligence can be used in identifying suitable target companies. Defined by Lisle and Bartlam (1999) as a "search and screen," the CI process can be put to use searching for targets that meet very specifically defined criteria. Learning the strategic intentions of the acquirer is an obvious place to start:

- Is the M&A supposed to move the company in a particular direction, correct an existing problem, or both?
- Defend a business area that is being threatened?

- Leverage existing products and capabilities within the present market, or provide entry into a new market?
- Is the M&A an effort to improve profitability or just add market share?

Once a "wish list" has been drawn up, the CI analyst can evaluate and rank potential candidates for senior executive consideration.

An added advantage to using a CI professional for ranking potential M&A candidates is that possible targets can be approached anonymously. Anonymity can eliminate competition for targets and, as a result, help to reduce costs (Lisle & Bartlam, 1999).

Employing CI in an Environmental Analysis

Antitrust laws should be of particular concern if the M&A: (a) Is large enough to adversely impact the market as a whole, (b) sufficiently concentrates the market, and (c) is horizontal in nature. The other combinations are vertical (a merger of supplier and purchaser) or conglomerate (firms that have no vertical or horizontal relationship). With a horizontal merger, the firms previously directly competed against each other. This is the type of M&A activity that has been predominantly challenged, because it has a reasonable probability of substantially lessening competition. If a CI analyst determines that your proposal is likely to be challenged by a regulating body, time, effort, and money can be saved.

An excellent illustration of the importance of environmental analysis involved Coca-Cola's planned acquisition of the non-U.S. soft-drink arm of the British company, Cadbury Schweppes. Even though the two groups' drinks were already distributed by a single company (Coca-Cola Schweppes Beverages), they ran into opposition. In countries such as Germany, where Coke had more than half the market, regulators were unwilling to allow the U.S. group to add another 1 or 2 percentage points by acquiring the Schweppes brands. As a result, Coca-Cola and Cadbury were forced by European Union competition authorities to revise the deal and scale back their plans. Popular reports suggested that Cadbury's CEO was surprised about the degree of resistance the company experienced.

Considerations in an International Context

Competitive intelligence can help with determining the appropriate and accepted ways of going about the M&A process in foreign countries in order to save time, money, and possible embarrassment.

In Japan, M&As are not yet totally accepted as a legitimate commercial transaction. This is discussed in the article "Competitive Intelligence in the Acquisition of Japanese and German Companies" (DiCicco, 1993). At the extreme, it is considered antisocial behavior. Middle managers take a dim view of upper management or owners deciding to sell the firm without consultation; publicly announced offers are thought to be disruptive and are only accepted if owners and employees agree to the sale. The tactics used to acquire companies in Japan mimic their culture, which can be in stark contrast to North American

Table 13.1
KEY CI VARIABLES FOR ACQUISITIONS OF JAPANESE COMPANIES

Technology and hidden assets valuation

As in North America, Japanese firms often have land that is undervalued on the books. This would normally be taken care of in valuation procedures. Technology valuation, however, is not performed as a component of goodwill, and DiCicco (1993) warns that a technology-pricing model should be used by the CI department.

The "real" distribution and sales network

Unravel the complex distribution network of the target, and acquire equity ownership in a key distributor. In this way, you can propose equity ownership in the target when exports reach a certain goal.

Ownership lineage

Monitor aging, childless owners. They have no one to pass on the business to and would therefore be more willing to sell.

Timing

Relationships need to be built up over time. It is these relationships that determine whether a deal can be transacted. For example, a popular method is mutually profitable technology licensing. It provides a "win–win" situation, which the Japanese like. The Japanese company is appointed as a licensee and then provided with technology improvements. A major equity stake can be discussed once sales reach a certain goal.

Alliances with the target's main bank

Banks play a more central role in Japan with regards to match-making. A suggested first step in M&A is to determine the main bank connections and officers who are friendly to the own-ers of the acquisition target. The main bank can then introduce the pair confidentially and often acts as an advisor.

Window dressing

Firms may look desirable but acquirers should employ CI in uncovering any falsified finan-cial statements. For example, a red flag might be the discovery of accommodation notes appearing on promissory-note data in banks.

Gaining control from a distance

A strategy that has been employed abroad is using CI to determine who owns convertible bonds offshore. These bonds are bought on a confidential basis and ownership is not regis-tered in Tokyo. The bonds can then be used to control and take over the company without ever having to go into Japan.

Source: DiCicco, 1993. Reprinted with the permission of the Society of Competitive Intelligence Professionals.

culture and therefore would not be innately obvious. Loyalty, group advice, politeness, and patience are listed as key attributes in the success of this process.

North American companies often use the wrong type of CI information in dealing with Japanese companies. Table 13.1 lists some of the key variables in successful CI gathering for acquiring Japanese companies. Table 13.2 summa-rizes the value of information for M&As. The conclusion: Additional informa-tion reduces risk.

Table 13.2
VALUE OF INFORMATION FOR M&As

Illuminate unknowns

Used to supplement due diligence, CI can help the acquiring firm by providing information that due diligence does not. Some areas of interest might include:

- Target's market share. (Is it what the target claims?)
- Technological developments in the industry. (Does it appear that the target's product or service is going to become obsolete?)
- Status of important customers. (Are they planning to migrate to another supplier in the not-too-distant future, or is this action likely to cause them to migrate?)

Prevent surprises

CI can be used to explore whether proposed M&A activity could result in an antitrust violation. This is a concern if the proposed deal:

- Is large enough to significantly impact the market as a whole.
- Sufficiently concentrates the market.
- Is horizontal in nature (organizations were formerly competitors).

CI can help prevent other surprises such as:

- Tougher than expected competition.
- Narrower than expected profit margins.

Provide alternatives

CI can help the acquiring firm to explore other alternatives beside M&A that could help them reach their goal(s). Having feasible alternatives and knowing their relative costs may help management more accurately determine the value of the target.

Result: Additional information decreases risk.

THE FOUR CORNERSTONES OF SYNERGY:
AN EXCELLENT FRAMEWORK FOR COMPETITIVE INTELLIGENCE

Synergy

Synergy is the only logical explanation as to why executives would pay a premium for a company that its shareholders could purchase on their own at market price. Synergy is defined as: "Increases in competitiveness and resulting cash flows beyond what the two companies are expected to accomplish independently" (Sirower, 1997). Although simple in principle, synergy has been difficult to achieve in practice. The value of a firm as determined by the market and reflected in its share price already contains expectations about future performance. When two companies become one, even with no premium having been paid, the combined entity must outperform previously held expectations in order to create shareholder value. If a premium has been paid by the acquirer, this makes the task even more difficult.

Companies often enter into mergers or acquisitions with information that is insufficient for allowing them to make plans to capture the synergies that they need in order to be successful (Sirower, 1997). Other information should also be collected to assist the acquirer in determining whether synergies can be achieved and what steps the company needs to take in order to achieve them. This "soft" data can be provided by CI. Executives often talk about the great strategic "fit" that the two companies have, ignoring the fact that this alone will not create performance improvements.

Additionally, management's understanding of the possible synergies and their resulting value can help them determine an appropriate price. How can a company know what price to pay for a target if it doesn't know what value it can expect in return?

Sirower's (1997) framework recognizes four components of synergy, which he calls "cornerstones." These include: 1) strategic vision; 2) operating strategy; 3) systems integration; and 4) power and culture. He argues that the presence of all four components will not guarantee synergies, but if one of the cornerstones is missing, synergy is impossible. Although he does not refer to CI in his book, it is clear that this framework can easily be utilized by CI professionals to help acquirers in the M&A process.

APPLYING COMPETITIVE INTELLIGENCE TO THE FOUR CORNERSTONES OF THE SYNERGY MODEL

Strategic Vision

Creating or developing a strategic vision is probably the one area where little help is needed from CI. Management and investment bankers have aptly demonstrated their skills in coming up with enticing vision statements that they use to generate support for their plans.

Competitive intelligence can be helpful in ensuring that the strategy behind the vision is sound. In *Strategic Acquisitions*, Robinson and Peterson (1995) warn that

> [t]ransaction specialists [investment bankers, accountants, lawyers, etc.] are essential to completing the acquisition but won't assure success in meeting your business objective. You must control the acquisition process since you, the business manager, are responsible for directing the business strategy and it is your money being spent to accomplish the task.

On the basis of the information provided by CI, the acquirer may decide that the target is not suitable, the market is not worth going into, or that a combination of concerns make the achievement of anticipated synergies unlikely.

An example of where this information could have been useful was the Sears decision to become a "one-stop shop" for financial services. After acquiring Dean Witter and Coldwell Banker, and spending $250 million above the initial price of the acquisitions, Sears found that its strategy was not yielding synergy.

The financial products that Sears was trying to sell were not ideally suited to the environment and manner in which they were being sold. In fact, each of the financial products required distinctly different marketing, sales, and distribution channels. Simple marketing research might have prevented this loss. Customers clearly did not want one-stop financial shopping.

Operating Strategy

Given that most companies do little in the way of pre-acquisition planning, most combined entities have no formal operating strategy on the day the deal is completed (Sirower, 1997). The operating strategy must respond to the following contestability questions:

- What can be further sustained or improved along the value chains of the businesses that competitors cannot challenge?
- How can competitors be attacked and disabled?

Competitive intelligence not only *can* answer these questions but *should* answer them, and before a merger or acquisition gets to the point where price is seriously being discussed.

Specifically, how is this merger going to make life more difficult for the competition? If the merging companies cannot answer this until months after the deal has been done, then they will be sitting ducks while competitors respond to the change in the competitive environment. Competitors are not going to stand idly by and watch two companies merge without anticipating and taking reactive or even proactive measures.

One example where a vertical integration had taken place was Lockheed Martin's purchase of Loral, an electronics supplier. In response, McDonnell Douglas decided to pull support from its competitor indirectly by switching suppliers, no longer sourcing their components through Loral. This move surprised the Lockheed Martin CEO. Had some CI been done regarding the possible effects of the merger on customer attitudes, this problem might have been foreseen long before the deal was completed and some action taken to protect Loral. In terms of synergy, not only did Lockheed Martin have to perform better than the market expectations, it had to do so with the handicap of the loss of a major account.

Systems Integration

This involves the implementation of the acquisition or merger. How can the two systems be successfully combined and, in turn, support the operating strategy? If a part of the synergy involves cost savings through economies of scale, then this synergy cornerstone is key.

There are five types of possible integration environments (Sirower, 1997):

- The company is acquired as a stand-alone
- The company is acquired as a stand-alone but with a change in strategy
- The target is to become part of the acquirer's operations

- The target and the acquirer are to be completely integrated
- The target takes over the acquirer's existing business, which is integrated into the target's environment.

Each type of integration poses different problems and an adjustment period is to be expected. However, remaining unaware of integration's effect on the overall business *before* the systems are combined can put the merger at risk. At the very least, CI could help to alleviate some of the more obvious problems involved in integration. If the problems cannot be solved altogether, they can be anticipated in order to avert disaster.

Power and Culture

How can the power and culture groups in an organization be combined to improve performance? The implicit assumption has been that if cultures were managed well there would be resultant performance gains. The issue is not whether the cultures are similar or different, but "whether the changes necessary to support the strategy will clash with either culture" (Sirower, 1997). Are the rewards and incentives structured so that the employees cooperate within the individual businesses and across the combined entity?

Corporate culture is arguably the most important factor with regard to the success or failure of mergers and acquisitions. According to Ken Smith, head of Mitchell Madison Group's M&A practice in Toronto, "companies often inadvertently pick away at the cultures of the acquired firms, destroying the very attributes that attracted the merger in the first place" (Crone, 1999).

The emerging culture must support the new strategy of the combined company if the M&A is to be successful. However, that which made the target attractive in the first place must not be lost. Acquiring companies sometimes forget that the target had value as a stand-alone. That value must be maintained in the immediate future and grown over the long term. If the target was attractive because of its creativity or entrepreneurial focus, then the acquirer needs to determine what cultural factors supported those attractive qualities. Competitive intelligence can be useful here. Magazine articles can serve as a good starting point for understanding an organization's culture, but there is no substitute for personal interviews. Talking with a wide range of staff is the best way to understand the target's culture in detail, to discover if it has changed, and why.

WHY HAVEN'T OTHERS MADE THE CI–M&A CONNECTION?

There are a number of reasons why companies engaging in M&As haven't made an effort to employ CI. Table 13.3 lists these reasons.

Table 13.3
BARRIERS TO THE CI/M&A CONNECTION

1. Management hubris

Pride and self-confidence of management carried to an extreme results in acquisition premiums that make it impossible for the combined entity to be successful in shareholders' terms (Roll, 1988).

2. Agency Problem—The principal (shareholders) possesses an asset and employs an agent (management) to increase its value. Problems can arise because the agent does not always prefer to take the action that the principal would prefer.

There is a conflict of interest between management and shareholders. Management compensation, prestige, power, and job security can be linked to increasing the size of the organization, which is easily done through M&A. This problem is compounded by the fact that the shareholders of the acquiring firm have no legal recourse in the event of management overspending on an acquisition.

3. Inexperience

A major acquisition is a rare event for most companies. Management may be unaware of the fundamentals of the problem (Sirower, 1997).

4. Time

In the fervent, auction-like atmosphere of most acquisitions, time is a key factor. There may be little time to gather appropriate, useful information.

IMPLICATIONS FOR THE CI PROFESSIONAL

The obvious suggestion is that you will need to make senior executives aware of the contribution that CI can make with regards to the M&A process.

To combat the obstacle of time, try to get involved in the M&A process as early as possible so that you have sufficient time to gather the required intelligence. Even with a reasonable amount of lead time, you will likely need to analyze the situation and prioritize the information you feel will be most useful. Sensitivity to managerial preference can play a key role here. Because of the possibility of the "Hubris Hypothesis" (Roll, 1988), it may be likely that much of the time put into gathering information to determine whether or not the union makes strategic sense could be wasted. The best contribution that can be made by CI in this case is to gather information on the implementation/integration issues—such as how the systems can best be integrated, anticipating possible people and culture issues and examining the future operating strategy—in order to assist in as smooth and successful a transition as possible.

A proactive CI professional can start the process early if he or she anticipates M&A activity. If your company has a history of M&As or it has become apparent that it is a possibility, the CI professional can start early by performing some scenario analysis. What strategic directions is this company likely to take in the next two to five years? Which companies might be attractive targets? If time and information are limited, the CI professional could detail the attributes of some possible imaginary targets. The product of this type of intelligence would be a series of templates for each strategic direction prepared in advance. This would help shorten the amount of time needed to perform the necessary analysis once a merger or acquisition is being considered.

IMPLICATIONS FOR SENIOR EXECUTIVES

Senior executives need to be sensitive to the fact that M&As most often fail to create shareholder value. Different types of information are needed to supplement due-diligence procedures, and senior managers need to seek out the assistance of CI professionals to help in the M&A process. They should keep the CI professional aware of the possible strategic directions of the company as well as possible attractive targets. In the event that time is limited, a senior executive might want to discuss areas of the M&A where information is most needed from the CI professional. If there are concerns about the elements of synergy, information about strategic issues or the implementation/integration issues may be required.

CONCLUSION

Due diligence—the type of information that is gathered during M&A procedures—is not adversarial in nature. It needs to be supplemented with specific kinds of "soft" data that CI can provide in the pre-acquisition or pre-merger stages. This is evidenced by the repeated failure of M&As to increase shareholder value. By providing different kinds of information, CI can make an extremely valuable contribution to the success of mergers and acquisitions.

REFERENCES

Business Wire. (1999). "Post Merger & Acquisition Integration Excellence Study to be Sponsored by Best Practices, LLC," *Business Wire* (June 24).

Crone, G. (1999). "Merging Companies is Easy, Merging Corporate Cultures is Hard," *Financial Post (National Post)* 1(113): C5.

DiCicco, R. (1993). "Competitive Intelligence in the Acquisition of Japanese and German Companies," in *Global Perspectives on CI*, ed. J.E. Prescott and P.T. Gibbons. Alexandria, VA: Society of Competitive Intelligence Professionals.

Keenan, M., and L.J. White. (1982). *Mergers and Acquisitions.* Toronto: Lexington Books.

Lisle, C., and J. Bartlam. (1999). "Can the Target Pass the Competitive Intelligence Test?" *Mergers and Acquisitions* 33(4): 27.

Robinson, B.R., and W. Peterson. (1995). *Strategic Acquisitions: A Guide To Growing and Enhancing the Value of Your Business.* New York: Irwin Professional Press.

Roll, R. (1988). "The International Crash of October 1987," *Financial Analysts Journal* (September/October): 19–35. Reprinted from *Black Monday and the Future of Financial Markets*, ed. A. Meltzer. Homewood, IL: Dow-Jones-Irwin.

Sirower, M.L. (1997). *The Synergy Trap: How Companies Lose the Acquisition Game.* New York: Free Press.

14

New Product Development and Competitive Intelligence

Hamid Noori, Brenda McWilliams, Gene Deszca, and Hugh Munro

INTRODUCTION

Breakthrough products (BTPs) have been found to contribute significantly to corporate profits and market position. However, because such products are designed to meet needs that may not yet be apparent in the market and have no historical point of reference, traditional market-forecasting techniques are unable to provide accurate predictions of market success for them. An alternative to traditional approaches is explored, which involves combining forecasts of quantifiable environmental variables with qualitative analysis of uncertainties through scenario creation and investigation. This "umbrella approach" assesses future goals, needs, desires, and product-development directions, and works backward from the future scenario to the present to determine what steps must be completed. The goal is to incorporate current information into a corporation's product development process and to determine which pathway it should follow.

THE COMPETITIVE CHALLENGE OF BREAKTHROUGH PRODUCTS

In 1983 Motorola introduced the world to the first publicly available cellular telephone, supported by a communications infrastructure that allowed users the wireless capacity to stay in touch with anyone who had access to a telephone. The introduction of that "breakthrough" product (BTP) came after more than a decade of development and $150 million investment. This product has changed the way the world communicates and has grown into a highly profitable part of the Motorola business—greater than $300 million in profits in 1990 (Lynne, Morone, & Paulson, 1996). Nevertheless, are there things that could have been done to alleviate the financial costs and/or reduce the development time, while increasing the certainty of the success of the product?

New-product-development executives face the challenge of managing product and market uncertainty and ambiguity every day. Their goal is to introduce the "right" product at the "right" time. But how are these product-development conditions determined and met successfully?

In the case of "breakthrough" products—those that are unique to the market—the failure rates can be expected to be particularly problematic. The rewards, however, are significant. Competitive market pressures are combining with the rapid pace of technological development to make innovation increasingly important in firms' overall strategies. Consequently, BTPs are becoming a significant tool with which firms can leverage competitive advantage. During the 1989–1993 period, breakthrough products accounted for only 10 percent of new-product introductions, but generated 24 percent of new product profits (Martin, 1995). Furthermore, the development of breakthrough products is an essential weapon in meeting the challenges of global competition (Lynne, Morone, & Paulson, 1996) and leadership in the marketplace.

Consider the impact the development of breakthrough products has had on the following firms: Motorola (cellular phones), Sony (consumer electronics), Chrysler (minivan), and Corning (fiber optics). Each of these firms' ability to understand the future of their markets and the applications of the products they were developing helped them redefine and create markets. What drove this knowledge? According to Lynne, Morone, and Paulson (1996), it was a "probe and learn" process in which early versions of the product were introduced or tested, information was gathered, and the next iteration was developed. This, however, can be a very long and expensive process. Are there other approaches that would allow firms to accelerate their learning and develop the "right" BTPs in a more expeditious manner?

TRADITIONAL FORECASTING APPROACHES: GAPS, SHORTCOMINGS, AND OPPORTUNITIES

Firms can employ a wide range of techniques to develop premarket forecasts for new products. Such techniques range from highly objective quantitative approaches to more subjective qualitative techniques, from complicated computer-modeling processes to simply asking the customer for its opinions and ideas. Some well-known approaches to forecasting include time-series analysis, logit models, and conjoint models on the quantitative side, and purchase-intention surveys, simulated test markets, and focus groups on the more qualitative side. However, these techniques all have certain prerequisites or input requirements that cannot be met when the forecast is being developed for a break-through product.

The innovativeness that distinguishes BTPs from product extensions and incremental innovations makes forecasting their success much more trouble-some. Traditional applications of market-research methods, both quantitative and qualitative, fail to account for the following:

- Consumers are generally not aware of the future needs BTPs are designed to meet and the environments in which they will be used

- Breakthrough products often have applications beyond those initially envi-sioned. The developers may be unaware of the needs the product can serve, the potential customer makeup, or the environments in which it will be used

- The technologies on which the products are based are in the evolutionary phase

- Breakthrough products are unlike anything currently available in the market, resulting in an absence of historical data on which to base projections

- The success of BTPs may depend on the pre-existence of necessary infrastruc-ture or support mechanisms, which do not currently exist.

The forecasting problem is compounded by the fact that all of these uncer-tainties interact (Schoemaker, 1995). Thus, any forecast for BTPs must be able to account for technological changes, information diffusion, customer response, competitive reactions, infrastructure support, regulatory/political requirements, and the relationships between all of these factors. This is where existing market-research and -forecasting approaches fail.

As noted above, the lack of historical data (because BTPs are, by definition, unique to the market) makes quantitative models difficult to employ. Further-more, qualitative approaches, which often rely on customer input, are con-strained by the customers' lack of understanding of the needs BTPs will fulfill and by their inability to see beyond their current environment. Customers' famil-iarity and experience with products that already exist often interfere with their ability to understand entirely new products that address unarticulated needs, offer a whole new set of benefits and potential uses, create or expand product cate-gories, and/or create cross-market competition. The Chrysler minivan, for exam-ple, was not based on stated market needs, but on insight into future market trends. Table 14.1 provides a summary of the key characteristics of BTPs that differentiate them from other new products.

There have been attempts over the last few years to improve the success of premarket forecasting for BTPs by finding alternative methods of capturing the customer's voice and purchase intentions. Approaches such as diffusion models, visioning, lead-user analysis (von Hippel, 1989), empathetic design (Leonard-Barton, 1994), customer immersion (Campanelli, 1993), and, most recently, information acceleration (Urban, Weinberg, & Hauser, 1996) have all been applied to the BTP forecasting problem. An analysis of these methodologies (Noori, Deszca, & Munro, 1997) indicates that visioning techniques and infor-

Table 14.1
ATTRIBUTES OF BREAKTHROUGH PRODUCTS

Market/Customer

- New to customer
- Tied to emerging customer trends
- Shift market structures to create new customers (Urban et al., 1996)
- Require customer learning, acculturation, and behavior change (Lynne et al., 1996; Urban et al., 1996)
- Longer diffusion process (Lynne et al., 1996)
- Create or expand a new category and/or create cross-category competition

Product

- Unpredictable evolution (Lynne et al., 1996)
- Exist outside current product hierarchy
- Precede the establishment of a dominant design (Leonard-Barton, 1994; Lynne et al., 1996)
- Offer unique benefits

Technology

- Infrastructure creation or change may be necessary (Lynne et al., 1996; Urban et al., 1996)
- Represent or incorporate new, innovative technologies (Lynne et al., 1996; Urban et al., 1996)
- May embody new processes

mation acceleration are the leading market-assessment approaches for use in the development of BTPs. Due to their inherent flexibility, these two methodologies cover a broader range of issues than other approaches and attempt to address matters related to the market, product, and technology categories identified in table 14.1. The other methodologies are more focused on one aspect of the product development process. For example, lead-user analysis, empathetic design, and customer immersion all largely concentrate on market-category issues and are primarily concerned with the interpretation and incorporation of the customer's voice into the development process. While the inclusion of the customer's voice is very important, the development of BTPs also requires the consideration of other issues and variables.

THE NEXT GENERATION: AN UMBRELLA APPROACH

What is required for the development of useful, premarket forecasts for BTPs is not entirely new techniques or complicated modeling approaches, but rather an extension of current methodologies employed around a new frame of thinking. Rather than basing the BTP forecasts on existing markets and customers, companies should start in the future at their desired state and work backward to develop the products, markets, and infrastructure/regulatory approvals necessary to link that future to the present. This process requires the implementation of a three-stage technique comprised of scenario analysis, backcasting, and continuous monitoring, integrated under a single approach to product development. In essence, this is an "umbrella" approach to BTP development that combines and integrates the strengths of various tools into one comprehensive methodology (Noori, Deszca, & Munro, 1997).

The umbrella methodology represents a disciplined approach to the ongoing development of market and competitive intelligence (CI) concerning new products and services. By definition, it asks managers to get outside their existing frames of reference and think broadly about what is possible, what would be required to turn such possibilities into reality, where the risks lie, and where relevant information resides. It is a process that advocates the incorporation and integration of information from diverse sources in ways that make it possible to monitor developments in real time and make adjustments to scenarios, critical-path activities, and ongoing initiatives.

Each stage of the umbrella approach to BTP development collects essential information that is useful on its own, but is even more powerful when linked to the other two stages. In the scenario-analysis stage, managers determine how the future might look under various assumptions and use these scenarios to limit the range of future uncertainty. The next stage, backcasting, is used to determine what would have to happen, over time, to increase the likelihood of the scenario becoming a reality, thus developing action-oriented pathways between the present and the future. Continuous monitoring, which takes place during the entire product-development cycle, allows firms to recognize and influence which of their defined futures is unfolding. Together, these elements comprise a BTP "forecasting" process. It can be implemented at the point of ideation, evolved over time, actively monitored, and utilized for decision-making purposes.

This framework can incorporate a number of tools as information inputs, including many of the traditional market-forecasting techniques described earlier. The scope of inquiry depends upon the budget, the nature of breakthrough product, its stage of development, and the commitment of the individual firm to this disciplined approach to market assessment. Because this is an information-based approach, it relies on the abilities of managers and their employees to systematically and effectively collect, analyze, and act on new information. This approach is also dependent on the existence of a flexible product-development and -introduction process, which can incorporate changes in market information in an effective and timely manner (McWilliams, 1996).

Managing Information Costs: Secondary Sources

The proposed model benefits from primary information that is firm and product specific, such as that related to product-design issues and customer input. However, secondary information sources can prove very useful for the purposes of monitoring developments related to socioeconomics, technology, products, and competitors, and as a supplement to ensure objectivity and consistency

(Ginter & Duncan, 1990). For example, current and forecasted values for general economic, social, political, and technological variables are accessible from government publications, as well as those of other organizations that conduct research in these areas. Even competitive analysis can be undertaken using only secondary data (see Wang [1995] for an illustration).

Thus a great deal of the information required to implement the umbrella methodology can be quite easily collected from secondary sources. This is particularly true in today's "information age," which is characterized by the breadth of timely information available on the Internet and through on-line research databases. The value of secondary information is clearly illustrated in the Motorola case example given below.

IMPLEMENTING THE UMBRELLA APPROACH TO BTP DEVELOPMENT: HOW IT WORKS

The umbrella approach to BTP development is more about learning a new way of conceptualizing and managing market information than learning new modeling techniques or complex algorithms. As information is collected and processed through each of the three key stages, the firm gains a greater level of awareness about the factors that will facilitate and inhibit the successful development and launch of BTPs. In the description provided below, the development of the Motorola cellular telephone is used to illustrate how the umbrella methodology is implemented. This case example is provided for illustration purposes only and is based on secondary information about past events. The depiction of the implementation process will demonstrate how the approach could be used for BTPs in the future.

Stage One: Scenario Analysis

Scenario analysis has gained a significant amount of exposure and support in its application to long-range planning (Schoemaker, 1995). For a BTP, this approach asks managers to imagine different worlds where, as a result of various sets of customers' future requirements, alternative versions of the product would be successful. The products are differentiated from one another on the basis of the needs they address through their technical attributes and functions.

Scenario analysis forces managers to consider the factors influencing their current environment and to project how these will behave in the future. Areas of influence can primarily be classified under one of five headings: economic, social, political, technological, and internal.

The attempt at forecasting these behaviors will result in the identification of either key trends or areas of uncertainty, and will help to define the future customer needs the product must be designed to meet. Trends are a result of those influences whose future behavior can be predicted with some degree of confidence, and therefore will be consistent across all future scenarios. The uncertainties, on the other hand, represent those aspects of future behavior that have

Table 14.2
MOTOROLA KEY INFLUENCES

Influence	Trend	Uncertainty
The demand for mobile radiotelephone service was growing rapidly. Overcrowding of the radio spectrum was leading to increased dissatisfaction with the existing service.	√	
The boundaries between the different applications of radio-communications service were blurring and beginning to overlap.	√	
Sales of portable products (two-way radios and pagers) would continue to exceed those of mobile units, and microelectronics technology will continue to advance.		√
The trend toward more-open economies was expanding access to global markets.		√
Will the (American) Federal Communications Commission (FCC) finalize allocation of the radio spectrum among the competing uses such that radio common carriers have sufficient access?		√
Will the FCC take longer than five years to finalize the allocation of the spectrum?		√
The market structure of the wireless-communications industry was essentially a duopoly (American Telegraph and Telephone [AT&T] and Motorola) and concern with preserving competition was growing.	√	
The FCC was struggling with alternative allocations of the radio spectrum for a number of competing uses (television, police, taxis, radio communication).	√	
Will the market for mobile and portable radiotelephones extend beyond the existing commercial and industrial markets?		√
Will the cellular telephone with the most features possible (and therefore a higher price) optimize customer adoption?		√

values or outcomes that are completely unknown and therefore mark the true distinctions between the scenarios (Schoemaker, 1995). The result of the analysis is the "product possibility domain," which contains alternative versions of the BTP, each meeting a particular set of customer needs and evolving from each of the scenarios.

In the Motorola case example, there was a number of factors at work during the development period that influenced the future market for the product. Some of these key influences and their role as a trend or uncertainty are outlined in table 14.2.

In addition, a full review of Motorola's operating environment at the time would have provided additional business-trend-assessment data for use in scenario determination (see McWilliams [1996] for a full review). By combining

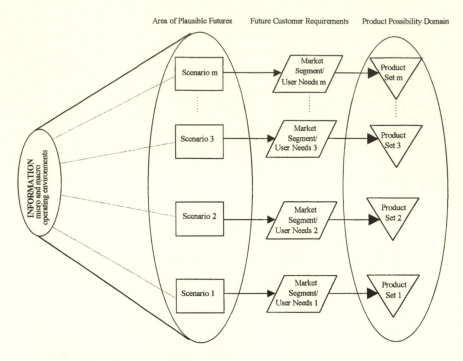

FIGURE 14.1 Product possibility map.

these trends with possible uncertainty outcomes, future scenarios can be derived, each meeting different sets of customer needs and implying different product definitions (see figure 14.1).

The process of scenario generation is not complicated, although it does involve a great deal of effort and thought on the part of the participants. Schoemaker (1995) provides a general outline of the steps necessary to generate a feasible and consistent set of scenarios; figure 14.1 illustrates these scenarios. Various tools have been identified in the literature that can be used at each stage of the scenario-analysis procedure to enable efficient and complete information-collection. This matrix should include variables that are internal to the firm, as well as those that characterize the firm's operating environment.

The process of identifying the relevant variables and their relationships should be based on a group/team approach. This team should include the decision-makers at the firm, other members of the firm whom the outcome may affect, and consultants from outside the organization who are specialists in the various areas of influence (e.g., a sociologist, an economist, a political scientist, a technologist). In addition, the firm should view its customers and suppliers (and others) as potential sources of information (Schoemaker, 1995). Within this team construction, there are a number of approaches available to achieve a consensus on the nature of the various relationships. For example, methods such as Delphi and Nominal Group Process (NGP) and tools such as Decision Support

Systems (DSS) and computer-supported cooperative workstations may be very useful in conducting this exercise.

One point that firms should bear in mind, however, is that when an odd number of scenarios is provided (e.g., 3 or 5), there is a tendency to gravitate toward the middle scenario, since it often represents a balance between two extremes. In order to avoid this, firms should consider an even number of scenarios (Wang, 1995). Additionally, there may be innumerable scenario alternatives that the firm deems as possible. Scenario analysis is concerned with limiting that number to those that are plausible and that clearly represent separate end-states. It is not useful for the firm to consider pathways that lead to relatively similar end-states, because the outcomes would not be sufficiently different to warrant the analysis.

The process of scenario analysis enables the company to bound its possible futures, and therefore reduce the uncertainty inherent in the long-range BTP-development process (Schoemaker, 1995). That is, by specifically delineating possible and plausible outcomes, firms can limit the number of future possibilities to be considered. Furthermore, it allows managers to make more informed decisions by accounting for a greater range of possibilities than the single "most likely" outcome produced by traditional forecasting methods (Wang, 1995).

Stage Two: Backcasting

Following the construction of the product-possibility domain, consisting of "m" possible alternative scenarios, the next step deals with *backcasting*. Backcasting, a normative approach that starts with the future and works back toward the present, was originally used in developing energy policy (Robinson, 1990). More recently, it has been applied to strategic management and competitive intelligence (CI) (Wang, 1995). The purpose of backcasting is to define a path between the present and a possible future, so as to determine what steps must be taken or what events must be realized in order for that future to take place. Backcasting works by starting at a particular future scenario and defining backward, step by step, what outcomes must be fulfilled or what factors must exist in order to link the future with the present (Godet, 1986).

Backcasting analysis allows us to better understand how environmental factors must evolve in order for a particular product to be successful "n years" in the future. The pathway between ideation and product introduction is a function of the end product—the future world in which it is assessed to be successful—and the current environment. Thus different versions of the product may or may not incorporate the same steps necessary to reach the alternative end-points. Figure 14.2 illustrates the backcasting path linking the Dyna Tac 8000x (which was subsequently the first cellular phone made publicly available) with the original ideation stage.

Stage Three: Continuous Monitoring of the Environment

The value of the umbrella methodology over time is dependent on the process of continuous monitoring or scanning of the identified critical environmental fac-

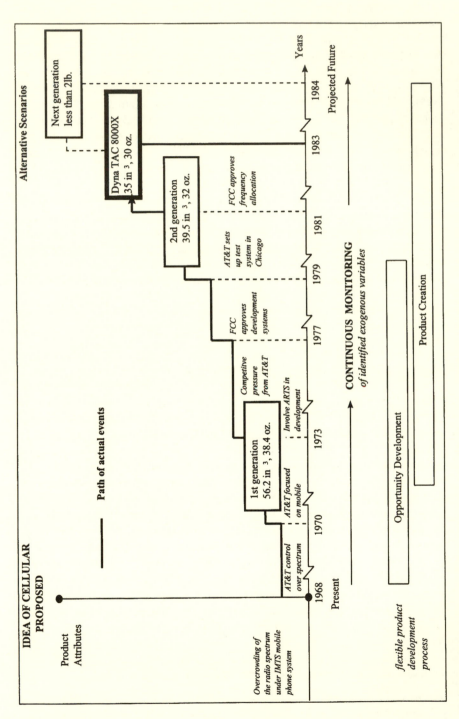

Figure 14.2 Diagrammatic simulation of the Motorola cellular phone.

tors. The signals emanating from the general market and macroenvironment, as well as from customers, must be monitored at each stage of the firm's progression toward the possible future end-points in order to reveal which future is unfolding (Schoemaker, 1995). Continuous and dynamic monitoring enables firms to incorporate the most current information available into their product-development processes and make decisions accordingly.

This process is dependent on the existence of a flexible product-development process, as described by Iansiti (1995), whereby firms "gather and rapidly respond to new knowledge about technical and market information *as a project evolves*." This type of BTP-development process is necessary in order to take advantage of the information backcasting reveals.

The integrative nature of the umbrella methodology provides benefits over using a single approach. Taking advantage of a number of techniques helps enrich the information available in the model and, therefore, improves its accuracy. This approach can take advantage of existing approaches (such as information acceleration, empathetic design, probe and learn) during different stages of the development process, allowing the company to cultivate an increasingly sophisticated sense of customer needs. In addition, the umbrella methodology can be constructed upon a base of secondary information. Therefore resource constraints, which might otherwise impede the quality of the forecast made, are more easily accommodated. This inherent flexibility allows the developers to take advantage of the most appropriate and accessible market-sensing tool at different points in time and integrates that information under one comprehensive methodology.

HOW THE UMBRELLA APPROACH ADDRESSES THE PROBLEMS OF BTP DEVELOPMENT

The benefits realized by employing the umbrella approach to BTP development are based on three primary characteristics of the process: First, it raises the level of awareness within the firm, alerting management to changes in the environment that may impact the product-development process. It also creates an awareness of how environmental trends and uncertainties can influence the needs customers will have in the future, and indicates what changes in the product-development strategy will be necessary to meet those needs (table 14.3). Second, it provides a systematic approach that clearly maps the necessary steps from the successful product introduction point back to the present. Therefore it reduces the uncertainty associated with developing BTPs without relying solely on forecasting techniques that are often ill-suited to the task. Finally, the integrative nature of this approach enhances competitive and market intelligence by providing benefits over using a single forecasting technique. Taking advantage of a number of techniques helps to increase the information in the model and therefore improves its accuracy.

Table 14.3
ADDRESSING THE CHALLENGES IN BTP DEVELOPMENT

BTP Development Challenge	How the Umbrella Approach Addresses the Challenge
Customers are not aware of the needs BTPs will meet in the future	• By identifying key trends and uncertainties, management becomes aware of what customer future needs might be • By recognizing that needs are at least partially conditioned by environmental factors • By not relying solely on customer input, which may be biased by current experiences
Changing market structures implies that products may have more than one application	• By imagining different futures where the product can be successful in one or more markets and forcing managers to consider alternatives
Customer learning is required	• By identifying where current customer knowledge is deficient and allowing the firm to take action to educate customers
Changes in customer behavior may be necessary	• By allowing the company to see what behavior changes are necessary for product success under each scenario • By realizing that once necessary changes are identified, the company can influence the environment and customers by lobbying, advertising, etc.
Introduction depends on the existence of an enabling infrastructure	• By clarifying what the infrastructure needs will be • By alerting the company to possible ways of ensuring the infrastructure is put in place
Competition is becoming more and more intense	• By alerting the company to actions of competitors that may be signals of the strategic path the competitors are following • By alerting the company to indirect competitors who may otherwise have been ignored
Government intervention and regulations may affect the success of a new technology that is being introduced	• By raising the awareness as to the political movements that may impact on product introduction and help manage the lobbying and/or regulatory approval process

HOLES AND LEAKS IN THE UMBRELLA: HOW TO RECOGNIZE AND AVOID THEM

There is a number of issues that must be recognized and addressed by the firm in order to ensure that the umbrella approach is successfully implemented. Furthermore, because this methodology is an on-going process rather than an event, these issues must be continuously reviewed to ensure that the quality of the process is maintained.

Information Management

The umbrella approach is an information-based framework. It essentially provides a systematic guideline for collecting, analyzing, and utilizing information to improve and guide the development of BTPs. The real issue for the firm, however, is to decide what information will be most useful and on which variables it will collect information. Consequently, firms must be selective, since more will not necessarily be better, particularly in the face of cost and time constraints.

It is not enough to simply collect information—it also must be assessed, integrated into the development process, and used. Managers and employees must develop the skills and methods necessary to effectively and efficiently manage the information-collection and -analysis process. This may require, for example, the creation of a database where information can be stored, retrieved, and analyzed quickly and accurately. It may also require the creation of a new position within the company that is responsible for continuously monitoring the environment for new, relevant information and assembling and disseminating it to decision-makers—precisely the role of the CI specialist.

Creating and Utilizing an Expert Team

The quality of the team of experts is critical to the success of this approach, because it is responsible for identifying and analyzing the relevant trends and uncertainties, and for generating the end-state scenarios. Consequently, it is important for the firm to create a team that has the right mix of competencies/perspectives and that can function effectively.

There is a number of well-know difficulties in team-based activities that must be managed (Noori, 1995). For example, members may be geographically dispersed; there may be tensions across different functions; and some members may be more dominating than others. Risk propensities have been known to shift and decision-quality impaired if the process is not managed effectively. As a result, a concerted effort through selection and team building must be taken to ensure that the core team performs effectively, particularly given its key role in the development process.

Time

In the past, the new-product-development literature has focused a great deal of research on the issue of *time*. The goal has typically been to reduce measures such as "time to market" and "time to break even." This approach inherently views time as being controllable by the firm. However, in the case of BTPs, many of the factors that influence the time necessary to develop and introduce a product are outside the firm's control. Therefore timelines cannot be set in absolute terms, but rather must be flexible and adjustable (in both directions).

Firms can, however, still attempt to influence those forces that impact on time in order to change the product-development timeline. The pro-active and environmentally aware nature of the umbrella approach implies that firms should concentrate on bringing about the realization of the factors necessary to reach the desired end-state.

ACKNOWLEDGMENT

The first author wishes to thank the Research Committee of the Hong Kong Polytechnic University for the support of this work.

REFERENCES

Campanelli, M. (1993). "Taking a Long Look at Focus Groups," *Sales and Marketing Management* 145(4): 9.

Ginter, P.M., and W.J. Duncan. (1990). "Macro-environmental Analysis for Strategic Management," *Long-Range Planning* 23(6): 91–100.

Godet, M. (1986). "Introduction to la Prospective," *Futures* 18(2): 134–57.

Iansiti, M. (1995). "Shooting the Rapids: Managing Product Development in Turbulent Environments," *California Management Review* 38(1): 37–58.

Leonard-Barton, D. (1994). "Empathetic Design and Experimental Modeling: Explorations into Really New Products," *Market Science Institute Report* (94-124): 19–21.

Lynne, G.S., J.G. Morone, and A.S. Paulson. (1996). "Marketing and Discontinuous Innovation: The Probe and Learn Process," *California Management Review* 38(3): 8–37.

Martin, J. (1995). "Ignore Your Customer," *Fortune* 131(8): 121–26.

McWilliams, B. (1996). "Choosing the 'Right' Breakthrough Product/Service: An Application of Scenario Analysis and Backcasting." M.A. thesis, Wilfrid Laurier University, Waterloo, Ontario.

Noori, H. (1995). "The Design of an Integrated Group Decision Support System for Technology Assessment," *R&D Management* 25(3): 309–22.

Noori, H., G. Deszca, and H. Munro. (1997). "Developing Breakthrough Products: Challenges and Options for Market Assessment." Working paper, Wilfrid Laurier University, Waterloo, Ontario.

Robinson, J.B. (1990). "Futures Under a Glass: A Recipe for People Who Hate to Predict," *Futures* 22(8): 820–42.

Schoemaker, P.J.H. (1995). "Scenario Planning: A Tool for Strategic Thinking," *Sloan Management Review* 36(2): 25–40.

Urban, G.L., B.D. Weinberg, and J.R. Hauser. (1996). "Premarket Forecasting of Really New Products," *Journal of Marketing* 60(1): 47–60.

von Hippel, E. (1989). "New Product Ideas from 'Lead Users,'" *Research/Technology Management* 32(3): 24–27.

Wang, C.K. (1995). "Organizational Competence Analysis in Strategy Formulation: An Application to the Information Technology Industry." Doctoral thesis, University of Waterloo, Waterloo, Ontario.

15

The Need for Business Intelligence Tools to Provide Business Intelligence Solutions

Beth Ringdahl

INTRODUCTION

The competitive advantage that can be gained by the company that is best able to manage its information resources cannot be underestimated. Business intelligence (BI) tools have provided strategic advantages in allowing better decision-making in areas such as marketing, customer analysis, and operations. Competitive intelligence (CI) professionals can utilize these tools to accurately analyze and interpret industry trends and competitor activities. Existing tools allow an understanding of what's driving the business; however, the current development of a new generation of tools is necessary to enable modeling and forecasting that provides actionable intelligence that directly impacts the bottom line. This chapter provides a nontechnical analysis of ways that business users and statisticians can collaborate to make more effective, business-oriented BI applications, and insight into why past systems have failed. It also provides a brief discussion of new technologies that will allow greater precision in understanding customer behavior and other internal and external factors that affect the business.

THE NEED FOR BUSINESS INTELLIGENCE (BI) SYSTEMS

Tyson (1998) elaborates on the necessity for a "perpetual strategy" in managing an organization's customers, competitors, suppliers, strategic alliances, future opportunities, and future threats in order to maximize competitive knowledge.

Table 15.1

OPPORTUNITIES IDENTIFIED THROUGH BUSINESS INTELLIGENCE APPLICATIONS

1. Analysis of market trends

2. Customer profitability and segmentation

3. Target marketing and campaign management

4. Customer churn analysis or retention

5. Credit risk management

6. Fraud and abuse prevention

7. Analysis for cross-selling (introduction of new products) and up-selling (increased quantities) and distribution channels

8. Collection analysis

9. Category management

10. Retail-network management, inventory management and logistics

11. Product/portfolio profitability

12. Cost analysis

13. Customer service

14. Streamlining business and manufacturing operations

15. Customized products and services

Source: Adapted from Saarenvirta (1998).

Increased competition and rapid changes in the marketplace demand rapid and effective knowledge-based decision-making. Statistical tools that can enhance this process provide a competitive advantage. A large portion of the current literature focuses on data mining, a component of Decision Support Systems (DSS). Therefore many of the examples used in this chapter are taken from the data-mining literature.

Business intelligence applications have predominantly been used to describe and explain a company's business by analyzing trends associated with the market, customers and competitors, identifying causes for changes in revenues or costs, and forecasting demand. Table 15.1 outlines the major business opportunities provided through effective information management by BI tools. Table 15.2 outlines major industries that have successfully used BI tools and the opportunities these applications have provided.

THE GAP BETWEEN BUSINESS-USERS AND STATISTICIANS

Since business intelligence software is still evolving, a gap exists between the needs and understanding of the business user and the statistician who developed the models (table 15.3). Originally, these tools were seen as magical solutions in which data could be inputted, and out would pour meaningful, useful relationships. In reality, relationships are much more complex. Mathematical models are

Table 15.2

BUSINESS INTELLIGENCE TOOLS: INDUSTRIES AND OPPORTUNITIES

Opportunities	Financial Services	Telecommunications	Utilities	Insurance	Health Care	Retail	Hospitality/Resort
1. Market trend analysis	✓	✓		✓		✓	✓
2. Segmentation	✓	✓	✓	✓	✓	✓	✓
3. Target marketing	✓	✓	✓	✓	✓	✓	✓
4. Churn analysis	✓	✓	✓	✓			
5. Credit risk management	✓			✓		✓	
6. Fraud prevention	✓			✓	✓		
7. Cross- and up-selling	✓	✓		✓	✓	✓	✓
8. Collection analysis	✓	✓		✓		✓	
9. Category management	✓	✓		✓		✓	✓
10. Retail network management						✓	✓
11. Product profitability	✓	✓	✓	✓	✓	✓	✓
12. Cost analysis	✓	✓	✓	✓	✓	✓	✓
13. Customer service	✓	✓	✓	✓	✓	✓	✓
14. Streamlining operations				✓			
15. Customized service	✓					✓	✓

Table 15.3
BUSINESS-USER–STATISTICIAN GAP

Needs of the Business-User	Understanding of the Business-User	Gap Existing Between Business-User and Statistician
1. Built-in understanding of the business problem	Thorough knowledge of the market allows accurate formulation of the problem	Statistician emphasizes technology and perceives a statistical modeling problem that may require analysis by means of a sophisticated skill set
2. Ease of use	Data processing and results must be formulated in business terms	Commonality of user terminology and technical terminology may be required
3. Data must be easily accessible	Data warehouse must be practical, scalable, and allow easy integration for relational database products	Data often requires translation from varied sources and formats
4. Accurate, meaningful interpretations must be generated for business insight	Output in terms of sales, revenues, costs, or profitability	Statistician's view as statistical parameters used to generate complex models
5. Practical, accurate reports are required for information dissemination	Questions must be answered without understanding database complexities	Applications should provide powerful, analytical capabilities with a simple user interface

readily generated; however, it is only by applying sound business principles that decisionable and meaningful insights can be found. End-users should be consulted in developing BI tools in order for statisticians to understand business processes from the end-user's perspective, as well as understand the environment in which the system will be applied (Anand, 1998). Business-users will have an inherent knowledge about the data set, and the incorporation of this knowledge will improve the efficiency and effectiveness of analysis.

Tools must be designed to provide decision-making-process simplicity. The objectives in using these tools include:

- Providing access to critical data obtainable in a format suitable for decision-making needs
- Analyzing trends, highlights, or exceptions associated with the market, customers and competitors
- Understanding the economics that drive changes in sales revenues or costs. This knowledge identifies key variables and economic opportunities that form the basis of new competitive advantages
- Forecasting sales revenues and/or costs
- Providing actionable intelligence to improve the business.

Tools should simplify representations to the business-user without reducing the complexity of the model or the power of the analysis. Business reports should be generated to improve overall understanding without the need to understand database complexities. Summary reports that quickly identify trends can be produced with the objective of "perspective not precision" (Tyson, 1998). For example, the Cognos Corporation identifies an "Information Sweet Spot," recognizing that information-value plateaus at a certain level, and that it is not economically advantageous to delve any deeper (Cognos Corporation, 1999).

THE GAP FROM DESCRIPTION TO PRESCRIPTION

Khabaza and Mallen (1998) describe the "chasm of representation" as the gap that exists between data and the business reality it represents. Older custom applications required extensive involvement by the information systems (IS) department and an extensive knowledge of structured query language (SQL). Newer applications are more user-friendly and allow models to be generated across multiple dimensions using intuitive navigation and investigation. The evolution of business intelligence applications is outlined in table 15.4.

The early generation of data-processing tools allowed businesses to access data and provide status reports that could be used to more effectively run routine

Table 15.4

**STEPS INVOLVED IN THE EVOLUTION OF
DATA-MINING/BUSINESS INTELLIGENCE TOOLS**

Evolutionary Stage	Business Question	Enabling Technologies	Characteristics
Data collection (1960s)	"What was my total revenue in the last five years?"	Computers, tapes, disks	Retrospective, static data delivery
Data access (1980s)	"What were unit sales per state last month?"	Relational databases (RDBMS), Structured Query Language (SQL)	Retrospective, dynamic data delivery at record level
Date warehousing and decision support (1990s)	"What were unit sales per state last month? Drill down to individual cities."	On-line analytic processing (OLAP), multidimensional databases, data warehouses	Retrospective, dynamic data delivery at multiple levels
Data-mining/business intelligence tools (emerging today)	"What's likely to happen in a particular city next month? Why?"	Advanced algorithms, multiprocessor computers, massive databases	Prospective, proactive information delivery
Future	"What interventions can be made to improve the situation?"	User-friendly and business-oriented interfaces and applications	

Source: Adapted from Thearling (1998).

business operations. As more powerful tools were developed, insights were gained into what factors were driving the business. The latest tools allow interpretation, modeling, and forecasting that provide opportunities to improve the business by incorporating this analysis into the corporate strategy. However, a great gap exists between the ability to describe situations and the necessary analysis to prescribe a solution. Mathematical models can be used to effectively identify and describe problems. It is only by filtering models through rational business rules and logic that insightful actionable knowledge can be used to present opportunities that improve the business. Inherent organizational knowledge, industry knowledge, and the personal knowledge and intuition of business professionals will be more effectively incorporated through collaboration, mathematical modeling, and forecasting tools.

WHY PROJECTS HAVE FAILED

A 1997 U.S. report (Rao, 1998) estimated that 70 percent of U.S. data-warehouse projects experienced disappointing results due to unpredicted costs, delayed timeframes, limited return on investment, and the amount of practical information generated. Unexpected costs arise as a result of the great deal of technical expertise required to analyze and understand the data, build and test models, and allow contingencies for technical failures. Time delays may occur, since high levels of organizational commitment are required to standardize data-systems that are often implemented across functional areas with very different strategic goals. Return on investment may be disappointing, since the overall project can often take years to implement, in which time the business environment, key personnel, or management preferences may change. Disappointments in the amount of practical information generated are especially evident where objectives were improperly defined or where analysis indicated significant trends without the capabilities to explain why they were happening. Three major reasons for project failures are:

- *Underestimating the complexities* of effectively establishing and implementing all stages in the business intelligence structure
- *Misinterpretation of data and trends* generated by business intelligence tools
- *Divergent interests* of the various stakeholders, including the statistician or applications developer, tool vendors, consultants, and the business user.

The scope of each of these three reasons for project failure and their possible solutions are as follows:

Underestimating the Complexities

An over-enthusiastic corporate culture looking for a magic solution may underestimate the complexities of establishing a data-warehouse and subsequent analytical systems. Management may become enamored with "tools" rather than business objectives. Technology implementation must fit into overall organizational structure, including human resources, culture, management preferences, and existing information systems. Business-users must be involved in all stages of system design and implementation in order to formulate appropriate questions and provide viable solutions. Projects that are initiated with no clear business objective are vulnerable to failure. External factors such as changes in the business environment can introduce complexities and change the relevancy of the original objectives of the project.

SOLUTIONS:

- Conduct assessments of the needs of the entire organization and design a total system that is practical and scalable

- Management must foster corporate buy-in and ensure that users at all levels have some say in its development and implementation. This may allow the system to be more effectively integrated into the existing business process with minimal disturbance to existing operations

- Conduct a smaller pilot project to determine if expectations are realistic

- Ensure that realistic budgets and human resources are allocated for the on-going sustainability of the data warehouse, analytical tools, and dissemination of results.

Misinterpretation of Data

Misinterpretation of data and incorrect assumptions can result in ineffective decision-making and negative consequences to the business process (Makulowich, 1997). The data-gathering process may be subject to inherent errors and artifacts of the business process. Complex results are not always understood or interpreted correctly. It is human nature to occasionally fixate on false patterns, or neglect patterns that are real but seem unbelievable. Skills in statistics, database management, and business analysis contribute equally to the accurate analysis and interpretation of results.

SOLUTIONS:

- Structure business problems to answer the right questions

- Collaborate with tool vendors to establish the optimal system and provide the simplest, most effective solution

- Data-gathering process must be planned and appropriate for the organization

- Provide adequate staff training.

Divergent Stakeholder Interests

Although end-users, applications developers, tool vendors, and consultants all have a vested interest in the success of the industry, the downfalls associated with the BI technology have received a great deal of publicity. Users blame the technology, not its implementation. Application developers defend their technology but blame its implementation. Tool vendors want to sell the magic solution. They may downplay the effort and skill required to effectively implement a system that will produce high-quality results, wanting their products to be perceived as user-friendly business solutions. In the past, individual software vendors were reluctant to provide an end-to-end solution encompassing database support and integration of applications. Consultants or service providers want to be perceived as experts in solving complex mathematical models. It is in their best interest to encourage the perception that the process is too mathematically challenging for the average user.

SOLUTIONS:

- Collaboration will foster greater communication for the development of an optimal system

- Advances in developing a common terminology will increase understanding between parties

- The organization itself must be knowledgeable and cognizant of needs and choices in implementing the system

- Greater numbers of successful projects will foster trust among the various players.

BRIDGING THE GAPS

Many factors should be considered in order to optimize the ability of BI tools to provide valuable information for strategic decision-making. Major factors outlined below are discussed further in the following section:

- The need for teamwork and collaboration
- The need for clearly defined objectives
- The need for complete, accurate, accessible, and integrated databases
- CRISP-DM, a CRoss-Industry Standard Process for Data Mining, provides a common reference standard for establishing projects.

Teamwork and Collaboration

Systems should be developed by a team of professionals to meet the user's systems design and applications needs. The team should consist of the chief information officer (CIO), business and industry experts, data-mining practitioners, applications developers, and the ultimate system end-users. The CIO must provide vision for the organization, since its structure and culture will determine how the system will be received and utilized. By working with end-users, statisticians could learn to employ simple and business-oriented language to describe analytical processes. A common vocabulary between business users and software developers will demystify complexities for both parties. Systems can be designed to more effectively input financial information; statisticians should learn to think in terms of "maximizing profit" rather than "minimizing Root Mean Square (RMS) error" (Thearling, 1998). Enhancements in the user interface would allow more simplified analysis, allowing technology to become invisible. Simple design features could allow the user to make trade-offs between model precision and time available for the analysis. The user could judge whether or not he or she is most interested in overall trends or precision of the model. By working together, there is enhanced user confidence and familiarity with the system. It is important to record and deploy new expertise gained from information-sharing to ensure that future projects benefit from the experience.

Clearly Defined Objectives

Another key to system development is to systematically identify key business issues and their dynamics and determine what solutions are needed. Industry and business experts must effectively communicate objectives and parameters for modeling purposes. Focusing on how the business process is structured should increase efficiency and the likelihood of tangible benefits. If business problems are inadequately formulated, patterns emerge that may not be defined by any relevant trends. The tool must be effectively integrated into the existing business process so that it can be effectively implemented with minimal disturbance to existing operations.

Precise definitions of objectives may assist in taking the steps from understanding what is driving the business to determining ways to improve the business. Masand and Mani (1998) have developed a system known as CHAMP (CHurn Analysis, Modeling and Prediction), an automated system to predict customer behavior on a large scale. They recognized the need for the system not only to identify churners, but also to provide insight into what intervention could be made to effectively reduce the churn rate. Although BI tools can effectively describe the characteristics of churners, marketing needs to know why people churn in the hopes of preventing it in the future.

Database Development

Companies are spending millions of dollars developing data-warehouses that are the heart of the system. Alliances with suppliers and customers, as well as management's need to have an overall integrated view of the business and industry, result in the need for flexibility in supporting diverse data-sources. Data-gathering must be systematic and practical, since data is collected from varied sources and formats. The collection and storage of data must be driven by decision-making needs. Databases must be free of errors to prevent idiosyncrasies. They should be designed to allow seamless integration of local files and remote databases. Systems need to be scalable to handle mass volumes of data.

The Standard Process Model for Data Mining

The establishment of a data-mining project can be a formidable task. John (1998) outlines the benefits of establishing a common data-mining process model.

CRISP-DM was developed with the objective of increasing the use and effectiveness of data mining in Europe. The process focuses on the end-user rather than the technology. "It is intended to lean more towards describing *what* general tasks should be performed rather than *how* they should be done. The developed model is intended to be industry and tool neutral" (John, 1998).

A detailed outline presents the normal course of a standard data-mining process and provides a common reference for all stakeholders to discuss data-mining projects. It provides an overview of the lifecycle of a data-mining project and various tasks that need to be implemented during the following six phases:

- *Business understanding* to define project objectives in terms of a data-mining problem
- *Data understanding* that encompasses data collection, analysis of data quality, and familiarization with the data-set
- *Data preparation* includes data-cleanup and transformation for analysis
- *Modeling* techniques and parameters are selected and calibrated to generate optimal values
- *Evaluation* of the model and results to ensure that they answer the original business objectives
- *Deployment* of the knowledge in a usable form.

The model also provides guidelines and solutions to problems that occur in project management. Benefits from the use of the model include the development of projects that are more efficient, accurate, time efficient, and less costly. Better planning results in increased confidence for data relevancy and interpretation of results. Greater numbers of successful projects will lead to increased adoption of the technology by other organizations.

How Companies Can Benefit in the Future

Business intelligence tools allow managers to model the complexities of today's business environments and maximize the return on their investment in information technology. As interpretation of trends in corporate information becomes more accurate, companies will compete more effectively. Intangible benefits are numerous—they include increased business flexibility and knowledge of customer behavior. Employees may be more motivated, since information is readily accessible at all levels for better decision-making.

The evolution of current BI tools has made great progress in fulfilling the needs of the business-user outlined in table 15.4. The ultimate goal is to design software that encompasses a mass audience with a wide range of user abilities, providing a user-friendly interface that is web-enabled and automated to maximize productivity and uses intelligent agents to assist in the sort-and-query process (Thearling, 1998). Systems are being designed that can be directly accessed by business users without the need for IS-support staff or statistical analysts for modeling and interpretation. Software companies with different applications capabilities have formed alliances to offer end-to-end solutions. IBM offers a complete set of tools for the entire business process (White, 2000). Applications developers are recognizing the value of vertical applications that are designed to meet the needs of a particular industry.

New technologies are being developed that will result in product enhancements for more powerful analysis geared to end-users. Software applications are being developed that better incorporate time-series for predictive modeling. "Wizards" can be incorporated to guide users so they can stay on track with less effort. The Internet is providing a new paradigm in the way information is accessed and shared. The Internet can provide real-time data that will be extremely useful for applications such as direct marketing. Web access will allow suppliers and customers to access and input data throughout the supply chain. Some experts project that in time, databases and business transactions will become synonymous (Makulowich, 1997).

Knowledge management has been used extensively to enhance customer relationships by better understanding customer behavior and changes in market conditions. It would be valuable to incorporate more qualitative data into business modeling. New interactive platforms such as call centers, the Internet, kiosk systems, and interactive television will result in massive amounts of data generated through customer interactions. New developments in text mining will allow customer feedback to be transcribed and analyzed. Speech patterns and emotion detectors can recognize the mood of customers. Consumer reactions can be traced by following navigational paths throughout a website, and sites can be designed accordingly. Although still in its infancy, these technologies present great opportunities to listen and act upon customers' needs and suggestions.

An emerging revolution in data mining is the development of intelligent agents that conduct environmental scanning. These agents can gather, filter, classify, and analyze information. Knowledge agents have the ability to transform data into meaningful information, generally through data-mining principles. An example of this technology is "automated alerts," which find managerially important information within a huge database (Bayer, 1998). Alerts identify changes in the competitive environment that a business-user can act upon if they are deemed to be significant. This technology is especially useful for an industry such as the packaged-goods market in which thousands of events need to be tracked simultaneously. Users can be alerted to short-term market-share changes, introduction of new competitive items, and competitor pricing and promotional activities. However, users can be overwhelmed by the amount of data generated in these analyses. Intelligent information-delivery systems can analyze and prioritize the significance of the alerts. Once again, this system relies on key inputs from business-users to define effective decision criteria.

REFERENCES

Anand, T. (1998). "Skills and Tasks of a Data-Mining Practitioner," Position Papers from the Workshop, *Keys to the Commercial Success of Data Mining*, ed. K. Thearling and R. Stein, August 31 <http://www3.shore.net/~kht/workshop/papers.htm>.

Bayer, J. (1998). "Automated Alerts," Position Papers from the Workshop, *Keys to the Commercial Success of Data Mining*, ed. K. Thearling and R. Stein, August 31 <http://www3.shore.net/~kht/workshop/papers.htm>.

Cognos Corporation. (1999). *Delivering Warehouse Return on Investment with Business Intelligence*. Cognos Publications.

John, G. (1998). "Letting Business Users Loose," Position Papers from the Workshop, *Keys to the Commercial Success of Data Mining*, ed. K. Thearling and R. Stein, August 31 <http://www3.shore.net/~kht/workshop/papers.htm>.

Khabaza, T., and J. Mallen. (1998). "Hunching, Not Crunching: Data Mining and the Business User," Position Papers from the Workshop, *Keys to the Commercial Success of Data Mining*, ed. K. Thearling and R. Stein, August 31 <http://www3.shore.net/~kht/workshop/papers.htm>.

Makulowich, J. (1997). "Washington Technology On-line," Supplement to the *Washington Post*, October 23 <http://www.wtonline.com>.

Masand, B., and D.R. Mani. (1998). "Beyond Data Mining: Influencing the Business Process," Position Papers from the Workshop, *Keys to the Commercial Success of Data Mining*, ed. K. Thearling and R. Stein, August 31 <http://www3.shore.net/~kht/workshop/papers.htm>; <http://www.ncr.dk/CRISP>.

Rao, S.S. (1998). "Diaper-beer Syndrome," *Forbes* 161(7): 128–30.

Saarenvirta, G. (1998). "Data Mining to Improve Profitability," *CMA Magazine* 72(2): 9–12.

Thearling, K. (1998). "An Introduction to Data Mining—Discovering Hidden Value in Your Data Warehouse," Pilot Software <http://www3.shore.net/~kht/text/dmwhite/dmwhite.htm>.

Tyson, K.W.M. (1998). "Perpetual Strategy: A 21st Century Essential," *Strategy and Leadership* 26(1): 14–18.

White, C. (2000). "The IBM Business Intelligence Software Solution (Version 3)," Database Associates International. Inc., March <http://www.software.hosting.software.ibm.com>.

Part 4

COMPETITIVE INTELLIGENCE AND ITS APPLICATION IN SPECIFIC CONTEXTS

16

Identifying Competitive Intelligence Priorities in Biotechnology

Jayson Parker

INTRODUCTION

This chapter presents a framework for competitive intelligence (CI) practitioners that will allow them to dynamically modify competitive intelligence systems that are synchronized with product development for biotechnology companies. Such a system must reflect several considerations:

- product-development stage
- stakeholders
- resources.

Stakeholder considerations and the availability of resources are concomitants of the stage of product development. In light of this close linkage, changing stakeholders and resources will be discussed as they impact competitive intelligence needs once industry-relevant characteristics of biotechnology have been explained for the CI practitioner.

RELEVANCE

At issue is an allocation policy of resources to track competitors for biotechnology firms. Biotechnology firms, unlike large pharmaceutical firms, are distinguished by having small market capitalization of typically less than U.S.$200 million (Charette & Lewis, 1998) and no sales revenue (Haseltine, 1998). A CI system for these companies must reflect the virtual absence of professional managers in these firms as well as constraints in financing and staffing. What personnel should be involved with CI and how much time should be spent on CI issues?

Some senior managers have argued that there are no competitors in biotechnology (MacAdam, 1999). What criteria should be used in assessing potential competitors and what classes of sources should be monitored? Is CI only an issue once biotechnology companies have advanced their products into clinical trials?

A central CI issue is the stage of product development. This is a critical determinant of the resources devoted to monitoring different dimensions of the competitive environment. A company close to releasing a drug for general use by the public will have very different competitor concerns than a company still engaged in preclinical research. The stage of product development also impacts the resources available to biotechnology firms, and this must be reflected in a CI framework for establishing priorities.

In the end, the CI practitioner should be aware that competitor information required by biotechnology companies is a function of its product-development stage. The stage of product development exposes the company to different risks in the market. This must be addressed through a flexible system for allocating resources to monitor the firm's competitive sphere.

BIOTECHNOLOGY: OVERVIEW OF INDUSTRY-RELEVANT CHARACTERISTICS FOR COMPETITIVE INTELLIGENCE PRACTITIONERS

Biotechnology firms are not small pharmaceutical firms. Pharmaceutical firms have large product pipelines with a number of drugs at different phases of development. Some of these products are approved for human use and are generating revenue, while others are still subject to basic research. In contrast, biotechnology firms typically have one or a few products in their development pipeline (Haseltine, 1998). This allows analysts to classify these firms based on the stage of development for their most advanced product (Charette & Lewis, 1998). Such a taxonomy may look like table 16.1.

Product development progresses through several stages: preclinical research (animal); clinical trials (3 phases); and drug approval by the relevant regulatory body (the Health Protection Branch in Canada; the Food and Drug Administration in the United States [FDA]). Note that the probability of a new drug reaching the market for human use is less than 1.2 percent. Human testing alone may take 10 years to complete, independent of the time spent in basic research with animals.

Prior to the commencement of clinical trials, a patent must be filed covering the drug treatment in question (Haseltine, 1998; Heller & Eisenberg, 1998). As a result, the technology or drug is now a matter of public record. Further, such patents last 20 years from the time of filing that, on average, gives the company about 10 years following the successful completion of clinical trials to recoup its

Table 16.1

**BIOTECH COMPANY CLASSIFICATION BASED ON THE STATUS
OF THEIR MOST ADVANCED PRODUCT**

Company	Market Capitalization (US$)	Most Advanced Product	Status
Algene Biotech	41 million	Alzheimer gene identification	preclinical
Theratechnologies Inc.	63 million	TH 9506	phase I
Biomara	157 million	Theratope	phase II
Synsorb Biotech	203 million	Synsorb Pk	phase III

Source: Charette and Lewis (1998).

costs, including other projects that have failed, in addition to a profit, all discounted to the present.

Biotechnology companies do not have the resources to conduct their own clinical trials, so this is outsourced to contract research organizations (CROs)—firms that conduct clinical trials on behalf of these resource-starved biotechnology companies. They vary in their effectiveness and may be considered a resource in which biotechnology firms compete for access (Cann, 1999).

As product development progresses, distinguishing elements that put the company at risk with respect to its competitors also change. Briefly, these are:

• *Preclinical research*

　—Sunk costs: minimal at this point
　—Competitive risks:
　　§ competing laboratories may generate new research findings that point to alternative approaches
　　§ new patents that "compete" with research must be evaluated
　　§ other firms may file a patent covering the same technology faster

• *Phase I clinical trials*

　—Sunk costs: still minimal
　—Patent filing: technology now public record
　—Competitive risks:
　　§ competing laboratories obtain new research findings that point to alternative approaches
　　§ taking steps necessary to facilitate the success of the clinical trial
　　§ recruiting the best CRO to facilitate trials relative to competitors

• *Phase II clinical trials*

　—Sunk costs: now substantial
　—Initial public offering likely at this stage
　—Competitive risks:
　　§ strength of CRO conducting competitor clinical trials
　　§ new patent filings promising more effective treatments

§ ability of technology and targeted indication to attract investor interest relative
to competitors

- *Phase III clinical trials*
  —Sunk costs: now substantial
  —Competitive risks:
  § rapid trial completion allows more time to market drug before the patent expires
  § bioavailability: in what quantities and at what cost can the drug be manufac-
  tured?

- *Drug approval*
  —Sunk costs: now substantial
  —Competitive risks:
  § patent expiry: the threat of generics
  § patent extensions: competitive lobbying
  § capturing as much profit from drug sales (while remaining patent-protected)
  § competitor pricing
  § distribution and marketing: may have to outsource depending upon competitor
  resources
  § new means to minimize side effects (drug synergies, new routes of drug
  delivery).

EVOLUTION OF THE BIOTECH FIRM WITH PRODUCT DEVELOPMENT

There are also secondary effects of product development that affect a firm's relationship with competitors. As a biotech firm's most advanced product moves
through each phase described for drug testing and development, there are corresponding events that transpire in step for the firm as a whole (table 16.2) associated with its stakeholders, sources of financing, and human resources. Key stakeholders are investors, human patients in clinical trials, and employees of the firm.

Changes in the firm's stakeholders affect the priorities assigned to tracking
different types of competitor information. Further, as the firm evolves with
development of its lead product, its capital structure begins to change, reflecting
a lower company risk. Biotech firms having an investor base with progressively
less tolerance for risk often curtail their involvement in high-risk projects. Risk-
averse investors may impact the firm's ability to compete with companies less
advanced in product development but backed by stakeholders that have a much
higher tolerance for project risk. The extreme ("the future" in table 16.2) may be
the future of some biotech firms: as their pipeline grows, they demonstrate stability in earnings and eventually are able to attract bondholders as stakeholders
in the company.

In the early stages of product development, biotech firms are almost entirely
composed of scientists (e.g., Entellos Inc., located in Menlo Park, California). As
the firm's resources grow, both through a broader investor base and sales revenue, it can take on professional managers as well as specialized staff (table
16.2). As human resources expand, more specialized staff can be recruited such
as full time CI personnel (e.g., Genentech, located in San Francisco, California).

Table 16.2
CHANGING STAKEHOLDERS WITH PRODUCT DEVELOPMENT
IN BIOTECHNOLOGY

Product-Development Stage	Financing and Capital Structure	Principal Human Resources	Competitive Information Needs
Preclinical research	angel investors; venture capitalists; parent company	scientists	new research; recent patent filings; competitor alliances
Phase I clinical trials	angel investors; venture capitalists; parent company	scientists; patients	CRO employed by competitors; new patent filings
Phase II clinical trials	initial public offering: shareholders and venture capitalists	scientists; patients; managers	public awareness of technology and indication
Phase III clinical trials	equity and venture capitalists	scientists; patients; managers	competitor bioavailability; speed of trial completion
Approval	equity; venture capitalists	scientists; patients; managers; specialized business staff	competitor distribution agreements; competitor pricing
The future	equity; bond holders; preferred shares	scientists; patients; managers; specialized business staff; mid-level management	competitive lobbying for and against patent extensions; competitor testing of drug synergies

Source: Based on interviews with senior biotechnology managers (MacAdam, 1999; Meikle, 1999; Nower, 1999; Shincariol, 1999).

IMPLICATIONS

Biotechnology presents a unique challenge for CI practitioners. Any CI system implemented within a biotechnology firm will have to be changed over intervals as short as one year (e.g., the length of time of phase I clinical trials). Accordingly, the priorities and resources assigned to different types of competitive intelligence change continually.

COMPETITIVE INTELLIGENCE AREAS:
FIVE SPHERES OF CONCERN IN BIOTECHNOLOGY

Before discussing an allocation policy, we will briefly review five spheres of CI information that reflect the stages of product development:

- Basic research (and patent portfolios, key scientists)
- Alliances (and licensing, technology purchases, and consortia membership)
- Clinical research
- Market positioning
- Regulatory power.

Basic Research

In this instance, basic-research findings are monitored from laboratories working with either similar technologies or that are focusing on the same problem (Shincariol, 1999). This task is enormous. For example, the Society for Neuroscience's annual meeting typically features 30,000 neuroscientists from around the world presenting their latest findings (see <http://www.jneurosci.org/>). Relevant research findings for a firm may be spread across several different segments of this research field. For example, in the case of cocaine addiction, relevant reports may be found in cell-culture systems, behavioral neuroscience, brain imaging, cognitive psychology, anecdotal clinical reports, and electrophysiology, to name just a few. In general, new scientific findings at the basic research level can be monitored through a constellation of channels:

- Identifying the competitor's portfolio of patents
- Refereed publications
- Conferences
- Graduate theses and academic-defense appearances.

Alliances

It is essential to monitor competitor alliances. Alliances allow competitors to share research-and-development costs so that their combined resources and complimentary capabilities (core competencies) may allow more rapid progress on a particular problem. In its larger form, alliances among groups of firms (or consortia) may bring this to new levels through the networking of resources and global staffing (e.g., Molecular Simulations' Pharmaceutical Development Consortium). Technology purchases and new licensing agreements can also dramatically change a competitor's strength. For example, in moving into a technology called anti-sense, Inex (located in Burnaby, British Columbia) recently purchased a portfolio of patents covering thousands of proprietary molecules of unknown clinical value. Alliance activity can be monitored through a combination of sources:

- Press releases
- Online searchable databases of alliances for biotech firms
- Industry newsletters
- Bloomberg financial news (not typically used).

Clinical Research

Information pertaining to clinical trials for competitors is important in bench-marking a firm's efforts. Online searchable databases allow one to identify all competitors currently conducting clinical trials for a given disease, their sample size, and dosage regimen (e.g., the Clinical Trials Monitor at <http://www.ctbintl.com/intct.htm>). Bioavailability of a drug is not directly accessible, but may be inferred from press releases and the size and pace of clinical trials. The CRO conducting clinical trials is typically indicated in the press release covering trial initiation. The CRO can carry some weight in the trial's probability of success (Cann, 1999). The results of the clinical trials at the end of each phase, as well as any interim difficulties, may be obtained from press releases or by visiting, in the case of the United States, the FDA website (<http://www.fda.gov/>).

Market Positioning

The fundamental question is the product's perception by the public and investor community. Does the company still command the public eye by virtue of the technology chosen ("gene rescue") or indication focused on ("AIDS") in relation to its competitors? A competitor using gene-rescue technology may be working on a different disease, or if it is focusing on the same disease, may be using a different technology. Thus the firm in question must monitor the status of its efforts relative to competitors in commanding public attention (Shincariol, 1999). Monitoring competitor product pipelines is also critical: Are competitors releasing new products into the market before the firm in question for the same disease state? This can be readily ascertained from press releases. Based on clinical-trial results and postmarket reactions to the release of an approved drug, what is the relative effectiveness of the drug? What is the magnitude and type of side effects reported by the public during mainstream use relative to competitors? How expensive is the drug relative to competitors (not a relevant issue in Canada, but certainly in the United States)? Information of this kind can be obtained in the United States at the FDA website (<http://www.fda.gov/>).

Regulatory Power

Particularly in the United States, changing regulatory environments can greatly impact competition among biotechnology firms (i.e., for the few with approved products at this time such as Human Genome Sciences, located in Rockville, Maryland). Regulatory change is relevant because it can be influenced through competitive lobbying by generic drug manufacturers and the original drug-development company. For example, Schering Plough is currently lobbying for its third extension on the patent life of its product Clariton, preventing generic-drug manufacturers from entering the market and introducing price competition. Schering-Plough has recently been successful in obtaining this extension, and has also been successful in fighting antitrust allegations associated with the bundling of its high-priced drug, Ribavirin, with other less-demanded drugs. (CBS News, 1999). These are just a few of the issues that a firm nearing approval

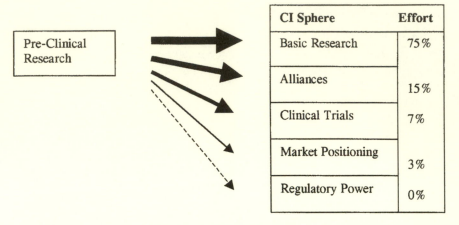

CI Sphere	Effort
Basic Research	75%
Alliances	15%
Clinical Trials	7%
Market Positioning	3%
Regulatory Power	0%

FIGURE 16.1 Stage 1: preclinical allocation policy.

of its drug has to monitor, both in seeking to maintain its product in the market-place and to recoup investment in the face of competitors that evoke antitrust allegations or block patent-life extensions.

ALLOCATION POLICY FOR COMPETITIVE INTELLIGENCE RESOURCES

In this final section we will examine the trade-offs in attention paid to each of the above five areas as functions of product development for a biotechnology firm. There are two principal arguments: To illustrate how competitive-intelligence priorities vary across the product-development process; and second, a schema to allow firms to formalize a priori how they should allocate these priorities now and in the future. Allocations are presented in rank-order relations; while actual numerical assignments convey this, their specific values should not be taken literally. Finally, allocation policies are derived in part from what is currently the practice, even if they result from largely unconscious decisions on the part of biotech firms, and in part from a proposal as to what should be the case.

Stage 1: Preclinical Research

During the preclinical research stage scientists are, in essence, the only real employees of the firm. Angel or venture-capital investors provide financing, while professional-management advice, if any, is outsourced (Meikle, 1999). The critical priority during this phase is the promise of the research finding in relation to competing laboratories. Reflecting one group of principal stakeholders (scientists), there is a natural tendency to focus on competitor research activities, which overshadows longer-term issues pertaining to market positioning (Meikle, 1999). Incorporated in the allocation policy proposed are the views of these stakeholders (figure 16.1).

The second group of stakeholders (investors) also takes a longer view of the firm's marketplace prospects and will demand answers from scientists along these lines. Therefore allocation to clinical trials of competitors and market positioning receives some attention during the preclinical phase (figure 16.1).

Alliances receive the most attention during the preclinical stage, since they have their greatest benefit during the research-and-development phase. If competitor alliances threaten the company, it can respond through greater research and development, either by itself or through its alliances. Alliances can be formed for other purposes (e.g., distribution), but given the overwhelming value assigned to innovation in this industry (MacAdam, 1999; Meikle, 1999; Nower, 1999; Shincariol, 1999), its effects would be most dramatic during the preclinical research phase.

Stage 2: Phase I Clinical Trials

Sunk costs are relatively low at this point. The firm still has considerable flexibility, investor patience permitting. As a result, considerable effort is still paid to basic research findings, since the firm still has the option of filing for a new investigational drug and abandoning the current effort if it can come up with a better idea.

The highest failure rate occurs during stage 2, in comparison with subsequent stages. A continued focus on basic research allows the firm to distribute its risks by having additional projects in the queue. For such a project to contribute to competitive advantage, basic-research activities of other firms must be closely monitored.

Now that the firm has entered clinical trials, it pays more attention to the progress of competitors currently engaged in clinical trials (figure 16.2). To a lesser extent, longer-term issues such as regulatory power receive attention in the context of its competitors. Regulatory power has low priority, given the high failure rate of phase I clinical trials.

Stakeholders expand during this phase to include patients (which may also be thought of as a resource). Since patient involvement is voluntary, the firm must have a product with sufficient potential to command this group's participation. Patients as stakeholders will demand close attention to reported side effects of similar technologies in use by competitors that have already engaged in clinical trials. These stakeholders may encourage the firm in question to be more aware of its competitors' problems using similar technology during clinical trials.

Stage 3: Clinical Trials II and III

While these phases have some differing risk characteristics, there is sufficient similarity to treat them with one CI-allocation policy (figure 16.3). Stakeholders change during phase II clinical trials. Biotech companies typically go public during this phase (Nower, 1999), replacing much of the capital put forward by venture capitalists with common shares. The company also acquires stakeholders in the form of professional managers, largely because it can now afford them (Meikle, 1999). This increase in managerial resources contributes to the com-

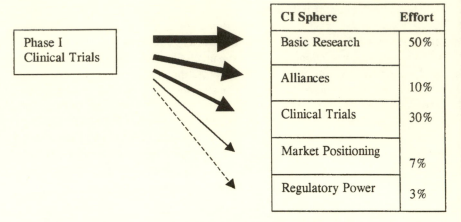

FIGURE 16.2 Stage 2: phase I clinical-trial allocation policy.

pany's competitive advantage, since its management team is now much stronger. Conversely, CI on similar developments for competitors should also be monitored ("clinical trials" in allocation policy, figure 16.3). In assessing the strength of competitors' senior-management teams, lead-product development has now gone far enough that competitors can be evaluated by their ability to meet stated milestones (Shincariol, 1999).

Basic research still receives considerable attention. Since these companies are evaluated at many points along the pipeline, they should have new projects in progress. This necessitates a minimum allocation to CI in basic research that demands a fair size of the company's resources to facilitate new project development.

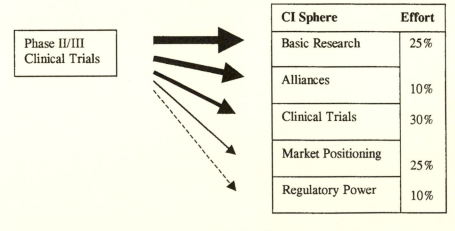

FIGURE 16.3 Stage 3: phases II/III clinical-trial allocation policy.

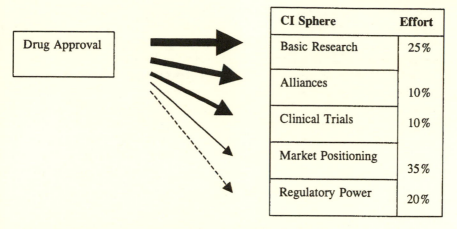

CI Sphere	Effort
Basic Research	25%
Alliances	10%
Clinical Trials	10%
Market Positioning	35%
Regulatory Power	20%

FIGURE 16.4 Stage 4: product-approval allocation policy.

Competitive intelligence resources allocated to market positioning increases dramatically. As the company nears its final ruling from the regulatory body in question (e.g., the FDA), it must prepare for more practical competitor issues such as price of production, distribution, and brand equity. For example, if a competitor appears to be negotiating a possible license or sale of the product under development to a large pharmaceutical company, the product in question becomes a much larger threat, with greater resources behind it (e.g., distribution, manufacturing, and brand recognition). Such a move may prompt the biotech firm in question to consider pursuing a similar avenue.

Stage 4: Product-Approval Allocation Policy

In this final phase (figure 16.4), CI on basic research remains strong. However, market-positioning information and awareness of lobbying activities by competitors with respect to regulatory issues (patent extension, antitrust allegations) are monitored with greater vigilance. The continued CI emphasis on basic research reflects the need to initiate another drug candidate into the pipeline.

IMPLEMENTATION

The constrained resources of biotechnology do not allow for professional managers until product development has advanced considerably (e.g., table 16.2). Full-time CI staff is out of the question, as management resources are scarce enough (Meikle, 1999). Competitive intelligence is a responsibility that has to be assumed by all the firm's personnel. This already happens to some extent as scientists focus on CI in basic research, while professional managers appear to be more concerned with information on competitor market positioning.

It is important that firms recognize that their CI priorities will change, commensurate with the advancement of their lead product, and that such changes should be deliberate rather than reactive. Some firms may decide on very different allocation policies than those proposed. As long as firms formally review their allocation policies with the changing status of their lead (or only) drugs, more effective monitoring of competitor activities may be achieved. For example, in discussion with a senior executive from Entellos Inc., which will soon market computer simulations of physiological states such as AIDs, it was revealed that he was unaware of Physiome Sciences Inc. (located in Princeton, New Jersey), another company that is currently marketing such simulations, albeit for different physiological processes (Holtzman, 1999). The existence of such corporate blindspots exemplifies the need for deliberate CI priority-changes commensurate with product development.

IMPLICATIONS FOR THE COMPETITIVE INTELLIGENCE PRACTITIONER

Competitive intelligence professionals may benefit from this framework, because it can be tailored for each biotechnology company. Allocation policies may reflect the unique circumstances that management feels currently or potentially confront the company. Such review processes may benefit companies, since this framework does not require large capital expenditures but rather institutionalized review within the firm allocating staffing resources among varied spheres of concern (e.g., basic research, regulatory power, clinical trials) that impinge on the firm in question.

OBSTACLES

As alluded to in earlier parts of this chapter, biotechnology firms by and large do not yet have revenue-generating products on the market. It is very difficult to discuss the allocation of resources for firms that feel they are already financially stretched. The case must be made that changing CI priorities commensurate with product development places the firm in a better position to answer the concerns of its changing stakeholder base (i.e., investors, recruited managers, and patients).

Given the central role of scientists as stakeholders in biotechnology, there is a tendency to overemphasize the technology while failing to observe some generalities from the investors' (other stakeholders) point of view (Shincariol, 1999). For example, Mr. MacAdam, chief executive officer (CEO) of TM Bioscience, feels that his company's chip-technology lab has "no competitors." The CEO of Entellos has responded similarly (Holtzman, 1999; MacAdam, 1999). Firms that fail to recognize competitors of either their own technology or the direction they have targeted will be difficult "sells" for CI practitioners. Some may have to be convinced of this more basic reality before formal allocation policies for CI can be discussed.

REFERENCES

Cann, B. (1999). Vice president, sales and marketing, clinical services, MDS Inc. Personal communication, February 15.

CBS News. (1999). *Fighting Drug Bundling.* CBS News <http://www/CBS.com>.

Charette, C., and K. Lewis. (1998). "Biotechnology and Pharmaceuticals" (research report, April 2). Toronto: Nesbitt Burns.

Haseltine, B. (1998). "Beyond the Behemoths," *Economist* 346(8056): 57–78.

Heller, M.A., and R.S. Eisenberg. (1998). "Can Patents Deter Innovation? The Anticommons in Biomedical Research," *Science* 280(5364): 698–701.

Holtzman, S. (1999). CEO and president, Entellos Inc. Personal communication, May 13.

MacAdam, D. (1999). CEO and president, TM Bioscience. Personal communication, March 1.

Meikle, L.T. (1999). CEO and president, Biocatalyst Yorkton. Personal communication, March 9.

Nower, L.B. (1999). Partner, Health Care and Life Sciences, KPMG. Personal communication, April 7.

Shincariol, A.L. (1999). CEO and president, Novopharm Biotech. Personal communication, March 29.

17

Making Competitive Intelligence Work for the Small Business

Perry Broome

INTRODUCTION

This chapter explores reasons why small businesses need competitive intelligence (CI), and why few small businesses have implemented CI programs. It will focus on ways that small businesses can make the CI process efficient and cost effective. The CI needs of small businesses are analyzed in relation to the organization's strategy. A framework for assessing the costs of market and competitive data is provided. Suggestions for utilizing employees in the CI process are presented.

WHY DO BUSINESSES HAVE PROBLEMS DEVELOPING COMPETITIVE INTELLIGENCE PROGRAMS?

There are many problems associated with current business intelligence practices. Many organizations fail to see the value of CI. Management attitudes, corporate cultures, and previous research failures lead some organizations to believe that CI is unnecessary.

Many managers believe they have no competition. Some managers cannot get past their daily operational problems to concern themselves with the long term. Some leaders believe their companies are so successful that they need not worry about the competition. To ignore the competition through naiveté or arrogance invites problems. With the speed of technological change and the globalization of commerce rapidly increasing, profits are attracting competition in all industries.

Of the companies that *do* appreciate the potential value of CI, few can see past the difficulties in performing a cost–benefit analysis. Even though many organizations gather competitor information, few have formal CI programs in place. A 1997 survey of CI practitioners revealed that less than 60 percent of their organizations had programs in place to generate CI (Allgaier & Powell, 1998). The survey respondents were individuals who provided in-house CI expertise. Overall, the number of companies actively practicing CI is estimated to be between 10 and 15 percent (DeWitt, 1997).

Companies that implement programs often do so ineffectively. Some organizations do a poor job of identifying competitors (Clark, 1998). Many companies never get past the data-gathering stage. Often CI programs fail, because companies do not understand their own strengths and weaknesses, their competitors' capabilities, or the wants and needs of their customers.

In small businesses, resource constraints are the biggest reason for the lack of CI success. Few organizations have unlimited funds with which to pursue market research and competitive intelligence. Departments and divisions have to justify all operating-and-research expenditures.

The biggest problem in justifying a CI program is the inability to perform a meaningful cost–benefit analysis. Competitive intelligence is similar to market research in that a hypothesis can be formulated and the costs of implementing the CI program can be reasonably estimated. Costs will be susceptible to greater managerial control in smaller businesses where financial resources are often scarce. Most CI benefits cannot be accurately quantified until the work is done and the analysis is complete.

ADAPTING COMPETITIVE INTELLIGENCE PROGRAMS TO SMALL BUSINESSES

Competitive intelligence processes and techniques must be developed to deliver value for small business. The effectiveness of CI will depend on the efficiency of the collection and analysis of information, the quality and execution of the actionable recommendations, and the benefits ultimately realized.

Most small businesses can make the data-collection-and-analysis steps of its CI program effective and efficient. An organization's decision-making and strategy-execution skills vary with the quality and amount of human and financial resources. Small-business leaders can be trained to improve their analysis and decision-making skills. The benefits of CI programs can be estimated in terms of increased or protected margins or market share.

MAKING DATA COLLECTION EFFICIENT

The cost of gathering and analyzing data depends on the amount and availability of data required and the cost of its retrieval. The question is, how much data does a small business need?

To determine CI needs, small businesses can focus on the owner's perspective (goals, strategy, and mission) and the data-collection-and-analysis process (Pablubiak, 1996). In order to make CI cost-justifiable, the CI process may be designed in a modular format. For example, modular components could include an employee survey, customer survey, prospect survey, industry sources, and government sources. Costs and benefits can be identified at each stage of the process. The value of the intelligence produced at each stage can be viewed relative to the cost, priority, frequency, designer, process executor, and marketing strategy. This modular design can facilitate starting and stopping the CI process for cash flow or other reasons.

The appeal of a modular design is the flexibility it adds to the CI program. However, there are potential problems with this design. The industry and competitor data needed to predict and counter competitor actions seldom come from one or a few sources. Numerous bits of information from different sources have to be pieced together to formulate actionable intelligence (Dutka, 1998). It may be difficult to quantify the benefits of each individual data-source if the process is stopped after a particular module.

There are merits to designing a CI program based on the owner's perspective. The amount of data required should be a function of the organization's strategy. Strategy can be summarized in terms of four related components: goals, product-market focus, competitive premise, and business-systems focus (Fry & Killing, 1996). An organization's goals and product-market focus should determine a firm's data and analysis requirements. The resulting intelligence can then determine a company's competitive premise.

Most organizations pursue both hard and soft goals. Common hard goals include target levels of growth, profitability, and market share. The two ends of the spectrum for profitability are the maximization of shareholder value (offensive goals), and the maintenance of a positive cash flow (defensive goals). For organizations with defensive goals, the motivation may be simply to prevent elimination from the market, as opposed to a more offensive approach designed to lead the market.

Product market focus refers to the products an organization plans to sell and the specific markets targeted. Geographic markets can range from a local trading area to a global perspective.

Companies pursuing global markets require greater amounts of data and analysis. Each market will have local political, economic, and social issues to address. Profitable global markets attract more competitors. Higher costs accompanying the increased level of information required in global markets may consume too much of the limited financial resources of many small businesses.

Companies focusing on local markets may still have many potential com-

Geographic Market Focus

		Local	Global
	Offensive	Medium Needs	Highest Needs
Business Goals	Defensive	Lowest Needs	High Needs

FIGURE **17.1** Intelligence information needs based on business strategy.

petitors, but the effort to gather data on the known threats will be reduced because of a smaller geographic focus.

Based on the assumption that different strategies result in different intelligence needs, data-gathering efforts are summarized in figure 17.1.

How much do varying strategies determine competitor- and market-information requirements? Does the goal of protecting a small local market significantly reduce intelligence data needs?

Management preferences regarding organization size or amount of invested capital often result in defensive goals for small business. Many organizations are able to survive pursuing defensive goals, especially in businesses involving low technology and on-site service. For these organizations, CI routines are still required to ensure that the company's value proposition remains superior in the eyes of all customers.

A targeted product or market focus will alter the type of information a company needs in its CI program, but will not eliminate the need for CI. Just because an organization may be satisfied with maintaining a small piece of a market doesn't mean that competitors will ignore that piece or allow the company to survive.

Companies can gather and analyze an endless supply of information on their environments and competitors. The process can be organized by classifying CI needs based on five competitive forces (Porter, 1980): 1) Threats to profitability posed by forces outside of a firm's current group of competitors include potential new entrants to the marketplace, product substitutes, suppliers, and customers; 2) new entrants can become direct competitors; 3) substitutes are indirect competitors; 4) suppliers and customers can become competitors through vertical integration; and 5) suppliers and customers can also threaten margins without becoming competitors.

Small businesses seeking data on their industries and competitors have to weigh the value of the data against the cost. The cost of data is comprised of the price an organization will pay to subscribe to or purchase specific information, plus the time and effort required to capture the data.

Some data are available for no monetary price, but a high level of effort is required to assess, convert, analyze, and disseminate it. Newspaper subscriptions, periodicals, and Internet access can be relatively inexpensive. However, there are so much data available from these sources (and it overlaps) that a lot of effort can be required to sift through and capture relevant information. The subscription price can be small relative to the labor costs associated with using these sources.

Information specific to an industry or competitor can often be purchased from trade associations, industry analysts, and securities analysts. Reports from these sources may combine data with some degree of analysis. However, along with the ease of retrieval comes a price. Obtaining expert information can be very efficient. but an organization has to weigh the cost of the information against the benefits derived from it. The timeliness of the information must also be considered—stale data may be worthless, regardless of the source.

For example, if a competitor is publicly traded, sufficient public financial data may be available for someone to gather cost information, categorize it, and perform sensitivity, break-even, and other analysis. Time is required to gather the data. Accounting and financial expertise is needed to perform the analysis. Alternatively, a securities analyst or industry expert may have all of the available data and expertise to provide the information. In fact, he or she may have completed the analysis already in the context of another project.

The data required for a comprehensive analysis of a competitor are more detailed and often more difficult to obtain. Often the best sources for this type of data are industry associates, including suppliers, customers, employees, and other competitors. Data from these sources may be free, but can take time to gather. Success in extracting competitor information from these sources will depend on the relationships an organization can establish within its industry.

Companies have to choose between spending money to receive information immediately or spending time to gather the information on their own. Figure 17.2 shows the price/effort relationship associated with some potential sources of data.

The preferred source for many pieces of intelligence information is dependent on the urgency of the need and the human and financial resources of the organization. The cost and availability of business intelligence data continue to improve. Most of the information an organization needs is in the public domain. However, most small businesses do not have the resources and expertise to track down and analyze the relevant pieces.

Customers, suppliers, and competitor employees collectively possess most of the competitor information companies seek. Much of this information can be gathered by the employees of a small business during regular interactions in the marketplace. An effective approach to data collection for small businesses is to use employees to gather most of the direct competitor information, and to use reasonably priced sources for industry and macroeconomic data.

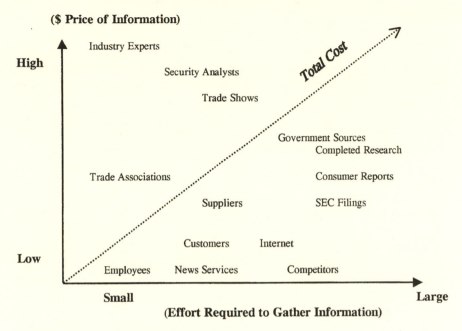

FIGURE 17.2 Cost of information.

USING THE SALES FORCE AND OTHER EMPLOYEES TO GATHER COMPETITIVE INTELLIGENCE DATA

All employees have the opportunity and capability to capture customer and competitive data. Small businesses can have an advantage in leveraging this capability because of their size. With fewer employees, less-complicated organizational structures, and broader job descriptions, small businesses should enjoy superior internal information flows.

Small-business leaders have to foster cultures that value the capturing and sharing of knowledge. Everyone in the organization has to understand his or her role in CI and how it can impact the future of the organization (Berger, 1997).

Members of a company's sales- and service-distribution systems have the best opportunity to gather business and competitor intelligence. They have regular contact with customers and should be constantly assessing satisfaction levels and identifying unmet needs. The sales force often interacts with competitors at industry functions, trade shows, and during bidding competitions.

Many companies do not use the sales force in the intelligence-gathering process, even though it is generally acknowledged that the sales force should be an organization's primary source of sales and marketing intelligence. The Allgaier and Powell (1998) survey revealed that 41.3 percent of respondents reported using sales training to improve the communication of competitor information. These results reflect the common practice of headquarters telling the field staff how its customers and competitors are behaving, instead of the sales force sending information in the opposite direction.

Another 1997 study by the Futures Group determined that companies were increasing their competitive data-gathering efforts, but were not translating new data into useful information (Cohen, 1998). As a result, salespeople end up with lots of data, but they do not know what to do with it.

Several steps can be taken to make a sales-force intelligence-gathering system effective. Buy-in is required for the success of any strategy. Employees' efforts are optimized when they believe in and support an organization's mission and strategy. Aligning salespeople with company strategy can be difficult, even though few employees personally have more at stake. The competition "steals" their customers and reduces their paychecks on a daily basis. The sales force has a lot at stake in understanding the competition and motivating management to pro-act.

Small businesses can improve sales-force participation in the CI process by ensuring that their compensation system motivates and rewards intelligence-producing behavior. Often, what gets measured, gets done. Measurement is necessary, but not sufficient to motivate proper behaviors in intelligence gathering.

One way to motivate and facilitate sales-force intelligence gathering is to financially support attendance at industry functions, seminars, and trade shows. Salespeople often want to attend events but may be hesitant if the cost represents a personal expense. By supporting attendance, a company can reward the employee while facilitating the gathering of information. As the company builds CI into its corporate and sales culture, these rewards can motivate and improve intelligence gathering. Larger businesses often reward top sales performers by sending them to off-site meetings and conferences with their company peers. Small business can provide similar rewards and enjoy the added benefit of intelligence-gathering opportunities at industry functions.

Some organizations alter their sales-compensation systems to motivate intelligence-gathering behaviors. For example, one personal-computer supplier ties a portion of its representative's pay to the level of documentation the representative submits on its clients' technology business plan, business needs, and relationships with key executives (Marchetti, 1998). The company also benefits from having the information documented if the representative leaves the organization.

Often in smaller businesses salespeople are required to perform many administrative duties that they view as nonproductive. They consider customer contact as the key to generating sales and commissions. Productive salespeople attempt to maximize the time they spend on that activity. They have to be motivated and coached to plan their time effectively in order to gather intelligence from customers, competitors, and other industry players.

Sales-call reports are often used in activities-management programs (Montgomery & Weinberg, 1998). These reports help representatives document their efforts and facilitate follow-up. Win/loss databases are used to record results of sales presentations (Allgaier & Powell, 1998). The reasons for sales success or failure can be analyzed to identify market trends or training needs. The data can also be synthesized and distributed as sales aids and proof statements to assist representatives in their sales process (Berger, 1996).

Intelligence reporting should also be incorporated into a company's perform-ance-appraisal process (Dutka, 1998). Making it a requirement to document cus-tomer and competitor information may improve a salesperson's results. Note-taking can reinforce the notion to the customer that the salesperson is genuinely interested in understanding and meeting customer needs (Schiffman, 1995). Note-taking also improves the volume and accuracy of information gathered.

Another important component of an employee intelligence-gathering pro-gram is the reporting mechanism. Ideally, the sales force will possess the tech-nology and skills to efficiently record information remotely. Many organizations build or purchase contact-management software to capture, record, and report data (Prior, 1996). Some database-management systems are used to facilitate intelligence gathering. A 1997 survey of firms with computerized intelligence functions determined that Microsoft Access, Lotus Notes, Wincite, and Intranets were the four most-popular tools used in intelligence programs (Fuld, 1998).

FROM DATA TO ACTIONABLE INTELLIGENCE

The final steps in the CI program involve analysis, recommendations, intelli-gence dissemination, and action. These are the steps where most CI programs experience declining effectiveness. Like all other organizations, small businesses will have to ensure that these steps are completed with the same commitment employed in the information-gathering stages.

Resources often constrain these efforts of small business. Sometimes special skills such as financial analysis, statistical analysis, or in-depth industry knowl-edge are required to piece together information into actionable intelligence. Once again, the small firm may have to obtain training to improve analysis skills, or seek outside help with the analysis.

There are several tools available for use in the analysis stage: *Lead-user analysis* focuses on users who adapt a company's products to meet their needs. These users often end up being the company's core future customers. Companies can engage in scenario planning to anticipate possible future competitive envi-ronments.

Other analysis tools include *competitive conjecture*, *SWOT analysis* (strengths, weaknesses, opportunities, threats), *war-gaming*, *simulation*, *modeling*, and *mar-ket-pattern recognition* (Allgaier & Powell, 1998; Clark, 1998). Some of these tools require special analytical expertise or computing capacity. The perceived value of the intelligence gained has to be weighed against the cost of outsourcing some of the analysis function. Whatever the form of analysis, the company has to synthesize information and predict the identities and strategies of its future com-petitors.

With the appropriate analysis skills in place, a small firm will have an advan-tage in moving effectively through to the recommendation stage. Small busi-nesses typically have fewer employees, fewer organizational levels, and fewer communication blocks to overcome. Employees of small firms often have broader roles and responsibilities. This can make it easier to pull together individuals who represent all aspects of the organization. A broad perspective can lead to more stimulating discussions and thoughtful decisions.

The firm's small size may also help facilitate the inclusion of more members of the sales and service teams in the analysis stage. Sales and service people are closer to the customer and may provide the best representation of the customer's perspective.

DISSEMINATING INTELLIGENCE

Small firms can be more effective and efficient in distributing intelligence. Fewer communication links allow for more information to be easily shared.

Many forms of intelligence can be distributed online. Pull technology is useful for distributing intelligence information (Stewart, 1999). It allows for the storage of information that can be read, downloaded, or printed as required by employees. Intranets facilitate the use of pull technology.

CONCLUSION

No organization is immune to the rapidly changing competitive landscape. Small businesses face many of the same competitive pressures and threats as larger businesses. All businesses have to anticipate the future competitive environment and design their strategies to ensure survival and success.

Small businesses have similar CI requirements, but fewer financial and human resources than those of large organizations. Small businesses must involve *all* employees in the CI process, including the sales force, because it is the most intimate with the marketplace and the customer. The sales force will need training, technology, motivation, and rewards to effectively participate in the CI program.

Gaps in the expertise needed to perform some of the CI analysis have to be overcome so that all the steps of the CI process can be completed. The outsourcing of some intelligence processes may be required. The dissemination of intelligence should be more efficient in small organizations due to their reduced size and complexity.

Small business must achieve alignment with a CI culture and perform CI efficiently in order to realize the benefits of implementing a CI program. With an organized and efficient intelligence-gathering, analysis, and distribution process in place, a small business will be better positioned to identify changes in the competitive environment and formulate strategies to address them.

REFERENCES

Allgaier, C., and T. Powell. (1998). "Enhancing Sales and Marketing Effectiveness through Competitive Intelligence," *Competitive Intelligence Review* 9(2): 29–41.

Berger, A. (1996). "How to Support Your Sales Force With Competitive Intelligence," *Competitive Intelligence Review* 7(4): 81–83.

———. (1997). "Small but Powerful: Six Steps for Conducting Competitive Intelligence Successfully at a Medium-Sized Firm," *Competitive Intelligence Review* 8(4): 75–77.

Clark, B. (1998). "Managing Competitive Interactions," *Marketing Management* 7(4): 9–20.

Cohen, A. (1998). "The Misuse of Competitive Intelligence," *Sales and Marketing Management* 150(3): 13.

DeWitt, M. (1997). *Competitive Intelligence Competitive Advantage.* Grand Rapids, MI: Abacus.

Dutka, A. (1998). *Competitive Intelligence for the Competitive Edge.* Chicago: NTC.

Fry, J., and J. Killing. (1996). *Strategic Analysis and Action.* Scarborough, ON: Prentice-Hall.

Fuld, L.M. (1998). "1998 Customer Satisfaction Report and Survey," *Competitive Intelligence Magazine* 1(3): 18–33.

Marchetti, M. (1998). "Paying Salespeople for Information," *Sales and Marketing Management* 151(7): 16.

Montgomery, D., and C. Weinberg. (1998). "Toward Strategic Intelligence Systems," *Marketing Management* 7(4): 44–52.

Pablubiak, P. (1996). "Competitive Intelligence for the Small Firm: Where Is the Value?" *Competitive Intelligence Review* 7(1): 17–22.

Porter, M. (1980). *Competitive Strategy: Techniques for Analyzing Industries and Competitors.* New York: Free Press.

Prior, V. (1996). "Contacts Database: Your Most Useful Intelligence Tool," *Competitive Intelligence Review* 7(3): 75–77.

Schiffman, S. (1995). *The 25 Most Common Sales Mistakes and How to Avoid Them.* Holbrook, MA: Adams Media Corporation.

Stewart, T. (1999). *Intellectual Capital.* New York: Doubleday.

18

Re-Designing the Competitive Intelligence Capability within a Financial Institution

Ross O. Armstrong

INTRODUCTION

This chapter will discuss the deployment of the competitive intelligence (CI) capability in a leading global financial institution. As a "knowledge-based system," the design takes into account the needs and uses of information, and presents challenges for organizational design. Specifically, this chapter will:

- Review the competitive intelligence needs and uses for the company
- Define key organizational relationships
- Develop a plan to re-design the competitive intelligence capability.

The organization, with over 1,500 branches, utilizes sophisticated financial- and management-information tools to assist clients in more than 50 countries. As business needs change, the organization develops innovative products and services to deliver value to the clients' bottom line. The financial institution's electronic services division (ESD) offers electronic cash and information-management services to enhance its corporate-clients' working capital, improve information flows, and simplify administrative procedures. These services enable its clients to make timely, informed, and effective decisions concerning their assets and resources.

ORGANIZATIONAL STRUCTURE

Traditionally, the financial institution has generated strong revenues based on retail/commercial loans and other interest-bearing products. The ESD evolved in response to the need for new products. The corporate, commercial, and electronic services divisions all have a range of products and services to sell and an organizational structure to support this effort.

Nature of Sales

Revenues generated by commercial and corporate financing are credit-based and largely "transactional" in nature. This "retail side" exhibits characteristics of a mature industry and focuses on issues involving commoditization and price. Compensation for the sales staff incorporates transactional measures—sales of credit-based products. Sales of the electronic services require considerable knowledge about the client's operational needs. This usually requires a relationship developed over a period of months or years.

Sales Force

The sales efforts were previously divided broadly into two streams:

- The corporate-market sales force, which focuses on the largest corporations
- The commercial-market sales force, which is distributed among the close to three-dozen commercial finance centers and focuses on medium-to-large corporations and a range of independent businesses.

Approximately 80 account managers promote the full range of services, from the largest commercial accounts to medium-sized independent businesses. It is important to understand that account managers from corporate or commercial divisions provide the sales activities for the ESD. Account managers receive product-support materials and provide "cross-selling" efforts. The sales force dedicates the majority of its time to corporate and commercial products and services. Only a small portion of its time and effort is spent promoting ESD's products and services.

COMPETITIVE INTELLIGENCE REQUIREMENTS

The intensity of competition is increasing rapidly. There are potential mergers of financial institutions and entry of insurance companies into financial markets. There is considerable multipoint competition, wherein the financial institution competes with a particular competitor across numerous products and services.

In response to this changing environment management wanted to develop a distributed CI network, one that was more widely dispersed and generated more effective intelligence. This required staff across the organization to acquire and communicate the information.

A series of interviews were undertaken to assess the nature of information needs and uses in order to facilitate the reorganization of the CI resource. These discussions are summarized below.

INFORMATION NEEDS AND USES

Information about Competitors

The financial institution wanted to know how competitors' pricing was structured, threshold levels for profits, and decisions about discounts. It wanted to develop competitor-specific pricing models to generate various scenarios. Similarly, management wished to obtain information about competitors' product lines, selling structures, and selling effectiveness. Information about competitor's strengths and weaknesses could prove invaluable to strategy development and market-positioning efforts. Managers also wanted to adopt a formal scanning process to learn more about both current and potential competitors.

Information about Customers

The organization desired information that would differentiate it (in its customers' eyes) from competitors—to understand how the market perceived it and its products, and how well it related to customers' needs. Customer-specific information would include the institution's contact history, linkages to appropriate corporate financial officers, sales-development history, and customer history with competitors.

Account managers wanted to be able to determine the expiration of service contracts for potential and actual clients. Competitive information generates more successful proposals by helping to determine not only who is in the running for deals, but enabling the financial institution to run a model of the competitors' pricing structure. Such information can also assist in analyzing lost opportunities—who got what and why.

Information about the Financial Marketplace

Continuous market scanning will identify potential competitors, new products and services, and issues that will affect the institution's customers or competitors. A variety of market statistics (such as regional-market penetration) will provide early indications of competitor activity. Benchmarks will assist in understanding customer and competitor processes.

COMPETITIVE INTELLIGENCE DIRECTIONS

For several years, the marketing department within the ESD had maintained a repository of information about competitors' products and services, pricing, and customer information. One individual was responsible for this information, and questions were deferred to this person. There were high risks of maintaining the CI capability within the hands of one person. The ESD wished to establish a process by which CI would be acquired, analyzed, and communicated—and lead to more effective decision-making. This led it to consider advances in the field of *knowledge management.*

KNOWLEDGE MANAGEMENT

Knowledge management involves facilitating and managing knowledge-related activities—its creation, capture, transformation, and use (Wiig, 1997). Competitive intelligence is specific knowledge that needs to be effectively managed.

"Knowledge is the overwhelmingly important productive resource in terms of its contribution to value-added and its strategic significance" (Grant, 1997). The activities that add value to most products and services are technological know-how, product design, marketing presentation, understanding the customer, creativity, and innovation. The ability to manage one's *organizational knowledge*—defined as processed information embedded in routines and processes that enable action (Myers, 1996)—can lead to a significant competitive advantage. Such a competitive advantage can be seen in many firms that have not only a great span of knowledge, but also a more sophisticated integration mechanism. Rivals find it increasingly difficult to replicate these processes.

WHAT IS KNOWLEDGE?

The definition of *knowledge,* most simply put, is "the capacity to act" (Sveiby, 1997). This capacity to act is created continuously by a *process-of-knowing*: It is a fluid mix of framed experience, values, contextual information, and expert insight that provides a framework for evaluating and incorporating new experiences and information (Davenport & Prusak, 1998).

There are several characteristics of knowledge. It is tacit, being formed in a social (i.e., personal) and individual context. Knowledge is action-oriented, fluid, and constantly changing. It is the process by which individuals gather fragmented clues from sensory perception and memory. People make sense of reality by categorizing these clues into theories, feelings, and values. Knowledge born of experience recognizes familiar patterns and makes connections.

Moingeon and Edmondson (1996) suggest an important distinction between learning "how" and learning "why." Learning *how* (when relatively clear criteria are present) and learning *why* (in diagnosing the whole system, evaluating opportunities to change governing values or contexts) are both important—each is appropriate in qualitatively different situations. In terms of application:

• *Learning how* involves the application of routines characterized by imitation and error-correction behaviors. It is difficult to imitate such a complex array of administrative and human skills

• *Learning why* is the application of a set of routines characterized by asking questions about contexts and systems and the intelligent application of analysis and diagnostic tools.

How Is Knowledge Organized?

The emerging area of theory and research into the role of knowledge within organizations has been described as the "knowledge-based view of the firm." The role of the firm had been described in the following way:

> If individuals must specialize in knowledge acquisition and if producing goods and services requires the application of many types of knowledge, production must be organized so as to assemble these many types of knowledge while preserving specialization by individuals. The firm is an institution which exists to resolve this dilemma: it permits individuals to specialize in developing specialized expertise while establishing mechanisms through which individuals coordinate to integrate their different knowledge bases in the transformation of inputs into outputs. (Grant, 1997)

Individuals are the primary agents of knowledge creation and are the principal repositories of knowledge (especially for tacit knowledge). In fact, as much as 75 percent of human intelligence necessary to address senior management's stated intelligence needs resides within individuals in the company (Sawka, Francis, & Herring, 1995).

Knowledge may be tacit, shared in a group or team (either consciously or in either group or individual performance), or embodied as explicit and distributable information (Demarest, 1997). Individuals and interrelationships, therefore, are key to knowledge generation, transmission, and use.

Knowledge within Organizations

Nonaka and Takeuchi (1995) proposed that knowledge-creating businesses have a nonhierarchical, self-organizing structure working in tandem with a hierarchical structure. This "hypertext organization"—an analogy borrowed from computer science—consists of multiple layers that should be interpreted as different "contexts."

The contexts comprise three interconnected layers: business system, project team, and knowledge base. The bureaucratic business-system layer is where routines are efficiently carried out. Upon this level, a project-team layer is superimposed: It is here that knowledge from short-term projects is created. Nonaka and Takeuchi (1995) suggest that the third layer—the repository of corporate knowledge—uses corporate strategy, corporate vision, and culture to define the context within which to tap tacit knowledge. The ability to switch among the different contexts swiftly and flexibly ultimately determines the organizational capability for knowledge creation.

Infrastructure is needed to facilitate the knowledge-building processes effectively. Demarest (1997) identified three classes of infrastructure concerns: The first one involves cultural issues such as reward structures and job security. The second, operational infrastructure, includes changes to a traditional human-resources organization, such as job ladders, compensation, work locale, and command-and-control structures. Technical infrastructure (including information technology) is the third area.

TRANSFERRING KNOWLEDGE

One's ability to share knowledge is central to our discussion. Improving cross-functional integration within the organization to ensure customer responsiveness is critical and directly related to the firm's competitiveness and profitability (Lapierre & Henault, 1996). Several key models of integration are noted.

Kahn (1996) described integration of knowledge:

- *Interaction:* Represents the structural nature of cross-departmental activities. Such activities address formally coordinated initiatives between departments, including routine meetings, planned teleconferences, routine conference calls, and the flow of standard documentation. Such activities are structural in that they regulate communication through frequency of occurrence, adherence to routine schedules, plans and/or policy.

- *Collaboration:* Represents unstructured affective nature of interdepartmental relationships. Collaboration is defined as an effective, volitional, shared process where departments work together, have mutual understanding, a common vision, shared resources, and collective goals. Collaboration represents a higher level of integration because such activities are intangible, not easily regulated, and difficult to sustain.

The underlying philosophy of each process is relevant to the present discussion. Underlying integration is a transaction-based philosophy, which favors structured communications (e.g., meetings), contact that is temporary and desires to maximize benefits while minimizing the cost of contact. The philosophy underpinning collaboration mirrors a relationship-marketing philosophy: emphasis on continuous relationships, strategic alignment through shared vision, collective goals, joint rewards, and an informal structure to manage the relationship (Kahn, 1996).

Grant (1997) cites other mechanisms of knowledge integration:

- *Transfer* takes place more efficiently

- *Direction* is exemplified when specialists in one area of knowledge issue rules, directives, and operating procedures to guide the behavior of non-specialists in other fields

- *Sequencing* allows an individual to coordinate his or her knowledge application without direct transfer taking place

• *Routines* are regular patterns of coordinated activity involving multiple individuals storing organizational experience in a form that allows for rapid transfer of experience to new situations.

An organization must recognize where knowledge lies before it can be transferred; "warrants," described by Brown and Duguid (1998), are standards of judgment whereby people distinguish what is worthwhile and valid from what is not—they show people what to attend to. Leonard-Barton (1995) proposed that in managing the absorption of knowledge, managers must not only create porous boundaries to expose their company to new ideas from the outside, but must scan broadly. It is here that the warrants may direct attention to new ideas and concepts.

Knowledge dispersed throughout the organization poses a significant challenge for centralized decision-making: The organization bears significant costs to gather and deliver it to the decision-maker (Cowen & Ellig, 1995). Examples of successful firms that use dispersed structures include Motorola (Galvin, 1997), Hewlett-Packard (Moss Kanter, 1996), and Buckman Laboratories (Buckman, 1998). Halal (1997) studied decentralized structures at MCI, Xerox, and Johnson & Johnson; structures at Federal Express and 3M were reported by Grant (1997). Creation of multidisciplinary teams to undertake specific projects or to support knowledge transfer is frequently reported (Ghoshal & Westney, 1991; Harkleroad, 1994). Other structures have utilized the concept of matrix management, knowledge "brokers" (Snow, Miles, & Coleman, 1995), "liaison representatives" (Prescott, 1987), or "common interest groups" (Allee, 1997).

KNOWLEDGE AND TECHNOLOGY

Technology is an important component of the knowledge-base level in the hypertext organization. Technology taps the explicit knowledge generated in the other two layers, while vision and culture tap the tacit knowledge.

A host of tools, equipment, technology supports, and physical structures is available to assist in managing the company's knowledge (Allee, 1997). CIBC, Motorola, and Buckman Laboratories have used physical structures such as learning centers. Some firms use technological solutions such as groupware (e.g., Lotus Notes) or Intranets. Davenport, De Long, and Beers (1998) described three basic types of repositories: *external knowledge* (for example, competitor intelligence); *structured internal knowledge* (such as research reports, product-oriented marketing materials, and techniques and methods); and *informal internal knowledge* (such as discussion databases full of "lessons learned").

The changing role of technology in knowledge management has evolved from researching technology itself (technical reports, product prototypes, patents, etc.) to the process of human interactions—*knowledge generation* (Amidon, 1998). Companies that value knowledge are mapping out guides to in-house expertise.

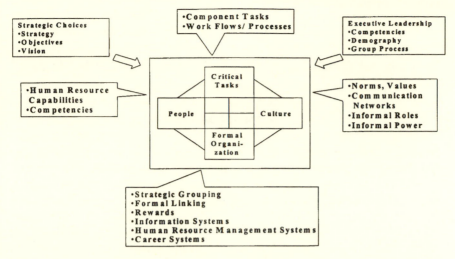

Figure within:

Strategic Choices
•Strategy
•Objectives
•Vision

•Component Tasks
•Work Flows/ Processes

Executive Leadership
•Competencies
•Demography
•Group Process

•Human Resource Capabilities
•Competencies

Critical Tasks

People ── Culture

Formal Organi- zation

•Norms, Values
•Communication Networks
•Informal Roles
•Informal Power

•Strategic Grouping
•Formal Linking
•Rewards
•Information Systems
•Human Resource Management Systems
•Career Systems

FIGURE 18.1 A congruence model of organizations. (*Source:* Nadler [1995]; Tushman & O'Reilly [1997].)

KNOWLEDGE SYSTEM DESIGN

CI Capability—Redesign

Asking the following fundamental questions will assist both in understanding the internal and external environments of a firm, and in the design and implementation of effective processes to manage the firm's knowledge:

• Does our knowledge produce economically valuable performances?
• How do we create knowledge as part of our business practices?
• How do we maintain and enhance our knowledge?
• How do we embody knowledge in products, services, processes, and cultures?
• How do we organize the company to recognize that anyone, anywhere can contribute to the solution of any problem?
• How do we organize around the flow of information rather than geography?

ORGANIZATIONAL CONGRUENCE

A key consideration is the degree of "fit" of the solution to the organization. Nadler's and Tushman and O'Reilly's model of organizational "fit" is effective in identifying the relationship within the organization, represented by the building blocks at the center of figure 18.1. In the organization's present capability there is a disturbing lack of congruence between several of the building blocks. There is formal linking of transactional (retail) business and the relationship-based business (ESD). However, group processes, competencies, corporate values, and rewards do not support this linkage. This presents a serious challenge to the financial institution, in that it must align and support these different processes effectively. Resolution of these issues supersedes the redistribution of the CI capability.

RECOMMENDATIONS

In the following section a number of organizational issues that needs to be addressed is identified according to Nonaka and Takeuchi's (1995) context levels:

Project Team Level

- A pilot project to distribute CI capability should be divided into a series of steps or phases.

- A project team should be established to address issues, plan the development, and oversee the implementation of the plan. The team should comprise sales representatives responsible for ESD, management from appropriate divisions, staff from the centralized CI unit, and information-systems staff. Leadership support must be ensured.

- Team members should provide liaison with their functional departments for design, implementation, and ongoing monitoring. This peripheral participation will assist with both the implementation and refinement of the re-designed capability and generate communities of practice for developing new capabilities.

- Utilize a model of organizational "fit" to evaluate how well the CI process or resource will fit with key organizational components such as culture, people, management preferences, and strategies.

Business-System Level

- Review the issue of cross-selling the ESD's products and services. Historically, there has been great corporate focus on "transactional" sales, but there is an emerging tendency to focus on the emerging importance of "relationship selling." The financial institution needs to determine how to effectively manage these two approaches. One approach might be to increase sales specialization—create a quick-response team of relationship experts to be called upon to develop an account's profitability.

- The organization must ensure that the desired sales behaviors are being reinforced. The account manager's portfolio includes credit-based products that generate quick returns and are easily measured for performance bonuses; the portfolio also includes ESD products and services, which usually require negotiation and fine tuning. The reward system for the former is based on sales volume, and sales activities are geared accordingly. For the latter, a much longer time period is required and measures of the value of the relationship should be developed, such as sales potential.

- The intelligence-gathering capabilities of the sales force must be enhanced through a focused training program.

- Clarity and purpose in the development of organizational routines cannot be overemphasized. The financial institution needs to adapt current business processes (routines) to include:
  - —environmental scanning
  - —recording and distribution of sales-call reports
  - —development and use of sales proposals.

- The organization needs to set the standards for what *is* and *is not* important to attend to and to instill these standards in its front-line sales staff.

Knowledge-Base Level

- Intelligence needs to be made actionable by effective analysis (Harkleroad, 1994) and integrated into the organizational context (Nonaka & Takeuchi, 1995). The knowledge-base level of the organization is the foundation for context. The corporate vision and strategy guide the processes at the other two levels. It is here that the knowledge acquired by the organization becomes competitive intelligence. This specialized function requires expertise: putting the knowledge into context should remain with the centralized CI unit.

- A corporate Intranet (Prescott, 1997) should be developed. The financial institution had tested the use of "bulletin boards" in sharing information among staff. A comprehensive internal survey was conducted regarding the sharing of information.

- A competitive intelligence/knowledge database needs to be developed to distribute the capability throughout the organization. Participation of the project team is only the first step. The "population" of the database and ongoing contribution to and use of the CI must be monitored and recognized.

- Identify impacts of the CI function on the performance of the business units and the organization as a whole.

SUMMARY AND CONCLUSIONS

The financial institution must adapt several organizational processes to support the sales force in managing customer relationships. Closer involvement with the customer generates opportunities to gain substantial knowledge—knowledge that must be integrated into the organization. To be useful, the knowledge must be re-categorized and enmeshed in an appropriate organizational context. While the knowledge acquisition and sharing is an important role for the sales force, the analysis and integration should remain a central function.

References

Allee, V. (1997). "12 Principles of Knowledge Management," *Training and Development* 51(11): 71–74.

Amidon, D.M. (1998). "The Evolving Community of Knowledge Practice: The Ken Awakening," *International Journal of Technology Management* 16(1/2/3): 45–63.

Brown, J.S., and P. Duguid. (1998). "Organizing Knowledge," *California Management Review* 40(3): 90–111.

Buckman, R.H. (1998). "Knowledge Sharing at Buckman Labs," *Journal of Business Strategy* 19(1): 11–15.

Cowen, T., and J. Ellig. (1995). "Market-based Management at Koch Industries: Discovery, Dissemination, and Integration of Knowledge," *Competitive Intelligence Review* 6(4): 4–13.

Davenport, T.H., D.W. De Long, and M.C. Beers. (1998). "Successful Knowledge Management Projects," *Sloan Management Review* 39(2): 43–57.

Davenport, T.H., and L. Prusak. (1998). *Working Knowledge*. Boston: Harvard Business School Press.

Demarest, M. (1997). "Understanding Knowledge Management," *Long-Range Planning* 30(3): 374–84.

Galvin, R.W. (1997). "Competitive Intelligence at Motorola," *Competitive Intelligence Review* 8(1): 3–6.

Ghoshal, S., and D.E. Westney. (1991). "Organizing Competitor Analysis Systems," *Strategic Management Journal* 12(1): 17–31.

Grant, R.M. (1997). "The Knowledge-Based View of the Firm: Implications for Management Practice," *Long-Range Planning* 30(3): 450–54.

Halal, W.E. (1997). "Organizational Intelligence: What Is It, and How Can Managers Use It?" *Strategy and Business* 9 (fourth quarter): 10–14.

Harkleroad, D. (1994). "Making Intelligence Analysis Actionable," *Competitive Intelligence Review* 5(2): 13–17.

Kahn, K.B. (1996). "Interdepartmental Integration: A Definition with Implications for Product Development Performance," *Journal of Product Innovation Management* 13(2): 137–51.

Lapierre, J., and B. Henault. (1996). "Bi-directional Information Transfer: An Imperative for Network and Marketing Integration in a Canadian Telecommunications Firm," *Journal of Product Innovation Management* 13(2): 152–66.

Leonard-Barton, D. (1995). *Wellsprings of Knowledge: Building and Sustaining the Sources of Innovation*. Boston: Harvard University Press.

Moingeon, B., and A. Edmondson, eds. (1996). *Organizational Learning and Competitive Advantage*. Thousand Oaks, CA: Sage Publications.

Moss Kanter, R. (1996). "When a Thousand Flowers Bloom: Structural, Collective, and Social Conditions for Innovation in Organizations," in *Knowledge Management and Organizational Design*, ed. Paul Myers. Boston: Butterworth-Heinemann.

Myers, P. (1996). "Knowledge Management and Organizational Design: An Introduction," in *Knowledge Management and Organizational Design*, ed. P. Myers. Boston: Butterworth-Heinemann.

Nadler, D.A. (1995). "A Congruence Model for Diagnosing Organizational Behavior," in *The Organizational Behavior Reader*, 6th ed., ed. D.A. Kolb, J.S. Osland, and I.M. Rubin. Englewood Cliffs, NJ: Prentice-Hall.

Nonaka, I., and H. Takeuchi. (1995). *The Knowledge-Creating Company.* New York: Oxford University Press.

Prescott, J.E. (1987). "A Process for Applying Analytic Models in Competitive Analysis," in *Strategic Planning and Management Handbook*, ed. W. King and D. Cleland. New York: Von Nostrand Reinhold.

————. (1997). "SCIP Panel Discussion: Symposium: Lessons Learned and the Road Ahead," *Competitive Intelligence Review* 8(1): 15.

Sawka, K.A., D.B. Francis, and J.P. Herring. (1995). "Evaluating Business Intelligence Systems: How Does Your Company Rate?" *Competitive Intelligence Review* 6(4): 22–25.

Snow, C.C., R.E. Miles, and H.J. Coleman Jr. (1995). "Managing 21st Century Network Organizations," in *The Organizational Behavior Reader*, 6th ed., ed. D.A. Kolb, J.S. Osland, and I.M. Rubin. Englewood Cliffs, NJ: Prentice-Hall.

Sveiby, K.E. (1997). *The New Organizational Wealth.* San Francisco: Berrett-Koehler Publishers.

Tushman, M.L., and C.A. O'Reilly III. (1997). *Winning Through Innovation: A Practical Guide to Leading Organizational Change and Renewal.* Boston: Harvard Business School Press.

Wiig, K.M. (1997). "Integrating Intellectual Capital and Knowledge Management," *Long-Range Planning* 30(3): 399–405.

19

Competitive Intelligence in Service Industries

Dawn E. Clarke

INTRODUCTION

The characteristics of a service are very different from the characteristics of a product. It is a logical extension, therefore, to assume that traditional product/manufacturing-focused competitive intelligence (CI) processes will differ when performing CI in service industries. The purpose of this chapter is to establish the similarities and the differences between CI in product-based and service-based industries. A discussion on service characteristics, industry success factors, and competitive threats in service industries culminates in the development of a CI value-chain concept in service industries. Finally, a framework for gathering information and competitive analysis of service industries is proposed, along with suggestions for future research.

COMPETITIVE INTELLIGENCE IN SERVICE INDUSTRIES

The goal of business is to maximize shareholder value. When a company can consistently achieve higher-than-average profitability levels it clearly has a competitive advantage in its industry. "In general, firms that engage in CI activities that increase the efficiency of information gathering and dissemination processes are likely to gain a competitive advantage over firms that do not" (Cory, 1996). The benefit of CI is its potential ability to generate a sustainable competitive advantage. The question remains: How many service businesses actively engage in competitive intelligence?

In service businesses, as in other types of businesses, the CI process can be

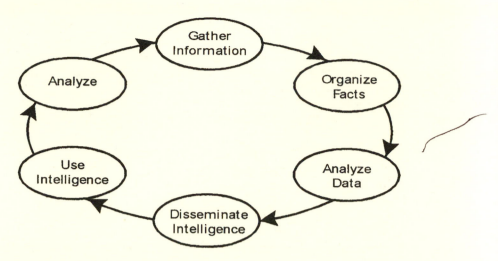

FIGURE 19.1 The competitive intelligence process.

depicted as a perpetual cycle of information gathering and analysis (see figure 19.1). Service businesses have many methods of continuously gathering information about their competitors and their customers. However, many service-industry companies have not yet discovered the true value of this information in terms of gaining a competitive advantage. Used effectively, the CI process could assist players in service industries to organize the facts they have gathered, to analyze the data, and to generate usable intelligence.

The new competitive landscape is characterized by increasing strategic discontinuities, blurring of industry boundaries, hypercompetitive markets, extreme emphasis on price, quality, and customer satisfaction, increasing focus on innovation and continuous learning, and changing career dynamics and employee expectations (Hitt, Keats, & DeMarie, 1998). A single leader once dominated many industries. For example, IBM once dominated the computer industry, and Xerox was the only name in photocopiers. In the new competitive landscape, environmental forces create an uneven playing field for these corporations. In this type of competitive environment, when strategic discontinuities occur frequently, these businesses are forced to develop strategic flexibility in order to survive. "Strategic flexibility is the ability to adjust or develop strategies to respond to external or internal changes" (Aaker, 1998). Diversification and effective utilization of resources are two of the ways service businesses can achieve strategic flexibility. Service industries are dynamic by nature. To gain or maintain any type of sustainable competitive advantage, a service business must achieve the ability to adapt and/or change course in order to predict, identify, and seize any window of opportunity that develops within the industry.

Both IBM and Xerox discovered that customer satisfaction was a key component to navigating in their new competitive landscapes. They each developed strategies that increased customer-service quality. These corporations used CI to gain competitive advantages by creating strategies to offer intangible assets to satisfy their customers. In fact, in the North American economy, "service—bold, fast, unexpected, innovative, and customized—is the ultimate strategic imperative" (Henkoff, 1994). This leads to the question: "Can CI be used to create sustainable competitive advantages in service industries?"

The primary characteristics that differentiate *services* from *goods* are:

- *Intangibility*
- *Heterogeneity:* nonstandardization
- *Inseparability:* of production and consumption
- *Perishability:* cannot be stored.

"A service is rendered. A service is experienced. A service cannot be stored on a shelf, touched, tasted, or tried on for size" (Shostack, 1977).

Successful service companies recognize that establishing relationships with customers and exceeding customer expectations are key elements to developing competitive advantages. According to Parasuraman, Zeithaml, and Berry's (1994) SERVQUAL model, the five dimensions of service are *reliability*, *tangibles*, *responsiveness*, *assurance*, and *empathy*. "Turning service quality into a powerful competitive weapon requires continuous striving for service superiority—consistently performing above the adequate service level and capitalizing on opportunities for exceeding the desired service level" (Parasuraman, Zeithaml, & Berry, 1994).

Customer satisfaction translates into profitability and growth. Satisfied customers tend to buy more often, to purchase more profitable services, and to defect less frequently. In service companies, defection rates are leading indicators of profit swings, and are highly influenced by service quality. As the real or perceived quality of a service increases, customer defection decreases and the number of first-time customers increases. Moreover, as service quality increases, overall costs decrease because costly service-recovery strategies do not need to be employed.

There is a known process for transforming service quality into profits. Service quality is the driving force behind lowering costs, improving customer retention, and attracting new customers. Businesses operating in service industries often generate very modest profit margins. Therefore attracting and retaining the right customer is imperative to lowering the cost of serving the business's customer base. The age-old sales adage that "the customer is always right" is increasingly fading from the new competitive landscape. Not every customer is the *right* customer for a service business. Some customers are very expensive to maintain; these customers actually increase costs, lower profits, and have the potential to decrease the quality of service experienced by others who are the correct fit for the business. The trend toward de-marketing certain customers is becoming more popular in service industries.

Service quality and service superiority are standards established according to customer perceptions and expectations. For service companies, the cost of quality is the cost of doing it right the first time. Long-term satisfied customers are increasingly generating more profits each year that they remain loyal to the service provider. Continuous improvement in service quality should not be viewed as a cost, but rather as an investment in a customer who generates more profit than the margin on a one-time sale.

Recent research suggests that both customers and service providers benefit from long-term relationships. For example, Gwinner, Gremler, and Bitner (1998) state that "[l]oyal customers can lead to increased revenues for the firm, result in predictable sales and profit streams, are more likely to purchase additional goods and services, typically lead to low customer turnover, and often generate new business for a firm via word-of-mouth recommendations." Their research suggests that customers involved in a long-term relationship receive three categories of benefits: confidence, social, and special treatment. They conclude that confidence benefits are what customers value the most and are the key to sustainable customer relationships. "Customers buy from people they know and trust" (Gwinner, Gremler, & Bitner, 1998).

Understanding the needs and desires of customers is essential to building relationships. Customer-focused CI activities can increase a service provider's probability of gaining a competitive advantage by identifying customer expectations and building long-term customer relationships. Many service providers in the hospitality industry—hotels and restaurants—gather intelligence on a regular basis. They seek to understand customers through the use of comment cards or customer-satisfaction surveys. Based on feedback, hotels may update services and amenities, and restaurants may offer improved service or change menu selections. A current example of this are the menu changes being introduced to the Canadian Swiss Chalet chain of restaurants. The company has traditionally maintained predominantly chicken-based menu selections. In the spring of 1999, based on customer comments and feedback from wait-staff, vegetarian selections were added to the menu. Over the next nine months, hamburgers, steak, and pasta selections were also added. These changes are a strategic response to industry competition. The strategy evolved from information gathering and analysis—competitive intelligence.

Airlines utilize CI tools to understand their customers, build relationships, and retain customers. American Airlines' SABRE system is the result of listening to customers' desire for a quick-and-efficient ticketing process. When first introduced, SABRE provided American Airlines a competitive advantage in its industry. Another airline, British Airways, stated in its 1994 Annual Report that its goal was "to be the best and most successful company in the airline industry." Its service strategy combines the development of identifiable brands with the delivery of top-quality customer service. In order to achieve this, British Airways developed its Customer Analysis and Retention System (CARESS). This information system was developed to ensure rapid response to customer complaints. Essentially, it is a tool to gather customer-focused competitive information.

Services marketers identify customer satisfaction as one of the fundamental keys to success or failure in the services industry. Thomas Stewart (1997) writes that "studies show that merely meeting customers' needs won't make them loyal. What it really takes is finding ways to make your service truly stand out." His article points out that satisfied customers will defect—not because they are not satisfied, but because they are not delighted with the service they have received. The defection of a satisfied customer is the result of the sum of each service encounter that the customer has with the service provider. "The gulf between satisfied customers and completely satisfied customers can swallow a business" (Stewart, 1997). Jones and Sasser (1995) caution that relying solely on customer-satisfaction surveys can be hazardous, because the results may not correctly identify *re*-purchasing behaviors. They identify customers as "a company's best friends and worst enemies," and have categorized customers as:

- *Loyalist/Apostle:* highly satisfied customer who exhibits supportive behavior and high levels of customer behavior
- *Defector/Terrorist:* an unhappy customer who has had a bad experience, defects, and tells everyone he or she knows about the experience
- *Mercenary:* highly satisfied customer who exhibits low commitment to the service provider—impulse buyer looking for low prices and fashion trends
- *Hostage:* an unhappy customer who is unable to switch service providers; he or she is a difficult and expensive customer.

Loyalists are the most desirable customers, making it important that a service provider identify ways to attract and retain them. On the other hand, hostages and defectors drive costs upward without contributing a profitable return. The CI process can be used to rid a service provider of these customers without alienating present or potential loyalists. The mercenary may provide a modest profit, but this type of customer is more expensive to maintain than a loyalist. It is important that the CI process maintain a watchful eye on the mercenary. The service provider should attempt to move the mercenary to the loyalist category without incurring excessive costs. Table 19.1 summarizes the cost, benefit, and CI implications of each customer category and demonstrates how the CI process can augment customer-satisfaction survey results to greatly enhance winning service strategies.

COMPETITIVE THREATS AND OPPORTUNITIES IN SERVICE INDUSTRIES

Competitive intelligence utilizes a variety of tools to identify and analyze competitive threats and opportunities. These tools vary in degrees of sophistication and technology. Information-gathering methods range from a relatively simple survey of competitors' press releases, to a more complex marketing-research project. Service companies are very familiar with marketing research. Most service organizations engage in some form of market research on a regular basis: customer-comment cards, customer-satisfaction surveys, or market-share data. Many service organizations confuse CI with marketing research. Although both CI and marketing research have elements in common, their focus, scope, and interpretation of information, among other things, are quite different.

Table 19.1

COMPETITIVE INTELLIGENCE IMPLICATIONS OF CUSTOMER TYPE

Customer Type	Profit Potential	Cost to Maintain	CI Implications
Loyalist/ Apostle	High	Low	• Most desirable customer • Gather intelligence on what services satisfy this customer and how to maintain loyalty
Defector/ Terrorist	Low	High	• Least desirable customer • Gather intelligence on how to mitigate the negative word-of-mouth during and subsequent to customer defection • Gather data on how to avoid making the same mistakes with other customers
Mercenary	Moderate	Moderate	• This customer is desirable if the cost to maintain is less than the customer's profitability • Gather data on this customer's transactions with competitors • Analyze transactions to ensure cost–benefit ratio is balanced in service provider's favor
Hostage	Low to Moderate	High	• Undesirable customer • Analyze customer's barriers to switching service providers and identify ways to remove the barriers

Marketing research is a service organization's link with its market environment. Much like CI, marketing research relies on gathering, analysis, and interpretation of information to identify threats and opportunities. Management uses this research for situational analysis and strategy development. However, marketing research is a static analysis and interpretation of a market environment at one point in time, and usually lacks useful inferences about competitive strategies in the marketplace. On the other hand, CI has a much broader focus and scope. Competitive intelligence is a dynamic process of gathering, analysis, interpretation, and utilization of *all* information connecting a service organization with its total environment.

Defining the competition is the first step toward gathering competitive information. Traditionally, competition has been identified as companies in similar businesses, selling similar services to the same set of customers. Increasingly, companies with related capabilities (selling substitutes to a service-provider's customer) have begun to surface as competitive threats. Market trends, technological developments, new customers' preferences, and competitors' capabilities have combined to create an environment from which new, nontraditional competitive threats have emerged (see figure 19.2).

An example of a nontraditional threat is the emergence of customers as a competitive threat to many service businesses. Table 19.2 shows the CI implications of customer behaviors that have affected the competitive nature of the market environment.

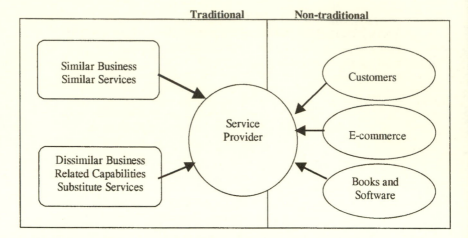

FIGURE 19.2 Traditional and nontraditional competitive threats in service industries.

According to a series of articles written by Deborah Sawyer (1996; 1997a, b), customers have the potential of becoming competitive threats when:

• There is too much competition—hypercompetition
• Customers have had bad experiences in the service encounter
• Customers exhibit ritual loyalty
• Customers exhibit a lack of knowledge.

Hypercompetition presents the customer with a vast array of services. In recent years, following deregulation of long-distance telephone services, customers have faced an onslaught of long-distance-service choices. Customers who had never considered switching service providers were suddenly given opportunities to consider features and service levels. As a result, prices in the industry fell rapidly. New competitors have not yet unseated the market-share leader because "too much competition translates for customers into too much choice: too many options, variations, prices, and possibilities, all of which create an unstable environment in which to buy" (Sawyer, 1996). Too much competition causes some customers to delay their purchase decisions. Competitive analysis may influence service providers with weak market share to exit the market. Conversely, analysis may identify an unoccupied market niche capable of creating a competitive advantage.

Customer ritual becomes a competitive threat when companies with sustainable competitive advantages are unable to win customers from inferior service providers: "Ritual represents customer loyalty your competitor has won, although this is not the same thing as saying the loyalty is deserved" (Sawyer, 1997a). Ritual involves relying on time-honored actions or ways of thinking. The older the habit, the more difficult it is to break established patterns. "It isn't

Table 19.2

**COMPETITIVE INTELLIGENCE IMPLICATIONS OF CUSTOMERS
AS COMPETITIVE THREATS**

Competitive Threat	CI Implication
Hypercompetition—when faced with too many choices, customers may delay their purchase decisions	• Service organization must be constantly aware of new and/or potential entrants to the market • Management must develop competitive strategies to differentiate their service(s) from those offered by the competition
Negative service experience—when a past service encounter has been a bad experience, customers tend to avoid future service encounters	• Competitive analysis of customer feedback will assist in the identification of deterioration in service quality • It will be necessary to analyze market share trends in order to infer whether negative experiences have driven customers to a competitor or from the market completely • Management must develop strategies to: —minimize negative service experience(s) for the organization's customers —encourage competitor's defectors to utilize organization's services
Ritual loyalty—when habitual buying patterns become synonymous with customer loyalty, customers may choose to purchase inferior services	• Competitive analysis of competitor's service quality correlated with industry market share analysis will assist in the identification of ritual loyalty • Management must develop strategies to: —consistently provide superior service quality —provide customer with incentives to switch service providers
Lack of knowledge—when unsure of how a service works (or what benefits the service offers) customers may be unwilling or unable to use the service	• Competitive intelligence should focus on the customer's level of knowledge • Competitive analysis will assist in the identification of barriers which prevent customer adoption of service(s) • Management must develop strategies to educate customers and remove existing barriers

enough to offer something attractive in terms of price, product, quality, or guarantees, you also have to find a way to diminish the ritual, and give the customer some reason to move outside of the tremendous comfort zone they have" (Sawyer, 1997b). In this case, traditional CI on the competitor is necessary to identify incentives for switching. A competitive analysis is focused on the competitors' customers in an attempt to discover ways to get them to try another company's service.

Customers' lack of knowledge is a competitive threat for providers of new, unique, or complex services. Traditional market research may indicate potential market share for a new service, but if the customers do not understand how the service works, or what the benefits are to the customer, lack of knowledge may translate to zero growth in market share. Competitive intelligence focused on the level of customer knowledge may identify this as a major competitive barrier to market entry, and allow]companies to factor it into their marketing plans accordingly.

Two other nontraditional competitive threats to service providers have emerged in the recent past: E-commerce and self-help books or software are making their presence known in service industries; particularly affected are traditional providers of professional services. Evidence of these new trends is on-line, secure access visits to the psychiatrist, and on-line consultations with lawyers—for a fee charged to the customer's credit card. Other competitively threatening items are software packages such as the *Canadian Legal Will Kit*, or do-it-yourself divorce kits.

Benefits of Using Competitive Intelligence in Service Industries

Competitive intelligence enables service companies to know what is happening in the marketplace in terms of the industry, the competition, and the customer. The new competitive landscape described by Hitt, Keats, and DeMarie (1998) depicts a dynamic, rapidly changing marketplace. Service companies must be able to keep pace and be able to respond appropriately.

In an atmosphere of constant adaptation and change it is sometimes difficult to justify the cost—in terms of money and manpower—of implementing and maintaining a CI process in a service organization. However, if the goal of business is to increase shareholder value, increased profits should be the goal of the service organization. When the end of the value chain is the company's bottom line, it is equally difficult to justify not having a CI program in place. Figure 19.3 is a proposed depiction of a service-industry value chain that includes the CI process.

The starting point of this value chain is the CI process. The primary goal of gathering and analyzing information is to generate usable intelligence that is both timely and factual. This process should assist management in making more informed decisions, thus facilitating improved strategy development. With a more focused strategy, a service organization has the potential to enhance the quality of service(s) offered to its customers. As discussed previously, increased service quality results in increased customer satisfaction, which tends to increase the level of customer retention. Any service organization that successfully encourages repeat business has the potential to enhance long-term relationships with customers. Long-term relationships have benefits for both the customer and the service organization. One of the benefits management realizes is the reduction in costs associated with servicing a long-term customer. Reduced costs and a stable customer base both tend to increase strategic flexibility and may lead to increased profits.

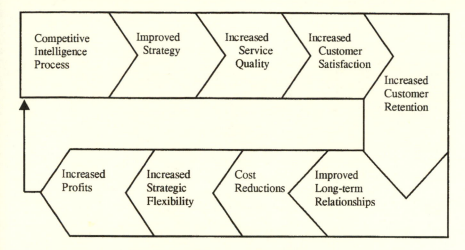

FIGURE 19.3 Competitive intelligence value chain in service industries.

COMPETITIVE INTELLIGENCE FRAMEWORK FOR SERVICE INDUSTRIES

The benefits derived from the CI value chain in service industries depend upon customer satisfaction and retention. Therefore customer analysis should form an integral part of the CI process in service industries. Figure 19.4 is a proposed framework for gathering and analyzing information in service industries.

The elements of this framework are sequential in nature, beginning with a broad examination of the service industry, and gradually refining the focus with each subsequent stage of the analysis. Competitive intelligence in any service organization should begin with a broad analysis of the industry environment, then narrow the focus slightly to analyze the service organization in relation to the environment. Once the service provider is aware of the organization's position in the industry, concurrent analysis of both competitors and customers will assist management in developing and implementing strategic decisions.

Table 19.3 identifies the objectives and outcomes of the analytical tools suggested for use in the CI framework. It should be noted that these tools were selected because they are relatively easy to apply in a service industry. Other CI tools could be substituted into the framework, but they may be more complicated and require dedicated organizational personnel. Many service organizations that would benefit from analyzing their competitors are small businesses with limited resources and are not likely to have the personnel to focus on in-depth competitive intelligence.

Environmental Analysis

As with product-based industries, the initial starting point is an analysis of the market environment in order to determine the profit potential of the service industry:

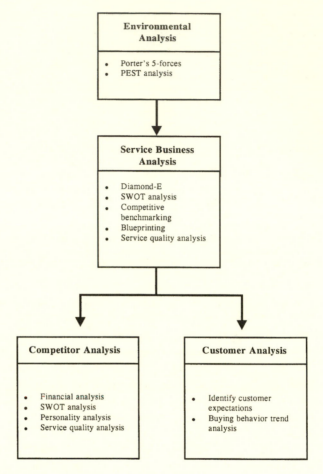

FIGURE 19.4 Competitive intelligence framework and tools for analyzing service industries.

- How profitable is this service industry?
- What are the factors critical for success in this industry?
- How is the industry evolving?

There is no point in planning the expansion of a barbershop in an isolated town with a population of 25 unless land developers have begun work on a 500-home subdivision. Industry analysis relies upon traditional competitive analysis tools—Porter's 5-forces model, and a political, economic, social, and technological (PEST) analysis. This initial step will begin to identify the competitive environment in which the service organization will work. Competitive analysis of the information should identify which resources are scarce and what untapped opportunities exist, as this is where sustainable competitive advantages can be created.

Table 19.3

OBJECTIVES AND INTENDED OUTCOMES OF ANALYTICAL TOOLS USED IN COMPETITIVE INTELLIGENCE FRAMEWORK

Analytical Tool	CI Objective	Intended Outcome
Environmental Analysis		
Porter's 5-forces	• Analyze strength of competitive rivalry • Determine the profitability of the industry	• Position service organization within the market environment where they operate
PEST	• Identify the political, economic, social, and technological policies and trends affecting the industry	• Develop an understanding of the environmental framework and boundaries for the service organization
Service-Business Analysis		
SERVO	• Analysis of the service organization, management preferences, resources, strategy, and how these elements fit with the market environment	• Develop a thorough understanding of business systems operating within service organization • Measure organizational performance
SWOT	• Identify the organizational strengths and weaknesses, as well as the environmental opportunities and threats	• Identify service gaps that may affect service quality and/or profitability • Identify scarce resources, unexploited opportunities, and sustainable competitive advantages
Competitive Benchmarking	• Identify similar organizational processes in other industries and compare the service organization with the best	
Blueprinting	• Develop a process blueprint to identify every aspect of the service organization's operations	
Service Quality	• Analyze the quality of service provided by the organization	
Competitor Analysis		
Financial Analysis	• Analyze the financial health and organizational stability of competitors	• Develop an understanding of competitors' business systems and predict possible reactions to changes in the market environment
SWOT	• Identify the strengths, weaknesses, opportunities, and threats faced by competitor organizations	• Develop a profile of competitor weaknesses and possible service gaps
Personality	• Analyze competitors' corporate culture, values, and past strategies	
Service Quality	• Analyze competitors' quality of service	
Customer Analysis		
Customer Expectations	• Identify the service and quality expectations and opinions of industry customers	• Develop a profile of customer behavior and a strategy to meet and exceed customer desires and expectations
Customer Behavior	• Analyze purchase behavior exhibited by customers	

Service-Business Analysis

Once the industry profitability has been established, competitive analysis should focus on the service organization itself. A SERVO analysis will enable the service provider to identify the degree of fit between the service organization and its competitive environment. This is followed by a Strengths, Weaknesses, Opportunities, Threats (SWOT) analysis: Will the strengths and weakness of the organization exploit the scarce resources in the service industry, or will the threats be insurmountable?

The use of competitive benchmarking in the service-business analysis will measure the organization's performance against best-in-class performance of other service and possibly nonservice companies. Competitive analysis takes a comprehensive look at the overall business and its strategy, but competitive benchmarking focuses on one specific function or process in the service business. The benchmarking effort asks the questions:

• Where do we need to improve the process?

• How do we improve the process?

The answers to these questions will enable the service provider to develop intelligence-based strategies to meet and exceed the performance of the competition. Competitive benchmarking sets targets and convinces organizations that they can meet them.

Benchmarking is outward focused, while an inward focus on processes can be gained by blueprinting the service encounter from beginning to end. A service blueprint is essentially a snapshot of the service: "Blueprinting helps to communicate the details of a service in ways that are useful to managers and employees, often revealing systems that might otherwise remain invisible" (Kingman-Brundage, 1992). Blueprints can efficiently and intelligently identify service gaps that, if left alone, may be costly to the profitability of the company.

The final analysis conducted of the service business is the service-quality competitive analysis model shown in figure 19.5. This analytical model has been created to recognize the dimensions of service identified in Parasuraman, Zeithaml, and Berry's research in service-quality measurement: "Since customers' service expectations seem to exist at both adequate and desired levels, firms need to measure two potential service-quality gaps: the gap between perceived service and *adequate* service, and the gap between perceived service and *desired* service" (Parasuraman, Zeithaml, & Berry, 1994). The following section builds upon the research of Parasuraman, Zeithaml, and Berry in order to develop a competitive analysis tool specifically for the service industries to measure service gaps. The CI model is an attempt to address the need for service businesses to continuously analyze their knowledge of customer expectations and level of customer service.

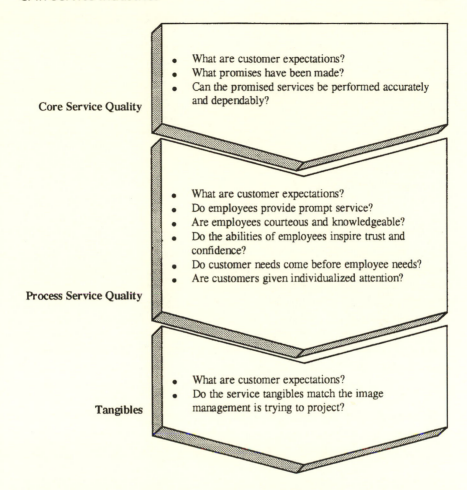

Core Service Quality

- What are customer expectations?
- What promises have been made?
- Can the promised services be performed accurately and dependably?

Process Service Quality

- What are customer expectations?
- Do employees provide prompt service?
- Are employees courteous and knowledgeable?
- Do the abilities of employees inspire trust and confidence?
- Do customer needs come before employee needs?
- Are customers given individualized attention?

Tangibles

- What are customer expectations?
- Do the service tangibles match the image management is trying to project?

FIGURE 19.5 Service-quality competitive analysis model.

Competitor Analysis

In order to avoid surprises and reduce competitive threats, competitor analysis is conducted by the service business. Traditional CI tools, especially financial and market analysis, help to identify where competitors are placed. Since customer satisfaction is essential to success in service industries, the service-quality competitive analysis is useful in identifying competitors' service gaps. An external view of this model may not be complete, but it will provide some insights to competitive advantages and/or disadvantages that the competition may have (see figure 19.5).

It is important to understand and describe the competitor's situation. It is equally important to understand and be able to predict how the competitor is likely to react in any given situation. Therefore a competitive analysis of the competitor's personality is essential to developing a strategy that will counteract competitor reaction. Competitive information to determine the personality of a competitor may include the following:

• Organizational structure

• Key decision-makers

• Ownership

• Business vision and goals

• Business strategies

• Market communications.

Customer Analysis

Last, but not least important, is the need for the CI process to analyze service-industry customers. In an industry where the ultimate goal is customer satisfaction, it is essential for a service provider to identify customers' expectations. In the conceptual service-industry framework, understanding customer expectations is an integral part of both service-business analysis and competitor analysis. The service-quality competitive analysis model's service dimensions each ask the question: "What are customer expectations?" The service provider that can correctly identify customer expectations for each dimension may have a competitive advantage in the industry—as long as he or she has the capabilities to meet and exceed those expectations. An analysis of customer-buying behavior and purchasing trends is another important aspect of customer analysis.

CONCLUSION

This chapter has identified general, abstract dimensions of CI in service industries. It has developed a value chain, a model for gathering information according to the five dimensions of service, and a conceptual framework to analyze the elements of service industries. Empirical research to demonstrate the value of these tools will enhance the learning of all CI professionals. Additionally, further empirical research will add to the somewhat sparse CI literature specifically written to increase the depth of CI knowledge in services industries.

An understanding of the unique qualities of the service industry—particularly the need to establish customer relationships and satisfy customer expectations—can be developed by researching the wealth of data found in the services-marketing literature. The proposed conceptual CI framework for service industries demonstrates how closely entwined the customer is with the service provider. Competitive intelligence in service industries cannot be effective unless the customer becomes an integral part of the CI process.

REFERENCES

Aaker, D.A. (1998). *Strategic Market Management.* New York: Wiley.

Cory, K.D. (1996). "Can Competitive Intelligence Lead to a Sustainable Competitive Advantage?" *Competitive Intelligence Review* 7(3): 45–55.

Gwinner, K.P., D.D. Gremler, and M.J. Bitner. (1998). "Relational Benefits in Services Industries: The Customer's Perspective," *Journal of the Academy of Marketing Science* 26(2): 101–14.

Henkoff, R. (1994). "Service Is Everybody's Business," *Fortune* 129(13): 48–60.

Hitt, M.A., B.W. Keats, and S.M. DeMarie. (1998). "Navigating in the New Competitive Landscape: Building Strategic Flexibility and Competitive Advantage in the 21st Century," *Academy of Management Executive* 12(4): 22–42.

Jones, T.O., and W.E. Sasser Jr. (1995). "Why Satisfied Customers Defect," *Harvard Business Review* 73(6): 88–99.

Kingman-Brundage, J. (1992). "The ABCs of Service System Blueprinting," in *Managing Services*, 2d ed., ed. C.H. Lovelock. Englewood Cliffs, NJ: Prentice-Hall.

Parasuraman, A., V. Zeithaml, and L. Berry. (1994). "Alternative Scales for Measuring Service Quality: A Comparative Assessment Based on Psychometric and Diagnostic Criteria," *Journal of Marketing* 70(3): 201–30.

Sawyer, D.C. (1996). "Competing Against Too Much Competition," *Competitive Intelligence Review* 7(2): 84–85.

———. (1997a) "Customer Ritual as a Competitive Threat," *Competitive Intelligence Review* 8(2): 83–84.

———. (1997b). "When Customers' Lack of Knowledge Is Your Biggest Competitive Threat," *Competitive Intelligence Review* 8(4): 78–79.

Shostack, G.L. (1977). "Breaking Free From Product Marketing," *Journal of Marketing* 41(2): 73–80.

Stewart, T.A. (1997). "A Satisfied Customer Isn't Enough," *Fortune* 136(2): 112–13.

20

Information Technology: Enabling Competitive Intelligence Adoption in Small-to-Medium Enterprises

J. Graeme Somerville

INTRODUCTION

Until recently, the information available to assist small and medium enterprises (SMEs) in assessing the issues associated with the implementation of competitive intelligence (CI) has been minimal. The literature is replete with examples, anecdotes, and studies of the implementation of CI in large organizations such as GM, AT&T, Motorola, and Nutrasweet. It appears that only large organizations have had the resources required to make the long-term investments needed for the creation and maintenance of CI. Experiences and insights have been gained within these large corporations with respect to the impact of CI on corporate strategy, tactics, organizational structures, and culture. Throughout the 1990s the business environment has become increasingly more complex, dynamic, and fast-paced. Sustainable competitive advantage, while hard fought for, is often short-lived.

Small-to-medium enterprises operate, thrive, and survive in the same competitive climate as their larger counterparts. In Canada, in 1997 SMEs with less than 500 employees accounted for 99.8 percent of all businesses and represented approximately 60 percent of business employment (Lagace, 1997). Small firms, according to the Canadian Federation of Independent Business (CFIB), demonstrate the greatest job creation during economic downturns and contribute the most to job growth during economic expansions (Lagace, 1997).

Now that larger firms have paved the way for the CI function within the enterprise, it is appropriate for SMEs to more fully explore its adoption. New information technologies—such as the Internet, the availability of Web-based services, the availability of outsourced CI services, and packaged CI application software—all contribute to make possible a CI function within SMEs. There are four new primary changes in CI: company size, technology and the Internet, knowledge management, and outsourcing (Hohhof, 1998). An increasing number of CI professionals is working as solo practitioners in SMEs (Hohhof, 1998). Knowledge management and decentralization of business intelligence are important trends for the future (Fuld et al., 1997). This chapter will discuss issues with respect to implementing CI infrastructure that is geared primarily to SMEs.

KNOWLEDGE MANAGEMENT WITHIN SMEs

Lotus Corporation defines *knowledge management* as the "systematic leveraging of information and expertise to improve organizational responsiveness, productivity, and competency" (Lotus Corporation, 1999). Knowledge has recently been recognized as important to wealth creation within firms and as an important corporate asset (Hohhof, 1998). This growing need for knowledge springs from increased global competition, the reduction of barriers to entry into a competitor's market, and the shortening of product lifecycles (Zanasi, 1998). Company survival and success are now determined by the rate at which companies learn and accumulate knowledge. If a firm's rate of learning is greater than that of its competitors, the firm has the potential for long-term success (Guimaraes & Armstrong, 1998).

One of the challenges faced by the CI function today is to effectively convert the large amount of information that is received. Information that does not get converted into intelligence will not be used in strategic decision-making processes. One estimate of the amount of information that is actually analyzed within corporations is 7 percent (Powell, 1997). In the SME, accumulation of information and its conversion into knowledge through analysis are often constrained due to human and financial resource issues.

THE ROLE OF INFORMATION TECHNOLOGY IN THE DEVELOPMENT OF COMPETITIVE INTELLIGENCE INFRASTRUCTURE FOR SMEs

One of the critical success factors for any sized firm that is considering the implementation of a CI function is to ensure that sufficient resources are applied to supporting the technical infrastructure. High-performance networks, the Internet, and new application software provide powerful tools for the CI professional. A 1999 CFIB study shows that the use of the Internet by SMEs has grown rapidly in the past four years. Member companies with 50–99 employees, and those with 100–499 employees, are connected to the Internet at rates of 80 and 88 percent, respectively (Mallett, 1999). While this study defined Internet connection in broad terms and did not indicate how the connectivity was used, it indicates that there has been a recognition and subsequent adoption of the Internet as a business tool by SMEs.

The Internet is one of the important elements in the CI toolkit for the gathering and dissemination of information. The top three reasons for Internet use by business are: to improve the quality of CI (70%); to increase the cost effectiveness of acquiring, disseminating, and using internal information (58%); and to adding value to existing products and services (55%) (Graef, 1997). Interestingly, Graef's study also indicated that attitudes of a surprising percentage of senior management (38%) toward the Internet were indifferent or negative. Senior-management commitment and support are required not only in the CI program itself, but also within its component parts.

A review of the CI literature reveals a number of important findings with respect to the contribution of well-designed information systems (IS). A 1998 study discussed the linkages between CI, business change, and IS support effectiveness (Guimaraes & Armstrong, 1998). The authors demonstrated that firms that possessed above-average effectiveness of their information systems were also those firms that were highly effective in implementing business change. Firms with above-average CI effectiveness also had a significantly higher level of business-change effectiveness than did those firms demonstrating below-average CI effectiveness. Finally, those firms with both CI and business-change effectiveness also had an above-average level of information-system-support effectiveness.

In his 1997 survey of the Internet, Graef explains that Internet technology is now in its third wave. The uses of the Internet have progressed from e-mail, monitoring competitors, and gaining access to public sources, through the second stage of Internet marketing and internal CI functions being marketed within the firm, to the third wave of collaborative intelligence. During this third phase, CI professionals will team up with their colleagues to leverage the firm's intellectual capital (Graef, 1997). In this phase, information technology plays an important role in information sharing and collaboration.

There is a number of tools that is available to all staff within the firm that will enable the adoption of CI application software. The basic assumption made here is that all staff involved in the CI function is equipped with workstations connected to the network. Those who travel are equipped with notebook computers, and every employee has access to e-mail and other corporate databases from anywhere that the Internet can be accessed. Technologies that support teams, when used as a primary communications vehicle, enable the building of team memory and provide a repository of shared records. Team members know where the information needs to be routed (or where the CI application is configured to route the information) and where to locate information (Zack & Serino, 1996). A well-structured store of information enables efficient access and distribution of information to team members.

One of the key developments that has emerged in the marketplace over the past decade is that of groupware technologies such as Lotus Notes/Domino and

Microsoft Exchange. The groupware concept was put forward by Lotus Corporation in the mid-1980s as a means to consolidate applications and functionality under the broad umbrella of communication and collaboration, bringing them together as a common set of services (Herardian, 1998). Groupware has evolved over the past decade from basic communication and collaboration, to a workflow engine that supports business-process reengineering, to a webserver and publishing platform, and, finally, to support knowledge management (Herardian, 1998). The key goals of the CI database(s) and software are: to provide a rich application environment for the end-users that supports any document and data-type; to enhance the collection and dissemination of information and knowledge through the organization; to support existing business workflow; to have sufficient flexibility to adapt to new and evolving business models; and, finally, to provide integration with other key elements of the corporate information-technology infrastructure and data.

Commercially available CI applications include such features as support for the majority of PC file-types, searching capabilities, and replication. Future CI applications will include capabilities such as:

- The ability to integrate intelligent agents that will automatically search user selected websites that provide a mechanism to regularly monitor secondary sources (Francis, Sawka, & Herring, 1995). This will reduce the amount of time that can sometimes occur in Web searches (Pawar & Sharda, 1997), and in undirected and informal viewing.

- The inclusion of workflow capabilities into the CI application. Ideally, the workflow should be sufficiently configurable so that business rules can be embedded and modified within the CI application to best reflect the organizational practices of the firm.

- The CI software should include a feedback mechanism from anywhere within the application. This will enhance the usability of the CI solution in the short run and assist with the long-term success of the CI infrastructure through ongoing involvement of the users.

- The use of configurable agents, which will provide a mechanism to monitor corporate-response goals for CI services, including research and analysis.

- The gathering and presentation of statistical information. The availability of the data will allow the manager of the CI function to understand *how* the information and knowledge has been used, *who used* the information, *who created* the information, and *how valuable* the CI information and knowledge is for strategic and tactical support of the firm. This data will be important feedback to the CI manager to tailor the supporting CI software and technology to best suit the organization. A feedback linkage is important in the evaluation of the CI function in order to identify and measure the intelligence being produced (Prescott, Herring, & Panfely, 1998).

- Support for on-line, real-time collaboration of CI professionals. For example, technology such as Sametime from Lotus will allow for synchronous collaboration. Any connected person within the name and address book of the firm (this includes customers, business partners, suppliers, and staff) with the Sametime software can collaborate in real-time via the messaging backbone (local area network [LAN], Internet, Intranet).

• The capability to integrate with document-management systems.

The good news is that the technology continues to evolve at a rapid pace. The features itemized above can be implemented using technology available today. The challenge for most SMEs is that they lack the necessary technical expertise to integrate various technologies in a cost-effective manner.

Information technology is not a panacea. It is important to distinguish between a technology that will enable both business processes and the people that will make a well-designed business-process work (Prince, 1998). Prince further states that effective CI includes the knowledge of how to gain rapid access to information, and that technological excellence alone is insufficient for business success. Information systems must learn to collect and distribute intelligence through all media, including voice mail, E-mail, and groupware. Getting actionable intelligence into the hands of users so that they can take action is one of the critical success factors of the CI function (Imperato, 1998). The business environment of today is characterized by unanticipated events, fluctuations in the global financial markets and changes in technology, and the sudden appearance of new, nontraditional competitors. Clearly, technology infrastructure plays a pivotal role in supporting all corporate functions and can enhance team interaction, collaboration, and information and knowledge sharing.

From the perspective of SMEs, the continued advancements of information technology are accompanied by ongoing reductions of the capital costs to acquire relatively sophisticated hardware and application software. The costs for data-storage, manipulation, and transmittal are falling, and the boundaries of what is feasible are expanding (Porter & Millar, 1985). Skills for supporting the infrastructure are now more readily available. For the small business that may not wish to make information-technology support a core competence, outsourcing of these functions is an option. An emerging trend in 1999 is the development of application service providers (ASPs), which offer hosted applications via the Internet. Organizations evaluating these services are principally concerned with security and ownership of data. Firms are increasingly dependent upon their information systems. A poor outsourcing agreement with a third party may not provide the needed support at a critical time.

ORGANIZATIONAL IMPLICATIONS

Implementation of a CI function within an SME requires careful consideration of the organization, the people, and the culture. Any strategic business process such as CI will require a level of individual and organizational discipline that may not have previously existed within the firm. The organization of the CI function, the tools, models, and analytical techniques are typically based on multiperson CI, either in a central department or coordinated divisional departments (Hohhof,

1998). Competitive intelligence units in smaller firms typically involve a solo CI practitioner who attempts to leverage the firm's existing analytical and information capabilities (Hohhof, 1998).

During the period when companies are growing quickly there are additional strains as new staff are added and must be trained, when employees who have been accustomed to working together may now be widely dispersed, when roles and responsibilities are changing, and when new disciplines and workflow are being adopted by the organization. Hamrefors (1998) put forward the notion of spontaneous environmental scanning (SES), which postulates that individuals will scan the environment based on their perceptions. The more SES that is conducted, the more experience can be developed within the individual and the organization. Repeated experiences then become tacit knowledge that will improve the individual's ability to detect weak signals in his or her task environment. An individual's perceptions change gradually through interaction with the environment. From an organizational standpoint, the more the environment makes sense to the individual, the more these impressions will guide his or her SES and ultimately the "perceptive strength" of the organization will be developed (Hamrefors, 1998). Hamrefors concludes by stating that targeted SES is a precondition for organizational change and learning.

There are a number of organizational design elements that can be incorporated into the design of the CI function that can alleviate some of the problems encountered with the implementation of CI. These include:

- *Development of a decentralized network:* Benchmark organizations are now creating decentralized organizations with centralized networks. Kodak, a large-company example, has instituted a managed matrix in which groups of individuals focus on key competitors and technologies. Contribution and analysis are decentralized, and ongoing meetings ensure that the groups remain effective (Prescott, Herring, & Panfely, 1998). The supporting technology will have a dramatic impact as to whether this decentralized approach can be implemented and managed effectively.

- *Embedding intelligence into the corporate culture:* Best-practices companies are sensitizing the firm to CI and providing the needed training to reinforce the importance of intelligence sharing within the culture (Prescott, Herring, & Panfely, 1998). Culture has been reported as having an impact on CI's utilization and positioning in the firm (Simon, 1997).

- *Understanding the skills of the individuals within the firm:* A key skill will be an individual's ability to quickly distill information received. Smaller units can be more productive if they have determined that is valuable information so that individuals within the firm can focus on targeted sources, services, and networking opportunities (Langabeer, 1998).

- *Team approaches to CI:* Understanding the competencies of individuals within the firm also will contribute to an identification of persons who may be able to make a contribution to the analysis and interpretation function of inbound information. After 1993, IBM consolidated its business intelligence functions using virtual teams that include both CI professionals and representatives from different functional areas (Behnke & Slayton, 1998). Rothberg (1997) suggests that cross-functional "shadow teams" be used to accumulate information about competitors that can be quickly turned into actionable intelligence. Francis, Sawka, and Herring (1995) also recommend cross-functional teams with members who are expert in finance, research and development, manufacturing, sales, and marketing.

- *Outsourcing of CI functions:* There is a trend reported within the past two years of outsourcing information collection and analysis. The firm will retain the expertise required to formulate the problem for research design, project management, and CI supplier selection (Hohhof, 1998). Bauman and Gelinne (1998) suggest that each request for CI services be reviewed in the context of outsourcing. The challenge, according to them, is to identify external resources that can provide cost-effective, quality research.

One of the key issues within SMEs is that there are limited human resources. Vigilance is needed to ensure that the human resources are effectively employed in their day-to-day capacities. Tools such as "shadow teams" could conceivably require significant amounts of time, to the detriment of the individuals' formal roles in the organization. Cross-functional teams will offer an expanded analytical capability within the firm for intelligence. Outsourcing of the data-gathering function will allow the firm to focus its energies on the more important research design, analysis, and presentation of intelligence information. Management commitment and continued support of the CI function also needs to include the provision of the necessary training in CI and development of individual analytical capabilities (Rothberg, 1997). The entire company must support the CI function, and the perpetual search for information must be embedded in the corporate culture. According to Fuld, the greatest challenge to CI is that it will not work unless everyone in the company contributes as well as consumes information (Harrison, 1998).

IMPLICATIONS FOR SMEs

In the short run, implementation of core CI functionality will support the day to day operational and tactical requirements of the firm. In the longer term, this accumulation of knowledge can be used to support strategy development within the firm. As the firm approaches the chaos of the "chasm" period of its evolution, it will need to make many tactical decisions to improve its position in the market and obtain a larger market share (Moore, 1991). Specific implications for SMEs include:

- Feedback mechanisms for CI users. These are critical, and will provide a means of identifying and focusing precious CI resources within the firm. An embedded feedback mechanism within CI application software will provide a convenient method for users to have input into CI functions, data, etc.

- A method of capturing information pertaining to the actual use of the CI database(s) is needed. If information is being processed that is deemed to have no value to the firm in the short or longer term, this information might potentially be eliminated from the CI process. Metrics must be captured as CI users consume and contribute to the CI databases. Regular review can ascertain how information and knowledge are being consumed and whether educational issues exist.

- Cost-effective data-gathering techniques. Push–pull techniques or intelligent agents (Buchwitz, 1998) will allow the gathering of information—particularly for web-based sources of information. One of the expectations of management is to be warned early about changes in the marketplace that will negatively impact a company's strategy (Sawka, 1998). Software agents can advise senior management of changed information on a rival's website. Regular monitoring of the websites of government agencies and regulatory bodies also provides critical early warning.

- Suitable technical resources to ensure maximum availability of CI information and knowledge bases. Insufficient support resources will reduce the effectiveness of the CI technology infrastructure.

- A lean CI function in an SME. Prescott (1989) suggests maintaining a list of individuals both internal and external to the organization who can assist in various projects.

- The integration of CI into the corporate culture. Due to the limited human resources of SMEs, many if not all employees will participate to some degree with the use of, or contribution to, CI databases. Contributions from sales representatives, customer-support personnel, and field-support personnel will allow for the development of a rich information environment. Senior management and other CI champions dispersed throughout the organization will need to continually reinforce the CI function's goals. The user-feedback mechanism mentioned above, if properly managed, will reinforce positive perceptions by the users and improve the overall CI database effectiveness.

CONCLUSIONS

We began by exploring the requirements for CI within SMEs and discussing trends in competitive intelligence. There are several key questions that the management of an SME needs to resolve: When does an in-house CI capability need to be implemented? In what type of CI function do we want to invest? Once these basic questions are answered, the CI function can be designed. Firms that are experiencing rapid growth and are approaching a transitional period in their evolution will find that a formal CI program will assist them as they enter uncharted waters. With the multitude of options available in the marketplace today with respect to CI software, outsourcing, and other services, many SMEs will be able to effectively implement a CI function.

From a review of the literature, there are positive developments with respect to the adoption of CI by SMEs. These developments include the following:

- A selection of CI software, which is available today and will provide everything from support of a library-type CI function to a full CI implementation. Packaged software lowers the barriers to entry for SMEs considering the adoption of a CI function.

- As noted by Hohhof (1998), there is an increasing number of single CI practitioners. As this trend develops, additional software and related services will become available.

- With an appropriate investment in infrastructure, CI software, and CI skills, there is an opportunity for small firms to become expert at CI. In one study, only 1–2 percent of participating firms could claim CI as a core capability (Fuld et al., 1997). One can postulate that even a small firm may develop superior CI skills relative to its larger competitors in the drive to seek competitive advantage.

- While the return on CI applications investment has been reported to be difficult to assess (Ghosal & Westney, 1991), Dashman's (1998) study estimates annual benefits of $370,000 for an investment in CI of $120,000 in a small firm. The recognition and quantification of return on investment (ROI) on CI now places the CI function in the same category as other business-investment decisions.

- Organizational structures such as cross-functional teams, shadow teams, etc., can offset the fewer numbers of dedicated CI staff. The manager responsible for the CI function can then optimize the use of internal and external resources to deliver value to the firm.

The barriers to SME implementation of CI have been largely eliminated. Small-to-medium enterprises can learn from the experiences of others and take advantage of the same capabilities from which larger corporations have benefited during the last two decades. Issues such as the impact of corporate culture, the need for effective support for the internal CI systems, and the need for the CI function to spend an appropriate amount of time converting information into knowledge will have to be carefully monitored. An approach to implementing CI should be as flexible as possible and adapt as the capabilities and requirements of the firm evolve. Corporate CI systems are now within the reach of many small-to-medium businesses.

References

Bauman, J.H., and M. Gelinne. (1998). "Maximizing the Use of CI Consultants: A Corporate Practitioner's Perspective, " *Competitive Intelligence Review* 9(3): 3–8.
Behnke, L., and P. Slayton. (1998). "Shaping a Corporate Competitive Intelligence Function at IBM," *Competitive Intelligence Review* 9(2): 4–9.

Buchwitz, L. (1998). *Monitoring Competitive Intelligence Using Internet Push Technology* <http://www.tor-pw1.netcom.ca~lillyb/CI_paper.html>.

Dashman, L. (1998). "The Value of an In-House Competitive Intelligence Department: A Business Plan Approach," *Competitive Intelligence Review* 9(2): 10–16.

Francis, D., K. Sawka, and J. Herring. (1995). "Competitors: Who to Watch, What to Watch, Who to Ignore and How to Tell the Difference?" *Competitive Intelligence Review* 6(3): 41–46.

Fuld, L.M., J.P. Herring, L. Kahaner, L.K. Knight, and J. Prescott. (1997). "Symposium: Lessons Learned and the Road Ahead," *Competitive Intelligence Review* 8(1): 7–15.

Ghosal, S., and D.E. Westney. (1991). "Organizational Competitor Analysis Systems," *Strategic Management Journal* 12(1): 17–31.

Graef, J. (1997). "Using the Internet for Competitive Intelligence: A Survey Report," *Competitive Intelligence Review* 8(4): 41–47.

Guimaraes, T., and C. Armstrong. (1998). "Exploring the Relations Between Competitive Intelligence, IS Support and Business Change," *Competitive Intelligence Review* 9(3): 45–54.

Hamrefors, S. (1998). "Spontaneous Environmental Scanning," *Competitive Intelligence Review* 9(3): 68–75.

Harrison, A. (1998). "Why IS Must Go Spying," *Software Magazine* 18(7): 1–8.

Herardian, R. (1998). "Will the Real Groupware Please Stand Up?" *DominoPower Magazine* (September): 1–4 <http://wwwdominopower.com/issues/issue199809/groupware001.html>.

Hohhof, B. (1998). "Finding the Wave: Shifts in the CI Model," *Competitive Intelligence Review* 9(1): 60–62.

Imperato, G. (1998). "Competitive Intelligence—Get Smart!" *Fastcompany* 14: 269.

Lagace, C. (1997). "Small Business Primer," Canadian Federation of Independent Business (April): 1–11 <http://www.cfib.ca/research/reports>.

Langabeer, J.A., II. (1998). "Achieving a Strategic Focus for Competitive Intelligence," *Competitive Intelligence Review* 9(1): 55–59.

Lotus Corporation. (1999). *Knowledge Management* <http://www.lotus.com/home.nsf/welcome/km>.

Mallett, T. (1999). "Virtually a Reality," Canadian Federation of Independent Business <www.cfib.ca.research/reports/virtual_e.asp>.

Moore, G.A. (1991). *Crossing the Chasm: Marketing and Selling Technology Products to Mainstream Customers.* New York: Harper Business.

Pawar, B., and R. Sharda. (1997). "Obtaining Business Intelligence on the Internet," *Long-Range Planning* 30(1): 110–21.

Porter, M., and V. Millar. (1985). "How Information Gives You Competitive Advantage," *Harvard Business Review* 63(4): 149–60.

Powell, T. (1997). "Competitive Knowledge Management: You Can't Reengineer What Was Never Engineered in the First Place," *Competitive Intelligence Review* 8(1): 40–47.

Prescott, J. (1989). "Competitive Intelligence: Its Role and Function in Organizations," in *Advances in Competitive Intelligence*, ed. J. Prescott. Alexandria, VA: Society of Competitive Intelligence Professionals.

Prescott, J., J. Herring, and P. Panfely. (1998). "Leveraging Information into Action: A Look into the Competitive and Business Intelligence Consortium Benchmarking Study," *Competitive Intelligence Review* 9(1): 4–10.

Prince, C. (1998). "Strategy and Tactics: A Primer for CI Professional," *Competitive Intelligence Review* 9(3): 15–24.

Rothberg, H.N. (1997). "Fortifying Competitive Intelligence Systems with Shadow Teams," *Competitive Intelligence Review* 8(2): 3–11.

Sawka, K.A. (1998). "Early Warning: The Decision-Makers Perspective," *Competitive Intelligence Review* 9(2): 63–65.

Simon, N.J. (1997). "Organizational Development: CI Is Not an Island," *Competitive Intelligence Review* 8(4): 80–82.

Zack, M., and M. Serino. (1996). "Supporting Team with Collaborative Technology," Lotus Development Corporation <http://www.lotus.com>.

Zanasi, A. (1998). "Competitive Intelligence through Data Mining Public Sources," *Competitive Intelligence Review* 9(1): 44–54.

ORGANIZATIONAL ISSUES
ASSOCIATED WITH
COMPETITIVE INTELLIGENCE

21

Corporate Community Culture and Counterintelligence

Suzanne Wiltshire

INTRODUCTION

In a world of total connectivity, your people are critical to your intelligence defense. For every new electronic security device that detects, scans, or records, there are three more that connect and send. Some new electronic device is born every minute of every day and immediately we need to innovate four more to interconnect, enable, upgrade, or be left out. Firewalls, transmission monitoring, and tight security control routine interactions. But keeping up with the latest and greatest security technology won't stop thieves if your employees invite them in.

CONNECTIVITY AND COUNTERINTELLIGENCE

Counterintelligence, according to *Webster's Dictionary*, is actions taken to counter enemy intelligence, espionage, or sabotage. Often, companies practice it as security with locks, passwords and entry codes, guards, computer-system firewalls, surveillance, and alarm systems.

Today we live in a world of connectivity, where phones, faxes, and the Internet provide critical interaction with customers and suppliers, personal friends, and family. The more interactions there are, the more the distinction blurs between what is business and what is not. The definitions of "proprietary" or "sensitive" also blur. What is in the best interest of the company and what constitutes a conflict of interest? Employees are faced with these decisions thousands of times a day, to the point where the questions stop being consciously asked. The employee makes an instant judgment, and carries on.

Since 1995 Internet traffic has doubled every six months, and wireless technology has mobilized business. One-time competitors are now strategic partners and allies. Employees are traveling and talking, meeting and collaborating, computing and sending, often from remote, unsecured locations, reliant on self-judgment. Therefore security, or the lack of it, ultimately lies with each individual. How can we monitor and secure this environment of connectivity? The answer is, we can't. But we can arm employees with a strong sense of corporate community culture and comprehensive knowledge of counterintelligence.

PREDICTABILITY

Predictability, which *Webster* defines as "foretelling based on observation or reasoning," is the basis of organizing for security and wealth. Howard Stevenson (1998) in his book *Do Lunch or Be Lunch* addresses decision-making in uncertainty. Based on Stevenson's observations, the amount of agreement between individuals about how things should be organized is what produces more predictability.

THE MOTIVE

The science and psychology of human motivation has long been studied and documented. Stevenson's list of organization for predictability progresses from individual direct actions, through increasing levels of interaction and agreement, to a state where a community exists that is bonded by shared vision and values.

Stevenson's list also correlates with another well-known theory of motivation, Maslow's *hierarchy of needs*. According to Maslow (1998), people seek *self-actualization*, which is a state in which individuals are self-motivated to achieve freedom of choice and responsibility of action through increased organization and agreement. Maslow recognized that self-actualization required very positive circumstances, and that negative circumstances (listed below) produced what he called "regressive forces of motivation" (Maslow, 1998):

- scarce resources
- inequitable organization or laws
- fear or anxiety
- loss leading to bereavement
- change
- bad communications
- suspicion
- dishonesty
- confusion of truth and honesty
- loss of gratifications (freedom, respect, love, safety, values, truth, beauty).

Maslow also recognized that for every trend in human nature, there was a countertrend. He wrote: "[I]t is perfectly true that every human being has a tendency to grow toward self-actualization; but it is just as true that every human being has a trend toward regression, toward fear of growth, toward not wanting self-actualization" (Maslow, 1998). By considering Maslow's regressive forces of motivation we see that under negative circumstances motivation can regress to seeking protection, reestablishing perceived equity, or seeking reprisal.

It is as if Maslow could predict the corporate trends of the 1990s. Stevenson (1998) conducted a poll and ranked the biggest contemporary threats to predictability in business (regressive forces of motivation) as perceived by employees as follows:

- Strategic restructuring   99.4 (respondents in thousands)
- Reengineering   47.9
- Continuous Improvement   10.0
- Virtual Companies   0.8
- Matrix Management   0.4 (no longer common today)

Regressive forces can create weaknesses in otherwise enlightened employees that make the company's intelligence vulnerable to threats from competitors and criminals.

Besides the motives of human nature are the motives of wealth. Technology has produced digital mirror images of every product and business process, creating a wealth of intelligence information. Customer information is no longer a one-time use, disposable item. It represents a potential lifetime of economic value. The value of corporate information, and therefore the stakes of either stealing or selling that information, just got a whole lot higher.

The Opportunity

Stevenson's model works extremely well when applied to counterintelligence. In figure 21.1, by mapping the possible threats to corporate intelligence over the corresponding agreement-seeking mechanisms, we see the appropriate defense tool matched to the potential threat. For example, the counteractivity to locks (power) is a physical security breach. The counteractivity to charisma (leadership) is deception; to common values (culture) is deflection; to incentives (management) is enticement; and to surveillance (management) is covert leaks. Companies that install technical security to block hackers, spies, and thieves only protect one domain on the plane of agreement.

The Internet is now used by 95 percent of Canadian businesses, according to a recent Ernst & Young survey (Ross, 1999). It is not only impossible for companies to restrict outside communication in today's interactive world of business, but to do so would strangle the company's livelihood. According to industry estimates, computer-intrusion attempts are tripling annually, and even though computer code is quite secure, the Ernst & Young survey found that 70 percent of

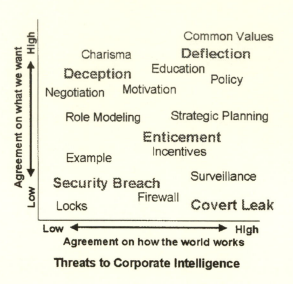

FIGURE 21.1 Counterintelligence: Defense tools matched to potential threats.

occurrences resulted in significant financial loss, 32 percent of which were over $1 million (Ross, 1999). David McMahon, a security analyst for Electronic Warfare Canada Inc., estimates that network administrators only catch about one in ten thousand hacks.

If companies can use sophisticated security that protects businesses in cyberspace, then why are there so many breaches? According to Charles Belford (1999), president of Management Smarts Inc., many executives suffer from technology tunnel vision. Chief executive officers (CEOs) support a management culture that looks suspiciously at managers that are too interested in information technology (IT). They treat IT as a mechanical piece of equipment, maintained by weird-looking, unintelligible people, a thing that has little to do with corporate strategy or capabilities.

Intellectual property is increasingly intrinsic and intuitive and comprises millions of bits of information—not only identifiable patents and copyrights. Most employees today have access to sensitive information. Intellectual theft is not only the theft of intellectual property, it is also the method of theft, which uses intellectual or psychological means such as *deception* and *enticement* (table 21.1).

Overt attack by outsiders is still a threat, and technical security is the appropriate response. However, the other three threats all involve employees. Bryan Lynch, a professional "white hat hacker" who audits corporate data-security, notes that "more than 70 percent of information theft and security breaches occur from inside" (Grier, 1999). Transfer of digital information can happen in a nanosecond, with no options for retrieval and few for damage control.

Most employees are incredibly naive or insensitive to issues of counterintelligence. They simply are not informed or trained. If asked, they would probably

Table 21.1
THREATS TO CORPORATE INTELLIGENCE

Threats	Weaknesses
Deception	Naive employees
Enticement	Dissatisfied employees
Covert action from inside the company	Disgruntled employees
Overt attack on property or systems	Criminal outsiders

have no idea what it is and would be shocked if told that it involves them. They think of counterintelligence as some dangerous, romantic, James Bondesque event that happens only in the movies.

Spies prey on naiveté. They are often passive collectors of information, doing nothing illegal (Davis, 1998). We all love to talk. A spy simply has to wait and listen, in open restaurants, on planes, and especially on the telephone. He waits for us to put out the garbage. Lee Lamothe (1999) gets paid to comb through garbage. He says: "It's a results-oriented business. Clients want information and they don't much care how I get it. . . . Garbage runs are a fruitful source of information."

Deception can be very difficult for employees to detect unless they are well trained. It may be a simple lie on the phone such as "I'm conducting an important survey" or "Peter (your boss) said that you would speak to me." Or an employee may receive a phone call from a supposed help-desk staffer. The caller sounds convincing and even mentions some personal detail to establish credibility. The employee is instructed to run a program sent through e-mail, which is actually a "Trojan Horse"—a program that surreptitiously relays corporate data to a "black hat hacker" (Grier, 1999).

Spies prey on employee dissatisfaction and greed. In March 1999, Motorola sued Intel and one of its own former employees for alleged industrial espionage (*Counterintelligence News and Developments*, 1999). The former Motorola employee, while director of the firm's development center for personal-computer microprocessors, allegedly kept Intel well informed of Motorola's trade secrets and development progress.

Enticement can also take the form of theft of the employees themselves and the valuable information they carry with them. Wal-Mart recently settled a lawsuit filed against Amazon.com for hiring away between 15 and 20 Wal-Mart technology workers, including the chief information officer, thereby illegally acquiring trade secrets about Wal-Mart's elaborate computing systems (*Counterintelligence News and Developments*, 1999). In Silicon Valley, engineers, enticed by riches, move freely from company to company, making it very difficult for companies to protect proprietary technology or information.

Intelligence protection ultimately depends on the motives of employees, their emotional and social state, and their level of counterintelligence awareness.

Technology used to mean *automation*—suddenly it means *information*. Billions of dollars are spent to seek and destroy crime using defensive computer technology. But how much is being spent on developing defensive psychology and sociology? How good is a technical security system if an inside employee decides to breach it or is naive?

MASLOW'S REGRESSIVE FORCES AT LARGE

Under recent competitive pressures of technology and globalization, corporations have struggled to survive. New structures and business practices have cut jobs and decentralized decision-making. The result is a great deal of workplace stress for bosses and employees. Some have not coped well.

Bad bosses *do* exist. Hard-charging change artists or egotistical, self-indulgent control freaks are often used by impatient, bottom-line-seeking boards of directors. Peter Frost and Sandra Robinson (1999), professors at the University of British Columbia, describe one CEO: "He walked all over people. He made fun of them; he intimidated them. He criticized work for no reason, and he changed plans daily." The result is organizational pain, "sadness, frustration, bitterness, and anger that are endemic to organizational life."

According to Bernadette Schell, author of the book *Stress and Emotional Dysfunction in Lives at the Top*, among top executives as much as 80 percent have some sort of imbalance and "at least 40 percent would have what I call quite intense mood disorder orientation. Narcissism is a big one" (Cole, 1999).

And then there are the good bosses who work for greedy shareholders. The near-universal acceptance of maximization of short-term shareholder wealth as the first obligation, and indeed the moral responsibility of management, obliterates any wishful notions of management's desire to support employees. In fact, downsizing is now expected as a natural condition of technology, even during the greatest economic boom in human history. For employees this translates into downsizing, change management, quarterly myopia, long work hours, and productivity-based compensation. In other words, employee stress. And where there is stress there is frustration.

SURVEILLANCE—TO PRY OR TO PROTECT?

Surveillance may be intrusive, but it is not illegal. Only one U.S. law addresses workplace privacy: the federal Electronic Communications Privacy Act, which forbids employer eavesdropping on employee telephone or e-mail conversations once it becomes clear that the content is personal. In Canada, although surveillance is not illegal, not disclosing its use may be (Johnson, 1999). Richard Nixon, an employment-law lawyer in Toronto, advises companies to make full disclosure of surveillance activities to employees. This prevents a violation of privacy both legally and morally (Gibb-Clark, 1999).

Since the late 1980s, near-ubiquitous monitoring has become increasingly affordable. According to the American Management Association International

(Greenberg, Canzoneri, & Smith, 1999), a growing number (two-thirds) of U.S. businesses use employee surveillance to protect business secrets, deter workplace crime, reduce employee misappropriation of company time and resources, and reduce corporate liability. After some Chevron Corporation employees sent a sexually harassing e-mail, the Chevron corporation was liable for US$2.2 million in damages, which probably could have been avoided with surveillance.

However, Beth Givens, director of the Privacy Rights Clearing House in San Diego, says that abuses of power run rampant (Stevens, 1999). She says that "if you are being monitored every hour of every day, there really is not a shred of dignity you can take home from your work situation."

Monitoring to increase productivity is also controversial. Management calls it *competitively necessary*; employees call it *intrusive and disrespectful* (Johnson, 1999). Dr. Julian Barling of Queen's University found that electronic surveillance produced feelings of injustice and was a leading source of workplace aggression (Gibb-Clark, 1999). Barling's study ranked "insecurity and a sense of injustice from electronic monitoring" as the major source of employee frustration and resentment, leading to aggressive behavior or violence. He concluded that above all, companies should "build a workplace that is fair and reasonable and allows people to function at their best."

LONE WOLVES GET EVEN

People want to be treated fairly. This is a basic component of Maslow's theory: Individuals want what they think they could have compared to what others possess. If inequity exists, then discomfort occurs and a person will try to rectify the situation.

This can be observed in society. In Canada, as taxes have risen, tax evasion has grown dramatically according to David Giles, Professor of Economics at the University of Victoria (MacKinnon, 1999). Given the opportunity, many otherwise law-abiding people have demonstrated that they will try to attain what they perceive to be equity even if it means resorting to illegal activity. In fact, Giles says there has been a general "downgrading of moral standards" shown by the growing underground economy in the United States, where the tax burden has changed little in 30 years. People simply look at their neighbors and say: "They're not paying it. Why should I?"

Only in tight cultural communities where values are shared do people want others to do better than they. For example, many Jewish and offshore Chinese communities operate on the assumption that honor for one is honor for all (Stevenson, 1998).

Employee emotional health is rarely considered by most companies, let alone valued or measured. Dr. Edgardo Perez, the chief executive officer (CEO) of an Ontario psychiatric-treatment center, says that "25 percent of white-collar workers and 40 percent of blue-collar workers had stress-related absences in the past year" (Cole, 1999). Imagine the stress-related lost productivity of employees still showing up for work!

RAGE CAN UNDERMINE COUNTERINTELLIGENCE

Rage is the outward destructive demonstration of anger in order to get even—a chair through a window, any act or threat of violence to people, property, or to the civility that binds us together (Cole, 1999). According to Gerry Smith, an employee-assistance consultant, incidents requiring trauma-team intervention, including workplace violence, have tripled over the past four years.

However, anger can be managed, according to Bill Wilkerson (Cole, 1999), who ran a crisis-management company for ten years. Employees can and will accept even a threat to the security of their employment as long as they clearly understand the reasons and believe the employer is acting fairly.

But anger that is held inside can escalate. Canadians are particularly fond of *passive aggression*—obstructionism, sarcasm, an embarrassing media leak, or a missing laptop (Cole, 1999). According to Wilkerson, a profound sense of unfairness exacerbated by insensitive bosses often triggers acts of industrial sabotage. The resentment builds into anger and then into rage, and at some point otherwise perfectly reasonable people who started out liking their jobs and caring about the people they work with start looking for ways to get even.

THE COUNTERINTELLIGENCE GAP

By applying three control tools (power, leadership, and management) to our model, we see that companies can create a counterintelligence defense system that covers most of the plane of agreement (figure 21.2).

But a large gap still remains. Business is currently rapid and unpredictable. Managers have decentralized authority, and flattened organizations have become more responsive and flexible. Without a hierarchy of control, empowered employees must make decisions as problems occur. And yet companies need them to act predictably in their best interest. This requires a high level of agreement and a sense of community value. Unless employees want to protect the company, it is not completely protected.

Stevenson's fourth tool of control is *culture*. High on his plane of agreement is where the tribes live and communities of mutual well being are built. Here is where values are discussed and agreed upon and the common good is universally recognized. To reach this place companies must quell the regressive forces. Employees, who are given the privilege of belonging, bear the obligation to contribute, support, and protect—here dwells predictability. Each individual thinks and acts alone, but the common accepted code of ethics and common purpose guide actions that are aligned and in agreement. The circle of wagons draws tight and the tribe protects its own (figure 21.3). Corporate-community culture is the missing line of defense in the counterintelligence practiced by most companies.

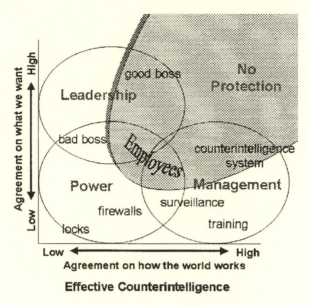

FIGURE 21.2 A counterintelligence defense system.

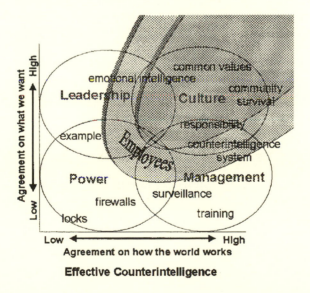

FIGURE 21.3 Corporate-community culture in counterintelligence.

BUILDING EFFECTIVE COUNTERINTELLIGENCE
BASED ON COMMUNITY CULTURE

$$\text{Effective Counterintelligence} = \frac{\text{Security} + \text{Management} + \text{Leadership}}{\text{Community Culture}}$$

Effective counterintelligence is a finely knit mesh of interlocking security devices, management-control systems, and empathetic leadership overlying a culture of community awareness and shared responsibility, values, and goals. All four of these tools interact to form a shield that deflects violations from without and from within.

Building a corporate-community culture requires strong leadership with emotional intelligence. Daniel Goleman (1998), co-chairman of the Consortium for Research on Emotional Intelligence, says that "without [emotional intelligence] a person can have the best training in the world, an incisive analytical mind and an endless supply of smart ideas, but he still won't make a great leader." Table 21.2 lists the hallmarks of emotional intelligence.

Harvard Business School Professor Rosabeth Moss Kanter (Church, 1999) says that the speed at which things happen today and the magnitude of the stakes make change an environmental factor, not an event. If there is a deep understanding that every employee plays a vital role in creating mutual benefit, and if there is respect for the unique nature of each contribution, then there will be appreciation and a sense of value and ownership that are worth pro-

Table 21.2
HALLMARKS OF EMOTIONAL INTELLIGENCE

Self-awareness	self-confidence realistic self-assessment admits failure and smiles
Self-control	honesty thinks before acting open to change
Motivation	passion to achieve unfailing optimism commitment
Empathy	serves all sensitive to others builds and retains talent
Social skill	builds networks friendly but persuasive leader of change

Source: adapted from Goleman (1998).

Table 21.3
STEPS TO RESOLVING DIFFERENCES

	Building Congruence
1. Rationality	Acknowledge emotions (yours and theirs), balance with reason
2. Understanding	Learn other viewpoints, opposing and expert
3. Communication	Consult before deciding, listen, explain
4. Reliability	Be trustworthy, but not wholly trusting
5. Persuasion (not coercion)	Explore ideas, convince on idea merits, not personal threats
6. Acceptance	Respect differences, deal seriously with all

Source: Fisher and Brown (1989).

tecting. However, such agreement is not easily built. Believing that it can be built and that it is worth building, is the first step. Redefining corporate values is the next.

Building congruence begins with the careful screening of potential employees for integrity, team values, and self-motivation. Then it requires open discussion, leadership, and mutual respect to extend agreement throughout the company (Fisher & Brown, 1989). The corporate strategy should focus on serving the customer. Functionally and emotionally, employees should support one another, working in unison of purpose and process. This is illustrated in table 21.3.

COUNTERINTELLIGENCE INTELLIGENCE

Arion Pattakos (1997) in his article "Keeping Company Secrets Secret" suggests eight steps to develop a comprehensive information-protection program:

- *Critical information analysis:* what information needs protection, according to potential damage in case of loss?
- *Threat analysis:* identify competitors (real and potential), foreign agents, activists, saboteurs. Identify possible methods of access
- *Vulnerability analysis:* identify weaknesses of present counterintelligence activities
- *Risk assessment:* rank threats according to value and vulnerability
- *Identification of controls:* determine protection concepts and estimated costs: prediction, avoidance, deterrence, detection, interception, containment, recovery, correction, etc. Determine appropriate controls: technical and physical security, personnel and procedural safeguards
- *Management decision:* allocate priority and implementation

- *Counterintelligence implementation plan:* time-driven with assignment of authority, responsibility
- *Effectiveness review:* periodic test and reevaluation plan.

Counterintelligence Program Checklist:

- Promote and practice an explicit code of ethics
- Value employees—be sensitive to their needs and stresses
- Align goals and values—reinforce them with actions and discussion
- Be passionate about winning the game strategically
- Set examples without exception
- Create a corporate community where people want to work
- Screen recruits for values and acceptance of responsibility
- Set clear, equitable company policies and procedures. Use detailed employee contracts
- Define ownership, information sensitivity, responsibilities
- Establish an information protection policy committee (IPPC); appoint officers
- Teach intellectual-theft methods and counterintelligence defense
- After probation and training, trust employees to use their best judgment
- Obtain employees' acknowledgment and consent before using surveillance
- Provide a physically secure environment
- Be suspicious, define violations, consequences
- Provide mentoring
- Investigate thoroughly and objectively before attributing blame
- Promote open and honest communication, and a trusting, supportive work environment
- Monitor corporate counterintelligence program risks, costs and benefits.

Recently, *Fortune Magazine* documented the failures of 37 CEOs: "So how does a CEO blow it? More than any other way, by failure to put the right people in the right job—and the related failure to fix people-problems in time . . . the failure is one of emotional strength." Jack Welch of the General Electric (GE) Corporation comments: "[T]he day we screw up the people thing, this company is over" (Charan & Colvin, 1999).

CONCLUSION

Few companies today would deny the competitive necessity and value of information technology (IT) to their business systems. However, many companies have failed to recognize the new vulnerabilities and stresses that IT carries with it. Good corporate-community culture is usually viewed as a "nice to have" thing, but few companies add it to the corporate valuation formula. Yet they certainly value intellectual property and go to great lengths to convince shareholders of its huge value. Risk management today comprises a sophisticated and expensive combination of practices, including insurance, currency hedging, security policies and devices, and even succession planning. As the value and use of IT in business increases, it becomes increasingly essential for companies to find new ways to manage the risk of losing their intangible and intellectual properties. No system is perfect, but how can any company practicing serious risk management not include corporate-community culture in their counterintelligence program?

REFERENCES

Belford, C. (1999). "Battle Just Half Over When Consultants Leave," *Globe and Mail* (September 30): T4.

Charan, R., and G. Colvin. (1999). "Why CEO's Fail," *Fortune* 139(12): 68–78.

Church, E. (1999). "CEO Forum," *Globe and Mail* (September 30): B11.

Cole, T. (1999). "All the Rage and Bad Boss," *Globe and Mail, Report on Business Magazine* (February): 50–57, 64–72.

Counterintelligence News and Developments. (1999). "Trade Secret Lawsuit Happenings," *Counterintelligence News and Developments* 2 (June). National Counterintelligence Centre (NACIC) <http://www.nacic.gov/cind/jun99.htm>.

Davis, J.W. (1998). "Spies on the Information Highway," *Counterintelligence News and Developments* 3 (September). National Counterintelligence Centre (NACIC) <http://www.nacic.gov/cind/sep98.htm#rtoc12>.

Fisher, R., and S. Brown. (1989). *Getting Together: Building Relationships as We Negotiate.* New York: Penguin Books.

Frost, P., and S. Robinson. (1999). "The Toxic Handler," *Harvard Business Review* 77(4): 97–106.

Gibb-Clark, M. (1999). "Research Maps Patterns of Workplace Aggression and When the Company Plays Big Brother," *Globe and Mail* (September 29): B18.

Goleman, D. (1998). "What Makes a Leader?" *Harvard Business Review* 76(6): 94.

Greenberg, E., C. Canzoneri, and C. Smith. (1999). *Workplace Monitoring and Surveillance.* New York: American Management Association International.

Grier, B. (1999). "Stealthy Hacker Dons White Hat," *Globe and Mail* (July 1): B24.

Johnson, T. (1999). "Quit Watching Me!" *Globe and Mail, Report on Business Magazine* (September): 58–62.

Lamothe, L. (1999). "Dirty Work," *Globe and Mail, Report on Business Magazine* (September): 34–35.

MacKinnon, M. (1999). "Underground Economy Takes a Big Bite," *Globe and Mail* (June 21): B1.

Maslow, A.H. (1998). *Maslow on Management.* New York: Wiley.

Pattakos, A.N. (1997). "Keeping Company Secrets Secret," *Competitive Intelligence Review* 8(3): 71–78.

Ross, J. (1999). "Canada Called 'Hacker Haven' for Criminals," *Globe and Mail* (May 17): A3.

Stevens, L. (1999). "Big Brother Invading Workplace," Fort Worth (Texas) *Star-Telegram* (September 29): M3.

Stevenson, H.H. (1998). *Do Lunch or Be Lunch.* Boston: Harvard Business School Press.

22

Understanding the Ethical Aspects of Competitive Intelligence

Shauna Hamilton and Craig S. Fleisher

INTRODUCTION

There is a view that competitive intelligence (CI) is an activity that is shadowy, unethical, and illegal. Images of trench coats, dumpster diving, listening trucks, and back-alley meetings are often found in newspaper articles about CI. Articles documenting these business practices, discussing large, multinational companies engaged in clandestine behavior, have not helped dispel these notions. Paine (1991) found that questionable intelligence-gathering fell into four categories: (1) misrepresentation; (2) attempts to influence the judgment of those entrusted with confidential information through such means as bribery; (3) covert surveillance; and (4) theft.

Meetings of CI professionals invariably touch upon ethical bases of performing their profession. For example, during its 1997 annual conference in San Diego, the Society of Competitive Intelligence Professionals (SCIP) conducted a law and ethics survey that asked 1,700 attendees what they would do in hypothetical situations. The results of its exercise, and the 728 responses (43 percent participation rate), were surprising in that: (1) newer SCIP members scored higher than more veteran members; (2) members with 5 years or more of experience were most correct, while those with between 2–3 years were the least correct; (3) members in firms that either had an ethics policy or general code of business conduct scored higher than those in firms lacking adequate guidelines; and (4) those who worked in firms with a specialized policy for conducting CI work scored substantially better than individuals whose firms did not (Sapia-Bosch & Tancer, 1998). The inclusion of ethics on the agenda was prompted by the importance of the issue to the CI community, and the belief that ethical lapses by CI practitioners often result from ignorance rather than intent (Sapia-Bosch & Tancer, 1998).

Is ethics really a problem in the CI community? Empirical research on the subject suggests that the answer is unclear. Business-ethics professors Trevino and Weaver performed a SCIP-sponsored literature review and study of ethical practices in CI. They found that while some organizations addressed CI ethics ". . . quite seriously, most CI practitioners felt left on their own, relying on personal background and intuition to make tough ethical decisions" (Trevino & Weaver, 1997). They further concluded that current ethical guidance was too vague to be truly helpful. Informal discussions with CI practitioners will show this finding to have a high degree of face validity. What then can be done to address these ethical concerns?

THE CALL FOR ETHICAL CODES IN COMPETITIVE INTELLIGENCE

With the introduction of the Economic Espionage Act (EEA) in 1996, many businesses have sought to realign their codes of conduct and corporate ethical codes to meet the due-diligence standard established by this new law. The EEA "makes it a federal crime to take, download, receive, or possess trade-secret information obtained without the owner's authorization" (Fine, 1997). Moreover, "if the information has been reasonably protected by the owner and has economic value from not being generally known, it meets the criteria of a trade secret under the EEA." Although this appears to be straightforward and not liable to confusion, what is "reasonable" is always subject to interpretation.

Interpretation is where the gray areas of ethical boundaries arise in CI. A 1997 study for SCIP revealed that there are many unresolved, open-to-question areas of information-gathering practices among CI professionals (Trevino & Weaver, 1997). Having only gained its popularity in the last two decades, CI is still an immature practice. A firm and universally accepted set of guidelines has not been established. Yet due to the very nature of the profession, ethical guidelines are needed to provide guidance and legitimacy. There is a growing awareness among practitioners and their managers of the need to adopt an agreed-upon set of standards. Although SCIP does provide its members with a Code of Ethics (see Code, following page), this may not be enough, especially for new or "lone ranger" CI practitioners who may not be aware of the practical difficulties in applying these guidelines to their practice or organization.

Fiora (1998) proposed that not only are ethical guidelines needed, but strong, successful implementation plans for those guidelines are even more essential. Fiora stated that "legal and ethical guidelines are the ground rules that all employees must follow in carrying out their business intelligence duties." It is critical that the guidelines mirror the ethical culture of the organization and that they conform to strict legal and ethical standards. By doing this, companies alle-

---

SCIP's Code of Ethics

To continually strive to increase respect and recognition for the profession.

To pursue one's duties with zeal and diligence while maintaining the highest degree of professionalism and avoiding all unethical practices.

To faithfully adhere to and abide by one's company policies, objectives, and guidelines.

To comply with all applicable laws.

To accurately disclose all relevant information, including one's identity and organization, prior to all interviews.

To fully respect all requests for confidentiality of information.

To promote and encourage full compliance with these ethical standards within one's company, with third-party contractors, and within the entire profession.

---

viate employee concerns about the firm's activities and help protect management from negative repercussions when employees do not conform to the guidelines or are caught engaging in illegal activity.

The 1997 SCIP study also stated that CI professionals should care about ethics. Because ethical failures can diminish a reputation, articulating ethical standards beforehand makes it easier to respond to future criticism. Additionally, a hallmark of a profession is the adoption of ethical standards. The study's future implications for the CI profession concluded that "it will become more and more crucial that members can identify the issues of concern and reach consensus about what is and is not appropriate" (Trevino & Weaver, 1997). Furthermore, one individual or organization's activities can bring negative publicity to an entire profession.

By the sheer amount of literature available on this subject (all stressing the same need for ethical codes within the CI profession), it is easy to forget about the other side of the argument. In order to understand the basis of any counter-opinion, however, it is essential to first understand ethics and ethical theory, and then to examine some of the advantages and disadvantages of ethical codes and standards.

Ethics—A Concise Primer

It is not our intention in this chapter to provide an entire synopsis of ethical theory and how it relates to business. It is important, however, to provide some context and definitions if we are to achieve a better understanding of the value of ethical codes in CI practice. The following section outlines some of the more common definitions of ethical theory, and some of the newer philosophical approaches.

Polls by organizations such as Gallup show that the public has low regard for the ethics of business managers. Business ethics generally concerns others' judgments about the rightness or wrongness of managerial behavior. The difficulty in ethics is in understanding how these judgments are fashioned and which standards or norms should be used. Four important ethics questions are: (1) What is?; (2) What ought to be?; (3) How can we move from what is to what ought to be?; and (4) What is our motivation in this transition? (Carroll & Buccholtz, 2000).

The subject of business ethics may be addressed at several levels: personal, organizational, industrial, and societal. Ethics discussions frequently come down to questions about obligations and responsibilities, and the conflicts existing between them. A number of different ethical principles serve to guide personal decision-making. The three most common philosophical principles applied to one's decisions are: (1) *justice*—assessments of the *fairness* of the distribution of benefits and costs; (2) *rights*—assessments of whether basic human *rights are being respected*; and (3) *utilitarianism*—assessments of the *aggregate benefits and costs*. Each of these approaches, though elegant in theory, can be difficult to apply in practice. For example, problems are frequently encountered in measuring benefits and costs, balancing conflicting basic rights, and gaining agreement on what constitutes "fair" distributions.

Morality and Ethics

Morality consists of the rules and principles of one's moral conduct. It is an individual phenomenon that tries to define right from wrong. Ethical theory is the self-reflection or justification that goes beyond the established set of morality defined by a culture or society. It allows for criticism or questions about the established rules of moral conduct and societal values. In other words, morality is about what resides in the individual, whereas ethics is how morality exists within relationships.

Virtue ethics descend from theories proposed by Plato and Aristotle. They move away from the obligation and rights-based nature of moral responsibility defined above to that of virtuous characteristics or dispositions, in other words, of *being*. People acquire virtues in the same way they would acquire such skills as cooking or carpentry. Aristotle believed that virtue is cultivated and made part of a person like a language or culture. Virtue ethics, then, propose that people are raised and educated to become virtuous in character and can choose between right and wrong by nature of their disposition.

Organizational Applications of Ethics

The previous discussion of ethics focused on the individual decision-maker. Rarely in CI would the decision-maker be acting solely on his or her own behalf. More frequently, he or she is operating as agent for a principal, or an employing organization.

A number of organizational factors can impact an individual's behavior. The behavior of one's superiors and peers and industry ethical practices have been demonstrated to be the most important influences on a firm's ethical climate, whereas society's moral climate and personal needs were shown to be less important (Carroll & Buccholtz, 2000). The results of recent studies have further demonstrated that businesspersons have been feeling increased pressures to perform, placing them under increasing stress to perform unethically (Jones, 1999). Additional behaviors of one's peers or superiors that create questionable ethical atmospheres include amoral decision-making, unethical practices, acceptance of legality as the standard of behavior, "bottom-line" mentality and expectations of loyalty and conformity, absence of ethical leadership, reward systems that overemphasize profits or sales, insensitivity toward how subordinates perceive pressure to meet goals, and inadequate formal policies. (Carroll & Buccholtz, 2000).

There are many common mechanisms that organizations utilize in order to improve their ethical climate. Among the most common of the methods for institutionalizing ethics would include ethics audits, ethics training, whistle-blowing mechanisms, disciplining violators, codes of conduct or ethics, ethical decision-making processes, establishing realistic objectives, establishing ethics programs and ethics-officer roles, and effective communication (Carroll & Buccholtz, 2000). Although each of these has been shown to be valuable in some contexts for improving the ethical climate, we will focus in this chapter particularly on codes of ethics. This method has received the lion's share of visibility in CI circles and can apply to sole practitioners (i.e., CI consultants) or practitioners within organizations (i.e., CI employees).

ETHICAL CODES: GOOD, BAD, OR JUST USELESS?

Top management has the responsibility for establishing standards of behavior and for effectively communicating these standards to everybody in the organization. A classic means for fulfilling this responsibility is through the use of codes of ethics or conduct. A phenomenon of the past two decades, these codes are in use at over 95 percent of all major corporations today, and the central questions in their effectiveness center around the managerial policies and attitudes associated with their use (Edwards, 1994).

Self-regulation is often cited by chief executive officers as being a more desirable option compared to government regulation. Business managers believe they have the expertise and acumen necessary to check their activities and that they can regulate themselves better than any government or "big-brother"-like organization. This being said, it is simple to see why codes of ethics are one of the more popular forms of self-regulation in business.

Ethical codes provide industry-wide advantages that are accepted by both businesses and consumers. The first advantage is that they provide guidance in ethically ambiguous situations. If employees are unsure of what course of action they should take when faced with an ethical dilemma, they can always rely on their company's guidelines for assistance. Codes can also provide a check on autocratic power. For example, if a manager is asking a subordinate to perform an activity that he or she is uncomfortable doing, the employee, in theory, can rely on the ethical code as a way of checking the position–power the manager has by reminding the manager that his or her suggestion goes against company policy. Ethical codes also help an organization's decision-makers to specify the social responsibilities of the business itself. They can enable a company to act morally when it would not have otherwise been able to due to competitive pressures. Last but not least, codes can also provide the advantages of legal protection for the company, increased company pride and loyalty, increased consumer goodwill, improved loss-prevention, and improved product quality and productivity (Ethics Resource Center, 1990).

However, ethical codes also have many disadvantages that inhibit them from achieving these advantages. The most obvious disadvantage is that, although ethical codes provide guidance and rules, they do not provide assurance that those guidelines will be adhered to or enforced. To bring about an ethical climate that all organizational members will believe in, violators of the accepted ethical norms must be disciplined. Business has, to date, demonstrated an unwillingness to discipline code violators (Carroll & Buccholtz, 2000). More importantly, codes are generally vague and ambiguous: This potentially restricts them from being enforced and also defeats their primary objective.

In reality, many codes are ineffective because people fail to respect them, and because they remove personal responsibility for behaving ethically. Part of the reason for this could be due to the problems companies have in implementing ethical codes. A lot of effort goes into writing ethical guidelines, but these manuals often get forgotten on dusty shelves. This is partly attributable to the unfortunate reality that employees who are supposed to be guided by codes are seldom involved in their creation.

Companies need to focus on the implementation of ethical guidelines rather than simply on their development. An organization can exert pressure on its employees to either behave ethically or unethically. Rather than making ethical conduct the tacit knowledge of every employee, Kirk Tyson's Eight-Step Implementation Plan (Tyson, 1996) suggests overt monitoring of intelligence activities and the employees gathering that intelligence. This plan raises the real issue of whether a company's culture or overt force is superior in delivering effective implementation of ethical codes. A strong ethical culture will emphasize correct behavior through the use of training, guidance, and top-management support. In the absence of a strong ethical culture, overt force may be necessary to prevent ethics problems.

ETHICAL THEORY AND EMPOWERMENT: ARE THEY CONNECTED?

One of the biggest trends currently in management is *empowerment*. But as a buzzword, *empowerment* has been badly defined and overemphasized. A new theory that begins where the role of empowerment failed is *value-based management*.

Value-based management has its roots in ethical theory and proposes to shape behavior by giving back personal responsibility to individual employees of a firm. Its basic philosophy is to reduce detailed regulation, control, and sanctioning, and to rely more strongly on the ability of the individual decision-maker to act rationally towards stated goals, policies, and values of the corporation (Jensen, 1999). It emphasizes that by restricting behavior through formal, written, and enforced rules, the exact opposite of the desired outcome is often the reality.

BUSINESS METAPHORS

How one firm perceives its ethical responsibilities or boundaries can be at least partly determined by how that firm views business. There are two views that are commonly seen in the CI literature: They are the *war metaphor* and the *game metaphor* views.

Under the *war metaphor*, decision-makers view business as war, where defeat of the enemy is the ultimate goal. Those acting under this view would use any means to win and would not perceive harm done to the enemy as being unethical.

The *game metaphor* describes business as a game where the competition is the opponent and the game is played out in the arena of the competitive marketplace under the auspices of marketplace guidance and rules. Success in the game is based on outwitting the competition by playing hard but fair and following the rules. Of course, if CI is to be treated as a true game of strategy, it would be fair to assume that it needs formalized, or at least commonly understood, agreed-upon rules.

THE EFFECT OF FORMALIZED RULES: DO THEY ERODE PERSONAL RESPONSIBILITY?

Some of the theories behind value-based management lie in the notion of *institutionalized responsibility*. Have we, as a society, succumbed to placing all moral and ethical responsibility on the institutions and governments that regulate our persons to the point where individual moral responsibility has been inevitably eroded? Looking at the evidence of the current trend for rules being used to replace individual responsible behavior, it might be viewed as such.

If a firm was to establish ethical guidelines for its intelligence unit, and the corporate culture supported ethical responsibility, CI employees operating in that unit could cease to make personal moral judgments in situations that could gain the company valuable information. According to the directors of CREDO, the Center for Research on Business Ethics at Denmark's Aarhus School of Business, "it is an open question whether ethical guidelines actually promote ethical behavior or whether they in fact limit ethical behavior to the observance of clauses found in the guidelines" (Petersen, 1999).

Ethical guidelines could actually promote the opposite behavior. It is human nature for individuals to push the boundaries of established limits as they traverse through the moral mazes of an organization and its environmental interactions (Jackall, 1989). Therefore it is probable that some individuals would look for the loopholes in the guidelines and put the firm at risk in their intelligence-gathering activities. A corporate culture that emphasizes individual responsibility would be effective at reducing the likelihood of either incident if that value-based responsibility was supported and enforced throughout the firm.

Corporations that implement ethical codes to guide their intelligence units may in effect get the opposite behavior from their employees than from what they set out to achieve. In effect, self-regulation at the business level might not be the best solution for eliciting ethical behavior in CI. Self-regulation at the industry level, though, through the adoption of a professional standard, might be a better route for CI professionals to pursue.

THE ROLE OF PROFESSIONAL STANDARDS: ARE THEY THE ANSWER?

Another form of self-regulation can be found in the creation of professional standards. These are more of an industrial regulation than a business regulation described by ethical codes. Professional standards are also widely accepted and are more commonly known in the medical, legal, and accounting professions.

Professional practice standards hold the obligations and responsibilities of a community of practice to be the formation of a type of moral conduct. Professional standards are used throughout business to minimize the uncertainty that consumers may feel when obtaining service from someone with expert knowledge. They are also used by the court system to determine the extent of a service failure or negligence in order to establish the amount of liability that should be assessed.

However, despite the proliferation of professional standards in the business community, it does have some fundamental flaws. For example, how much consensus is required for a norm to become a standard practice? Moreover, there is insufficient research as to the effectiveness of instituted standards. Although these experts in their fields set these standards, empirical research has not conclusively determined if these standards contain sufficient amounts of precaution or awareness for their particular contexts (Cressey & Moore, 1983).

Another factor that needs to be taken into consideration about ethical codes and professional standards is that they can, at times, be in conflict with one another. For example, some professional engineers prefer to work in companies that do not enforce ethical codes of conduct so that they are never in conflict with the professional standards established by the Society for Professional Engineers. Part of SCIP's Code of Ethics states that members should faithfully adhere to and abide by one's company policies, objectives, and guidelines. Yet this statement may put CI professionals in a quandary if their company does not operate as ethically as the SCIP code outlines.

PROFESSIONAL DESIGNATION:
IMPORTANT IN THE SCHEME OF THINGS?

One of the requirements of being designated a professional is to have an established community-wide, agreed-upon set of standards or guidelines of "professional" behavior. These standards or guidelines can contribute to the legitimacy of a discipline from the perspective of external stakeholders (Fleisher, 1998). Ethical guidelines also help to provide a level playing field for practitioners. The 1997 SCIP study about current ethical practices within the CI profession stated, with regard to establishing a universal ethical guideline that, "the payoff would be growing public approval for the profession and trust among practitioners and other stakeholders" (Trevino & Weaver, 1997).

This is important to CI professionals, as there is a lot of confusion about their profession and how it differs from corporate spying and surveillance. But industrial espionage is unethical and often illegal, and CI professionals are quick to point out that they feel that these tactics are largely, if not wholly, unnecessary. Most CI information is gleaned from publicly available sources, then analyzed and pieced together to obtain an overall picture of a competitor or industry. Effective CI practitioners do not need to undertake covert activities to obtain the valuable information they need (McBride, 1997).

The largest concern about ethics being expressed by CI practitioners seems to come more from a need to have the profession recognized by external stakeholders as being legitimate and ethical. If that is true, an outcry for firms to establish ethical codes in their intelligence units is not necessary, but an adoption of a standard that CI professionals both within and outside corporations can adhere to is essential.

CONCLUSION

As the CI profession matures, it becomes important that its practitioners can identify issues of importance, and can reach consensus about what is and is not appropriate. This chapter has promoted and encouraged a standard professional code among all CI practitioners that puts the onus for ethical conduct on individual responsibility. This approach is a better direction for the future than attempts to instill moral behavior through rule-based ethical codes at the business level. An industry-wide standard that CI professionals can believe in and have access to will provide the market not only with a level understanding of the playing field, but a reputation for professionalism. Nevertheless, any code in and of itself is only a necessary but not a sufficient means for assuring ethical CI behavior.

Emphasis and responsibility on the principles of SCIP would help prevent future conflict between an ethical standard at the professional level and an ethical code at the company level. Consumers and businesses tend to put a lot of faith in professional standards, and although they have their weaknesses and like laws are constantly evolving, they are the best option for satisfying the needs of current CI professionals without eroding the moral responsibility that they are intended to promote.

REFERENCES

Carroll, A., and A. Buccholtz. (2000). *Business and Society: Ethics and Stakeholder Management*, 4th ed. Cincinnati: Southwestern College Publishing.

Cressey, D.R., and C.R. Moore. (1983). "Managerial Values and Codes of Ethics," *California Management Review* 25(4): 57–58.

Edwards, G. (1994). "And the Survey Said . . ." in *Business Ethics: Generating Trust in the 1990s and Beyond*, ed. S.J. Garone. New York: Conference Board.

Ethics Resource Center. (1990). *Creating a Workable Company Code of Ethics*. Washington, DC: Ethics Resource Center.

Fine, N.R. (1997). "The Economic Espionage Act: Turning Fear into Compliance," *Competitive Intelligence Review* 8(3): 20–24.

Fiora, B. (1998). "Ethical Business Intelligence is NOT Mission Impossible," *Strategy and Leadership* 26(1): 40–41.

Fleisher, C.S. (1998). "Do Public Affairs Practitioners Constitute a Profession?" *Proceedings of the Fifth Annual International Public Relations Symposium*, Bled, Slovenia.

Jackall, R. (1989). *Moral Mazes*. New York: Oxford University Press.

Jensen, P.B. (1999). "A Value and Integrity Based Strategy to Consolidate Organization, Marketing and Communication—The Case of Jyske Bank." Working paper, CREDO/Department of Organization and Management, Aarhus (Denmark) School of Business.

Jones, D. (1999). "48% of Workers Admit to Illegal or Unethical Acts," *USA Today* (April 4–6): 1A–2A.

McBride, H. (1997). "They Snoop to Conquer," *Canadian Business* 70(8): 45–47.

Paine, L.S. (1991). "Corporate Policy and the Ethics of Competitor Intelligence Gathering," *Journal of Business Ethics* 10(6): 423–36.

Petersen, V.C. (1999). "The Careless Society—Or the Erosion of Responsibility." Working paper, CREDO/Department of Organization and Management, Aarhus (Denmark) School of Business.

Sapia-Bosch, A., and R. Tancer. (1998). "Navigating Through the Legal/Ethical Gray Zone," *Competitive Intelligence Magazine* 1(1): 31–36.

Trevino, L.K., and G.R. Weaver. (1997). "Ethical Issues in Competitive Intelligence Practice: Consensus, Conflicts, and Challenges," *Competitive Intelligence Review* 8(1): 61–72.

Tyson, K.W.M. (1996). "The Problem with Ethics: Implementation," *Competitive Intelligence Review* 7(supplement 1): S15–S17.

23

Competitive Intelligence and Organizational Change

Conor Vibert

INTRODUCTION

Throughout life, change insists on appearing, and it will often insist on being difficult to deal with. Organizations faced with change have the added difficulty of sustaining an image of stability—otherwise they are left vulnerable to their competitors. A corporation's unsuccessful adaptation is obvious when the replacement design does not fit with the environment. This chapter demonstrates how on-line analysts might spot and interpret signs of impending corporate change before they occur. It does so by matching important on-line indicators with the organizational dynamics of transformative capacity, in-house ability to determine outcomes, interests, underlying beliefs and worldviews, and operating environments (Hinings & Greenwood, 1988). These organizational dynamics are responsible for destabilizing an active operating entity and take the form of a capacity to transform ideas into concrete actions, a set of power holders, political interests that differ among internal competing factions, and underlying values that capture the attention of important internal stakeholders.

TRANSFORMATIVE CAPACITY

What is a firm capable of? What can it do? What true skill-sets does it possess? Answers to these questions are extremely important but not always obvious, even to corporate insiders. Unfortunately, in many instances, capability is most apparent when it is no longer in place. At first glance, the resignation of an airline-industry analyst may appear to some observers to be a minor setback. The seemingly overwhelming amount of commentary available to investors seeking to profit from the activities of the transportation sector might make such a loss seem inconsequential. However, were one to examine the history of this particular brokerage firm, one might recognize the historical market dominance of the corporation in question in offering advice to cash-plentiful clients. In a volatile marketplace, a lack of such expertise can lead to paralysis when swift and thoughtful decision-making is most in need.

When seeking to assess a change in the capabilities of an organization, competitive intelligence (CI) professionals should consider the ongoing level of effort toward innovation, the potential impact of new alliance agreements or long-term contracts, the existence of any extended product- or service-quality concerns, but especially the existence of in-house individuals whose expertise and experience include that of managing the form of change under consideration.

Innovation

How might innovation be assessed? One means is to monitor a company's patent application and filing activity using the U.S. Patent and Trademark Office (USPTO) on-line database (<http://www.uspto.gov/>) or the user-friendly patent server found on the IBM website (<http://www.patents.ibm.com/ibm.html>). Be wary of any recent reduction in the frequency of patent or copyright filings, or an increase in the number of filings by competitors. These signs may be indicative of an organization with few strong ideas for the future or a competitor on the march. The USPTO offers up-to-date information regarding patent registration; unfortunately, it mentions little about pending patents. Extensive discussion of the uses of the USPTO website databases is beyond the scope of this chapter; however, a simple but rough count of a firm's patenting activity can be obtained by typing in the company name under "Assignee" in the search box. If there are any current patents, they will be listed chronologically.

Innovative behavior can be indicated by other means. The Transium Business Intelligence website (<http://databex.transium.com/>) sorts articles by terms such as new-product development, test marketing, and patents. Recent innovative activity may be documented or summarized in these abstracts. Along with the selected articles offered by Hoovers Online (<http://www.hoovers.com/>), this search tool will point an analyst to electronic journals dedicated to the industry of interest. A query of articles in these journals may offer an assessment of the company and its products or services.

Alliances

New contractual relationships or alliance agreements can signal a change in organizational capacity or a redirection of existing strategy, especially when "Davids" seek to collaborate with apparent "Goliaths." In situations such as these, an alliance agreement may point to a previous product-line deficiency in a larger firm that is being overcome by an alignment with a younger niche-market player. It also often signals a new strategic direction for the smaller firm. For instance, consider the hypothetical example of a mid-sized management-consulting firm that enters into an agreement to provide 2,000 well-trained technical-service representatives to meet the needs of customers of a large but still growing personal-computer manufacturer. For the management-consulting firm, this initiative may indicate a move away from a generalist market to one that is solely technical in nature; for the computer manufacturer, it may provide a means for participation in all segments of the industry value-chain while removing an important reason in the minds of potential clients for not purchasing its products.

A number of portals is useful for identifying new collaborative relationships. For technology-oriented firms, *Red Herring* magazine's (<http://www.herring.com/>) on-line version lists alliance partners in its company profiles. Searching by company name or industry, and doing so chronologically using sites such as PR Newswire (<http://www.prnewswire.com/>), CNNfn (<http://www.cnnfn.com/>), or Transium Business Intelligence (<http://databex.transium.com/>), should also highlight any existing, formal, and/or collaborative relationships. Another option is simply to examine the website of the firm in question. If a search feature is offered, try querying the database using terms such as "alliances," "joint ventures," or "collaborative relationships."

Quality

Quality problems are not an issue most managers like to discuss. Negative publicity of this nature is also not normally corporately sponsored or disseminated. Thus analysts must make use of proxy measures. At least five approaches are extremely effective in this regard. A first approach is to use a generic search engine such as Yahoo! (<http://www.yahoo.com/>) or Infoseek (<http://infoseek.go.com/>) and conduct a keyword search by product, service, and company name. A story might simply pop up.

A second means is to explore on-line consumer reports regarding specific products or services. Silence, or an absence of positive publicity, may be indicative of deeper operational concerns, ranging from an inappropriate product design to substandard parts or poor assembly. A number of portals offer on-line consumer reports: These include Product Review Net (<http://www.productreviewnet.com/home.html>) and Consumer World (<http://www.consumerworld.org/>). Free product comparisons using the services of Compare may be located on the consumer economy page of the Yahoo! search-engine portal (<http://www.yahoo.com/>).

A third idea is to use an on-line investigative tool such as Transium Business Intelligence (<http://databex.transium.com/>). Search the available article abstracts by company name, then use the "Function" category to sort the articles. In many instances, abstracts will be categorized under headings such as "product reviews," "product launch," and "product quality," which can speed up an analysis.

Finally, one further means to assess the ongoing strength of a firm's product and service offerings is to check the warning notices carried by organizations such as the Better Business Bureau, the Consumer Safety Protection Commission, the Food and Drug Administration, and the Federal Aviation Administration. Look carefully for a history of repeated product recalls.

IN-HOUSE ABILITY TO DETERMINE OUTCOMES

Among the most important signals of an organizational transformation is a shift in the internal corporate power-structure. Who, really, is influential? Power is a topic extensively researched by sociologists, but rarely explored by business academics. In many cases, as power-holders change, so too does strategic direction. Although numerous perspectives abound, for the purpose of this chapter powerful individuals are those who acquire important resources, absorb organizational uncertainty, do visible things, occupy offices with considerable formal authority, and make the firm dependent upon themselves for the successful completion of certain key activities (Pfeffer, 1992). Awareness and monitoring of the activity of individuals who meet these criteria can provide insight into important alterations to come. Unfortunately, an in-depth analysis of this important topic is beyond the scope of this chapter. However, a few rules of thumb are helpful.

Authority

Authority can also be referred to as the level of an individual in the corporate hierarchy. For information on the status quo, look to the firm's homepage, for its "S1 registration form" if it exists, or for its most recent "DEF 14A proxy statement." For changes, look closely at the corporate press-releases for hiring announcements or the "SEC 8K Statements of Material Change" filed by the company.

Visibility

Powerful individuals do visible things. They are written up in the press and are important enough for the firm to expend resources to tell their story. Means of identifying visible employees include examining corporate press-releases for mention of key individuals by using tools such as the company homepage or specialty portals such as Business Wire (<http://www.businesswire.com/>) or PR Newswire (<http://www.prnewswire.com/>). Another angle is to use a business news source such as CNNfn (<http://www.cnnfn.com/>) to search for stories by the company name, then look for who is mentioned in the stories.

Dependence

Who is the company dependent on for its continued success? Answers to this question are often associated with important skill sets, personal ability, or connections. Who has important family connections that keep the company tied in to ongoing revenue-generation opportunities? Who has experience participating in the firm's previous mergers or acquisitions? Who understands where to find new customers or future customers? One approach is to look for personal profiles on the corporate website, in the firm's U.S. Securities Exchange Commission (SEC) "DEF 14A proxy statement," or in its "S1 registration form" (if one exists). When did the individual start with the company? Where did he or she come from? Why is he or she at that level in the company? What are his or her previous successes?

Uncertainty Absorption and Resource Acquisition

Who are the corporate heroes? Who are the previous corporate successes associated with? Who brought in the big clients? Who saved the company from bankruptcy or staved-off creditors while a turnaround was being implemented? Again, look for heroic stories in the press releases found on the company website, or make use of a search engine such as Northern Light (<http://www.northernlight.com/>) and find popular press stories. What do they say? If closely examining the company's "SEC 10K Annual Report," answer the question: "Whose area of the firm is growing?" Which executive is tasked with managing that area?

INTERESTS

Along with capacity and power, researchers may also want to be aware of any changes to the nature of internal stakeholder interests. Hiring and insider-trading activity may offer insight into this important concern. In instances of corporate growth, researchers may want to make note of whose department or division has been on the receiving end of any new positions or resources. The "employment opportunities" area of a company homepage, a specialized job-placement portal such as the Monster Board (<http://www.monster.com/>) or on-line local newspapers accessed through websites such as that of News Directory (<http://www.newsdirectory.com/>) are good places to begin a search. Look for hiring activity that is out of the ordinary. This can mean hiring for newly created positions involving nontraditional skill sets, or heavier-than-normal hiring for positions involving more-traditional skill sets.

However, hiring activity may not always be a good sign. A sure sign of a problem within a firm is evidence of an ongoing inability to retain valued employees. Look for a seemingly never-ending stream of job advertisements or new executive-hiring announcements without any corresponding changes in strategic behavior or logical justification. Most importantly, pay particular attention to departures from the executive suite. These are not always announced, yet once a search effort has been completed, the identities of successful candidates are normally publicized.

UNDERLYING BELIEFS AND WORLDVIEWS

Analysts seeking to spot a transformation in the making should pay attention to the values of the organization's human stakeholders—especially those that clearly deviate from the ones espoused by its top-management team (Meyerson

& Martin, 1987). How important are values? One need simply to think of corporations such as Microsoft (that consistently lure the best and brightest of college and university graduates) to realize the role of underlying corporate beliefs in differentiating an industry leader from its followers. Where might one find textual versions of espoused values? Try company websites, especially ones that are dedicated to the hiring of new recruits.

Overly negative, ongoing commentary regarding an organization should not be ignored. Signals of value shifts may take the form of illicit corporate behavior, or may be apparent in on-line discussion forums. Corporations are rife with disgruntled insiders or former employees who often seek a forum for sharing their viewpoints. These views may be worth gold to a competitor. Yahoo! offers a message board (<http://www.yahoo.com/>) that may help distinguish corporate from employee views of the company. At this site, type in a ticker symbol and look for the on-line message board. Portals such as The Raging Bull (<http://www.ragingbull.com/>) and The Motley Fool (<http://www.fool.com/>) specialize in discussion of particular stocks and industries and are well worth an investigation. Other discussion forums can be found using services such as DejaNews (<http://x28.deja.com/>) or Hotbot (<http://hotbot.lycos.com/>).

Another sign of values inconsistent with those of a corporation is evidence of widespread corruption or illegal activity. Where should a search begin for signs of illicit behavior? Try the on-line business press. An article search using a general-information portal such as Northern Light (<http://www.northernlight.com/>) or a news source such as CNNfn (<http://www.cnnfn.com/>) or Reuters (<http://www.reuters.com/>) may be the quickest route to uncovering any dirt. A different angle is to check out the media that lawyers read, such as the Legal News Network (<http://www.legalnewsnet.com/>). This offers a long list of corporate lawsuits in the news. Another interesting site is that of *Lawyer's Weekly* on-line magazine (<http://www.lweekly.com/sub.htm>). In this magazine one can search by keywords (such as the company name). The advantage or disadvantage here, of course, is that one may get a spin on events from legal commentators. In other cases, making use of the search capabilities of Law Crawler (<http://www.o.walworth.wi.us/lawcrawler.html>) is an option. Transcripts of court cases falling within the federal court system may be queried by company name. Cases falling under the jurisdiction of state and local systems may be accessed by using links from this research portal. This latter ability is most useful when investigating companies with offices or plants in more than one location.

EXTERNAL OPERATING ENVIRONMENTS

Do operating environments matter? In few instances would a response of "no" ring true? Indeed, one need simply think of the recent rejection by the Canadian government of a merger agreement between the Royal Bank of Canada and the Bank of Montreal to appreciate the significance of the phrase "no organization is an island unto itself." Major regulatory changes rarely leave players unaffected (Tushman, Newman, & Romanelli, 1988). Worrisome for any manager should be ongoing competitor activity in the areas of mergers and acquisitions, initial public offerings, or government lobbying that comes as a surprise. In terms of the internal operating environment, outside analysts should also be particularly interested in firms in the midsts of extended financial declines. This can indicate ongoing organizational crises.

Corporations may have no choice but to respond to major alterations in the competitive environment. These changes may not be obvious, as in a program of gradual share acquisition of a marginal competitor by a much larger operating entity. However, they may be quite visible: Ownership alterations, new industry entrants, mergers and acquisitions, and regulatory change are all important examples of industry alteration.

Mergers and Acquisitions

These examples can be identified by a number of means. The SEC website (<http://www.sec.gov/>) offers access to its most recent filings. Firms that choose to merge are obliged to report such activity to the SEC by using Form SC13D as well as Form 8K, which is a statement of material changes. Hoovers IPO (initial public offering) Central (<http://www.hoovers.com/ipo/>) offers researchers a searchable database that identifies firms whose shares have only recently started trading, as well as those who have filed an S1 Prospectus Form, but have not yet begun to trade on U.S. stock exchanges. Initial public offerings may be queried by geographic location, company name, industry, and underwriter. IPO Central is, of course, a shortcut to the real source, the SEC EDGAR database. Another interesting site is operated by *Red Herring* magazine (<http://www.herring.com/>). Considered by many as the bible of the venture-capital profession, it is extremely effective at monitoring merger-and-acquisition activity as well as documenting the development of IPOs in the area of technology. However, of all the sources, perhaps the most timely are those of the growing legion of business-information portals, many of which report merger-and-acquisition announcements almost instantly.

Regulatory Change

As noted above, regulatory change is also an important form of competitive alteration. Tracking these changes or proposed changes can be a difficult and time-consuming task, but one good approach is to read what the lawyers read, paying attention to the stories found on the Legal News Network (<http://www.legalnewsnet.com/>). A second approach is to examine the portal of the regulatory agency or department of interest. Commonly used portals include those of the U.S. Securities and Exchange Commission (SEC) (<http://www.sec.gov/>), the U.S. Federal Communication Commission (FCC) (<http://www.fcc.gov/>), the U.S. Food and Drug Administration (FDA) (<http://www.fda.gov/>), and the U.S. Environmental Protection Agency (EPA) (<http://www.epa.gov/>). Proposed changes and lobbying activity are normally well documented. Although the content of each website differs, many allow users to view letters submitted by interested parties or opinions rendered by the authority. In each site, look for section headings such as "press releases," "dockets," or "statements." Researchers should also be on the lookout for links titled "reading room" or "Freedom of Information Act."

Industry Associations

One last possibility for identifying important upcoming changes to a competitive environment is to examine the website of the relevant industry associations. The American Society of Association Executives offers access (through its "Gateway to Associations" link <http://www.asae.org/main/>) to a large number of national associations.

Many of these homepages provide a searchable database of press releases, formal statements, and executive speeches. Formal statements are often nothing more than responses to regulatory-change proposals or consensus suggestions for altering the industry's operating environment. In many instances, these websites clearly identify the major issues or challenges facing their managers and can be very informative when they take the form of "state of the industry" addresses.

INTERNAL OPERATING ENVIRONMENTS

While top-management teams ignore industry alterations at their own peril, few competent boards of directors ignore a more ominous internal sign than that of repeated poor financial performance or performance below industry standards. Financial statements can easily be found on the Internet if the stocks of the company under inspection are publicly traded on an American stock exchange. A good place to start is the SEC's homepage (<http://www.sec.gov/>). Forms such as a "10K company annual report," a "10Q quarterly financial report," and an "8K statement of material changes" will document any extended decline. Other tracking tools are numerous. Portals such as Market Guide (<http://www.marketguide.com/MGI/>), Zack's Investment Research (<http://aw.zacks.com/>), and Just Quotes (<http://www.justquotes.com/>) provide tools, charts, financial statements, and share-price indicators that allow almost instant comparisons to industry- and competitor-performance measures.

Other signals of a change in the offing include organizational inertia or executive complacency (Starbuck, Greve, & Hedberg, 1978). Characteristics associated with these include a change in corporate press-release frequency, uncharacteristically heavy and negative discussion of the company's prospects in the on-line discussion forums, extended product- or service-quality concerns, and a continuing departure of key personnel. While most of these signals were discussed earlier, the important question to consider is: "Why are these concerns not being resolved?" or "Why are they still lingering?"

Look for obvious news stories such as those that document periods of extended decline, openly question managerial inaction, discuss nonfavorable changes in market share, or praise the rise to dominance of a competitor. Analysts

Table 23.1
SPOTTING CHANGE USING ON-LINE SOURCES

Issue	Evidence	Theoretical Construct	Source
Does the company have the expertise to manage a change?	• The team may be weak • An examination of executive profiles found on the company's website, recent proxy statements and the original S1 form suggests that most of their expertise is in running companies operating in tranquil competitive environments • None of the members have managed the integration of a merger or a major restructuring aside from growth	Transformative capacity	SEC DEF 14A statement, 10K annual report, S1 registration statement Companies Online
Is the company's workforce unified behind top management?	• The mission statement of the company suggests that employees are the corporation's most important resource • Yet a monitoring of on-line discussion related to the corporation provides evidence from at least eight individuals who identify themselves as employees that the internal culture of the company is chaotic and tense • An examination of on-line hiring announcements suggests that employee turnover is extremely high and above that of its major competitors	Underlying beliefs and worldviews	Companies Online The Motley Fool Monster Board
Whose influence is growing in the company?	• An examination of the corporate hiring announcements suggests a growing role in the company for technical service representatives • This suggests an effort to move into a new area of the value chain in pursuit of higher profits and increasing influence for the vice president of customer relations	Interests	Monster Board
Do the same executives still call the shots?	• The chief financial officer (CFO) may be losing influence • A close examination of corporate press releases for the past year and a chronology of popular-press stories over the same time period indicate that the CFO, although still employed by the firm, has not been mentioned publicly in news releases for seven months	In-house ability to determine outcomes	Northern Light Companies Online
Is financial performance acceptable and being managed appropriately?	• An examination of recent share-price performance indicates 24 consecutive months of downward pressure. An examination of the last two annual reports and last four quarterly reports suggests net income figures that are not growing • No changes to the top management team are evident • No new product launches have been disclosed	Internal and external operating environments	SEC DEF 14A statement, 10K annual report, 10Q quarterly report, and 8K statement of material changes JustQuotes, Companies Online

should also be on the lookout for what is not mentioned. Corporations normally announce new executive-hiring initiatives, important promotions, or major improvement initiatives. Analysts should be concerned if initiatives such as these are not evident when performance is below the industry average. Silence or inactivity on the communications front can point to inactivity, internal paralysis, or turmoil.

Where might one look? Start a search on the company homepage and look for the press-release section. Company homepages can be accessed through portals such as Company Link (<http://www.companylink.com/>) or Companies Online (<http://www.companiesonline.com/>). External delivery sources such as PR Newswire (<http://www.prnewswire.com/>) or Business Wire (<http://www.businesswire.com/>) are excellent public-relations-material providers and offer users the opportunity to search by company name or industry. Look at the Hoovers Online portal (<http://www.hoovers.com/>). A search by company name should provide a company capsule. Examine the selected stories at the bottom of the page. Another option is to peruse the sorted article abstracts available through the Transium Business Intelligence portal (<http://databex.transium.com/>). Again, search by the company name and then sort the abstracts using the function option; this breaks the stories into categories such as financial forecasts, strategy, market development, etc. A third option is to use the Northern Light search engine (<http://www.northernlight.com/>): This portal clearly identifies information sources, allowing analysts to distinguish press releases from independent assessments and monitor corporate reactions to important competitive challenges.

CONCLUSIONS

This concludes our discussion of the potential role of the free on-line resources of the World Wide Web for identifying signals of change in an organization. Table 23.1 illustrates an example of how on-line researchers might capture some of the information necessary to undertake such an assessment.

REFERENCES

Hinings, C., and R. Greenwood. (1988). *The Dynamics of Strategic Change*. London: Basil Blackwell.

Meyerson, D., and J. Martin (1987). "Cultural Change: An Integration of Three Different Views," *Journal of Management Studies* 24(6): 623–47.

Pfeffer, J. (1992). *Managing with Power*. Boston: Harvard Business School Press.

Starbuck, W., A. Greve, and B. Hedberg. (1978). "Responding to Crisis," *Journal of Business Administration* 9(2): 111–78.

Tushman, M., W. Newman, and E. Romanelli. (1988). "Convergence and Upheaval: Managing the Unsteady Pace of Organizational Evolution," in *Readings in the Management of Innovation*, ed. M. Tushman and W. Moore. New York: Harper Business.

24

The Future of Competitive Intelligence

David L. Blenkhorn and Craig S. Fleisher

INTRODUCTION

It is an ideal time to look ahead as we reach the final chapter of our book, *Managing Frontiers in Competitive Intelligence*. We have tried to provide at least a glimpse of what competitive intelligence (CI) presently looks like on the leading edges of its management and practice, its relationship to functional business areas, its application in specific contexts, and with respect to organizational issues associated with CI. In this chapter we intend to do a little crystal-ball gazing. We should note two caveats in attempting this difficult feat: 1) our crystal ball, like many other experts in their fields, retains some opaqueness; and 2) we do not subscribe to the "seersucker theory" that says that for every seer, there is a sucker.

Our intent is to address this topic in two parts. We first describe the key directions we see facing senior organizational decision-makers and policy-makers, then suggest how these trends may impact and be impacted by the practice and management of CI.

FIVE CRUCIAL DIRECTIONS FOR TODAY'S TOP MANAGERS

We want to describe the five critical trends we see facing senior executives. In order to understand where CI may be headed, it is particularly important to understand its primary customers (e.g., senior decision-makers) are headed. We think it is important to describe directions, including opportunities and challenges, facing organizational executives and senior management. As such, we will describe how general managers (GMs) or managing directors (MDs) ensure that their organizations are able to capitalize on the most appropriate opportunities, while meeting or avoiding the challenges to its existing business. General managers must act effectively in the current and longer term along at least four primary dimensions: setting direction, building capabilities, implementing change, and assessing performance. It is to these themes that our discussion regarding opportunities and challenges will be directed.

Evolving environmental dynamics, discontinuities, and complexity have challenged the standard management thinking that existed into the late 1990s. Although this chapter's writers do not subscribe to "fad surfing" (Shapiro, 1996), there is a number of important directions facing senior decision-makers that needs mentioning. For sake of conciseness, we will organize this discussion around five key themes. We feel these five directions will most significantly affect managerial activities and practitioners in the near future (next 3 to 5 years), if they are not affecting them already; consequently, they will also be of greatest influence to the development of CI management and practice in the coming decade.

NEW ECONOMIC GROWTH

We are in the midst of a dramatic change in which we are moving from an industrial, capital-driven economy to a knowledge-based, postcapital, third-wave one (Drucker, 1994; Hope & Hope, 1997).

Opportunities

New economic growth offers management many new opportunities to innovate and diffuse innovations into the marketplace (Brown & Eisenhardt, 1995; Kotha, 1995). New economic growth will also require and allow managers to "frame bust" or "paradigm bend" in organic mind-sets as opposed to machine mind-sets (DeGeus, 1997). Management in postcapitalist organizations will seek to institutionalize innovative capabilities, thus shaping the future rather than reacting to it (Fahey & Randall, 1998; Hamel & Pralahad, 1996). Management that can sustain innovation in products and services will provide their organizations with a primary source of competitive advantage (Leonard-Barton, 1995). Employees, customers, and investors are eager for a new source of intellectual leadership; managements that provides foresight and a compelling view of the future can be beacons that motivate their organizations (Pralahad, 1997).

Challenges

Managers need to find ways besides downscoping, downsizing, or reengineering, which some described as "dumbsizing," to boost profits. Strategy during the leaner times has traditionally been nothing more than financial manipulation through a series of mergers and acquisitions (Kanter, 1997) and will need to be more sophisticated if organizations hope to succeed (Pralahad, 1997). Today's managers will have to create or generate real wealth, not just transfer it (Senge, 1999). Managers will have to demonstrate and communicate performance despite having to work with assessment tools that are obsolete and not supported by generally accepted principles (Kaplan & Norton, 1996).

Impacts for Competitive Intelligence

The many changes organizations face from new economic growth should ideally be foreseen in advance of the competition by top decision-makers. Top managers should be trying to shape the future rather than reacting to it. This will allow proactive decisions to be made with respect to products/services, customers or markets served, and possibly the future direction of the organization itself. New industries and boundaries may emerge that will threaten or replace existing ones. These new industries may threaten existing products/services, or the very existence of the firm itself. Where should we look to get indications of these "winds of change"? Ongoing, comprehensive environmental scanning by the CI function takes on an increasingly important role—not in its traditional form, but with new insights into what constitutes the new signals of change and their meaning. Top managers who can be "ahead of the wave" will be the first ones to succeed in the new economic growth.

Senior management needs a very innovative team in place to capitalize upon the ramifications of new economic growth. What are the types of intellectual capital with the mind-sets best suited to respond to the challenges of the future in general, and in our industry in particular? Where can these people be found? Which educational institutions are best educating their students to succeed in the future? How can we best orient and prepare our employees to address both the industry evolution and revolution? The CI function can best obtain and interpret information to answer these and other questions related to the "frame busting" and "paradigm bending" necessary to succeed in the future.

The CI function will benefit from this direction. Organizations are increasingly moving toward intangible and inimitable forms of innovation that utilize their intellectual assets or capital, as opposed to purely financial or physical capital. Competitive intelligence is well entrenched in intellectual methods for identifying opportunities through analysis and for deciphering uncertain futures in actionable ways. Because of this move toward growth through inventiveness and innovation, we would expect successful CI professionals to rapidly grow in importance and prominence within new economy organizations.

ADVANCING INFORMATION AND COMMUNICATION TECHNOLOGIES (ICT)

Information is both the medium of exchange for generative organizational learning and its source of power (Marshall, 1997). Significant technological trends and characteristics affecting managers include: 1) the increasing rate of information and communication technologies (ICT) change and diffusion; 2) the information age and economy; and 3) the increasing power of computers and communications technology. Information and communication technologies will continue to shrink time and space (Harmon, 1997).

Opportunities

Management will use ICT to provide stakeholders with larger volumes of data in a more user-friendly and timely manner than ever before (Thorp, 1999). Companies will realize value from ICT if their managers can figure out how to leverage it both internally and externally to generate profits (Gates, 1999). Evolving ICT such as global-positioning systems (GPS), digital-video discs (DVD), direct-to-home satellite TV (DTH), enterprise resource planning (ERP), and wireless and Internet-based phones all offer managers more efficient and effective ways to interconnect dispersed stakeholders. Managers will have chances to promote the convergence of information and communication technologies in ways to transfer and augment organizational knowledge (Garvin, 1993).

Challenges

Most managers have been forced to react to the impact of advances in communications and technology in their businesses because they do not understand its implications. More information does not equate with more knowledge (Quinn, 1992). Entire industries and companies can be eliminated in a short time due to competition from businesses using so-called "disruptive technologies" such as the Internet (Christenson, 1997). Appropriate boundaries must be placed on the potentially anticompetitive or even antisocial actions of ICT-empowered employees (Simons, 1994). Management must learn to deal with the high level of uncertainty and risk of choosing the "wrong" ICT solutions (Dixit & Pindyck, 1995). Last but not least, managers will need to seek the elusive balance between "tech" and "touch."

Impacts for Competitive Intelligence

The challenge for the CI function of advancing ICT is not the identification of new information sources or lack of information, but information overload and its correct interpretation. The increased technological capabilities can actually complicate rather than simplify the CI role of making sense from much more data emanating from many more sources.

   The CI function will have to scope out the latest ICT before it is available in the marketplace to ensure that leading-edge techniques will be utilized. Competitive intelligence managers should encourage leading-edge ICT providers (both hardware and software) to utilize the CI manager's organization as a "lead user" or "beta test site" for their new products/services. In this way, the ICT manufacturers will be working with real-life "solutions" to CI challenges as their primary research evolves into usable and tested software and hardware.

   The interpretation of the information function takes on a more complex and significant role as managers learn how to leverage this new and more relevant information to generate increased profits. Advances in ICT can assist managers in the interpretation role as "intelligent software" (i.e., an agent) is utilized for information retrieval and to make sense of increasing volumes of incoming data. Even with advancing levels of ICT, there will still be an important need for highly intelligent CI professionals to perform the final synthesis on the information and subsequent analysis performed by the technology itself. Make no mistake about it—ICT will not replace the need for CI professionals, but enhance it.

As higher levels of technological sophistication become available, the CI function must not lose the proper balance between "tech" and "touch"; the role of technology in CI is to make the function more efficient and user-friendly, not more complicated. Ideally, CI should drive ICT, not vice-versa. This also raises a hurdle for CI functions and professionals, since many of the systems being used organization-wide are being selected and authorized by individuals with little sensitivity to CI concerns or needs. To remain on top of this direction, CI will have to take a far more active involvement and leadership role than it has demonstrated so far with its organizational colleagues in the information systems (IS), information technology (IT), operations, and communication-technology areas.

Counterintelligence also takes on a new dimension with ICT. Competitors now have increased capabilities to invade your organization electronically, not to mention the problems caused by employees who can easily send out proprietary information with the click of a mouse. Once-secure databases and information systems are now vulnerable as a result of ICT being utilized for clandestine and nefarious purposes. Because of this direction, the CI function and professional will take on an even more vigilant role in counterintelligence activities to secure the organization against these security concerns.

INCREASING GLOBALIZATION

Globalization and the development of cross-border relationships transcend the existence of multinational companies, and they also affect local businesses in domestic markets. Globalization has largely been due to worldwide economic development and trade agreements (such as those overseen by the World Trade Organization [WTO]) that entail the opening of domestic markets to foreign firms. Intensive globalization has led to a global restructuring of industries— benefiting some, while harming other competitors.

Opportunities

Managers can develop global mind-sets and exploit market opportunities in new geographic areas (Stanat, 1998). Companies will have to learn how to utilize new and diverse sets of decision-making resources and talents that will need to be gathered on a global, not national, stage (Kanter, 1997). Managers will be involved in an expanding set of partnerships in the form of global alliances, joint ventures, partnerships, know-how, and marketing agreements (Drucker, 1997). Managers will be able to approach problem-solving and decision-making as a universal search—to learn beyond internal and external boundaries and embrace the effort to seek markets, competencies, and resources from around the globe (Somerville & Mroz, 1997). Managers will have new opportunities to bring people together from around the globe with a wide range of specialized knowledge in community-like atmospheres where they can achieve and be productive (Drucker, 1997).

Challenges

Managers cannot understand their industries by focusing solely on domestic markets and firms (Hitt, Hoskisson, & Kim, 1997). Managers must remain vigilant and aware of "foreign" competitors who can quickly enter their markets and establish competitive positions (Schuster, 1997). Managers are challenged to adopt ethical and responsible business practices in areas in which their own codes and standards may not be accepted (DeGeorge, 1993). Managers must be cognizant of the social and political unrest that often accompanies changes taking place in the economic sphere (Marcus, 1996). Management will have to acquire higher levels of intercultural competence and sensitivity (Pralahad, 1997).

Impacts for Competitive Intelligence

The CI function must monitor the globe well enough so that potential competition from new geographic areas is identified in advance of its becoming a reality. As developing economies mature, their industries and companies can become formidable to the traditional players in the field. An organization with an effective CI function should not be blindsided by these threats from global competition. For example, the social and political unrest in many corners of the globe are most often not random, unpredictable events (Fleisher, 1999). An effective CI program should not be caught off-guard—it should alert key managers of pending "hot spots" and the attendant actions that should be undertaken long before turmoil erupts. This CI role will only increase in prominence.

As firms expand their globalization efforts through alliances, joint ventures, and partnerships, a thorough due-diligence is necessary on the proposed partner(s). The CI function is well positioned to provide input that complements the traditional financial statements and other information provided by the company in order to learn the proposed partner's real agenda, culture, and track record. Some observers even think that we should get rid of the "competitive" out of CI and replace it with "cooperative"! We think that this may be among the most important roles for CI in the future, since alliances and networks will be far more critical to competition than they have been in the past.

Globalization considerably broadens the horizon of organizations in the areas of markets, sourcing raw materials, parts and services, and human talent—in other words, all along the value constellation (Gupta, 1994). The CI function, with its antennae widely spread, can obtain information and analysis on these matters on a global scale, rather than simply on a domestic one. This often provides better value to the firm, impacting the bottom line. It also increases the need for the CI function to take the lead on making sure the firm has global-intelligence systems and attitudes in place to take advantage of this direction. Those functions and professionals who fail to provide this global perspective will quickly lose their organizational currency.

ACCELERATING PACE OF CHANGE

Many high-profile companies of the 1980s (e.g., Apple, BHP, Wang) differed greatly from those of the 1990s (e.g., Microsoft, Enron, AOL). Personal computers, electronic networks, and the World Wide Web were in their infancy a decade ago. Hitt (1998) suggests that a multiplication of the amount of change that occurred between 1984 and 1997 by thirtyfold to fortyfold or more will determine the amount of change that will occur between 1997 and 2010. The world is changing fast, and many of these changes are likely to be unforeseen by most of us.

Opportunities

F. Robert Jacobs, author of *Real Time Strategic Change* (1994), states that "the most successful organizations of the future will be those that are capable of rapidly and effectively bringing about fundamental, lasting, system-wide changes." Change can bring about entirely new industries or products (Christenson, 1997). Change can also usher in more effective ways of managing than previously existed (Kotter, 1996). Highly changeable, complex, and dynamic competitive environments (i.e., hypercompetitive ones [D'Aveni, 1994]) allow managers to use new tactics that can undermine traditional advantages and reallocate industry profitability. Because of the pace of change, managers can utilize speed and agility as critical competitive weapons (Eisenhardt & Tabrizi, 1995). Managers with the ability to regularly recognize and develop the not-as-yet identified competencies that are in demand will be those who succeed (Somerville & Mroz, 1997). Finally, managers can be catalysts for the types of change their organizations require by assuming new or enhanced roles and responsibilities and energizing their organization's culture (Duques & Gaske, 1997).

Challenges

Most change efforts meet with some level of resistance from those who must change (O'Toole, 1996) and consequently fail (Somerville & Mroz, 1997). Certain groups will resist more stubbornly than others, frequently due to such relatively unalterable characteristics such as demographics (Conger, 1997). Managers often do not understand the sources of corporate inertia (such as blinders on their strategic frames, operational routines, dogmatic values, and shackled relationships) inhibiting their organizations (Sull, 1999). Some organizations are better designed to manage the impacts of change than others, although a majority lack the strategic flexibility needed to sustain competitive advantage over lengthy time periods (Hitt, Keats, & DeMarie, 1998). Last but not least, management will need to learn new ways of managing that require the empowerment of employees (Harmon, 1997), reconfigurable organizational structures (Galbraith, 1997), responsible (Pralahad, 1997) and situational (Hersey & Johnson, 1997) leadership to satisfactorily address continual change.

Impacts for Competitive Intelligence

The ability to identify and interpret the signals of impending major changes long before they occur are competencies greatly valued by top managers. Accurate models of predictive behavior are useful here. Predicting change is necessary but not sufficient information for top-level managers; also necessary is to provide scenarios as to how the change may impact your organization in areas such as products/services offered, markets covered, and eventual outcomes. The CI function, with continual environmental-scanning capabilities, is in a preferred position to monitor and make sense of those changes.

The CI function also has an internal role to play in the accelerating pace of change. Knowing your own organization's culture toward change is important when management plans major organizational changes. The ability of an organization to readily adopt and adapt to change may well be its sustainable competitive advantage. The CI function should be able to collect the right amount of internal data, turn it into information, and interpret the findings to provide valuable input to enable management to successfully nurture and manage this internal change. The CI function should help smooth the transition towards internal change.

However, not everything about this direction is expected to benefit CI. The shelf life of CI products, already short, will shorten even further. There will be less time to perform CI tasks, with immense pressure to complete today's jobs yesterday. Those functions and practitioners who are not able to achieve continuous reductions in their intelligence-process cycle time (IPCT—the duration of time occurring between the receipt of an intelligence request and providing satisfactory results to the CI client) will be at a growing disadvantage. Intelligence-process cycle time can be greatly reduced through the insightful application of automated information-gathering methods, although the analysis subprocess has not benefited as greatly in terms of cycle-time reduction. Additionally, the levels of uncertainty and risk from the accelerating pace of change perceived by decision-makers may cause them to be hesitant to move on the CI outputs provided.

GROWING IMPORTANCE OF LEARNING AND KNOWLEDGE

Knowledge has become key to personal and economic success and has replaced traditional factors of production such as natural resources, labor, and capital. Knowledge can account for a very large share of a firm's assets (Halal, 1998).

Opportunities

A key to competitive success will be for managers to develop intellectual capital in areas that will give their firms competitive advantages with targeted customers (Senge, 1994). Managers will have chances to develop new means to measure the stock of their employees' intellectual capital, since an accurate measurement of this asset may be a better indicator of the organization's future potential than any of the other assets currently measured on a company's books (Kaplan & Norton, 1996). Managers have opportunities to demonstrate the value of assessing, managing, and maximizing their organizations' reputation or stakeholder capital (external) and intellectual capital (internal) (Ind, 1997). Organizations will also have opportunities to utilize different intelligence types in new, marketable ways (Handy, 1995).

Challenges

Management must figure out how to reconfigure and adjust organizational structures, decision-making processes, reward systems, management-development approaches, and corporate cultures in order to cultivate organization-wide learning and open communications (Lei, Slocum, & Pitts, 1999). Few companies have appropriate systems to capture and apply the tacit know-how that exists within their employees (Leonard-Barton, 1995), which means that the loss of only a few key, gold-collared employees can create havoc with a company's ability to compete. Most companies lack the systems to value their organizations or employees' knowledge-capital and even unwittingly go about destroying knowledge (Nonaka & Takeuchi, 1995). Competitors can also exploit unprotected knowledge bases in new ways that require managers to be ever-vigilant with counterintelligence (Winkler, 1997). Managers will have to make determinations of how to allocate resources toward knowledge-development projects in the absence of commonly accepted standards (Quinn, 1992). Even though researchers have demonstrated that knowledge increases when information is shared, many managers still face cultural, political, or societal biases whereby individuals jealously guard the information they hold because they believe it is essential to acquiring or holding power. Last but not least, because the half-life of what we know is rapidly shortening, managers and management will be challenged to acquire extensive and continuous learning and training (Pralahad, 1997).

Impacts for Competitive Intelligence

Perhaps the only truly sustainable competitive advantage of an organization is that of being a so-called *knowledge* or *learning* organization. The CI function and practitioner can be a catalyst in learning and knowledge by providing responses to two questions: First, what should be learned by those in the organization, and who should learn what?, and second, what are the most effective techniques of learning, given the often diverse backgrounds (both educational and cultural) of the firm's employees?

Competitive intelligence can add value to the learning organization by discerning from the available new knowledge that portion that is most applicable to its organization to thrive and prosper. It should also help discern the most efficient learning methodologies to be internally utilized for maximum value to the firm. Therefore analysis will be a premium CI competence in the future.

Several clouds remain on this directional horizon for CI functions and practitioners. First, CI will constantly be challenged to tangibly demonstrate its value in economic or financial terms, because satisfactory methods to measure intellectual contribution to the organization do not exist. Second, CI will have to balance the conflicting needs of "need to know" and "doesn't need to know." Third, CI will likely need to continually outpace other functions and practitioners in the organization with respect to continuous learning, since it is often the organization's decision-making nerve center. Finally, good CI practitioners will be in high demand, creating the need for organizations to develop and institutionalize intelligence systems that can outlast any valuable individual.

SUMMARY

Although we recognize the presence of several key challenges in the directions facing management, we generally feel that the future for CI functions and practitioners is bright. We expect to revisit our views on direction and trends in the short term and hope that experience bears out our views and insights. We also hope that our review five years hence is as optimistic as today at the onset of the new millennium.

REFERENCES

Brown, S., and K. Eisenhardt. (1995). "Product Development: Past Research, Present Findings and Future Directions," *Academy of Management Review* 20(2): 343–78.

Christenson, C. (1997). *The Innovator's Dilemma: When New Technologies Cause Great Firms to Fail.* Boston: Harvard Business School Press.

Conger, J. (1997). "How Generational Shifts Will Transform Organizational Life," in *The Organization of the Future*, ed. F. Hesselbein, M. Goldsmith, and R. Beckhard. San Francisco: Jossey-Bass.

D'Aveni, R. (1994). *Hypercompetition: Managing the Dynamics of Strategic Maneuvering.* New York: Free Press.

DeGeorge, R. (1993). *Competing with Integrity in International Business.* New York: Oxford University Press.

DeGeus, A. (1997). *The Living Company.* Boston: Harvard Business School Press.

Dixit, A.K., and R.S. Pindyck. (1995). *Investment Under Uncertainty.* Princeton, NJ: Princeton University Press.

Drucker, P.F. (1994). *The Post-Capitalist Society.* New York: Harper Business.

———. (1997). *Management Challenges for the 21st Century.* New York: Harper Business.

Duques, R., and P. Gaske. (1997). "The 'Big' Organization of the Future," in *The Organization of the Future*, ed. F. Hesselbein, M. Goldsmith, and R. Beckhard. San Francisco: Jossey-Bass.

Eisenhardt, K.M., and B. Tabrizi. (1995). "Accelerating Adaptive Processes: Product Innovation in the Global Computer Industry," *Administrative Science Quarterly* 40(1): 84–110.

Fahey, L., and R. Randall. (1998). *Learning from the Future: Competitive Foresight Scenarios.* New York: Wiley.

Fleisher, C.S. (1999). "Public Policy Competitive Intelligence," *Competitive Intelligence Review* 10(2): 23–36.

Galbraith, J. (1997). "The Reconfigurable Organization," in *The Organization of the Future,* ed. F. Hesselbein, M. Goldsmith, and R. Beckhard. San Francisco: Jossey-Bass.

Garvin, D. (1993). "Building a Learning Organization," *Harvard Business Review* 71(4): 78–91.

Gates, W. (1999). *Business @ the Speed of Thought.* New York: Warner Books.

Gupta, A. (1994). "Business Unit Strategy: Managing the Strategy Business," in *The Portable MBA in Strategy,* ed. L. Fahey and R. Randall. New York: Wiley.

Halal, W.E. (1998). *The Infinite Resource: Creating and Leading the Knowledge Enterprise.* San Francisco: Jossey-Bass.

Hamel, G., and C. Pralahad. (1996). *Competing for the Future.* New York: Free Press.

Handy, C. (1995). *The Age of Paradox.* Boston: Harvard Business School Press.

Harmon, F. (1997). "Future Present," in *The Organization of the Future,* ed. F. Hesselbein, M. Goldsmith, and R. Beckhard. San Francisco: Jossey-Bass.

Hersey, P., and D. Johnson. (1997). "Situational Leadership in the Multicultural Organization," in *The Organization of the Future,* ed. F. Hesselbein, M. Goldsmith, and R. Beckhard. San Francisco: Jossey-Bass.

Hitt, M.A. (1998). "Twenty-First Century Organizations: Business Firms, Business Schools and the Academy," *Academy of Management Review* 23(2): 218–24.

Hitt, M., R. Hoskisson, and H. Kim. (1997). "International Diversification: Effects on Innovation and Firm Performance in Product Diversified Firms," *Academy of Management Journal* 40(4): 767–98.

Hitt, M.A., B.W. Keats, and S.M. DeMarie. (1998). "Navigating in the New Competitive Landscape: Building Strategic Flexibility and Competitive Advantage in the 21st Century," *Academy of Management Executive* 12(4): 22–42.

Hope, J., and T. Hope. (1997). *Competing in the Third Wave: The Ten Key Management Issues of the Information Age.* Boston: Harvard Business School Press.

Ind, N. (1997). *The Corporate Brand.* London: Macmillan Business.

Jacobs, F.R. (1994). *Real Time Strategic Change: How to Involve an Entire Organization in Fast and Far-Reaching Change.* San Francisco: Berrett-Koehler.

Kanter, R. (1997). "Restoring People to the Heart of the Organization of the Future," in *The Organization of the Future,* ed. F. Hesselbein, M. Goldsmith, and R. Beckhard. San Francisco: Jossey-Bass.

Kaplan, R.S., and D.P. Norton. (1996). *The Balanced Scorecard: Translating Strategy into Action.* Boston: Harvard Business School Press.

Kotha, S. (1995). "Mass Customization: Implementing the Emerging Paradigm for Competitive Advantage," *Strategic Management Journal* 16 (summer): 21–42.

Kotter, J. (1996). *Leading Change.* Boston: Harvard Business School Press.

Lei, D., J. Slocum, and R. Pitts. (1999). "Designing Organizations for Competitive Advantage: The Power of Unlearning and Learning," *Organization Dynamics* 27(3): 24–38.

Leonard-Barton, D. (1995). *Wellsprings of Knowledge.* Boston: Harvard Business School Press.

Marcus, A. (1996). *Business and Society: Strategy, Ethics and the Global Economy*, 2d ed. Chicago: Irwin.

Marshall, S. (1997). "Creating Sustainable Learning Communities," in *The Organization of the Future*, ed. F. Hesselbein, M. Goldsmith, and R. Beckhard. San Francisco: Jossey-Bass.

Nonaka, I., and H. Takeuchi. (1995). *The Knowledge-Creating Company.* New York: Oxford University Press.

O'Toole, J. (1996). *Leading Change: The Argument for a Values-Based Leadership.* New York: Ballantine Books.

Pralahad, C. (1997). "The Work of New Age Managers in the Emerging Competitive Landscape," in *The Organization of the Future*, ed. F. Hesselbein, M. Goldsmith, and R. Beckhard. San Francisco: Jossey-Bass.

Quinn, J. (1992). *The Intelligent Enterprise.* New York: Free Press.

Schuster, S. (1997). "Competing Globally," *Business Week* (June 23): 122–25.

Senge, P. (1994). *The Fifth Discipline: The Art and Practice of the Learning Organization.* New York: Doubleday/Currency.

———. (1999). *The Dance of Change: The Challenges to Sustaining Momentum in Learning Organizations.* New York: Doubleday/Currency.

Shapiro, E. (1996). *Fad Surfing in the Boardroom: Managing in the Age of Instant Answers.* Reading, MA: Perseus Press.

Simons, R. (1994). *Levers of Control: How Managers Use Innovative Control Systems to Drive Strategic Renewal.* Boston: Harvard Business School Press.

Somerville, I., and J. Mroz. (1997). "New Competencies for a New World," in *The Organization of the Future*, ed. F. Hesselbein, M. Goldsmith, and R. Beckhard. San Francisco: Jossey-Bass.

Stanat, R. (1998). *Global Gold: Panning for Profits in Foreign Markets.* New York: AMACOM.

Sull, D. (1999). "Why Good Companies Go Bad," *Harvard Business Review* 77(4): 42–56.

Thorp, J. (1999). *The Information Paradox: Realizing the Business Benefits of Information Technology.* New York: McGraw-Hill.

Winkler, I. (1997). *Corporate Espionage: What It Is, Why It Is Happening in Your Company, What You Must Do About It.* Rocklin, CA: Prima Publications.

Selected Bibliography

Part One: Overview of CI Management and Practices

Aaker, D.A. (1998). *Developing Business Strategies.* New York: Wiley.

Barndt, W.D., Jr. (1997). *The Demand Side of Competitive Intelligence: The Missing Link.* Alexandria, VA: Society of Competitive Intelligence Professionals.

Bernhardt, D. (1993). "Counterintelligence: Defending Your Company's Secrets," in *Perfectly Legal Competitor Intelligence: How to Get It, Use It and Profit from It,* ed. D. Bernhardt. London: FT Pitman Publishing.

Clark, B. (1998). "Managing Competitive Interactions," *Marketing Management* 7(4): 9–20.

Collis, D.J., and C.A. Montgomery. (1995). "Competing on Resources," *Harvard Business Review* 73(4): 118–28.

Cory, K. (1996). "Can Competitive Intelligence Lead to a Sustainable Competitive Advantage?" *Competitive Intelligence Review* 7(3): 45–55.

DeGeus, A. (1997). *The Living Company.* Boston: Harvard Business School Press.

DeWitt, M. (1997). *Competitive Intelligence Competitive Advantage.* Grand Rapids, MI: Abacus.

Dutka, A. (1998). *Competitive Intelligence for the Competitive Edge.* Chicago: NTC.

Ettorre, Barbara. (1995). "Managing Competitive Intelligence," *Management Review* 84(10): 15–19.

Fahey, L. (1999). *Competitors: Outwitting, Outmaneuvering, and Outperforming.* New York: Wiley.

Fuld, L.M. (1991). "Total Quality Through Intelligence Programs," *Competitive Intelligence Review* 2(1): 8–11.

———. (1995). *The New Competitor Intelligence: The Complete Resource for Finding, Analyzing, and Using Information about Your Competitors.* New York: Wiley.

Gilad, B. (1996). *Business Blindspots.* London: Infonortics.

Grant, R.M. (1997). "The Knowledge-Based View of the Firm: Implications for Management Practice," *Long-Range Planning* 30(3): 450–54.

———. (1998). *Contemporary Strategy Analysis,* 3d ed. Malden, MA: Blackwell.

Hax, A., and N. Majluf. (1996). *The Strategy Concept and Process: A Pragmatic Approach*, 2d ed. Upper Saddle River, NJ: Prentice-Hall.

Herring, J.P. (1992). "The Role of Intelligence in Formulating Strategy," *Journal of Business Strategy* 13(5): 54–60.

Hitt, M.A., B.W. Keats, and S.M. DeMarie. (1998). "Navigating in the New Competitive Landscape: Building Strategic Flexibility and Competitive Advantage in the 21st Century," *Academy of Management Executive* 12(4): 22–42.

Imperato, G. (1998). "Competitive Intelligence—Get Smart!" *Fastcompany* 14: 269.

Kahaner, L.K. (1996). *Competitive Intelligence: How to Gather, Analyze, and Use Information to Move Your Business to the Top*. New York: Simon & Schuster.

Langabeer, J.A. II. (1998). "Achieving a Strategic Focus for Competitive Intelligence," *Competitive Intelligence Review* 9(1): 55–59.

McGonagle, J.J., and C.M. Vella. (1993). *Outsmarting the Competition: Practical Approaches to Finding and Outsmarting the Competition*. New York: McGraw-Hill.

———. (1998). *Protecting Your Company Against Competitive Intelligence*. Westport, CT: Quorum Books.

Nolan, J.A. III. (1997). "Confusing Counterintelligence With Security Can Wreck Your Afternoon," *Competitive Intelligence Review* 8(3): 53–61.

———. (1999). *Confidential: Uncover Your Competition's Top Business Secrets Legally and Quickly—And Protect Your Own*. New York: HarperCollins.

Pollard, A. (1999). *Competitor Intelligence—Strategy, Tools and Techniques for Competitive Advantage*. London: Financial Times–Pitman Publishing.

Porter, M.E. (1996). "What is Strategy?" *Harvard Business Review* 74(6): 61–78.

Prescott, J.E. (1995). "The Evolution of Competitive Intelligence," *International Review of Strategic Management* 6(1): 71–90.

Prescott, J.E., and C.S. Fleisher. (1991). "SCIP: Who We Are, What We Do," *Competitive Intelligence Review* 2(1): 22–27.

Prescott, J.E., and G. Bhardwaj. (1995). "Competitive Intelligence Practices: A Survey," *Competitive Intelligence Review* 6(2): 4–14.

Prince, C. (1998). "Strategy and Tactics: A Primer for CI Professional," *Competitive Intelligence Review* 9(3): 15–24.

Salmon, R., and Y. de Linares. (1999). *Competitive Intelligence: Scanning the Global Environment*. Washington, DC: Brookings Institution Press.

Sawka, K. (1998). "Early Warning: The Decision-Makers Perspective," *Competitive Intelligence Review* 9(2): 63–65.

Shaker, S., and M. Gembicki. (1999). *The War Room Guide to Competitive Intelligence*. New York: McGraw-Hill.

Sun-Tzu. (1988). *The Art of War*. Oxford: Oxford University Press.

Tyson, K.W.M. (1998). "Perpetual Strategy: A 21st Century Essential," *Strategy and Leadership* 26(1): 14–18.

———. (1998). *The Complete Guide to Competitive Intelligence*. Lisle, IL: Kirk Tyson International.

Winkler, I. (1997). *Corporate Espionage: What It Is, Why It Is Happening in Your Company, What You Must Do About It*. Roseville, CA: Prima Publishing.

Part Two: Improving the CI Process

Albrecht, K. (1999). *Corporate Radar: Tracking the Forces That Are Shaping Your Business*. New York: AMACOM.

American Product and Quality Center (APQC), Consortium Report. (1998). *Managing Competitive Intelligence Knowledge in a Global Economy* <http://www.apcq.org>.

Barndt, W.D., Jr. (1994). *User-Directed Competitive Intelligence: Closing the Gap Between Supply and Demand.* Westport, CT: Quorum Books.

Bates, M.E. (1999). *Super Searchers Do Business: The Online Secrets of Top Business Researchers.* Medford, NJ: Information Today, Inc.

Baumard, P. (1994). "The Intelligence Dead End: How You Present It!" *Competitive Intelligence Review* 5(2): 53–55.

Blenkhorn, D., and B. Gaber. (1995). "The Use of 'Warm Fuzzies' to Assess Organizational Effectiveness," *Journal of General Management* 21(2): 40–51.

Buchwitz, L. (1998). *Monitoring Competitive Intelligence Using Internet Push Technology* <http://tor-pw1.netcom.ca/~lillyb/CI_paper.html>.

Burwell, H. (1999). *Online Competitive Intelligence: Increase Your Profits Using Cyber-Intelligence.* Tempe, AZ: Facts on Demand Press.

Cabena, P., P. Hadjinian, R. Stadler, J. Verhees, and A. Zanasi. (1997). *Discovering Data Mining: From Concept to Implementation.* Upper Saddle River, NJ: IBM and Prentice-Hall.

Calishain, T., and J. Nystron. (1998). *Official Netscape Guide to Internet Research*, 2d ed. Toronto: Coriolis Group.

Evans, P.B., and T.S. Wurster. (1997). "Strategy and the New Economics of Information," *Harvard Business Review* 75(5): 71–82.

Fahey, L., and R. Randall. (1998). *Learning from the Future: Competitive Foresight Scenarios.* New York: Wiley.

Fleisher, C.S. (1991). "Applying Quality Process Evaluation to the CI Function," *Competitive Intelligence Review* 2(1): 5–8.

Fleisher, C.S., and B. Bensoussan (2000). "A FAROUT Way to Manage CI Analysis," *Competitive Intelligence Magazine* 3(2): 37–40.

———. (forthcoming). *Business and Competitive Analysis for Strategic Management.* Upper Saddle River, NJ: Prentice-Hall.

Fuld, L.M. (1994). "Talk It, Show It, Write It," *Competitive Intelligence Review* 5(2): 56–57.

———. (1998). *The Fuld War Room: The Ultimate in Competitive Intelligence* (multimedia software). Cambridge, MA: Fuld & Company/Montreal: Iron Horse Multimedia.

Ghoshal, S., and S. Kim. (1986). "Building Effective Intelligence Systems for Competitive Advantage," *Sloan Management Review* 28(1): 49–58.

Gilad, B., and J.P. Herring, eds. (1996). "The Art and Science of Business Intelligence Analysis: Intelligence Analysis and Its Applications," in *Advances in Applied Business Strategy*, supplement 2A, B. Greenwich, CT: JAI Press.

Graef, J. (1996). "Sharing Business Intelligence on the World Wide Web," *Competitive Intelligence Review* 7(1): 52–61.

———. (1997). "Using the Internet for Competitive Intelligence: A Survey Report," *Competitive Intelligence Review* 8(4): 41–47.

Hamrefors, S. (1998). "Spontaneous Environmental Scanning," *Competitive Intelligence Review* 9(3): 68–75.

Hannon, J.M., and Y. Sano. (1995). "Customer-Driven Human Resources Practices in Japan," *Human Resource Planning* 17(3): 37–53.

Harkleroad, D. (1994). "Making Intelligence Analysis Actionable," *Competitive Intelligence Review* 5(2): 13–17.

Herring, J.P. (1996). *Measuring the Effectiveness of Competitive Intelligence: Assessing and Communicating CI's Value to Your Organization.* Alexandria, VA: Society of Competitive Intelligence Professionals.

———. (1998). "What Is Intelligence Analysis?" *Competitive Intelligence Magazine* 1(2): 13–16.

———. (1999). "Key Intelligence Topics: A Process to Identify and Define Intelligence Needs," *Competitive Intelligence Review* 10(2): 4–14.

Hussey, D. E., and P. V. Jenster. (1999). *Competitor Intelligence: Turning Analysis into Success,* Wiley Series in Practical Strategy. New York: Wiley.

Kaplan, R.S., and D.P. Norton. (1996). "Linking the Balanced Scorecard to Strategy," *California Management Review* 39(1): 53–79.

Kassler, H. (1997). "Mining the Internet for Competitive Intelligence," *Online* 21(5): 34–45.

Langley, A. (1995). "Between Paralysis by Analysis and Extinction by Instinct," *Sloan Management Review* 36(3): 63–76.

Linville, R.L. (1996). *CI Boot Camp.* Johnson City, NY: Competitive Horizons.

O'Dell, C., and C.J. Grayson Jr. (1996). *Identifying and Transferring Internal Best Practices.* American Product and Quality Center (APQC) Best Practices White Paper Report <http://www.store.apqc.org/cgi-bin/vsc.exe/Jacket/cmifwp.htm?E+Book Store>.

Oster, S.M. (1999). *Modern Competitive Analysis,* 3d ed. Oxford: Oxford University Press.

Pawar, B., and R. Sharda. (1997). "Obtaining Business Intelligence on the Internet," *Long-Range Planning* 30(1): 110–21.

Prescott, J., J. Herring, and P. Panfely. (1998). "Leveraging Information into Action: A Look into the Competitive and Business Intelligence Consortium Benchmarking Study," *Competitive Intelligence Review* 9(1): 4–10.

Rothberg, H.N. (1997). "Fortifying Competitive Intelligence Systems with Shadow Teams," *Competitive Intelligence Review* 8(2): 3–11.

Sankey, M.L., and J.R. Flowers, ed. (1999). *Public Records Online: The National Guide to Private and Government Online Sources of Public Records,* 2d ed. Tempe, AZ: Facts on Demand Press.

Sawka, K.A. (1999). "Finding Intelligence Analysts," *Competitive Intelligence Magazine* 2(1): 41–42.

Sawka, K.A., D.B. Francis, and J.P. Herring. (1995). "Evaluating Business Intelligence Systems: How Does Your Company Rate?" *Competitive Intelligence Review* 6(4): 22–25.

Schlein, M., J.R. Flowers, and S.K. Kisaichi, ed. (1999). *Find It Online: The Complete Guide to Online Research.* Tempe, AZ: Facts on Demand Press.

Schoemaker, P.J.H. (1995). "Scenario Planning: A Tool for Strategic Thinking," *Sloan Management Review* 36(2): 25–40.

Werther, G. (1998). "Doing Business in the New World Disorder: The Problem with Precision," *Competitive Intelligence Magazine* 1(2): 24–26.

Wyckoff, T. (1999). *Benchmarking Competitive Intelligence.* Washington, DC: Special Libraries Association.

Zahra, S., and S. Chaples. (1993). "Blind Spots in Competitive Analysis," *Academy of Management Executive* 7(2): 7–28.

Zanasi, A. (1998). "Competitive Intelligence through Data Mining Public Sources," *Competitive Intelligence Review* 9(1): 44–54.

Part Three: CI and Its Relationship with Business Functions and Processes

Allee, V. (1997). "12 Principles of Knowledge Management," *Training and Development* 51(11): 71–74.

Allgaier, C., and T. Powell. (1998). "Enhancing Sales and Marketing Effectiveness through Competitive Intelligence," *Competitive Intelligence Review* 9(2): 29–41.

Berger, A. (1996). "How to Support Your Sales Force With Competitive Intelligence," *Competitive Intelligence Review* 7(4): 81–83.

Birkett, W.P. (1995). "Management Accounting and Knowledge Management: Management Accountants Are Becoming Strategic Resource Managers," *Management Accounting* 77(5): 44–48.

Brown, J.S., and P. Duguid. (1998). "Organizing Knowledge," *California Management Review* 40(3): 90–111.

Cartwright, D.L., P.D. Boughton, and S.W. Miller. (1995). "Competitive Intelligence Systems: Relationships to Strategic Orientation and Perceived Usefulness," *Journal of Managerial Issues* 7(4): 420–34.

Christenson, C. (1997). *The Innovator's Dilemma: When New Technologies Cause Great Firms to Fail.* Boston: Harvard Business School Press.

Coburn, M.M. (1999). *Competitive Technical Intelligence: A Guide to Design, Analysis, and Action.* Oxford: Oxford University Press.

Cohen, A. (1998). "The Misuse of Competitive Intelligence," *Sales and Marketing Management* 150(3): 13.

Davenport, T.H., and L. Prusak. (1998). *Working Knowledge.* Boston: Harvard Business School Press.

Davenport, T.H., D.W. De Long, and M.C. Beers. (1998). "Successful Knowledge Management Projects," *Sloan Management Review* 39(2): 43–57.

Demarest, M. (1997). "Understanding Knowledge Management," *Long-Range Planning* 30(3): 374–84.

Dugal, M. (1998). "CI Product Line: A Tool for Enhancing User Acceptance of CI," *Competitive Intelligence Review* 9(2): 17–25.

Eger, M.C. (1996). "The CEO and the CI Professional: Big Impact Partners," in *Advances in Applied Business Strategy*, supplement 2A, ed. B. Gilad and J.P. Herring. Greenwich, CT: JAI Press.

Guimaraes, T., and C. Armstrong. (1998). "Exploring the Relations Between Competitive Intelligence, IS Support and Business Change," *Competitive Intelligence Review* 9(3): 45–54.

Halal, W.E. (1998). *The Infinite Resource: Creating and Leading the Knowledge Enterprise.* San Francisco: Jossey-Bass.

Leonard-Barton, D. (1995). *Wellsprings of Knowledge.* Boston: Harvard Business School Press.

Lynne, G.S., J.G. Morone, and A.S. Paulson. (1996). "Marketing and Discontinuous Innovation: The Probe and Learn Process," *California Management Review* 38(3): 8–37.

Marchetti, M. (1998). "Paying Salespeople for Information," *Sales and Marketing Management*, 151(7): 16.

Moingeon, B., and A. Edmondson, eds. (1996). *Organizational Learning and Competitive Advantage.* Thousand Oaks, CA: Sage Publications.

Myers, P. (1996). "Knowledge Management and Organizational Design: An Introduction," in *Knowledge Management and Organizational Design*, ed. P. Myers. Boston: Butterworth-Heinemann.

Nonaka, I., and H. Takeuchi. (1995). *The Knowledge-Creating Company*. New York: Oxford University Press.

Powell, T. (1997). "Competitive Knowledge Management: You Can't Reengineer What Was Never Engineered in the First Place," *Competitive Intelligence Review* 8(1): 40–47.

Prior, V. (1996). "Contacts Database: Your Most Useful Intelligence Tool," *Competitive Intelligence Review* 7(3): 75–77.

Saarenvirta, G. (1998). "Data Mining to Improve Profitability," *CMA Magazine* 72(2): 9–12.

Sirower, M.L. (1997). *The Synergy Trap: How Companies Lose the Acquisition Game*. New York: Free Press.

Snow, C.C., R.E. Miles, and H.J. Coleman Jr. (1995). "Managing 21st Century Network Organizations," in *The Organizational Behavior Reader*, 6th ed., ed. D.A. Kolb, J.S. Osland, and I.M. Rubin. Englewood Cliffs, NJ: Prentice-Hall.

Stewart, T. (1999). *Intellectual Capital*. New York: Doubleday.

Sullivan, M. (1997). "Using Competitive Intelligence to Develop a Strategic Management Action-Oriented Measurement System," *Competitive Intelligence Review* 8(2): 34–43.

Sveiby, K.E. (1997). *The New Organizational Wealth*. San Francisco: Berrett-Koehler Publishers.

Wiig, K.M. (1997). "Integrating Intellectual Capital and Knowledge Management," *Long-Range Planning* 30(3): 399–405.

Part Four: CI and Its Application in Specific Contexts

Ashton, W.B., and R.A. Klavans. (1997). *Keeping Abreast of Science and Technology: Technical Intelligence for Business*. Columbus, OH: Batelle Press.

Behnke, L., and P. Slayton. (1998). "Shaping a Corporate Competitive Intelligence Function at IBM," *Competitive Intelligence Review* 9(2): 4–9.

Berger, A. (1997). "Small but Powerful: Six Steps for Conducting Competitive Intelligence Successfully at a Medium-Sized Firm," *Competitive Intelligence Review* 8(4): 75–77.

Bonthous, J.M. (1996). *Revealing the American Language of Intelligence*. Alexandria, VA: Society of Competitive Intelligence Professionals.

Brenner, M.S. (1996). "Technology Intelligence and Scouting," *Competitive Intelligence Review* 7(3): 20–27.

Cantrell, R. (1996). "Patent Intelligence—Information to Compete Before Products Are Launched," *Competitive Intelligence Review* 7(1): 65–69.

DeGeorge, R. (1993). *Competing with Integrity in International Business*. New York: Oxford University Press.

Fleisher, C.S. (1999). "Public Policy Competitive Intelligence," *Competitive Intelligence Review* 10(2): 23–36.

Flynn, R. (1994). "Nutrasweet Faces Competition: The Critical Role of Competitive Intelligence," *Competitive Intelligence Review* 5(4): 4–7.

Galvin, R.W. (1997). "Competitive Intelligence at Motorola," *Competitive Intelligence Review* 8(1): 3–6.

Hansen, J.P. (1996). *Japanese Intelligence: The Competitive Edge*. Washington, DC: NIBC Press.

Mogee, M.E. (1997). "Patents and Technology Intelligence," in *Keeping Abreast of Science and Technology: Technical Intelligence for Business*, ed. W.B. Ashton and R.A. Klavans. Columbus, OH: Battelle Press.

Prescott, J.E., and P.T. Gibbons. (1993). *Global Perspectives on Competitive Intelligence.* Alexandria, VA: Society of Competitive Intelligence Professionals.

Society of Competitive Intelligence Professional's 2nd Annual Competitive Technical Intelligence Symposium. (1999). "Developing Processes and Infrastructure to Meet Upper Management's CTI Needs: A Roundtable Discussion," *Competitive Intelligence Review* 10(3): 4–18.

Stanat, R. (1998). *Global Gold: Panning for Profits in Foreign Markets.* New York: AMACOM.

Vezmar, J.M. (1996). "Competitive Intelligence at Xerox," *Competitive Intelligence Review* 7(3): 15–18.

Part Five: Organizational Issues Associated with CI

Bauman, J.H., and M. Gelinne. (1998). "Maximizing the Use of CI Consultants: A Corporate Practitioner's Perspective," *Competitive Intelligence Review* 9(3): 3–8.

Berger, A. (1997). "Small but Powerful: Six Steps for Conducting Competitive Intelligence Successfully at a Medium-Sized Firm," *Competitive Intelligence Review* 8(4): 75–77.

Dashman, L. (1998). "The Value of an In-House Competitive Intelligence Department: A Business Plan Approach," *Competitive Intelligence Review* 9(2): 10–16.

Drucker, P.F. (1995). "The Information that Executives Truly Need," *Harvard Business Review* 73(1): 54–62.

———. (1997). *Management Challenges for the 21st Century.* New York: Harper Business.

Fine, N.R. (1997). "The Economic Espionage Act: Turning Fear into Compliance," *Competitive Intelligence Review* 8(3): 20–24.

Fiora, B. (1998). "Ethical Business Intelligence is NOT Mission Impossible," *Strategy and Leadership* 26(1): 40–41.

Frost, P., and S. Robinson. (1999). "The Toxic Handler," *Harvard Business Review* 77(4): 97–106.

Fuld, L.M. (1998). "1998 Customer Satisfaction Report and Survey," *Competitive Intelligence Magazine* 1(3): 18–33.

Fuld, L.M., J.P. Herring, L. Kahaner, L.K. Knight, and J. Prescott. (1997). "Symposium: Lessons Learned and the Road Ahead," *Competitive Intelligence Review* 8(1): 7–15.

Goleman, D. (1998). "What Makes a Leader?" *Harvard Business Review* 76(6): 94.

Hanson, J.R., and D. Krackhardt. (1993). "Informal Networks: The Company Behind the Chart," *Harvard Business Review* 71(4): 104–11.

Harkleroad, D. (1996). "Too Many Ostriches, Not Enough Eagles," *Competitive Intelligence Review* 7(1): 23–27.

———. (1998). "Ostriches and Eagles II," *Competitive Intelligence Review* 9(1): 13–19.

Hitt, M.A. (1998). "Twenty-First Century Organizations: Business Firms, Business Schools and the Academy," *Academy of Management Review* 23(2): 218–24.

Hope, J., and T. Hope. (1997). *Competing in the Third Wave: The Ten Key Management Issues of the Information Age.* Boston: Harvard Business School Press.

Kotter, J. (1996). *Leading Change.* Boston: Harvard Business School Press.

McGonagle, J.J. (1992). "Patterns of Development in CI Units," *Competitive Intelligence Review* 3(1): 11–12.

McGonagle, J.J., and C.M. Vella. (1996). *A New Archetype for Competitive Intelligence.* Westport, CT: Quorum Books.

―――. (1999). *The Internet Age of Competitive Intelligence.* Westport, CT: Quorum Books.

Miller, J.P., ed. (2000). *Millennium Intelligence: Understanding and Conducting Competitive Intelligence in the Digital Age.* Medford, NJ: Information Today.

Montgomery, D., and C. Weinberg. (1998). "Toward Strategic Intelligence Systems," *Marketing Management* 7(4): 44–52.

O'Toole, J. (1996). *Leading Change: The Argument for a Values-Based Leadership.* New York: Ballantine Books.

Pattakos, A.N. (1997). "Keeping Company Secrets Secret," *Competitive Intelligence Review* 8(3): 71–78.

Senge, P. (1999). *The Dance of Change: The Challenges to Sustaining Momentum in Learning Organizations.* New York: Doubleday/Currency.

Sharman, P. (1996). "Activity/Process Budgets: A Tool for Change Management," *CMA Magazine* 70(2): 21–24.

Simon, N.J. (1997). "Organizational Development: CI Is Not an Island," *Competitive Intelligence Review* 8(4): 80–82.

Simon, N.J., and A.B. Blixt. (1996). *Navigating in a Sea of Change: Perspectives on the Present and Future of Competitive Intelligence.* Alexandria, VA: Society of Competitive Intelligence Professionals.

Simons, R. (1994). *Levers of Control: How Managers Use Innovative Control Systems to Drive Strategic Renewal.* Boston: Harvard Business School Press.

Society of Competitive Intelligence Professionals. (1997). "Competencies for Intelligence Professionals," from the education-modules section of the Society of Competitive Intelligence Professionals (SCIP) website <http://www.scip.org>.

―――. (1997). *Navigating Through the Gray Zone: A Collection of Corporate Codes of Conduct and Ethical Guidelines.* Alexandria, VA: Society of Competitive Intelligence Professionals.

Sull, D. (1999). "Why Good Companies Go Bad," *Harvard Business Review* 77(4): 42–56.

Trevino, L.K., and G.R. Weaver. (1997). "Ethical Issues in Competitive Intelligence Practice: Consensus, Conflicts, and Challenges," *Competitive Intelligence Review* 8(1): 61–72.

Tushman, M.L., and C.A. O'Reilly III. (1997). *Winning Through Innovation: A Practical Guide to Leading Organizational Change and Renewal.* Boston: Harvard Business School Press.

Tyson, K.W.M. (1996). "The Problem with Ethics: Implementation," *Competitive Intelligence Review* 7(supplement 1): S15–S17.

―――. (1997). *Competition in the 21st Century.* Boca Raton, FL: St. Lucie Press.

Vella, C.M., and J.J. McGonagle. (1987). *Competitive Intelligence in the Computer Age.* Wesport, CT: Quorum Books.

Watts, R.J., A.L. Porter, and N.C. Newman. (1998). "Innovation Forecasting Using Bibliometrics," *Competitive Intelligence Review* 9(4): 11–19.

Youngblood, A.H. (1998). "CI: Focusing Management on What Matters," *Competitive Intelligence Review* 9(2): 1–2.

Index

About the Editors and Contributors

Ross O. Armstrong is a principal with Armstrong and Associates, Burlington, Ontario, a management-consulting firm specializing in knowledge management, competitive intelligence, and market research.

Peter Barrett is a technical sales representative with Grace Specialty Building Products, Brantford, Ontario, a global manufacturing division of W. R. Grace and Co.

David L. Blenkhorn is professor of marketing at the School of Business and Economics, Wilfrid Laurier University, Waterloo, Ontario. He teaches, researches, and consults with multinational companies in the areas of business-to-business and relationship marketing, competitive intelligence, and developing and managing global supply chains. His book *Reverse Marketing: The New Buyer–Supplier Relationship* (with M. Leenders) addresses the need for radical change to traditional buyer–supplier relationships.

Perry Broome is president of Market Share, a marketing research and consulting practice. He teaches courses in marketing and marketing research in the Business and Management Division, Fanshawe College, in London, Ontario.

Dawn E. Clarke is a service-engineering marketing specialist at Babcock & Wilcox Canada, Cambridge, Ontario, where she performs market, customer, and competitor analysis and develops marketing strategy.

Robert Cunningham is a research assistant at the School of Business and Economics, Wilfrid Laurier University, Waterloo, Ontario.

Gene Deszca is professor of business at the School of Business and Economics, Wilfrid Laurier University, Waterloo, Ontario. He teaches and researches in the areas of organizational behavior and change.

CRAIG S. FLEISHER is dean of the Faculty of Business, University of New Brunswick, Saint John. He is on the editorial board of the *Competitive Intelligence Review*, was coordinator for the Society of Competitive Intelligence Professionals (SCIP) Canadian Technology Triangle chapter, and teaches, researches, and consults with multinational firms in the areas of managing competitive intelligence, corporate public affairs, and e-business strategy.

ALAIN FRANCQ is marketing manager at Virtek Vision Corporation, Waterloo, Ontario, where he is responsible for marketing strategy, channel management, marketing communications, market research, and competitive intelligence. He teaches a course in strategic planning in the Marketing in Science and Technology Program, Conestoga College, Kitchener, Ontario.

SHAUNA HAMILTON is a consultant at Info-Prod Research (Middle East) Limited, Tel Aviv, Israel, where she develops bilateral business and trade opportunities between Canada and the Middle East.

VICTOR KNIP is manager of special projects with the Ontario Community Newspapers Association, Burlington.

JULIA MADDEN is a steering committee member of the newly formed Society of Competitive Intelligence Professionals (SCIP) Canadian Technology Triangle chapter, Waterloo, Ontario.

TABATHA MARTINS is strategic-marketing analyst at Mortice Kern Systems (MKS) Incorporated, Waterloo, Ontario, where she is responsible for researching and evaluating e-business strategic direction.

RICHARD MCCLURG is a consultant with InDIMENSIONS Consulting Group, an e-business strategy and on-line development consulting firm located in Waterloo, Ontario.

BRENDA MCWILLIAMS is manager of marketing services at Federal Express Canada Limited, Mississauga, Ontario.

HUGH MUNRO is professor of business at the School of Business and Economics, Wilfrid Laurier University, Waterloo, Ontario. He teaches and researches in the areas of new-product development, e-commerce, and international business.

JEFFREY MURPHY is a research analyst with InDIMENSIONS Consulting Group, an e-business strategy and on-line development consulting firm located in Waterloo, Ontario.

HAMID NOORI is professor of technology and operations management at the School of Business and Economics, Wilfrid Laurier University, Waterloo, Ontario. He teaches and researches in the areas of operations management and the management of new technologies.

JAYSON PARKER is a senior analyst at AIC Limited, a large mutual-fund organization, where he advises on biotechnology and pharmaceutical companies for investment.

BETH RINGDAHL is a report analyst at Ernex Marketing Technologies Incorporated, Burnaby, British Columbia.

VICTORIA TURNER SHOEMAKER is the manager of business development for Kitchener Utilities, Kitchener, Ontario.

J. GRAEME SOMERVILLE is vice president, marketing for JPH International Inc., a Waterloo, Ontario, software firm specializing in solutions for local governments and utilities across North America.

ANGUS STEWART is a marketing-research analyst for MC2 Learning Systems Incorporated, a Toronto-based software company specializing in messaging technology including groupware and unified messaging (UM) products.

CONOR VIBERT is assistant professor of business policy at the Fred C. Manning School of Business, Acadia University, Wolfville, Nova Scotia, where he teaches and researches in the areas of business policy, change management, and organization theory. He is the author of *Web-Based Analysis for Competitive Intelligence* (Quorum Books, 2000).

SUZANNE WILTSHIRE heads the consulting firm, FutureNow Incorporated, Brantford, Ontario, where she assists preinitial public offering (IPO) technology firms to implement effective business-development strategies.